HOLLYWOOD'S ARTISTS

Film and Culture

FILM AND CULTURE

A series of Columbia University Press
Edited by John Belton

For a complete list of titles, see pages 299–303.

Hollywood's Artists

The Directors Guild of America and
the Construction of Authorship

Virginia Wright Wexman

Columbia University Press   New York

Columbia University Press
Publishers Since 1893
New York   Chichester, West Sussex
cup.columbia.edu
Copyright © 2020 Columbia University Press
All rights reserved

Library of Congress Cataloging-in-Publication Data
Names: Wexman, Virginia Wright, author.
Title: Hollywood's artists : the Directors Guild of America and the construction of authorship / Virginia Wright Wexman.
Description: New York : Columbia University Press, [2020] | Series: Film and culture | Includes bibliographical references and index.
Identifiers: LCCN 2019052936 (print) | LCCN 2019052937 (ebook) | ISBN 9780231195683 (cloth) | ISBN 9780231195690 (paperback) | ISBN 9780231551434 (ebook)
Subjects: LCSH: Directors Guild of America—History. | Motion picture producers and directors—United States—History. | Motion pictures—Production and direction—United States—History. | Motion picture industry—United States—History.
Classification: LCC PN1995.9.P7 W477 2020 (print) | LCC PN1995.9.P7 (ebook) | DDC 791.4302/330922—dc23
LC record available at https://lccn.loc.gov/2019052936
LC ebook record available at https://lccn.loc.gov/2019052937

Cover design: Milenda Nan Ok Lee
Cover image: Moviepix Collection / John Kobal Foundation / © Getty Images

Contents

Acknowledgments — vii

Introduction — 1

CHAPTER ONE
Directors as Artists: The DGA Rides the Wave — 10

CHAPTER TWO
Charisma and Competition: The DGA Stakes Its Claim — 38

CHAPTER THREE
Recognition: The DGA Takes Credit — 65

CHAPTER FOUR
Politics: The DGA Stages HUAC — 86

CHAPTER FIVE
Law: The DGA and Artists as Owners — 106

Conclusion — 118

Appendix A: Beyond Creative Rights 121
Appendix B: Chronology of the Directors Guild of America 131
Appendix C: Officers of the Directors Guild of America 153
Appendix D: Chronology of the Artists Rights Foundation 155
Notes 163
Bibliography 239
Index 277

Acknowledgments

My understanding of issues facing the Directors Guild of America has been aided by the opportunity to interview many people with significant roles in the organization. These interviews, all conducted in 2001, were arranged by Gina Blumenfeld, then the Guild's special projects executive, to whom I owe special thanks. Anthropologist Sherry Ortner has written about the difficulties inherent in gleaning information from members of an industry long famous for its predilection to control its image.[1] I was fortunate in not encountering any of the difficulties Ortner enumerates, finding many people who gave generously of their time and helped me to appreciate the human element that grounds the work the DGA does. I had lengthy discussions with four of the Guild's former presidents: Gene Reynolds, Arthur Hiller, Gilbert Cates, and Martha Coolidge. DGA board member and future president Paris Barclay shared his thoughts on the organization's efforts to advance the careers of its minority members, and Elliot Silverstein, who then headed up the Artists Rights Foundation, patiently elucidated some of the legal intricacies his group was grappling with at the time. The DGA's executive director, Jay Roth, and associate executive director, Warren Adler, also talked with me at length. All of these native informants spoke eloquently and with great pride about the Guild's creative rights achievements.

During the long journey this project has taken on the road to publication, my efforts have also been aided by myriad colleagues, librarians, archivists, friends, and family members—too many to mention. However, I must offer special thanks to Jane Gaines, who read some early drafts of the manuscript and offered wise and encouraging critiques. Tony Gardner and Robert Marshall guided me through the Directors Guild files deposited in the Oviatt Library Special Collections department at California State University, Northridge. Ned Comstock at the University of Southern California Library and Jenny Romero at the Margaret Herrick Library both went above and beyond expectations to locate relevant materials for me. Colleagues at an array of events at which I read papers about the DGA, including the Columbia University Film Seminar, the Chicago Film Seminar, the University of Illinois English Department Symposium, and several Society for Cinema and Media Studies conferences, proffered useful suggestions.

After I submitted a draft of the manuscript to Columbia University Press, the editors worked with me creatively and carefully on the final refinements.

The contributions of my husband, John Huntington, could never be quantified; suffice it to say, this book would never have been possible without his continued support, input, and advice.

Introduction

> It is a question of describing the gradual emergence of the entire set of social conditions which make possible the character of the artist as a producer of the fetish which is the work of art.
> —PIERRE BOURDIEU

> There can be no definitive critique of genius or talent that doesn't first take into consideration the social determinism, the historical combination of circumstances, and the technological background which to a large extent determine it.
> —ANDRÉ BAZIN

> I, for one, am sure that the super-author of pictures will in the not too distant future rise like a colossus in our midst.
> —JESSE L. LASKY

Today, the stock of Hollywood directors is high. Some observers see the trend as a long-overdue recognition of film artists whose shaping hand has, in the past, often been unjustly ignored by a philistine public and a mendacious corporate industry. A more economically oriented line of thought looks to the breakup of the old studio system and the rise of the independent film movement in the 1970s and 1980s as the key to unlocking the power of directorial talent. Other commentators see Hollywood's growing emphasis on marketing as a gift to directors, whose names are now routinely used to help sell the films they helm. The new knowledge that film critics and scholars have produced, most notably the focus on directors championed by auteurists, has played a role as well. In addition, directors have been given a boost by a growing film festival culture that promotes the names of favored cineastes. But another factor is rarely mentioned in discussions of the prominence of Hollywood directors in today's public realm: the active role played by their institutional base, the Directors Guild of America (DGA).[1]

The preeminent place Hollywood directors occupy both in the film industry and in the public mind was not predetermined; it was enabled by trends within the culture at large and, as this book demonstrates, it was fought for by the DGA, through its creative rights program. From the moment of the Guild's founding—and even before—creative rights have been a central preoccupation of Hollywood directors, driving an agenda that has enjoyed remarkable success over the years. Its goal is to make directors into artists.

From the time a dozen major directors founded it in 1935, the DGA has grown to become a many-faceted organization with more than 1,500 members, including assistant directors and unit managers as well as directors. It is the smallest of the three major talent groups in Hollywood (the actors and writers are the other two). Yet, by the turn of the millennium, references to the DGA in the Hollywood trade press routinely included the adjective "powerful." The Guild draws its strength from several sources. Like the actors, the directors can force a work stoppage. Moreover, the managerial aspects of directors' jobs on the set and their role as liaisons between the artisans who create movies and the business interests that finance them give DGA members a strategic advantage over the writers, actors, and "below-the-line" participants.

Despite its commanding position in the Hollywood hierarchy, however, the Directors Guild has received little serious scrutiny, while the Screen Actors Guild (SAG) and the Screen Writers Guild have both been subjects of book-length studies.[2] Published work on the Directors Guild approaches it as a traditional union, concerned with obtaining higher wages and better working conditions, especially for its most underprivileged members.[3] But viewing the DGA simply as another labor organization overlooks what is most distinctive about it: its creative rights mission.

From the time of its inception, the DGA has focused on the goal of positioning Hollywood directors as artists. The key element in the Guild's creative rights program was contributed by Frank Capra, who introduced the slogan "One man, one film" as a guiding principle in the early days of the organization. Capra's phrase reflected the cultural assumption that art is the expression of a single person and challenged the DGA to apply this principle to Hollywood cinema. The Guild wants its members to be seen not simply as supervisors of popular entertainments but as authors in the high art tradition. It has pursued this goal on several fronts, gaining ever-greater control for directors over the entire filmmaking process, mounting public relations activities to shape the way in which they are perceived, and controlling the configuration of movie credits. During the House Un-American Activities Committee (HUAC) era, the DGA refined its image of directors as artists by associating that image with ideas about virility and social commitment. During the last part of the twentieth century, the Guild took its creative rights mission in yet another direction by lobbying for laws that would give directors control over their films after they were released. The DGA's work in these spheres has dovetailed with economic, technological, social, and political changes to alter the way in which mainstream American movies are made and received.

My approach blends theoretical concerns with focused archival research, emphasizing the role of human agency as it is situated within institutional and societal contexts. In the process, I have drawn extensively on formulations put forward by theorists who have examined the cultural discourses surrounding creative work. Michel Foucault's essay "What Is an Author?" has inspired scholars across the humanities to turn to the subject of authorship in order to address the silences that lie behind a historical, solitary genius model of creative endeavor.[4] Pierre Bourdieu's studies of the cultural formations surrounding artistic production also inform my arguments.[5] In addition, I have been inspired by examinations of the movie industry by scholars such as Thomas Schatz, John Thornton Caldwell, and Jerome Christiansen, which focus on the social and institutional underpinnings of Hollywood cinema.[6] The paradigms these scholars have adopted embrace the historical specifics and cultural exigencies informing popular ideas about what art is and how it is created.

Throughout its history, the DGA has striven to bring its members into conformance with reigning cultural assumptions about art and artists. As Bourdieu has pointed out, in modern Western societies "the artist is the first and last source of the value of his work."[7] This value arose from a historical process that evolved over time. M. H. Abrams's classic study *The Mirror and the Lamp* traces the way in which attention to the figure of the artist grew out of the idea of the originary genius that developed during the Romantic period, when the view of art as an imitation of nature gave way to an idea of art as the expression of the imagination of its creator. Scholars such as Stephen Greenblatt and Rudolf Wittkower have explored the origins of this notion in the Renaissance concept of self-fashioning. During this period, as Svetlana Alpers has shown, Rembrandt's name became a brand as the work done by others in his studio was marginalized. Other scholars, such as Martha Woodmansee and Mark Rose, have suggested that, in the literary arena, the social groundwork for the Romantic theory of the artist was laid out in eighteenth-century court battles over the legal rights to books; in the course of these battles, arguments were circulated claiming that authors had the right to be thought of as owners of their work.[8]

Implicit in all these developments was a growing emphasis placed on the artist as a symbol of individuality and freedom, qualities highly esteemed in Western societies. As Bourdieu emphasizes, the highest place is reserved for artists like Vincent van Gogh, who pursue their calling despite the lack of economic benefits. In a cultural climate such as ours, works of art have been increasingly valued as icons that represent the complex inner lives of those who produce them. *Hollywood's Artists* draws on all these cultural assumptions in the course of examining the creative rights mission of the DGA. The book as a whole focuses primarily on cinema rather than on television or more recent media platforms in which DGA members are involved, because cinema is the area that the Guild's creative rights agenda was designed to address and the one in which this agenda has been most effectively carried out.

Chapter 1, "Directors as Artists," begins by exploring the way in which the Guild's creative rights objectives have been supported by trends in the industry and in the culture as a whole. Hollywood has long positioned its prestige productions as legitimate artistic enterprises and has increasingly promoted the idea that directors should be considered the authors who create them. Beginning in the 1970s and 1980s, the indie film movement focused even more centrally on the creative centrality of directors. Developments outside of the industry itself, especially the growing influence of auteur criticism during the 1960s and afterwards, furthered the directors' cause as well. The DGA's own policies have worked in tandem with such trends in several ways. Due largely to the Guild's efforts, directors have gained increasing control over the filmmaking process. In addition, the organization's promotional efforts involve an array of programs, including award ceremonies and various cultural activities, which are designed to help shape public attitudes toward directors as artists. In all these efforts, the Guild has been guided by Frank Capra's principle that a lone director is responsible for whatever artistic merit a film may have.

Chapter 2, "Charisma and Competition," describes the way in which the Guild's commitment to singular authorship dovetails with an image of directors as charismatic leaders. This image has affected directors' relationships with their most prominent creative partners: producers, actors, and writers. Producers have, for the most part, bought into the DGA's mission to present directors as singular authors, understanding it both as an opportunity to promote directors as brand names that could increase a film's bottom line and as an intangible value that could be used as a bargaining chip to negotiate lower directorial salaries.

However, the Guild's agenda has created friction with other groups of artisans with whom directors must interact. Stars have sometimes used their power to seize control of productions from directors. Screenwriters have mounted vigorous and protracted efforts to gain more control over their films, only to be repeatedly outmaneuvered by the DGA—even as writers have superseded directors in the realm of television. Directors have traditionally held jurisdiction over all below-the-line talent, including cinematographers, production designers, and art directors, but they came into conflict with editors (the only ones who don't work alongside them on the set) when directors' cuts of films became popular as reissues during the 1980s. In addition to placing their coworkers in subordinate positions, the image of directors as charismatic leaders links them with popular conceptions about masculinity and has disadvantaged women who have sought to enter the profession. The complex media landscape of the digital era has created further complications by introducing new constituencies, including consumers, into the mix of creators. Such developments have cast a bright light on the contradiction at the heart of the Guild's "one man, one film" principle.

Chapter 3, "Recognition," traces the Guild's efforts to control the way in which a director's participation in a given production is announced on screen. Here again, Capra's mantra has directed DGA policy, ensuring that, except in rare instances, only a single director will be credited for any given film, even if more than one has worked on it. To protect the integrity of this credit, in 1969 the Guild invented a fictional name, Allen Smithee, which could be used for the on-screen directorial credit of DGA members who wished to disown films they had directed. The Guild's stance on the so-called possessory credit, a recurring hot-button issue between the DGA and the Writers Guild, is also addressed in this chapter.

Chapter 4, "Politics," focuses on the way in which the DGA has constructed a narrative about a dramatic event in its past, a Guild meeting that occurred during the House Un-American Activities Committee investigations of the movie industry. At this time, the DGA considered requiring all its members to sign an oath of loyalty to the United States government. The matter quickly became tangled up in the internal politics of the organization, and soon Cecil B. DeMille launched a move to recall Guild president Joseph L. Mankiewicz. The recall was debated at a seven-hour meeting held at the Beverly Hills Hotel on the night of October 22, 1950. Many of the Guild's most prominent members, including John Ford, Joseph L. Mankiewicz, William Wyler, John Huston, Cecil B. DeMille, and, most notably, Frank Capra, repeatedly changed their positions at key moments during this fraught time. Guild members created a story about this event that suppressed such inconsistencies in order to shape it into a Hollywood melodrama featuring a clear-cut hero (Ford) and villain (DeMille) as well as an uplifting ending. Their tale portrayed Guild members as artists who were manly, patriotic, and socially committed.

Chapter 5, "Law," is devoted to the Guild's attempt to control what happens to films after they enter the marketplace. Here, the distinction between creative authors and legal authors comes into play. In the 1980s, a technology emerged that allowed the owners of old black-and-white movies to rerelease them in colorized versions. Led by Fred Zinnemann and others, the Guild attempted to ban colorization, but this project soon evolved into a drive to pass legislation granting directors ownership rights over films, an initiative modeled on the artists' moral rights doctrine that prevails in Continental Europe.

To achieve its goal, the Guild established a semiautonomous organization called the Artists Rights Foundation (ARF), headed by longtime Guild creative rights activist Elliot Silverstein. Though the foundation did manage to persuade the U.S. Congress to establish a national registry of American films thought worthy of preservation in their original form, more far-reaching legislation that would grant ownership rights to directors and other creative personnel remained beyond its reach. This project thus set an outer limit to the DGA's creative rights aspirations.

Hollywood's Artists concludes by describing the major bread-and-butter issues that form the context in which the DGA's creative rights agenda has evolved. The organization negotiates and oversees numerous programs centered on financial matters and issues connected with working conditions, including base salaries, royalty payments (called residuals), a pension plan, work schedules, and safety standards. In the 1960s the organization set up training programs for assistant directors, and in the 1980s it launched a series of initiatives aimed at seeking better employment opportunities for its disadvantaged members. Emerging technologies have necessitated new kinds of labor agreements focused on residual payments for new delivery platforms such as DVDs and internet streaming. In addition, runaway productions, filmed outside of Hollywood, have proliferated in an increasingly globalized environment as producers scour the world for fresh locations and cheap sources of labor. All of these Guild concerns form a background to the creative rights agenda that the organization has always seen as its main purpose.

The arguments put forward in *Hollywood's Artists* draw on a wide range of resources: documents in the DGA files deposited at California State University at Northridge, an array of archival materials, personal papers and biographies of various key players, histories of the industry, and articles in the trade and popular press. I have quoted freely from such materials, for the directors themselves have been both insightful and articulate in commenting on their organization, and journalists have written copiously about the group. I also have cited examples from

Hollywood films that take up themes of directors' creative prerogatives, in the belief that such works typically reflect attitudes within the industry.

My understanding of issues facing the DGA has been aided by the opportunity to interview many people with significant roles in the organization. Anthropologist Sherry Ortner has written about the difficulties inherent in gleaning information from members of an industry long famous for its predilection to control its image.[9] I was fortunate in not encountering any of the difficulties Ortner enumerates, finding many people who gave generously of their time and helped me to appreciate the human element that grounds the work of the DGA. I had lengthy discussions with four of the Guild's former presidents: Gene Reynolds, Arthur Hiller, Gilbert Cates, and Martha Coolidge. DGA board member and future president Paris Barclay shared his thoughts on the organization's efforts to advance the careers of its minority members, and Elliott Silverstein, who at the time headed up the Artists Rights Foundation, patiently elucidated some of the legal intricacies with which his group was grappling at the time. The DGA's executive director, Jay Roth, and associate executive director, Warren Adler, also talked with me at length. All of these native informants spoke eloquently about the Guild's creative rights achievements.

Like Hollywood directors themselves, I, too, have taken on the mantle of authorship by writing this book, and like them, I am situated within history and culture. As a feminist, I have been drawn to study the way in which the image of charismatic leadership that the DGA has fostered for its members has affected female directors. On another front, because I was a university student during a time when college film societies flourished, my filmgoing habits are largely driven by auteurist presumptions about the importance of directorial signatures. Further, as someone trained as an academic in the middle of the twentieth century, I am more likely to frequent museums than rock music clubs or video game websites, and I watch films in theaters rather than on a smartphone. My relationship to art and entertainment is thus that of a passive observer rather than an active participant, and in this regard, I differ from many of those who have come of age in the new millennium. In this book, I examine the historical underpinnings of such cultural predilections.

The subtitle of this book refers to authorship as a cultural construction. However, though the perception of Hollywood directors as creative artists may have been furthered by the creative rights mission of their guild, as well as by larger cultural trends, it is also true that each director comes to his or her work with unique abilities, predilections, and concerns. Though filmmakers interact with their surroundings throughout their lives and during the creative process itself, every participant in the making of a movie brings something exceptional to the table. This book honors that reality even as it examines an institution that has been instrumental in shaping the way in which artistry in Hollywood has come to be understood.

CHAPTER ONE

Directors as Artists

The DGA Rides the Wave

> The Guild got together not for more money, but for creative rights.... And I always felt that the DGA was the premiere guild of the entertainment industry because of this unique attitude.
> —GILBERT CATES, PRESIDENT OF THE DIRECTORS GUILD OF AMERICA, 1994–1996

> Every author, as far as he is great and at the same time original, has had the task of creating the taste by which he is to be enjoyed.
> —WILLIAM WORDSWORTH

Unlike writers and actors, who organized to protect salaries and working conditions, directors have always seen control over the creative process as the central mission for their guild. They are the only Hollywood union that negotiates creative matters separately from other labor issues, and they entrust such negotiations to a committee made up of members, not staff. This unique emphasis arises out of the directors' sense of who they are. As anthropologist Hortense Powdermaker observed, in her 1950 study of Hollywood culture, successful directors have always been distinct from other members of the Hollywood community in that they are "primarily motivated by the desire to produce an excellent film, and more concerned about their craft and art than with profits."[1]

ORIGINS: A GUILD, NOT A UNION

The Directors Guild of America's focus on creative rights arises from the very notion of what a guild is. First established in the Middle Ages, the guild system enabled artisans to band together in fellowships to further the group's common interests and control the quality of what they produced. Through apprenticeship programs, such guilds limited access to the crafts they represented and established standards that governed the activities of all members of the organization.[2] In America, the Jeffersonian principle of the independent citizen linked the guild ethos to democratic ideals so that the medieval standard of mutual support was joined with a republican notion of citizenship that carried with it associations of personal responsibility and pride. Within this ideological framework, labor unions in nineteenth-century America fostered ethical standards that valued both fellowship and worker autonomy. Though it was a source of controversy, this worker pride helped business owners because it raised the level of productivity.[3]

The industrial revolution that transformed labor conditions at the end of the nineteenth century ended this mode of union-based artisanal pride as technology and assembly line production methods forced people into jobs in which wages and working conditions became the only areas where labor could realistically hope to make gains. The Directors Guild, however, revived the guild ethos that had prevailed in an earlier era, focusing its efforts on enhancing the position of directors both within the film industry and in the culture at large. One Guild president, George Sidney, made the link between medieval guilds and the DGA founders explicit, stating, "They had in mind those sixteenth-century craftsmen that focused on talent and quality and brought everybody together."[4] Longtime DGA activist Fred Zinnemann also explained the DGA in such terms: "The essence of a guild is achievement and performance, the best possible, the most excellent performance, without ceiling on time and effort. This was as true of the old silversmiths as it is of the directors."[5] Directors, however, went beyond models established by the old guild framework in order to identify themselves not just as skilled workers but also as inspired creative artists in the tradition of nineteenth-century poets and painters.

Even though the DGA put its guild identity front and center, it came into being at a historical moment in which traditional union concerns were part of the cultural landscape, and it had to adapt its agenda accordingly. The organization coalesced amid a flood of union activity that was an outgrowth of the federal government's New Deal policies during the 1930s. President Franklin Roosevelt had put forward a legislative program that included the National Industrial Recovery Act, which sought to regulate the relations between workers and management, and the National Labor Relations Act (the Wagner Act), which required employers to bargain with recognized unions. As part of its initiative to support the efforts of organized labor, the federal government also set up the National Labor Relations Board (NLRB), endowing this office with the power to ratify the right of workers to unionize.

Yet, even with such supportive national policies, Los Angeles was not an easy city in which to organize, for it had a history of strong antilabor sentiment. In 1890, a printers' strike settlement established a tradition of open shop, which gave employers the right to hire nonunion workers. In 1910, labor activists were accused of bombing the *Los Angeles Times* building, creating a considerable backlash against workers. By 1920, labor costs in Los Angeles were 25 percent to 50 percent lower than those of New York. By the mid-1930s, however, the pace of union activity had picked up, and from 1936 to 1938 union membership in the young city jumped from less than 20,000 to 125,000 (of about 600,000 workers in all job sectors).[6]

Despite this rise in numbers, labor organizations both in Los Angeles and elsewhere around the country continued to experience problems, and motion picture workers were no exception. By the 1920s, corruption and gangsterism had infiltrated the International Alliance of Theatrical Stage Employees, to which many industry craftspeople belonged. Many of the prime movers in the formation of the Writers Guild were reputed to be members of the Communist Party, and many were Jewish. Thus, antiunion forces could—and did—draw on widespread fears about gangsterism as well as prejudices against Communists and Jews.[7] In 1927, under the leadership of MGM's Louis B. Mayer, the studios attempted to thwart the move toward labor organizing among its workers by setting up a company union, the Academy of Motion Picture Arts and Sciences. By the midthirties, however, it had become clear to most members of the Hollywood community that the Academy had been designed in large part to ensure that decisions about levels of compensation and authority over the work process would remain in the hands of the studio bosses.[8]

The challenging social climate notwithstanding, the three major film industry talent groups—writers, actors, and directors—persisted in their efforts to unionize. They had strong motivation, for in Hollywood, where personal relationships are crucial, fraternal associations play a key role; unionization, with its opportunities for networking, thus fit comfortably into the culture of the business.[9] As early as 1914, the screenwriters formed the Photoplay Authors' League, an offshoot of the Authors League of America, which had begun in 1912. Though the league collapsed in 1919, what is now called the Writers Guild of America (WGA) came into being the following year.[10] At the height of the Depression, in the spring of 1933, a series of major financial setbacks in the film industry prompted the studios to institute across-the-board pay cuts, triggering the formation of the Screen Actors Guild. A few months later, the WGA, which had been virtually destroyed by studio interference and internal political squabbles, was reactivated.

The directors, for their part, had their own prehistory of organizational efforts.[11] These initiatives focused on issues of status, networking, and creative control rather than on money and job security, foreshadowing the distinctive preoccupations that would later characterize the DGA itself. From 1915 to 1926, a group called the Motion Picture Directors Association flourished. This organization was social and charitable in nature. Its four aims were "to maintain the honor and dignity of the profession; to improve the moral, social, and intellectual standing of all persons connected with the motion picture producing business; to cultivate social intercourse among its members; and to aid and assist all worthy distressed members."[12] It was avowedly not a union and rejected the overtures of the American Federation of Labor to affiliate with it. "We were not joined together to fight the [motion picture] business," wrote J. Searle Dawley, one of the group's members. "Our idea was to be of some service to the [motion picture] art."[13] The group emphasized its commitment to the idea of directors as artists in a song that began, "I'm an artist with a cap-i-tal A; I'm a member of the MPDA."[14]

Directors as Artists 13

The association had branches in both Los Angeles and New York, and at one time about 150 directors, virtually all of those in the business, belonged to it. Between 1924 and 1927, the group published a journal initially called *The Director* and later *The Motion Picture Director*. In 1924, members of the association partnered with Blue Ribbon Pictures to launch a plan to fund a handful of movies over which the directors would exercise full control.[15] This effort was thwarted when producers threatened a blacklist.[16] Once the Academy of Motion Picture Arts and Sciences was organized, in 1926, most directors shifted their allegiance to the new organization, and the Motion Picture Directors Association was dissolved.

Other attempts at organizing to gain creative control followed. In 1931, four directors—Frank Borzage, Cecil B. DeMille, Lewis Milestone, and King Vidor—formed Directors Guild Inc., with the intention of producing independent films. Directors Guild Inc. represented a variation on the model United Artists had established in 1919 to distribute the productions of its filmmaker-owners. Though the group's plan was never carried out, the four partners did draft a "Directors Declaration of Independence," thereby announcing their goal of gaining greater power for directors. "It is the writer and director who make a picture," wrote DeMille at the time, "not the executive in his office."[17] All four of these filmmakers subsequently became founding members of what eventually became the Directors Guild of America, and DeMille and Vidor were two of the major forces charting the course of the DGA during its formative years.

In the same year, producers David O. Selznick and Walter Wanger hatched a similar scheme for independent production, with the goal of providing more autonomy for directors. Selznick explained, "Under the factory system of production you rob the director of his individualism, and this being a creative industry, that is harmful to the quality."[18] In 1937, King Vidor attempted to launch yet another directors group, this time with Lewis Milestone, Gregory La Cava, and Howard Hawks. Called Screen Directors Inc., it was structured as a directors' cooperative and planned to release films through RKO.[19] However, it was soon apparent to Vidor, as it was to most other directors, that their best hope of gaining control over their work lay in unionization.

What is now called the Directors Guild of America was founded at the end of 1935, more than two years after the writers and actors had organized. The issue that galvanized the directors into action was not money; it was creative authority. The autonomy many of them had enjoyed during the 1920s had steadily eroded during the 1930s, due in part to new bank oversight of the studios.[20] The push for greater efficiency put more authority in the hands of executives, who used it to limit directors' creative input. In 1933, both Universal Studios and Paramount Pictures announced that they would assign directors to projects as needed, allowing them no choice of material and no preparation time. This policy was particularly ominous coming from Paramount, for it was the studio that had previously given the greatest power to celebrated directors like Ernst Lubitsch, Joseph von Sternberg, Cecil B. DeMille, Leo McCarey, and Rouben Mamoulian.[21]

There was also increasing evidence, especially at Warner Bros., of the growth of an assembly line system of production in which multiple directors would be assigned to a single film, a fate that had already befallen the writers. Busby Berkeley's work at the studio in the early thirties, which often involved creating musical production numbers that could be inserted into films directed by others, provided a model for this scheme, as did Raoul Walsh's position as the Warners' "tank man" in charge of all scenes that were shot in the studio's water tank.[22] Sam Marx, head of MGM's scenario department during the 1930s, stated that "team spirit was implicit in the studio's directing staff," by which he meant that MGM directors were expected to fill in for one another as needed and as assigned.[23] When sound came in, dialogue directors were hired, which further eroded directors' power.[24] Finally, the studios had taken on the project of branding their productions through the use of distinctive studio styles, which limited directors' ability to impose their own stylistic signatures. The bland, glossy appearance of MGM releases during this period exemplified this trend, as did the gritty, hard-edged look of Warner Bros. pictures.

A *Variety* report published in early 1936 enumerated the reasons behind the directors' organizational efforts:

> They want to make pictures in such a way that they will participate in the production practically from its creation. They want to be in on story conferences. They want to have a say on the selection of their casts, and they want to be in on the cutting of their pictures,

as they feel if they are given screen credit, they should also be given a right to protect their reputations on what reaches the screen. They claim that [producers and studio executives] have been trying to railroad them, that they have had assignments 24 hrs before a pic went into work. That they have had no chance in these cases to say whether they wanted to make them in factory style. That in these instances they were not even given a chance to use their own ideas in the making. They were given a script, with camera angles, etc., and told to get it out. Then when the picture was finished, they were not permitted to function as cutters. They were through with the picture. The studio producers cut it to suit themselves, with the directors advancing the claim that in most of these cases their creative ability was not demonstrated and that they were just automatons.[25]

John Ford had his own description of why the DGA was needed:

Changes are due in the motion picture industry from the director's standpoint. With the coming of sound, the "committee method," so-called, came into being. Previously, the method of making pictures had been the "combination method"—the producer, the writer, and the director. And the director started on the idea with the writer and followed through until it was completed on the screen.

My complaint toward the "committee method" is that no one man's idea is carried through in its entirety. The picture, by necessity, becomes a composite work. . . . Through the Directors Guild, we hope to eliminate the "committee method." We feel that the Guild fulfills a very great need.[26]

Frank Capra added his voice to the chorus advocating for greater directorial control. "Eighty percent of the directors today shoot scenes exactly as they are told to shoot them without any changes whatsoever," he complained in a 1939 letter to the *New York Times*. "Ninety percent of them have no voice in the story or in the editing."[27]

The DGA's organizing efforts began in earnest on December 23, 1935, at the house of King Vidor, who would become the Guild's first president. Joseph Newman, who worked with Vidor at MGM during this period, credits Vidor as "the father of the modern Directors Guild."[28] Frank Borzage, Howard Hawks, Lewis Milestone, Frank Tuttle, and William Wellman were among those who attended. The initial group may also have included Herbert Biberman, Lloyd Corrigan, John Cromwell, John Ford, William K. Howard, Henry King, Ernst Lubitsch, Gregory La Cava, Rowland V. Lee, Rouben Mamoulian, A. Edward Sutherland, Woody Van Dyke, and Richard Wallace.[29] At a subsequent meeting, on January 8, 1936, with five more in attendance, the group drafted its articles of incorporation, which were filed with the government on January 13. The following day, a hundred more applications for membership poured in. The Guild's first public meeting took place at the Hollywood Athletic Club on January 15, 1936.[30]

Though the Guild founders had much in common, they also had significant differences. Vidor, Milestone, and Biberman were leftists, while DeMille and Capra, the DGA's second president, were politically conservative. In response to pressure from its right-wing constituency, the Guild ultimately chose to remain independent of larger labor organizations. On January 22, 1936, the group fired its original lawyer, Laurence Beilenson, who also represented the WGA and the SAG (the latter organization was affiliated with the American Federation of Labor). Subsequently, at the behest of Capra, the group hired Mabel Walker Willebrandt, a conservative former United States assistant attorney general and a close friend of Louis B. Mayer, to represent them. Willebrandt arranged the group's NLRB hearings and drafted its first Basic Agreement.[31]

The successful directors who formed the core of the DGA and would lead it in the years to come were rich men for whom bread-and-butter union concerns were largely irrelevant. Seizing on this anomaly, the studio representatives argued that the directors were not eligible to unionize because of their salaries and status, comparing their situation to that of the design engineers at Chrysler Motors, whose application for recognition as a union had already been denied by the NLRB on the basis that they were already well compensated.[32] A 1936 article on the nascent organization reflected this view. It was titled "Hollywood's $100,000 a Year Union" and quoted an executive at the NLRB hearing who stated, "They already have big houses and swimming pools. What do they want? Two swimming pools?"[33] In response to such arguments, the DGA's Washington lawyer, Barry Brannon, pointed out that directors could not be considered management because they had no power to hire and fire. "In practice," Brannon explained, "a director may exert substantial influence in selection of cast or designation of members of the production unit. But this influence is exerted vicariously by means of recommendation and suggestion, and not as a matter of right by any authority given him under his contract."[34]

On May 19, 1937, four days after the Screen Actors Guild signed a contract with producers that focused on wages and working conditions, the directors decided to admit assistant directors and unit managers as junior members. By taking this step, the DGA increased its membership from 90 to 550 and reshaped its image in such a way as to make traditional union issues a more credible part of its agenda, thus ensuring that they would receive NLRB ratification. One can readily assume that the directors must have understood at this point that their ability to negotiate the creative rights agenda that lay at the heart of their move to organize would be greatly strengthened if carried out under the umbrella of a struggle for fair wages and humane working conditions, and that such concerns would apply most obviously to low-paid, overworked assistant directors and unit managers. The move also placed assistant directors and unit managers, who were responsible for matters of day-to-day budgeting and scheduling for all productions, under the wing of directors, thereby giving directors greater authority on the set. Moreover, as DGA member Elliot Silverstein later noted, the participation of the assistant directors and unit managers in the Guild made the threat of a strike far more potent, for though many studio executives may have believed that they could fill in for directors if the situation called for it, it was far more likely that a strike involving assistant directors and unit managers, whose duties included the complicated tasks of setting up shooting schedules and managing cadres of workers, could shut production down entirely.[35] Though the studios adamantly opposed the Guild's enlarged membership and the claim to increased directorial authority on the set that it implied, the government ratified the directors' revised conception of their organization.

Yet another reason for admitting the assistant directors and unit managers into the Guild was the directors' desire to ally themselves with other Hollywood craftspeople who were then unionizing. This motive is suggested in a speech delivered by Guild treasurer John Ford to the DGA membership, probably in early 1937. Ford said:

> We want to know why the hell so many brilliant directors and assistants are not working, I, for one, would like to cooperate with the other people in the game and find out what's at the bottom of this. I firmly believe that that kind of cooperation is plainly our duty unless we are satisfied to remain an insignificant and exclusive club. Let's try to get back to the old days—when the people on the set looked to the director for leadership. Let's pitch in with our co-workers and try and find a way out of this mess. Let['s] work in the industry, with the industry and for the industry. Let's not be high-hat—let's help the others.[36]

Ford's comments suggest that the directors wanted to position themselves as leaders of the groups of artisans who created Hollywood entertainment, rather than as part of the business interests that paid the bills.

Though this strategy ensured that the DGA would be recognized by the NLRB, the producers continued to stall. But the Guild's negotiating committee, by then under the leadership of the intrepid Frank Capra, forced a showdown by threatening to strike and boycott the Oscars unless the studios recognized their right to organize. On February 19, 1939, the studios, represented by the Motion Picture Producers Association, finally caved in and agreed to negotiate.[37] Thus the directors got their Guild, which enabled them to exploit the labor-friendly tenor of the times in order to graft some of their creative rights goals onto a more conventional union agenda. The breakthrough came none too soon, for most of the DGA's prime movers were soon to be called away to serve their country in World War II.

The star directors who negotiated with producers on behalf of the less privileged assistant directors and unit managers stood to gain little in the way of material advantages. Frank Capra did not hesitate to point this fact out to his fellow Guild members. In a letter to the DGA membership dated January 1, 1939, he wrote, "Practically all the men involved [in the negotiations] will get no direct benefit from the Guild."[38] Capra's remarks were somewhat disingenuous, however, for even if there were no significant material benefits in the offing for him and his A-list colleagues, important issues were at stake for them. At the November 7 DGA meeting of the previous year, in which the Guild's membership drive was discussed, he commented, "If we get preparation for story and the chance to make first cut, you don't think those two things are important to directors?"[39] Producer Pandro Berman, who sat on the other side of the negotiating table during this period, later recalled, "When the Directors Guild was formed, the directors tried to take advantage of the opportunity to take over all the authority. They wanted autonomy. They would have liked to have gotten rid of the producers entirely."[40] If the matter of salary was important for these already wealthy men, it was largely because of its symbolic meaning, for, as Rouben Mamoulian later stated, "A lot of directors were underpaid, and being underpaid also meant that they lacked authority in many fields where the director should have authority."[41]

The leadership role that made A-list directors responsible for negotiating wages and working conditions for less privileged members of the DGA strengthened the directors' dominance over the filmmaking process at the same time that it provided them with a recognized forum for advancing the cause of their own position as artists. But obligations to the Guild's lower ranks were not uppermost in the minds of the leaders. As DGA activist Robert Aldrich later recalled:

> For a long time [the Guild] was run by big-name directors in a benign, thoughtful, conservative way, but for their best interests. It was very difficult to make them understand that it was a vertical union, that they had to consider the welfare of a second assistant who was being exploited, who was not being paid proportionally to other craftsmen. It was very hard for them to come by the fact that, having involved the assistants, it was their responsibility to care for the assistants' concerns and welfare, just as they cared for their own.[42]

The DGA's first contract with producers, from 1939, states the purpose of the organization as "recognizing the director's creative function." The Guild's constitution reads in part:

> The director's professional function, called "directing" or "direction," is unique and all embracing. He reconceives the particular

entertainment or information form as it will appear in its entirety and vitally participates in all the phases of its preparation and execution. He is closely associated with all other creative talents and crafts involved in the production of the unit, and one of his major aims is to extract the utmost values from these talents and crafts and to present them to the public at their very best.

He works directly with all of the elements which constitute the variegated texture of a unit of entertainment or information: story, acting, dialogue, movements, music, song, dance, camera, photography, sound recording, scenery, costumes, props, make-up, etc.

The director's task is to contribute creatively to all these elements and to guide, mold and integrate them into one cohesive dramatic and aesthetic whole.[43]

The document gave directors a guaranteed preparation time prior to shooting and specified directorial consulting privileges on matters such as casting and editing. These safeguards of directorial authority over films have been strengthened with each new Guild agreement.

The DGA's creative rights mission came under a new set of pressures after World War II, when the organization became involved in heated negotiations over the new medium of television. TV has historically occupied a lower position on the cultural totem pole than film, and its directors have enjoyed little status, due to the conventions of the medium. The style of a given television series is typically set at the outset; directors of individual episodes must conform to the formula set down in the show's "bible."[44] Such directors function as journeymen who must follow the established pattern of the series, not as innovators who put their personal stamp on a unique work. Industry jargon labels their duties as guest shots. "In television your hands are usually tied," director Rob Bowman once confessed. "You're told, 'Don't get in the way of the dialogue.' In my view, you just give up to a life of anonymity as a television director."[45] Given this reality, TV directors have not historically harbored the creative rights aspirations of their cinematic colleagues; accordingly, they have been more interested in the benefits associated with union membership than by those offered by a guild. Incorporating such a group into the DGA was thus a fraught process.

In the beginning, jurisdiction was the issue. The DGA had been alert to the desirability of including TV in its purview since before the war. Director Joseph Lerner recalled "a meeting of the Directors Guild, sometime before the war, when directors were begging the Harry Cohns and the Zanucks to start up TV stations, and they were being told it wasn't their kind of business, it was a shitty medium, a six-inch picture, who was going to look at it?"[46] Undeterred by the studio bosses' resistance, during the late 1940s a number of prominent Guild members, including Ford, DeMille, and Hal Roach, had already set up production companies aimed at the TV market.[47]

In 1947, a New York–based union, the Radio and Television Directors Guild (RTDG), was formed; in 1948, it won a contract with the major New York City television stations, covering all staff directors. On March 19, 1950, the DGA entered the fray, announcing its intention to represent all television directors, and on July 30 of that year the Los Angeles–based Guild won a contract with a local TV station.[48] The RTDG quickly responded, filing a complaint against the DGA on September 18 accusing it of unfair labor practices. The next day, the DGA, retaliated, filing a counter-complaint that accused the rival group of being Communist dominated.[49] In December the NLRB dismissed both complaints, citing lack of evidence. This decision cleared the way for the DGA leaders to pursue their ambitions to represent television directors. The move came at a crucial moment for the Guild, for its membership at the time hovered just above six hundred and those who belonged believed that the group's future lay in its ability to add TV directors to its roster.[50]

Eventually, in 1960, the DGA and the RTDG merged, but the struggle had been a contentious one. And disagreements continued to simmer. Some centered on geographic issues, but more substantive differences soon emerged over what the Guild's primary mission should be.[51] Many members of the RTDG, which formerly had been affiliated with the American Federation of Labor, wanted a traditional union that would put wages and working conditions at the top of the agenda over the creative rights issues so dear to the hearts of their West Coast colleagues. In 1962, an East Coast group headed by Ted Corday sent the DGA policymakers a letter proposing that the Guild's constitution be rewritten in more union-like terms by allocating jobs in terms of seniority and allowing all members, not just senior members, to run for the presidency.⁵² Their action prompted Frank Capra to declare, at the next national board meeting, "We made a mistake. We don't want you [Easterners] in our guild."⁵³ Capra's sentiments were seconded by Fred Zinnemann, who addressed the DGA board around this time. He stated, "The umbrella of the DGA is too small to cover the opposing and incompatible concepts of guild and union."⁵⁴ George Sidney concurred. "They don't like our constitution and want to alter it along the lines of a union," he said. "But we won't go for it."⁵⁵

In 1964, the DGA formed a Creative Rights Committee under the chairmanship of Elliot Silverstein.⁵⁶ The title of the document the group produced, "The Directors' Bill of Rights," elaborated on the idea that creative control for directors was not a privilege but a right, alluding to the juridical traditions of Westernized nations with their various constitutions and thereby identifying directors as citizens of an enlightened polity.⁵⁷ Since its publication, virtually all of the goals listed in that document have become part of the standard contract for directors, including participation in the selection of all production elements and personnel, control of rehearsals and shooting, and authority over editing and scoring.

THE CULTURAL CONTEXT

Hollywood movies cannot be readily assimilated into traditional conceptions of art. They are manifestly produced by groups, not individuals. Moreover, mainstream films typically adhere to formulas associated with both the tropes of popular genres and the strict grammar of the classical Hollywood style. In addition, they are the products of a profit-oriented business enterprise. Such a production context is far removed from the Romantic vision of the artist as a solitary genius who expresses deeply personal preoccupations with no expectation of economic gain. Modernist aesthetic theories have further distanced Hollywood fare from accepted cultural conceptions of art because, as Lawrence Levine and others have shown, the modernist movement opened an unprecedented gulf between elite and popular arts, so that the mass audience Hollywood movies attract precludes such works from claiming aesthetic validity.⁵⁸

From the earliest days of cinema, the Hollywood industry has taken up the challenge presented by these cultural assumptions, positioning their prestige productions as legitimate artistic enterprises rather than vulgar amusements.[59] Sometimes this effort has involved strategies aimed at associating "the flickers" with the high arts. The abandoned barns and warehouses in which movies were made were called "studios." While the film business was still in its infancy, moguls like Jesse Lasky and Adoph Zukor borrowed subject matter from respected literary works and recruited stars from the worlds of opera, ballet, and the legitimate stage to add an aura of high culture to some of their productions. The lion logo for Goldwyn Pictures (later MGM), devised in 1917, included the motto "Ars gratia artis" (Art for art's sake).[60]

During the 1920s, movie palaces were designed to rival the grandeur of concert halls and opera houses. Founded in 1927, the Academy of Motion Picture Arts and Sciences, in addition to functioning as a company union, cultivated an aura of high culture in order to promote Hollywood movies as legitimate art. The organization took its name and inspiration from the learned societies that flourished during the Renaissance.[61] Its inaugural awards ceremony recognized the striking visual style of F. W. Murnau's *Sunrise* (1927) by giving it a special prize as Best Picture: Unique and Artistic Production.[62] In the 1940s, newspaper ads began to publish starting times for movies, which was intended to discourage the casual attendance patterns that had prevailed up to then. By implication, this practice defined each film as an artistic whole rather than a collection of sensational vignettes.

Though movie stars have remained at the center of most of the studios' promotional efforts, the quest to elevate more aesthetically ambitious productions led publicists to focus on creative authors who could be plausibly identified as the artists responsible for them.[63] Directors filled the bill for two reasons. First, they oversaw filming and brought all the disparate elements together and therefore could be seen as the unifying force that gave a picture coherence. This conception of the director's job was voiced by Cecil B. DeMille in a 1924 article he wrote for the publication of the Motion Picture Directors Association. A director's job, he stated, "is that of taking individual excellence made by artists, actors, designers, authors and cameramen and fashioning all these separate, perfect things into a perfect finished, SINGLE whole."[64] Second, directors could claim authorship of a movie's style insofar as they supervised staging, a job that encompassed both the configuration of a production's visual and sound elements and the quality of its performances.[65] The image of directors as stylists that this latter function implied could, in itself, be seen as crucial to their claim to be considered artists.[66] In an introduction to a series of essays on directors, put out by the DGA, Frank Capra paid tribute to both of these aspects of the director's job: "Only the director has the creative ability, and—more importantly—the *opportunity*, to meld all the components into a film that is stamped with his own style, pace, and thrust."[67]

Buying into these assumptions, the Hollywood studios cast the directors of their prestige productions as artists in the high culture mold.[68] At times, they pointed to the visual flair evident in a director's staging techniques. During the silent era, Paramount labeled the distinctive look of Cecil B. DeMille's films "Rembrandt lighting," while Metro trumpeted the art world origins of directors Maurice Tourneur and Rex Ingram.[69] The fan magazines played along. An article on D. W. Griffith that appeared in the October 1916 issue of *Photoplay* asserted:

> What Debussy and Richard Strauss and Puccini have done for music, what Manet and Monet did for painting, ... what William Dean Howells accomplished when he published *Silas Lapham*, ... something of the same as all these breaking of the fetters ... was done when Griffith created *Birth of a Nation*. For he had first sown and harvested a complete and perfect technique all his own; he applied this technique to an epical theme and a masterpiece panoplied in beauty sprang from his brain.[70]

The studios' efforts were subsequently supported by well-regarded cultural institutions like museums and universities, which began to include Hollywood cinema among their offerings and frequently organized film series and courses around directorial names. Columbia University began offering film courses in 1915, and New York's Museum of Modern Art launched its film library in 1935.[71]

After World War II, movie palaces were joined by art house cinemas dedicated to screening personal films made by international moviemakers.[72] At around the same time, film festivals came on the scene.

These organizations frequently give prizes to directors, and the director-heavy juries that make such awards create an aura of consecration, which Pierre Bourdieu identifies with art produced for other artists.[73] Movie reviewers took note of these trends and began to mention directors' names more and more frequently.[74]

Many directors advanced the studios' project of identifying them as the creative authors of movies by impressing their presence on the public. The advertisement D. W. Griffith took out in the *New York Daily Mirror* to announce his availability upon leaving the Biograph Company emphasized the stylistic contributions he had made to the development of film narrative, including insert shots, parallel editing, and similar techniques, as a way of asserting his stature as an artist.[75] Ironically, once Griffith had established his name with the public, Biograph took to capitalizing on his fame as well, proclaiming Griffith's role as the director of its film *The Battle of Elderbush Gulch*, shot in 1913 but released after the success of *Birth of a Nation* (1915) had made Biograph's former employee a star.[76]

Later directors devised additional strategies to make themselves widely known. Orson Welles and Charlie Chaplin appeared as actors in most of their films. Other directors have identified themselves as masters of particular genres, as John Ford did with Westerns and Ernst Lubitsch did with risqué comedies. Alfred Hitchcock made himself visible to the public through a range of techniques. He associated his name with a genre that came to be known as the Hitchcock thriller; he made cameo appearances near the beginning of all his productions; he encouraged the circulation of a readily recognizable caricature of himself; and, during the 1950s, he hosted a television series entitled *Alfred Hitchcock Presents*.[77]

The DGA took up the project of presenting directors as creative authors by launching its own public relations program. The 1939 DGA agreement states that "one of the Guild's purposes is to increase the public awareness of the Director's important creative contribution to entertainment."[78] The Guild publicized the names of its members through a range of public relations activities. By the late 1940s these activities were so fully institutionalized that, in 1948, then-president George Marshall could report in the annual financial statement, "Public relations has always been a subject of intense discussion in the Board

Room, and it has been felt that we should have some form of contact that would bring to the director the prestige and credit he is entitled to, particularly in the minds of the theatre-going public. With this thought in view an extensive campaign has started."[79] This effort was renewed in 1958, under president George Sidney, who stated, "The Guild is launching a full-scale publicity and public relations program designed to bring proper recognition to its members.... No year books, no almanacs, no extant publications contain your views of your work, and film making generally. But without them, we cannot hope to show the industry or the nation the focal role of the director in films."[80] By 1996, the Guild had established an in-house publicity department.[81]

To draw attention to the most notable work of its members, the DGA has sponsored many awards. Such gestures not only advertise to the industry and to the world at large the achievements of directors but also raise the consciousness of the DGA membership itself, helping directors in all media to conceptualize their positions as creative rather than simply managerial. In 1949, the Guild began to give awards for outstanding direction of individual films. As Marshall explained at the time, the purpose of such awards was, "to enhance the position of the director in the eyes of the press, the public, and the industry."[82] Gradually, a series of other awards was put into place, honoring television directors, assistant directors, unit managers, and directors of commercials. For a time, the Guild presented yet another award, this for directorial achievement by a foreign filmmaker.[83] The DGA also bestowed special achievement awards on Federico Fellini (1957) and Ingmar Bergman (1990), two of the premier figures in world cinema.

The DGA's promotional efforts also have engaged the critical community. In 1955, the Guild sponsored a poll that asked film reviewers to select "the ten greatest directorial achievements during the past fifty years."[84] On February 8, 1956, DGA executive secretary Joe Youngerman wrote to Frank Capra justifying this move. "Delmer Daves expressed his shock that of all the reviews, an almost infinitesimal percentage even mentioned the name of the director," Youngerman explained, "let alone give him credit for the success of films."[85] By 1964, the DGA had instituted a new award to recognize the movie critics themselves. To promote this award, the Guild created a radio advertisement in which Frank Capra and Alfred Hitchcock lauded the talents of reviewers. A draft of this spot was also to include statements by Cecil B. DeMille, such as "It may seem strange, but we directors find intelligent criticism very helpful in improving our pictures;" to which Capra was to have replied, "I'm learning more about movies than I imagined possible by going through these reviews"[86]

The Guild's public relations efforts got a further push in 1974, when Elia Kazan wrote a letter to the organization calling for a special projects initiative designed to "increase the prestige of the Guild and of our particular craft and art." He added, "Isn't that one of the main purposes of a Guild as distinct from a union?"[87] The Guild followed through on Kazan's suggestions by appointing a Special Projects Committee, which Robert Wise led from 1976 to 2000. The committee and its offshoot, the Educational and Benevolent Foundation, sponsored such projects as an oral history program and weekend retreats with notable directors.[88]

The DGA also has supported activities specifically designed to situate directors within the context of the high arts and in relation to the academic culture that is home to this tradition. During the 1940s, the Guild organized an exhibition at its headquarters of art from the private collections of its members, including works by Pablo Picasso, Auguste Renoir, Vincent van Gogh, and Henry Moore.[89] In 1950, the group also commissioned prominent Canadian artist Miriam Lyons Steinhart to paint a series of portraits of some of its most famous members, including Cecil B. DeMille, Joseph Mankiewicz, Albert Rogell, and Frank Capra; these were to have been auctioned off at a gala fundraiser.[90] In addition, in 1956 the Guild arranged a series of talks by directors at the San Francisco Museum of Art, and a few years later sponsored a screening series at the Museum of Modern Art in New York City, on the occasion of the DGA's fiftieth anniversary. A one-hour documentary entitled *Fifty Years of Action*, produced by the Guild and directed by Douglas M. Stewart Jr., accompanied the series.[91] Other DGA-sponsored public relations activities included a course on directing, offered through UCLA, and appearances by directors at universities nationwide.[92] Since 1978, the Guild has also sponsored an annual Film Educators Workshop, bringing college professors to Los Angeles for a two-week introduction to the art of filmmaking.

In 1989, the DGA constructed a new twenty-million-dollar headquarters designed by the prestigious architectural firm of Rochlin Baran and Balbona. Guild members viewed this project as an opportunity to impress their image as artists on a larger public through their sponsorship of an architectural work in the high art tradition. In the words of DGA founding member Rouben Mamoulian, the directors' plan was to create "a drop-dead building."[93] The resulting seven-story structure, located at 7920 Sunset Boulevard in West Hollywood, featured sleek curving shapes with a subtle pattern of stripes formed by granite in mauve and burgundy shades (figure 1.1). DGA president Gilbert Cates stated, "Its uniqueness will reflect the status, prestige and the position of the Directors Guild in the entertainment industry."[94] The DGA's new headquarters won two awards for Rochlin Baran and Balbona from the American Institute of Architects—one upon its completion in 1989 and another twenty-five years later. In the brochure issued on the occasion of its dedication, Mamoulian described it as "a symbol of the directors and what the directors do, and a building that will welcome through open doors not only our members but people from the outside."[95]

FIGURE 1.1 Headquarters of the Directors Guild of America. Photo by Kim Wexman

However, not everyone approved of the Guild's new home. In a critique published in the *Los Angeles Times* soon after it was dedicated, architectural critic Leon Whiteson observed, "The DGA headquarters is . . . deliberately at odds with its surroundings."[96] Unlike the unprepossessing structures housing the WGA and the SAG, which are nearby, the DGA's sculptural edifice stands apart from its eclectic, small-scale neighborhood. Though its windows overlook the street, a reflective bronze coating prevents passersby from looking in. Unlike the open door Mamoulian had envisioned, it appears as a formidable monolith. Within the industry, it is known as "fortress DGA."[97]

THE SINGULAR ARTIST

More than any other individual, Frank Capra shaped the DGA's creative rights agenda. He was at the forefront at every stage, leading early negotiations with the studios, serving as the group's second president, and then going on to chair numerous committees. Capra was in a unique position to advocate for the directors' cause, for he had attained a rare position of power in Hollywood before he joined the Guild. Harry Cohn, his boss at Columbia Pictures, had agreed to feature Capra's name rather than that of a major actor to market the studio's prestige productions and had given Capra considerable freedom in shaping the films he made there. Capra later recalled his initial interview with Cohn:

CAPRA: I don't want to talk business. You name the price, I'll name the conditions.
COHN: What do you mean, conditions?
CAPRA: I write the film. I direct the film. I edit the film. I put the sound track on the film. I put it in the can. All me.[98]

In the late 1920s, Capra had teamed up with Scoop Conlon, a publicist who had determined to focus his attention on directors and was engaged in promoting them as the behind-the-screen stars of moviemaking.[99] Capra and Conlon brought to the DGA's creative rights agenda the catchphrase "One man, one film." "Any art creation should be the product of one mind," Capra stated at the time. "With that mind there should be no interference."[100] He later elaborated on the idea as follows: "One man has to make the decision, one man says yes or no. That man should be the director."[101] Capra's autobiography returns again and again to the principle of the director as a solitary creator. He wrote, "The 'one man, one film' idea took hold slowly—against opposition from entrenched executives—and today many directors have a box office value as big, or bigger than the stars."[102] The phrase "One man, one film" and all that it implied was the key that enabled directors to create an image of themselves as artists.

In his autobiography and elsewhere, Capra repeatedly linked his mantra to elite cultural traditions. "One man makes one film," he stated on one occasion. "One painter, one painting."[103] By making such gestures toward canonical art forms, Capra swept aside the problematic issues of aesthetic merit and authorship raised by Hollywood cinema. But the slogan also did more: it reflected a value that the culture at large places on the lone artist as a symbol of bourgeois values.

Original artistic expression is honored in modern Western democracies in part because it supplies visible evidence of the uniqueness of each individual and the ability of each person to express themselves freely. As Peter Burger puts the matter, "During the period when essential fundamental principles of developing bourgeois society... were being recognized, art was seen as the only possible sphere in which man's lost wholeness could be recovered."[104] In the modern era, the free expression of singular creative talents in the West is often opposed to the restrictions placed on artists under socialist regimes, and the United States emphasizes these values more strongly than any other nation.[105] DGA members have always understood Capra's motto in these terms. In the Guild's earliest public statement, Capra asserted, "What built the motion pictures was individuality."[106] In an introduction written for an anthology of articles from *DGA Magazine*, John Ford wrote in a similar vein. "Directors, because of the nature of their profession (some might say the cussedness of their natures too), are among the greatest individualists in the world."[107] George Stevens likewise expressed these sentiments when he stated, "Directing is an individual thing. The more individual, the better."[108] In various interviews and books, Hollywood directors have also espoused the ideal of artistic freedom. "I always feel constrained in the presence of too many rules, severe rules," John Huston once commented. "They distress me. I like the sense of freedom."[109]

A model of filmmakers as solitary artists who are free to create conspicuously personal work has long existed in Europe, for Europeans identified film artistry with singular directors from an early era. David Bordwell has aptly labeled the European tradition of filmmaking "art cinema," as it fits neatly into the traditional mold established in the high arts.[110] Art cinema directors frequently take part in preparing scripts for their productions, giving a personal stamp to elements such as plotting and dialogue that audiences can readily identify. In addition, directors' control over casting allows certain performers to be read as directorial alter egos, as, for example, Jean-Pierre Léaud was for François Truffaut and Marcello Mastroianni was for Federico Fellini.[111] Further, filmmakers like Andrei Tarkovsky and Ingmar Bergman have produced works whose obscurity is assumed to express the inner lives of their makers.

Many Hollywood directors have fostered similar images as creative authors in the European art cinema mold by creating personas as embattled figures at odds with their industrial surroundings. Some, like Woody Allen, have employed a rhetoric of distance, claiming that the superficiality of the Hollywood industry makes it impossible for them to live in Los Angeles. In other instances, the distance mainstream American directors put between themselves and the movie business is symbolic. Erich von Stroheim became notorious for his battles with his studio bosses, which were centered on both the lavishness of the expenditures he required to achieve the effects he wanted and, in the case of his 1924 picture *Greed*, the commercially daunting eight-hour running time he insisted on to ensure the film's artistic integrity.[112] The years following the demise of the old-style studios saw an increasing number of directors following the path von Stroheim had marked out with *Greed*, declaring their detachment from market forces by producing movies that would not fit into the two-hour time limit conventionally slotted for theatrical showings.[113]

Besides distancing themselves from the impersonal machinery of the industry, some Hollywood directors also have sought to assert their affinity with the art cinema tradition of personal expression by explicitly identifying their films with their own lives. Steven Spielberg's career has been especially telling in this regard for, though his name is well known, it was initially associated with formulaic commercial exercises rather than idiosyncratic personal statements. Spielberg first attempted to reconfigure his image by tackling socially significant subjects in films like *The Color Purple* (1985) and *Empire of the Sun* (1987), but he received little critical recognition for these efforts. Only with his 1993 holocaust drama *Schindler's List* did Spielberg manage to change the terms in which he was viewed, as he was able to identify the story's weighty social theme with his own personal experiences as a Jew growing up in a community of gentiles.[114] In numerous interviews about this film, he recalled his childhood years. "I was embarrassed, I was self-conscious," he told one journalist. "I was always aware I stood out because of my Jewishness. In high school I got smacked and kicked around. Two bleeding noses. It was horrible."[115] Reviewers responded in kind to this carefully orchestrated publicity campaign. "*Schindler* is Spielberg's most personal and passionate film, an attempt to explore his Jewish heritage," wrote one.[116] Coincidentally or not, Spielberg won his first Academy Award for this picture.

In the 1960s and 1970s, the popularization of auteurism, which championed directors, gave a significant boost to the DGA's efforts to cast its members as creators in the high art tradition. Developed by a group of young critics associated with the Paris-based film journal *Cahiers du cinema*, the auteur theory was brought to the United States by Andrew Sarris, whose 1968 handbook *The American Cinema* was widely disseminated on American college campuses, nurturing a generation of young cinephiles who launched film societies in order to screen movies identified with directors anointed by the *Cahiers* group.[117]

American critics and journalists had been praising directors as early as 1915, when one writer opined, "The director is the man. The movie director has command of everything."[118] During the 1940s and 1950s, critics such as Otis Ferguson and Manny Farber voiced their commitment to a similarly director-centered approach, as did many other writers. The auteurists' French pedigree, however, endowed the group with impressive cultural capital, since Paris has long been positioned as a center of Western high art and has been a leading innovator in the visual arts at least since the nineteenth century. Paris also could claim a place as the center of film culture by virtue of the avant-garde cinema movements, ciné-clubs, and film journals that have flourished there since the 1920s.[119] France's position at the forefront of international cinephilia was further bolstered after World War II by the international preeminence of the Cannes Film Festival, which placed directors front and center.[120]

The auteur theory gained traction not just by virtue of its origin in France but also because the innovative methodology it employed furthered the project of enshrining directors as creative authors. The two central tenets of the movement resonated with larger cultural assumptions about the definition and significance of art in Western society. The first of these tenets was a focus on the director as a solitary artist; the second was its insistence on the primacy of style. Jean-Luc Godard, a founding member of the auteurist school, spoke to the first principle when he wrote, "The cinema is not a craft. It is an art. It does not mean teamwork. One is always alone; on the set as before a blank page."[121] In an earlier article in *Revue du cinéma*, the precursor to *Cahiers*, DGA member Irving Pichel expressed similar sentiments: "Creation is the work of one person."[122]

To justify their designation of the lone director as the crucial creative contributor to a film's artistry, the auteurists focused on style or, as they termed it, mise-en-scène.[123] This emphasis was evident in an article by *Cahiers* critic Fereydoun Hoveyda, who stated, "The originality of the auteur lies not in the subject matter he chooses, but in the technique he employs, i.e., the *mise en scène*, through which everything on the screen is expressed.... The task of the critic ... [is] to discover behind the images the particular 'manner' of the auteur."[124] The method these critics employed involved bypassing unprepossessing aspects of the works under review to focus on stylistic flourishes that appeared intermittently, engaging in what *Cahiers* editor Eric Rohmer called "la critique des beautés" (an appreciation of moments of beauty).[125] In order to identify such elements, they examined a director's entire body of work (the oeuvre) rather than confining themselves to individual films. As British auteur critic Peter Wollen put it, "It is only the analysis of the whole corpus which permits the moment of synthesis when the critic returns to the original film."[126]

The auteurist outlook soon captured the attention of the young, who began to take movies more seriously as art, embracing the highly personal cinema of European writer-directors such as Bergman and Fellini as well as the productions of auteurist-anointed Hollywood hit makers such as Hitchcock and Hawks. By the 1970s, this audience had created a new market for more director-driven American films, and a cadre of moviemakers with identifiably personal styles, including Martin Scorsese, Francis Ford Coppola, and Robert Altman, came to the fore.[127] Changes in the tax code also provided financial support for such films. What came to be known as the American indie film movement was given a further push in the 1980s and 1990s by the Sundance Film Festival, which showcased such films, and by production companies such as BBS, Miramax, and the Directors Company, which typically put directors front and center. In due course, major studios such as Twentieth Century Fox and Sony jumped on the bandwagon with specialty divisions like Fox Searchlight and Sony Pictures Classics, which were dedicated to making low-budget indie films that were promoted as personal visions of their directors.[128]

The DGA was quick to grasp the value of auteurism for advancing its mission. In 1968, William Wyler was quoted in the Guild's magazine. "In America the press has ignored us," he said. "In Europe the critics have been interested in directors and have made the public aware. But now at long last U.S. critics have become interested bringing readers with them."[129] Shortly thereafter, the Guild cosponsored a forum in New York City featuring a panel of directors and critics that included auteurist Andrew Sarris.[130] Elia Kazan's 1974 letter to the DGA board, calling for a committee that could publicize the work of its members, explicitly cited the auteur theory as a model the organization should encourage in the United States. The Guild organized a second forum in New York, in 1993, entitled "Auteur! Auteur! Thirty Years of the Auteur Theory in America." The event explicitly honored Andrew Sarris.[131]

To provide more tangible support for the indie film movement, the DGA put in place a multitiered payment schedule in 1984 to allow independent producers working on shoestring budgets to pay Guild membership dues at lower rates. This move made room in the Guild's ranks for indie filmmakers like John Sayles and Woody Allen. In a further effort to accommodate the interests of this group, an Independent Directors Committee, chaired by future DGA president Michael Apted, was formed in 1998. DGA-sponsored legislation passed in 2004 provided tax breaks for films budgeted at less than $15 million.[132]

As the auteurist preoccupation with directorial style gained the status of dogma among many cinephiles, it also became fodder for parody.

Robert Altman took up the challenge in *The Player* (1992), a satire about a Hollywood studio executive. *The Player* opens on a conversation between two movie studio workers about the beauties of directorial technique. One voices his admiration for the famous crane shot that opens *Touch of Evil*.

"The pictures they make these days are all MTV—cut, cut, cut," he complains. "The opening shot of Welles's *Touch of Evil* was six and a half minutes long . . . well, three or four, anyway. He set up the whole picture with that one tracking shot."

With an eight-minute running time, the single crane shot that captures this conversation and the action surrounding it is even longer than the one in *Touch of Evil*, and it is also more flamboyantly executed; thus, Altman casts himself, in a tongue-in-cheek manner, as an auteur more to be revered than Welles. "It's a very conceited thing, this shot with no cuts in it," the director later commented. "It's showing off."[133]

This examination of the Directors Guild of America's creative rights program documents a history of successes, emphasizing the way in which Frank Capra's "One man, one film" slogan has played a vital role in guiding the organization's agenda. Working in concert with larger trends both within the film industry and in the popular imagination, the DGA's efforts have helped overcome traditional biases against the idea of mainstream cinema as an art form and of Hollywood directors as artists.

However, as the twenty-first century got under way, new developments threatened directors' hard-won status as singular authors, in unanticipated ways. Streaming services like Amazon Studios and Netflix have blurred the hierarchical distinction between movies and TV, which was historically viewed more as an escapist diversion than a legitimate art form. Globalized corporations have assembled transmedia empires in which content migrates freely among many platforms, a development that scholars have labeled with terms such as "convergence" and "flow."

In response, prestigious film institutions have attempted to preserve the high-culture aura of cinema and its director-auteurs by insisting that only theatrical releases can come under their purview. In 2018, the Cannes Film Festival caused a stir by barring Netflix films that had not been released theatrically. In 2019, Steven Spielberg, in his role as a member of the governing board of the Academy of Motion Picture Arts and Sciences, threatened to propose that the Academy ban such films from Oscar consideration. "Once you commit to a television format, you're a TV movie," he commented, by way of explanation."[134] In June 2019, the DGA seconded this view by limiting its feature film prize to theatrical releases. In announcing the policy, Guild president Thomas Schlamme stated, "We celebrate the important role that theatrical cinema has played in bringing together audiences as they collectively experience films as the filmmakers intended them to be viewed."[135]

CHAPTER TWO

Charisma and Competition

The DGA Stakes Its Claim

> A real director should be absolute. He alone knows the effects he wants to produce, and he alone should have authority in the arrangement, cutting, titling or anything else which it may be found necessary to do to the finished product. What other artist has his creative work interfered with by someone else?
> —LOIS WEBER

> It is possible to plot a politics of cultural labor, possible to imagine a collective of authors, individuals who do not lose themselves when working with others.
> —MOLLY NESBIT

In a 1986 interview, the Directors Guild of America's chief creative rights negotiator, Gilbert Cates, cautioned a reporter not to confuse creative rights with creative control, but in truth the distinction is not easy to draw.[1] The very title "director" implies authority over others. This principle was explicitly stated by Elia Kazan in a DGA pamphlet entitled "What Makes a Director," where he is quoted as saying, "Directing, finally, is the exertion of your will over other people."[2] Directors often refer to themselves as "helmers," comparing their job to that of the captain of a ship; like a ship's crew, a movie crew is pictured as functioning under the command of a leader. Alternately, the moviemaking group may be likened to a symphony orchestra guided by a director-conductor's baton. DGA president Gene Reynolds drew on this analogy when he observed, "There are a hundred instruments but only one conductor."[3]

Military campaigns constitute another area of comparison. "The director is . . . the General in the film production army, guided by his 'battle plan' or 'blueprint,' the prepared script," John Ford once wrote.⁴ Francis Ford Coppola had his own variation on this idea, commenting, "The director is the ringmaster of a circus that is inventing itself."⁵

The directors' role as supervisors puts them at a disadvantage in their quest to be thought of as artists. Traditional artists, who putatively work in unfettered isolation, can stand for the Western ideal of freedom in terms of what Orlando Patterson has called "personal freedom"; their isolation even allows them to be held up as archetypes for such a value. By contrast, Hollywood directors are compromised not just by the institutional constraints under which they work in the corporate world of Hollywood but also by their position of power over other groups of artisans. Their situation conforms to Patterson's conception of a different kind of freedom, "sovereignal freedom," which he defines as "the power to do what one pleases with others."⁶

If characterizations of directors as captains, conductors, generals, and ringmasters depict them as leaders, the DGA's emphasis on creative rights issues has enabled them to be seen as the kind of leaders who have much in common with Max Weber's definition of those who wield charismatic authority. "Charismatic authority is understood as being irrational in the sense of being foreign to all rules," Weber writes. It is "a certain quality of an individual personality by virtue of which he is considered extraordinary and treated as endowed with supernatural, superhuman, or at least specifically exceptional powers or qualities, and on the basis of them, the individual is treated as a 'leader.'"⁷ Pierre Bourdieu associates this mode of leadership with the mystique of the artist: "Charismatic authority . . . directs the gaze towards the apparent producer and prevents us asking who has created this 'creator' and the magic power of transubstantiation with which the 'creator' is endowed."⁸ Such leaders are seen as gifted individuals who dominate others in part because they value intangible goals over pecuniary gain. Though the Guild has negotiated monetary benefits for its members, its emphasis on creative rights enables directors to be seen as leaders of this sort.

From the earliest days of moviemaking, many directors devised strategies designed to position themselves as commanding leaders. Directors occupy special chairs on movie sets and use megaphones that allow their voices to be heard above all others. Clothing and accessories may also be brought into play. Cecil B. DeMille's signature jodhpurs and whip served this purpose, as did D. W. Griffith's straw sombrero, F. W. Murnau's blue jumpsuit, and John Huston's slouch hat.[9] DeMille also employed a "chair boy" whose sole function was to place a chair when the director decided to sit (and if the boy failed, the whip could be used to correct him). If one wanted to speak with Joseph von Sternberg on the set, one wrote one's name on a large blackboard.[10]

CHARISMA AND HIERARCHY

Directors' ambition to be thought of as singular authors in the high art tradition has led them to propose various conceptualizations about the work they do that place their collaborators in subordinate roles. Fred Zinnemann advanced one such model in 1994: "The fact must be maintained that the *principal author* of a film is the director and that the others are associate authors, each responsible for his own department."[11] In a 1956 letter to Frank Capra, Joseph Youngerman offered a variation of this model, likening the creation of a movie to the birth of a baby and casting the director as its mother. "There is no intent to minimize the contributions of the other contributors," Youngerman wrote. "Let us say that the writer 'fathers' the film, the producer acts as obstetrician, and the director 'gives birth' to what you see."[12]

Despite such attempts to carve out a space for collaborators, the creative rights the DGA has won for its members have, in practice, placed directors in a questionable relationship to some of their coworkers, especially to above-the-line talents: producers, actors, and writers. For the most part, directors have avoided conflicts with below-the-line artisans, the only exception being editors, whose authority has been severely eroded by the increasingly widespread phenomenon of the director's cut. Each of these groups has responded differently to the position in which the DGA's creative rights agenda has placed them.[13]

Producers: Good Losers

The DGA's first public act consisted of an attack on producers and studio executives.[14] A report by DGA president Frank Capra published in the *New York Times* and the *Wall Street Journal* in 1938 harshly criticized the number of associate producers and other executives the studios had inserted into the filmmaking process. "The director has for ten years been steadily pushed out of his initiating role," the report asserted, "and has thereby been less able to offer the industry his technique, inspiration and mechanical skill."[15] Capra was not alone in his outrage at such interference. In 1935, John Ford voiced his ire at RKO when executives ordered additional scenes shot for *The Informer* without consulting him and had *The Plough and the Stars* recut without his permission.[16] Ford was again in high dudgeon the following year when Darryl Zanuck recut *The Prisoner of Shark Island*; he was joined in his threat to boycott Fox by Frank Lloyd, whose *Under Two Flags* had also fallen victim to Zanuck's editing shears.[17]

Producers were quick to respond to these attacks on their authority. In 1940, David O. Selznick wrote to the DGA president:

> The growing obsession of the one-man jobs is based on vanity, as some men who are attempting to write, direct, and produce will to their sorrow learn and, in fact, in some cases have already learned. The reaction is already setting in, and two or three splendid directors have had the good sense to give up their vanity rather than let it destroy them, and return to direction, working in collaboration with fine producers.[18]

Director King Vidor recalled how Selznick's ideas worked in practice. "He liked to use several directors on his big pictures," Vidor stated. "He thought that having several directors' names on the picture would make it seem very impressive. The [DGA] didn't want that to happen at all. . . . Selznick liked to put all of the second unit directors' names in the credits. Let's be honest, he wanted to belittle the importance of any one director."[19]

Despite the self-serving practices of Selznick and others like him, producers have watched their control over the filmmaking process steadily decline since the 1940s. Pandro S. Berman, whose producing career peaked during the 1930s, claimed in 1964, "When producers were supreme, Hollywood was at its peak. Now that the young director has taken over, Hollywood has gone to hell."[20] By 1950, anthropologist

Hortense Powdermaker could observe, "Normally the producer has the higher status, but an important director often outranks him."[21] The DGA has been an active player in this shifting balance of power, and as the years have passed, the organization has continued to make inroads. In 1996, the Guild's Code of Preferred Practices limited the number of executives authorized to give editorial suggestions to directors.[22]

The disappearance of the producers' traditional institutional bases has played a significant role in the power shift toward directors. The producers' interests were well supported under the traditional studio system, when the studio bargaining entity, the Alliance of Motion Picture and Television Producers (AMPTP), spoke for them.[23] However, after the Paramount antitrust decree of 1948, producers began to feel that the AMPTP represented the interests of the newly reconstituted studios, which were focused primarily on financing and distribution, at the expense of the producers who oversaw the making of specific films.[24] Another of the producers' strongholds, the Academy of Motion Picture Arts and Sciences, which was controlled by the studios, withdrew from interindustry conflicts following the organization of the talent guilds. As independent production increased during the 1940s, new producers' organizations emerged to supplement the AMPTP, which represented the major studios. These were the Society of Independent Motion Picture Producers, which represented twenty-five independents, and the Independent Motion Picture Producers Association, which represented thirty-two smaller independents. However, these entities occupied a weaker position in negotiations than the AMPTP.[25]

The power of producers was weakened by other factors as well. Talent agents began to play an increasingly active role in packaging film projects. In addition, new corporate structures favor directors over producers. Frequently, patchwork financing strategies spread the fiscal responsibility for a picture among several entities in widely scattered locations; directors, the ones actually on the scene as production moves forward, are the beneficiaries of such practices.[26] Moreover, producers often enter the field ill prepared for their jobs. Once the old-style studios broke up, their traditional training ground vanished. In recent years, some university film schools have attempted to fill this gap by developing their own producer training programs, but one still reads complaints in the trade press from those in the industry about producer incompetence. Assistant directors and unit production managers have sometimes taken up the slack, but they—partly due to DGA-negotiated industry-wide policy—increasingly report to directors.

The producers' position was also eroded when, beginning in the 1940s, a growing number of directors became their own producers. "Until 1938–39, this had been the position of only a few men—DeMille, Lloyd, [Ernst] Lubitsch, Capra," industry observer Leo Rosten pointed out in 1941, "but within three years there were added to the producer-director list such men as Wesley Ruggles, Leo McCarey, William Wellman, Gregory La Cava, Mervyn Leroy, George Stevens, Mitchell Leisen, John Ford, Mark Sandrich, Orson Welles, and others."[27] During the 1950s, other important directors, including Billy Wilder, George Sidney, and Robert Wise, also took on roles as producers. Still other big names, such as Alfred Hitchcock, cast their producers as functionaries while keeping ultimate control over their films in their own hands; innovative industry heavyweights such as Lew Wasserman often facilitated such deals. During the 1970s and 1980s, some directors, Sydney Pollack and Martin Scorsese among them, went even further by assuming positions as producers or executive producers of films directed by others, and a few, such as Robert Altman, Francis Ford Coppola, George Lucas, and Steven Spielberg, even founded their own studios.

Ultimately, the producers have lost out to the directors not simply because their institutional bases have disappeared but also because they have historically been more attuned to profits than to creative rights and have been willing to bargain away creative rights to augment profits. A striking example of this strategy occurred in 1973, when the DGA negotiated for the director's cut as part of the Directors' Bill of Rights. To allay the producers' fears that allowing directors to produce their own cut of a film would lengthen production time, Frank Capra, the Guild's lead negotiator, devised a plan whereby the DGA would guarantee that, if any director failed to meet postproduction deadlines, one of the dozen top directors in the industry would edit the film in question within the designated time frame, free of charge. "There was nothing compared to the looks on the faces of the negotiating teams on the other side of the table when this proposal was made to them," recalled Elliot Silverstein, who sat beside Capra on the Guild's negotiating team. "There was a silence.... Never before had a labor union said, 'Hey, we want to do something because we're interested in the quality of the work and we're not going to charge you for it.'"[28]

In the end, both sides have won. The directors have gained control while the producers have made more money by helping DGA members become marquee names that could sell films. In addition, by supporting the directors' efforts to advance their image as artists, the producers also enhanced the long-term profitability of their productions, for movies made by artists move beyond the realm of ephemeral entertainments to become enduring works of art that can be sold and resold over long periods of time.

Actors: Power Players

Of the three major Hollywood talent guilds, the Screen Actors Guild, is the closest to a traditional union, focusing for the most part on salaries and working conditions rather than on creative issues. All actors share an interest in such bread-and-butter concerns. Though a good deal of publicity surrounds the high salaries enjoyed by major Hollywood stars, most SAG members live a precarious hand-to-mouth existence. In his book on the Actors Guild, David Prindle reports that, in 1988, the annual income of most SAG members was under $2,000 and 85 percent were out of work at any given time.[29] Under the old-style studio system with its standard seven-year contracts, performers enjoyed more job security than they did later on, but even in those days unemployment was high, and those who were under contract lived in fear that changes in public taste or studio priorities would end their careers when their contracts expired.

Though the Actors Guild itself has been relatively uninvolved in creative rights issues, SAG members who are stars often care deeply about their control over the films they make. And in terms of Hollywood clout, leading actors outrank most directors. As veteran multihyphenate Tony Bill once put it, "If there's a conflict between the director and an actor, the big dog wins in our business. That dog is the star."[30]

The ascendancy of stars in the Hollywood pecking order was won during the silent period, as their visibility and glamour became a central element in the studios' publicity machinery and the fan press. Fortified by their box office prowess, these above-the-line performers have steadily gained greater influence over the movies in which they participate. To be sure, during the studio era, stars, like directors, were hemmed in by restrictive long-term studio contracts that hampered their ability to choose their preferred projects and collaborators. But once on the set, they took precedence over everyone else. As the classical studio system began to break apart in the 1950s, bankable actors began to set up their own production companies, a move that enabled them to hire and fire directors themselves.

Directors have often benefited from the relationships they have been able to forge with stars, who frequently request a trusted director as a condition of their participation in a given picture. But in these relationships the stars hold most of the cards and are capable of using directors as pawns. Stars can pull rank on directors not only because their names are usually more marketable but also because, unlike directors, they cannot be readily replaced once a production is under way. The movie *State and Main* (2000) dramatized the unrivaled power stars enjoy by virtue of their ability to cause a work stoppage when the leading lady in the film-within-the-film decides—after shooting has begun—that she needs more money to appear in a nude scene. The director is the person who must negotiate with her, recognizing that she has the upper hand, for if she quits, the production must shut down.

The desire of some stars to take complete charge of their movies prompted the DGA to tighten its policy of disallowing any of the personnel attached to a given picture to assume the directorial role if the original director departs after shooting has commenced. What came to be known as the Eastwood rule was triggered by the film *The Outlaw Josey Wales* (1976). The movie's efficiency-minded star, Clint Eastwood, who was also executive producer, bristled at perfectionistic director Philip Kaufman's slow pace. After Kaufman had prepared the production and shot some of the scenes, Eastwood fired him and took over. According to actress Sondra Locke, who had a featured role in the picture, "Kaufman's approach took more time and therefore more money, and with Clint, that was an impenetrable impasse."[31]

The DGA sought to rein in such intrusive star behavior by putting into place tougher rules that laid out conditions under which directors could be replaced, creating a stiffer fine and revoking the offender's right to a DGA membership card. "No person assigned to or performing in a particular motion picture before the director is replaced can replace the director," the Basic Agreement read in part. "Further, the director can only be replaced by a person who has previously directed a feature motion picture or not less than ninety minutes of television programming shown in the United States."[32] As a result of the new DGA-negotiated safeguards, the number of directorial replacements dropped from twenty-one in 1980 to eight in 1985, despite an increase in overall production.[33]

Writers: Resisters

The DGA is not the only Hollywood guild concerned with creative control; the Writers Guild of America also has put creative rights issues high on its agenda. More than any other group, screenwriters have chafed at the DGA's drive for creative control over the entire process of moviemaking, out of a conviction that writers, too, are creators. Writers create plots and dialogue that can be readily identified as original, and their scripts often include instructions for camera setups and the like as well.[34] A 1999 article in the WGA's publication *Written By* makes the case for screenwriters to claim authorship in no uncertain terms, stating, "We are the sine qua non, the ones whose personal vision and style create something from nothing but our own imaginations."[35]

Many directors support this view. Allan Dwan, whose directorial career in Hollywood spanned more than fifty years, once commented, "I think the story is the number one thing. The whole business is based on that."[36] Directors who are also writers concur. Joseph L. Mankiewicz once wrote, "A properly written screen play *has already been directed*—in his script, by the trained screen writer who has conceived his film in visual symbols and translated them into descriptive movement and the spoken word."[37] Preston Sturges also believed that writers were the cinema's primary creative force. In 1957, he wrote:

> When I went to Hollywood, I saw that directors were treated as Princes of the Blood, whereas writers worked in teams of six like piano movers. In the beginning I tried to prove that writers were easily as important as directors, then one day I realized it would be easier to become a Prince of the Blood myself than to

change the whole social order.... This did not change the relative merits of directors and writers (who are actually vastly more important), but it changed my salary and the way people treated me.[38]

If writers are to be thought of as film authors, what does that make directors? For some, directors become mere interpreters of the writer's work. Screenwriter Philip Dunne takes this position in his memoir, *Take Two*, arguing that if two different directors had made films from the same script, "there would have been differences, of course: completely different camera angles, different emphases, different shadings in the performances. But these differences wouldn't have been much greater than the differences you might detect if you listened to Jascha Heifetz play Beethoven's Violin Concerto and then to David Oistrakh or Yehudi Menuhin play the same work. In all the performing arts, individual interpretation is important, but never as important as the basic material."[39] Cecil B. DeMille's screenwriter brother, William, took a similar stance, though he was prepared to give directors more credit. "The function of the director will be to interpret, not create," he once stated. "But interpretation is so important that it may immeasurably add to the value of the finished product."[40]

Frank Capra had a different opinion about the writer–director relationship. He put it this way:

> The Screen Writers Guild really hates me. The idea of one man, one film doesn't go down with them. They feel that many people contribute to the making of a film. But for me it's one captain for a ship. 'In the beginning was the word'—that's the attitude of the writers, and it's true. Somebody has to write something. But you don't photograph the written work. You photograph people speaking, not people writing. Writing is just to give the actor something to do.[41]

In the struggle for dominance during the early days of cinema, it appeared that writers might come out on top. Unlike directors, whose craft can claim little in the way of a distinguished tradition, screenwriters can look at their work in the context of an illustrious history of high literary art from Sophocles to Joyce. In the early 1910s, most critics built on this history by singling out screenwriters as the authors of films. In a similar vein, production companies around the world frequently sought to convey an image of quality by adapting classic literary and dramatic works.[42] For similar reasons, well-known writers like Zane Grey, Jack London, and L. Frank Baum were able to capitalize on their name recognition by establishing their own production companies. In 1919, the Famous Players Film Company issued an elaborate thirty-two-page brochure that heralded the formation of a new body called Eminent Authors, which was to elevate filmmaking by associating it with canonical literary figures.[43] Academia picked up on the trend, honoring screenwriters as authors in a course offered at Columbia University during the 1910s and 1920s.[44] In 1929, one Hollywood executive claimed that "the dominant, I might say the menacing force in motion pictures [is] the scenario writer."[45] When sound arrived, writers became even more central to the production process, for then they contributed dialogue as well as narrative structure and intertitles. In 1940, screenwriter Dudley Nichols stated, "I devoutly believe it is the writer who has matured the film medium more than anyone else."[46]

European studios took up the cause of writers as well. In France, the Société Film d'Art adapted works by Charles Dickens, Goethe, Honoré de Balzac, and others. Italian film companies gestured toward works of literary distinction with early blockbusters like *Quo Vadis* (1913), adapted from a novel by Nobel laureate Henryk Sienkiewicz, and *Cabiria* (1914), which featured intertitles by the eminent Italian poet Gabriele D'Annunzio. During the 1930s, following the practice American reviewers had adopted two decades earlier, French critics began to honor scriptwriters as the authors of films.[47]

Despite this heartening beginning, however, several factors conspired to seal the writers' eventual fate as also-rans to the directors. The first scriptwriter, Roy L. McCardell, was hired by Biograph in 1897, long before Griffith made directing a recognized profession, but by 1915 intertitle specialists had split the screenwriter's role into two parts: structure and text.[48] The writers' authority was further diluted by the introduction of treatment scripts, which allowed producers, executives, and stars to make suggestions. Such practices broke up into several stages the process of preparing screenplays, and the Hollywood studios responded by adopting the practice of assigning several writers to work on scripts in tandem or serially. At Warner Bros., screenwriter Julius Epstein, one of the many writers who worked on *Casablanca*, described the practice: "You were assigned a script, and when you were through with it, the studio would give it to another writer. And someone else would polish it, and, if you were good at a particular thing, you would do that kind of scene on one picture and another and another."[49] The realities of moviemaking create additional disadvantages for writers, for decisions involving camera angles, film stock, lighting, and editing may call for specialized knowledge; moreover, locations are often far-flung, making those actually on the scene best able to make last-minute modifications necessitated by local conditions.

In their struggle for control over their work, screenwriters often have appealed to the traditions of theater, where writers are honored over directors. In 1950, screenwriter Howard Koch laid claim to this tradition when he wrote, "The screenplay must be given the same centrality and protection accorded the stage play under the Dramatists Guild contract."[50] In the theatrical world, where the scope of a production's visual and sound design is limited, dialogue and plotting take pride of place. Legal practices, too, have worked in favor of the playwrights. The Dramatists Guild's first contract, in 1919, gave them copyright for their work; producers could license a play, but they were required to consult the writers about directors, casting, and script changes. Screenplays, by contrast, are typically passed along to production executives who perform these functions, and copyright resides with the studios. Moreover, while playwrights customarily sit in on rehearsals, screenwriters are usually barred from movie sets, where their scripts are frequently rewritten by directors and actors. In addition, screenwriters rarely enjoy the privilege of reviewing the edited versions of the films they create. The writers' sense of their own stature has also worked to their disadvantage in Hollywood, as they have repeatedly excoriated screenwriting as a demeaning—if lucrative—falling away from their higher calling in the theatrical or literary arenas.[51]

Screenwriters faced a new set of roadblocks when the House Un-American Activities Committee turned its gaze on Hollywood, because the committee targeted screenwriters more than any other group. Some were imprisoned and many others were blacklisted.[52] In 1947, at the start of the HUAC hearings, director Sam Wood pointed a finger at writers as "the most dangerous group in the industry," charging that the Communists in Hollywood "operate by getting control of the writers and by blackballing those who don't follow the party line."[53] Seven of the ten Hollywood figures cited for contempt of Congress and sent to prison in 1947 were writers. Subsequently, in a 1952 arbitration proceeding with the WGA, the studios won the right to deny credits to writers tagged as Communists.

The popularization of the auteur theory that took root in the 1960s constituted a further setback for screenwriters insofar as it focused on the stylistic signatures of lone directors at the expense of the storytelling prowess of groups of writers. An article published in the WGA's magazine in 1999 called auteurism "a grotesque affront to common sense," a sentiment echoed by screenwriter William Goldman, who wrote, "I have never met another fellow technician, not a single cinematographer, or producer, or editor, who believes it."[54]

The writers' position on this question, however, has been inconsistent. At times, they have advocated for the recognition of writers as part of a team effort, while at other times they have championed the idea of writers as sole authors. The contradiction was apparent in a campaign statement made by WGA presidential candidate John Wells in 1999, in which he first appealed to the notion of group authorship, only to revert to the principle of individual authorship—but for writers rather than directors. "By claiming sole creative authorship the director denies all other artists involved in the motion picture their rightful due," Wells said, but then he went on to assert that "the writer is the author of the work, the creator."[55]

In 1994, screenwriters Scott Alexander and Larry Karaszewski offered an implied critique of the excesses of the auteurist approach in their script for *Ed Wood*, about a man famous for being the worst director of all time. Alexander and Karaszewski had been inspired by Rudolph Grey's 1991 biography of Wood, *Nightmare of Ecstasy*, the publication of which suggests the extent to which directors, even those without talent, have come to the forefront of public interest even as writers continue to be marginalized.[56] *Ed Wood* can be viewed as an argument against the idea that all directors are entitled to be considered artists. In a scene set in the legendary Hollywood restaurant Musso & Frank Grill, Wood meets Orson Welles. Welles assures his fellow director that "visions are worth fighting for," the implication being that all directorial visions, no matter how incoherent or trivial, lie at the center of film artistry.

Even as Alexander and Karaszewski's gentle satire questions the excesses of an auteurist creed that unthinkingly enshrines directors of any stripe as the sole creative force responsible for cinematic art, it also stands as evidence of the creative might of screenwriting teams. Though stylishly directed by Tim Burton, *Ed Wood* can be more readily associated with the sensibilities and interests of the Alexander–Karaszewski writing partnership, which has produced a number of similar studies of lowbrow cultural icons over the years, including *The People vs. Larry Flint* (1996), *Man on the Moon* (1999), *Big Eyes* (2014), *The People v. O. J. Simpson* (2016), and *Dolemite Is My Name* (2019). As Alexander once put it, *Ed Wood* represents "a semi-genre we created: the anti-great man."[57]

Despite the various challenges to their power and integrity that have emerged over the years, movie writers have continued to struggle for control over their work, and this mission has led to repeated clashes with the Directors Guild. In 1977, for example, the WGA proposed that screenwriters be given authority to approve script changes made on the set, prompting the DGA to resign from the Inter-Guild Council. Another crisis erupted in 1988, when the writers managed to negotiate a contract with independent producers that assured them of "meaningful consultation" on the choice of directors, major cast members, and locations. In 1990, the writers and directors called a temporary truce. But the issue arose again in 1994, when the writers put before producers a document entitled "The Screen Authors Agreement." This proposal gave writers the right to approve directors and stars, to be present on sets for dailies and during postproduction, and to see a cut after the directors' cut. Predictably, the directors came out strongly against it. In each of these cases, the directors prevailed.[58]

If the writers faced an uphill struggle in negotiations with the DGA over film-related issues, their battles over television told a different story. In the past, TV's smaller screens and distracted viewing conditions meant that dialogue, not pictures, took center stage. Nonetheless, in the network era, writers faced daunting odds: as in film, they customarily

Charisma and Competition 51

worked in groups, and individual episodes in continuing series were often scripted by freelancers.[59] As John Thornton Caldwell has noted, television's culture of collaboration in itself marks it as an inferior form: "The film industry has traditionally denigrated television for writing by committee, while assuming ownership for itself of the traditional creative marker of quality: sole authorship."[60]

Bowing to this reality, the TV industry worked to establish a sophisticated audience for its prestige productions by promoting individual writers like Paddy Chayefsky, Horton Foote, and Rod Serling, making them into household names. The advent of so-called quality TV in the 1970s accelerated the process of promoting such television writer-auteurs, and by the twenty-first century, TV writers like Shonda Rhimes and David Simon, now identified as "showrunners," gained celebrity status. By 2000, WGA president John Wells was urging his colleagues to acknowledge the contributions of directors. "Directors in episodic TV and long-form are not getting the level of respect they deserve," he stated in the WGA monthly *Written By*. "And often this mistreatment comes at the hands of WGA members."[61]

At the time of Wells's plea, however, the television landscape had already begun to shift in the direction of directors. Commercial-free cable channels, bigger screens, and the fact that people were now able to select shows to record for later viewing set the stage for television shows with distinctive visual styles and more attentive audiences. In response, beginning in the 1980s, television executives began to look to film directors to add prestige to their programming, a phenomenon that John Thornton Caldwell has labeled "auteur imports." A-list directorial names like Francis Ford Coppola, Steven Spielberg, George Lucas, David Lynch, Spike Lee, Barry Levinson, and Oliver Stone were among those recruited.[62] In 2002, NBC executive Ted Frank observed, "The selection of directors to do pilots is extremely important," citing as an example *The West Wing*, which partnered writer Aaron Sorkin with director Thomas Schlamme. Schlamme matched Sorkin's fast-paced verbal exchanges with long Steadicam two shots that moved quickly as the actors walked down hallways, a kinetic technique known as "walking and talking," which became a well-known signature of the show.[63]

During the same period writer Shawn Ryan, creator of the critically acclaimed television show *The Shield*, said, "The best decisions I made were at the very beginning, to give up power. I chose to give up power to the director in this case, and it got me the look of this show." Bill D'Elia, creator of *Ally McBeal*, concurs. "Series television looks better than ever," he observed. "And it's because the directors have become more important."[64] In addition, premium cable outlets like HBO elevated the status of miniseries and movies made specifically for television, paving the way for directorial signatures to be showcased in prestige productions such as *Mildred Pierce* (Todd Haynes, 2011) and *Behind the Candelabra* (Steven Soderbergh, 2013).

Yet even in these instances the name directors in question relied on the recognition they had won through the work they had done in cinema, which they could then carry over to television projects; as of 2019, no director whose career was confined to TV alone had yet achieved marquee status. The continued dominance of writer-producers in the struggle for creative laurels in the TV realm was reemphasized in 2019, when *Los Angeles Times* television critic Mary McNamara anointed *Game of Thrones* as "TV's greatest show of all time," awarding authorship credit to novelist George R. R. Martin, who had penned the original literary works on which the series was based, and to writer-showrunners D. B. Weiss and David Benioff.[65]

Editors: Cut Out

Traditionally, control over the shape of the theatrical release versions of Hollywood movies has rested with the producer, but during the studio era, editors wielded considerable control over the nitty-gritty of the cutting process. In 1969, Edward Dmytryk wrote a piece for *DGA Magazine* extolling the virtues of promoting a partnership between directors and editors, suggesting that directors adopt the practice of allowing editors on the set with them. The article got a quick response from editor Anthony Wollner. "Mr. Dmytryk states that in the one instance during his own editing career when he was told exactly where and how to cut, the result was a catastrophe," Wollner wrote. "There has been a trend in Hollywood toward ... director–editor relationships [in which the director is in charge] over the past few years. It frustrates the creative editor and deprives many films, both television and features, of their greatest artistic potential."[66]

The directors owe their growing authority over the editing process in part to the efforts of their Guild. A 1947 DGA report stated, "The cutting and editing of a picture has always been the subject of deepest concern to every director" and announced that "the Negotiating Committee will seek to have the director given control over cutting, editing and dubbing up to the first public preview." The report went on to describe the way in which the Guild had intervened in a recent dispute between Fritz Lang and Universal Pictures over *The Secret Beyond the Door*, which the studio had cut without Lang's permission. The DGA had been instrumental in resolving the dispute in Lang's favor. The report stated, "This Guild action paves the way toward increased protection for directors and their rights in relation to cutting and editing their films." The document concluded by quoting DGA president George Stevens: "The Guild is a 'strong man' in the industry. He is a 'big fellow.' Mr. Lang called on the Guild and 'the big fellow' walked into the office of Universal-International Pictures and accomplished something that very few individuals in the industry could accomplish."[67]

In 1973, the DGA won jurisdiction over the reediting of films for foreign theatrical showings. At the same time, the Guild partnered with the AMPTP in urging the networks to allow directors to supervise the reediting of movies shown on television.[68] In 1977, the directors achieved similar control over the editing of films shown on commercial airplanes.[69] At this time, Creative Rights Committee chair Elliot Silverstein told the press, "Our negotiations had nothing to do with limiting the rights of anybody else, particularly the editors."[70] This statement was clearly disingenuous, since the DGA document represented a serious attack on the traditional prerogatives of editors. Predictably, the editors protested, with one asking, "Who is the Directors Guild to impose a time limit on the editor's work?"[71]

The editors began at a disadvantage, because Hollywood bookkeeping conventions define them as below-the-line or craft workers, as opposed to the above-the-line talents, who are considered creative personnel. Seeing the handwriting on the wall, the editors have made the best of it. A 2002 article in *Cinemeditor Magazine*, "The Psychology of the Cutting Room," stated,

> We have to be aware that the light that shines on us dims the light shining on the director. We can never say that we saved a film. Neither will a director ever acknowledge that something like that happened because it takes away from his accomplishments. We have to keep a low profile.... The egos of directors, producers and especially actors are much more competitive than ours are.... Having said that, you should indulge your ego as much as possible in the solitude of your first assembly.... I always aim to become a director's best friend, temporarily at least, but preferably for life.[72]

As directors have gained clout as celebrities, more and more of them have been able to negotiate the right to preside over the final cut of the films they oversee. Many have taken advantage of this privilege to create movies that do not fit comfortably into exhibitor schedules. In 2006, Paul Dergarabedian, head of exhibitor relations at Universal Studios, voiced concern over the situation. "As directors have final-cut approval over the movie, I think we have seen some of the running times get bloated," he said, noting that the previous four movies directed by Michael Mann had average running times of more two and one-half hours, and all were box office disappointments.[73] The same year, Bryan Singer's final cut of *Superman Returns* clocked in at 154 minutes, prompting one blogger to comment, "I got married, raised a son and sent him off to college while *Superman* unrolled."[74]

The authority directors now have over the editing of their films was satirized in Albert Brooks's film *Modern Romance* (1981), which chronicles the misadventures of film editor Robert Cole as he works on cutting a low-budget science fiction feature. When David, the movie's director, enters the editing room, the two have a disagreement over whether a particular line ("You know nothing!") should be included. Robert offers a long, well-reasoned explanation about why this speech should be eliminated, but he is cut short when David states, "I love that line!," thereby ending the discussion.

The DGA's 1965 Directors' Bill of Rights guaranteed directors the right to produce a director's cut of their films.⁷⁵ In negotiating this right, the Guild was working toward establishing a distinct version of every film that could be identified as definitive because it had been approved by its director, following Capra's "one man, one film" principle. But in practice the director's cut provision means only that a director has the right to reedit an editor's initial rough cut. Such a version typically lacks finishing touches like pickup shots, visual effects, and original music. A producer subsequently oversees a team of editors who create the studio's final cut by adding these elements and shaping the film to conform to commercial criteria. As Alan Horn, then president of Warner Bros. commented in 2006, eliminating fifteen to twenty minutes from a director's cut "is not at all uncommon."⁷⁶ Thus, the definition of a director's cut as set forth in the Guild contract is a cut that would not typically be suitable for release.⁷⁷

The commercial potential inherent in the idea of the director's cut began to be seriously exploited after the introduction of videotapes, which enabled consumers to purchase movies to watch at home, in the mid-1970s. This technological innovation created a new market for rereleases. In 1980, Columbia issued *Close Encounters of the Third Kind: Special Edition*, a reedited version of the original release that Steven Spielberg had prepared.⁷⁸ The cultural cachet of the idea of the director's cut was definitively established with the 1992 video release of a reedited version of the 1982 cult favorite *Blade Runner*, explicitly labeled "The Director's Cut." As the idea of the director's cut has gained currency in the culture at large, films have been increasingly rereleased in altered versions labeled as directors' cuts and have become significant revenue streams for the industry.⁷⁹ In the process, directors have seen their prestige increase as the phenomenon of the director's cut has enabled them to become more closely identified with ideas about quality cinema and singular authorship.

Some director's cuts assembled after a film's initial release represent a director's desire to correct mistakes in the original version. Most Hollywood productions put tremendous pressure on directors to tailor their work to conform to commercially viable running times and to avoid censurable material while at the same time meeting scheduled release dates, even if the shooting schedule has been unexpectedly prolonged. Reactions to test screenings further complicate the process. As Terry Gilliam put it, "When you're finishing off a film it's the most stressful time in the filmmaking process. Everyone wants a success, especially the director. . . . And oftentimes with the benefit of hindsight, you find yourself asking, 'How could I have done that?' "[80] Thus, when Robert Wise claimed that the DVD recut of his film *Star Trek: The Motion Picture* (1979) as *Star Trek: Director's Edition* (2001) was "the film I really wanted," it was a credible statement.[81]

However, as the phenomenon of the director's cut gained currency, complications emerged. Some directors returned again and again to reedit their work. The most common strategy followed in such rereleases is to add scenes that were deleted in the original release version. For example, in 2001 Francis Ford Coppola added about thirty minutes to *Apocalypse Now*, recreating it as *Apocalypse Now: Redux*. David Fincher added seven minutes to his 2007 production *Zodiac* for a special screening at Lincoln Center.

In some instances, the director's "preferred" version is hard to determine. At the studio's request, Ridley Scott reedited *Alien* (1979) for DVD in 2002, just so that this new version could be labeled a director's cut. In a variation of this strategy, Zack Snyder produced two director's cuts of *Watchmen* within a few months of its initial theatrical release in winter 2009; the first was called "Director's Cut," the second "Ultimate Cut." Oliver Stone produced three director's cuts of *Alexander* (2004): one in 2005, another in 2007, and a third in 2013. Wolfgang Peterson produced two director's cuts of *Troy*, one in 2004 and the other for a screening at the Berlinale in 2007. The possibility of multiple versions can even be built into the filming process itself, as when Peter Jackson shot additional footage for each of the *Lord of the Rings* movies in anticipation of adding additional material for the eventual DVD release.

Sometimes a director's cut isn't even supervised by the director. The 2005 DVD release of *Pat Garrett and Billy the Kid*, for example, includes Sam Peckinpah's original rough cut, the studio-edited original release version, and a later version assembled by film historian Paul Seydor, which adds polish to the then-deceased director's rough cut. In the 1990s, the Guild officially bought into this expanded meaning of the term by successfully negotiating for the right for its members to be consulted on all reissues labeled as director's cuts.[82]

Once the cachet of the director's cut had been established, European directors took up the cause. But here, too, confusions emerged. An altered version of the German film *Das Boot* that added an hour to the 145-minute running time of the initial theatrical release version was marketed as a director's cut, even though the production originated in 1981 as a six-and-one-half-hour TV miniseries.[83] Similarly, Volker Schlöndorff produced a "director's cut" of *The Tin Drum* (1979) for a special screening at Cannes in 2010. "I always thought the original was the director's cut since I did it," he commented at the time. "But last year the lab was asking, we have sixty boxes of material—and every year the producers are paying for storage. How long do you want to keep it? I did not re-edit the whole movie; I just added a few scenes and a few surprises."[84]

At times, a director's cut may represent a struggle between two directors, as happened with *Superman II* in 1980. When Richard Lester replaced *Superman II*'s original director, Richard Donner, he reshot most of Donner's footage so that 75 percent of the original release version was Lester's material; Donner's director's cut edition, which came out on DVD in 2006, reversed the ratio. Alternately, a director's cut may represent a single director's changed perspective. For the rerelease of *The Last Picture Show* (1971) on LaserDisc in 1991, Peter Bogdanovich reedited the film to make the character played by Cybill Shepherd more sympathetic. "When I was younger, I don't think I understood the woman's point of view as well as I do now," Bogdanovich explained at the time. Reacting to such backpedaling on the part of his colleague, James Cameron subsequently commented, "You're getting into revisionism when a director's ideas have changed, when he redirects the film. That's not as valid."[85]

In short, though the DGA had originally envisioned the director's cut as a device for identifying a definitive version of a movie as the one overseen by the director, its lone creative author, the commercial exploitation of this phenomenon has led to a proliferation of versions that may or may not be produced under the auspices of a movie's director, and even when they are, may not represent a singular intention. One man, one film can—and often does—become many men, many films. Instead of enshrining a single author-ized version of a picture as the only valid one, the director's cut has exacerbated the problem of determining which iteration of the cinematic text is entitled to be considered definitive, and it has even problematized the question of who the director is. Thus, in wresting control over a film's final shape from the editors, the directors have introduced a new level of complication into Capra's mantra by destabilizing the fixed meaning that might otherwise be attached to a Hollywood movie considered as an object of art and, in the process, creating ambiguities about the identity of the creative author who made it.

As the twenty-first century began, Hollywood's conversion to digital technology was transforming the role of directors and leading them to rethink their relationships with coworkers. The DGA has responded to these technological innovations by offering training sessions for its members and by lobbying for appropriate compensation for directors as they engage with the challenges that have emerged. Among the new tools directors must master are digital cameras, which have changed conditions on the set. Digital cameras do not require elaborate lighting, allowing for quicker, more efficient filming; as a result, everyone is better able to conserve and focus their energy, thereby creating a more hospitable environment for directors in their role as managers of equipment and personnel. Furthermore, while a 35-millimeter camera is limited to ten minutes for a single take, digital cameras can run indefinitely, enabling directors to order lengthy takes. Comedy directors, especially, are inclined to exploit this option, letting the camera run on in hopes of capturing an unpredictable moment of spontaneous inspiration on the part of the actors. In such circumstances, editors may find themselves sorting through an ocean of footage in order to assemble a manageable rough cut, and directors must yield to the necessity of leaving much of this labor—and the decisions involved—to the editors.[86]

Digitalization has produced other innovations that threaten directors' authority. The proliferation of visual effects and digitized soundscapes means that many scenes are conceived in the form of collages put together by teams of specialists in far-flung locations, not under the director's eye. Patty Jenkins met this situation head-on in the course of helming her first effects-heavy movie, *Wonder Woman*, in 2017. "I went out and shot elements on the Amalfi coast of Italy, on film, exactly how I wanted it to look," she subsequently recalled. "The visual effects then had to match everything I'd filmed. Instead of it being a 'make up whatever island you want' free-for-all, where people could bend the rules about what a plant should look like, or how those cracks in the stone should be, we planted a flag. That helped every artist down the line see what they had to achieve in order to make the scene look real."[87]

The internet, with its focus on interactivity, constitutes another kind of challenge to the image of directors as singular artists by inviting users to participate in the creative process. Robotic creators have also been added to the mix. Such an expansion of authorial prerogatives has prompted new theories that further undermine Capra's one man, one film definition of media artistry. Henry Jenkins's studies of fan cultures and Lev Manovich's models of new media authorship are part of a growing trend that proposes updated modes of understanding how artistry and artists are defined.[88] While the success of the DGA's creative rights mission in helping to position directors as the auteurs behind Hollywood cinema is undeniable, its ability to achieve a similar status for its members in an era of new media incarnations has yet to be determined.

CHARISMA AND PATRIARCHY

As Karen Ward Maher has shown, popular beliefs about the relationship between charismatic leadership and physical prowess link directors to an image of masculinity; this association grows out of a larger cultural model that has been labeled "hegemonic masculinity," which defines itself in terms of hierarchy, rationality, the repression of emotions other than anger, and a propensity toward violence.[89] Women as well as men have bought into this cultural style. Lillian Gish asserted that directing was "no career for a lady," and Dorothy Arzner once remarked that she owed her success as a director to her masculine characteristics.[90] Penny Marshall made the connection between male directors and charismatic authority explicit when she commented, "With directing, I know people on movie sets want leadership, but I don't exude that captain-of-the-ship image."[91] Ida Lupino took a similar view. "I hate women who order men around," she once said. "I say, 'Darlings, Mother has a problem. I'd love to do this. Can you do it? It sounds kooky, but I want to do it. Now, can you do it for me?'"[92] The image of directors as individualistic leaders also disadvantaged women by distancing them from a culture of collaboration that was implicitly marked as feminine.[93] The careers of many of the women who have occupied the director's chair have perpetuated this stereotype. In the silent period, Alice Guy, Lois Weber, and Nell Shipman established reputations as team players who worked in close partnerships with their husbands. The trend has persisted into the sound era with marital pairings like Ida Lupino and Collier Young, Nancy Meyers and Charles Shyer, and Valerie Faris and Jonathan Dayton.[94]

The phenomenon of gender bias in Hollywood is complicated by the presence of powerful female stars. Often, however, people in the industry have treated such women not as fellow professionals but as prima donnas who need wrangling, an attitude that has often come into play when female actors clash with directors over creative issues. In the eroticized, sexually permissive environment of Hollywood, the professional qualifications of such women are easily slighted, given that so many owe their entry into the business to beauty pageants rather than to acting schools and have survived by resorting to the fabled Hollywood casting couch. After they have gained a foothold in the industry, red carpet events keep the focus on their sexualized bodies rather than on their professional skills. Once on the set, even established female stars may be marginalized by the freewheeling frat boy atmosphere that frequently prevails. In 2015, former DGA president Martha Coolidge commented on some of the most egregious practices prevalent in the industry. "There are . . . some men in this game for the sexual perks . . ." she told reporter David Robb. "So they are not going to hire women in any important positions. They're going to hire cute women that are their prey and conquests . . . [and] they don't want anyone watching who might say something to their wife or their boss."[95]

Women have been a central part of the industry from the earliest days, though many have been traditionally relegated to low-level jobs.[96] During the 1910s, however, many women worked as directors at major studios. Before the formation of the DGA, the Motion Picture Directors Association included at least four women, who were admitted as honorary members.[97] Arzner, who had carved out a successful career as a director in the late 1920s, was a director-member of the DGA during the 1930s and 1940s, and Lupino, who had established herself as a director by leveraging her clout as an actor and taking advantage of a chance opportunity, belonged to the organization at the director level during the 1950s. The Guild's longtime legal counsel Mabel Willebrandt also was female.

But these women were exceptions. For many years, the DGA cultivated an aura of masculine privilege. Guild stalwart John Rich commented that in the early days of the Guild, the air at board meetings "was thick with clouds of pipe and cigar smoke. The order of the day was cigars, the more expensive, the better."[98] During the membership crisis that hit the DGA during the 1950s, the group voted at one point to grant automatic membership in the organization to their sons.[99]

If such customs conformed to the testosterone-fueled tenor of most union practices of the time, when it came time to acknowledge female colleagues, the DGA put a distinctive spin on conventionally gendered language by overlaying it with Hollywood glamour-speak. For example, a 1965 newsletter contained an item entitled "Thirty-Eight Beautiful Distaffers (36-24-36)." It announced, "We are happy to report thirty-eight beautiful and charming but most professional female members."[100] Introducing Lupino as a presenter at the Guild's awards ceremony in 1961, Frank Capra described her as "our Guild's most handsome member ... one of the most exciting package deals of the year—brains, talent and beauty."[101] Lupino willingly played along with such attitudes. "The chief handicap [for women directors] is having to get up earlier, get your hair done and make-up on," she once said.[102]

In 1979, seven years after the WGA and SAG had launched similar efforts, the DGA formed a Women's Steering Committee, which compiled statistics on female hiring since 1941 and, at a press conference in June of 1981, reported on the deplorable record it had unearthed.[103] The Guild took action on the issue by pledging not to allow its members to work in states that had failed to ratify the Equal Rights Amendment.[104] Beginning in 1980, the Women's Steering Committee hosted meetings with industry executives in an effort to encourage them to hire more female directors, but negotiations fell apart when the issue of quotas was raised. Speaking of the various mixers and mentoring programs the group had sponsored over the years, Martha Coolidge commented in 1997, "The problem is, [the Guild members] are not the ones doing the hiring."[105]

In 1983, the Guild took a further step to advance gender equality by mounting lawsuits against Warner Bros. and Columbia Pictures for failing to establish a program of goals and timetables with the aim of hiring more female directors. However, the suit was thrown out of court in 1985 when the judge ruled that the Guild itself was also at fault for not having more women among its members and for not encouraging directors to hire more women as their assistants (one of the paths to becoming a director). The judge further charged that the DGA policy of insisting that only one director could work on a film had the effect of prohibiting on-the-job training.[106]

During the same period, two white male directors hit the Guild with a reverse discrimination suit, alleging that the DGA lobbied employers to hire women and minorities as second assistant directors. In that case, the judge ruled in the Guild's favor, writing, "The DGA has recognized that despite the existence of a readily identifiable pool of qualified women and racial minorities, signatory production companies historically have hired women and minority DGA members in numbers well below their representation in the DGA membership."[107]

As the twentieth century ended, the DGA continued to launch programs to promote gender equality. In 1995, the group inaugurated an annual diversity award to honor industry organizations that consistently hired women and minorities, and it began to compile records of the percentage of women and minority directors hired on a year-by-year basis. Despite such efforts, however, the Guild could claim only limited success. In 1983, only 9 percent of the Guild's membership was female, and by 2009 the percentage had gone up to just 13.4 percent.[108] It was not until 2002 that the group elected its first female president, Martha Coolidge, and 2010 was the first year in which the DGA awarded directorial honors in the feature film category to a woman—Kathryn Bigelow, for *The Hurt Locker*.[109]

By 2015, the American Civil Liberties Union had begun an investigation of gender discrimination within the Hollywood studios, alleging that the DGA fostered such discrimination by offering producers secret lists of recommended directors.[110] In response, the DGA inserted a clause in its contract negotiations requiring studios to include women and minorities in the interview process for all director jobs.[111] But the

DGA suffered a further setback in terms of public perception in 2017 when it lagged behind the Academy and the Producers Guild in addressing the charges of sexual harassment against producer-director Harvey Weinstein.[112]

Directors must dominate. That is the by-product of the style of charismatic leadership that the DGA has cultivated. This image has operated to minimize the input of other groups of artisans who make Hollywood movies, including producers, actors, writers, and editors, and its association with virility has imposed barriers for women who aspire to enter the profession. If the DGA's one man, one film principle has thus far been unable to impose itself in the realms of television and new media platforms where authorial agency is dispersed among many participants, it has nonetheless played a role in positioning such media as lesser modes of cultural endeavor. Capra's mantra continues to function as a cornerstone of cinema's honored place atop the vast array of entertainment options, largely by virtue of the aura supplied by the singular director-artists who are understood to have created it.

CHAPTER THREE

Recognition

The DGA Takes Credit

> At first, we weren't looking just for more money for directors. We wanted recognition: credits.
>
> —JOSEPH YOUNGERMAN, LONGTIME DGA EXECUTIVE SECRETARY

John Ford was fond of recounting a nightmare in which, as he died and approached heaven, he noticed a sign above the pearly gates that read "Produced by Darryl F. Zanuck."[1] Such an obsession with credits is not unique to Ford. Bernard Weinraub, a *New York Times* reporter with longstanding experience on the Hollywood scene, wrote in 1995, "If money is the driving force in Hollywood, credits on a movie screen are a close runner-up."[2] In a similar spirit, Hollywood entertainment lawyer Schuyler M. Moore has commented, "More acrimonious fights are fought over who gets what credit and in what order than over any other issue in the film industry."[3] And the satire of Hollywood mores, *Wag the Dog* (1999), created its climax out of the willingness of a producer to face death rather than the loss of a screen credit. "You think I did this for money?" asks the producer. "No. I did this for credit."[4]

Hollywood film productions work with a credit bible made up of pictorial charts. These charts have repeatedly constituted a flash point for all the major Hollywood talent groups, especially writers and directors. Money plays an important role in these struggles, for only those who receive screen credit are entitled to residual payments.[5] Perhaps even more importantly, credits define the nature of the contribution each creator has made to a finished film, and the accumulation of credits amounts to Hollywood's version of a professional résumé or calling card.[6]

For these reasons alone, the Directors Guild of America has cause to exercise tight control over the ways in which the names of its members appear on screen and in publicity. But the DGA's interest in credit allocation goes beyond a concern about residuals and résumé building; the image of the director is also at stake. The allocation and configuration of credits help to create the perception of the directors as artists. The directors' efforts in this realm build on a long history that has seen the names of creative authors play an ever-greater role in public discourse.

CREDITS AND THE NAMES OF AUTHORS

The DGA's activities around credits are part of a preoccupation with the names of authors that has become a focus of critical interest across the humanities. In his book *Paratexts: Thresholds of Interpretation*, Gérard Genette discusses how an author's name on the title page of a book functions as a generic marker that controls the way in which viewers understand the content that follows.[7] Such a marker works in a similar fashion when it appears on the credit roll of a Hollywood movie.

Michel Foucault has emphasized that authors' names operate in a historically specific manner, sometimes attaching themselves to certain discourses and, over time, shifting to others.[8] In general, more and more modes of creative endeavor have been identified with authors; today, even department store windows are sometimes signed.[9] Yet uncredited creations still exist.[10] In the twenty-first century, anonymous internet posting is on the rise. Another contemporary instance of unsigned art is advertising, which is presumably uncredited in order to keep the names of saleable commodities at the center of attention. However, when advertising artists move into film, their authorship may become more widely known. The credit sequences for *Vertigo*, by Saul Bass, and for *Seven*, by Kyle Cooper, both eminent graphic designers, are examples of this phenomenon; each received on-screen credit for his work. The Directors Guild took the lead in crediting individuals who create television commercials by adding this category to their annual awards in 1979.

In the early days of cinema, production companies suppressed the names of their creative employees, choosing instead to promote the names of the studios themselves as familiar brands that could lure consumers into theaters with a promise of quality. Such credits later appeared in the form of logos featuring iconic images like the MGM lion and the Paramount mountain.[11] A 1910 article on the Biograph Company in *Motion Picture World* suggested the effectiveness of the studios' strategy. While acknowledging the presence of various creative personnel, the writer credits the studio as a movie's author: "I do not know their staff, their producers, actors or anybody associated with the Company, yet mere mention of a Biograph picture seems to awaken in me a desire to see that picture. I have always felt I could get into the skin of their subjects and think as their producers and actors and photographers thought."[12]

It did not take long for the industry to respond to the public's curiosity about the people who actually created movies. By 1911, the Edison Company began to attach title cards to their productions that provided the names of cast members.[13] By 1912, advertising for films routinely included the names not only of stars and writers but also of directors, usually on the same title card, with the director's name at the bottom. As a consequence, the names of directors gradually became familiar to audiences. An article in the May 1924 issue of *Photoplay* documented the effect of such recognition; it was entitled, "Stars and Directors Whose Names Bring in the Public." Another *Photoplay* story, in December 1925, referred to D. W. Griffith as "the greatest unscreened star of the screen."[14] The directors themselves quickly grasped the value of this trend in furthering their careers. Biograph's refusal to credit Griffith either on screen or in advertising undoubtedly contributed to his decision to leave the company in 1913, and the man subsequently hailed as "the father of film" thereafter took care to emblazon his initials on the intertitles of every one of his productions.

Awarding credits to directors was complicated by the uncertainty about what their title should be. Though nineteenth-century theater directors had established name recognition, the movies, with their emphasis on visual storytelling, presented a new context.[15] As film historian Tom Gunning has stated, "Frequently early reviewers refer to the anonymous force responsible for [movies] as the 'stage manager.' But more frequently the term used is the one appearing in *Variety*'s announcement of [Wallace] McCutcheon's return to Biograph: *producer*."[16] This ambiguity reigned in the industry for some time. In 1928, for example, the Laurel and Hardy short *Two Tars* lists James Parrot as "director" and Leo McCarey as "supervising director"—another common designation during this period, which usually denoted someone who actually functioned as a producer.

The evolving nature of Cecil B. DeMille's early credits suggests the complexity of the problem directors faced. Carrying the name of a distinguished theatrical family associated with the storied stage producer David Belasco, DeMille was at first uncertain about how he could make the most of the cultural capital he brought with him into the new medium of cinema. His first difficulty lay in designating an appropriate title for himself. DeMille, along with his colleagues at Famous Players-Lasky, experimented with credits listing him as producer, writer, and even "picturizer" before deciding that "director" was the designation that best represented his position as the primary creative force behind his films.[17]

DeMille also faced the challenge of establishing his right to a credit whose size and placement would signal his superiority to the famous personalities with whom he worked. Credits on DeMille's early productions privileged the names of well-known novelists and stage actors over that of the director. Famous Players advertised itself as "Famous Players in Famous Plays," thereby proclaiming that literary authors and stars who were already celebrated in high art contexts like theater and opera, not directors, were the crucial elements in their productions. DeMille vied with opera diva Geraldine Farrar for top credit in the film adaptation of *Carmen* (1915). In the same year, ads for the adaptation of the stage hit *The Warrens of Virginia* played up the authorial claims of DeMille's brother, William, who had written the original play, and Belasco, who had mounted the production on Broadway. Their names appeared in large print while Cecil's credit as director came last, in much smaller type. Soon afterwards, however, his position was upgraded. "I think it a very good business move for us to build up [Cecil's] name . . ." Jesse Lasky wrote in 1915. "The public go to see a Griffith production, not because it may have a star in the cast, but because Griffith's name on it stands for so much . . . Let Cecil stage the plays that have no stars and his name in large type on the paper, advertising, etc., would undoubtedly in time take the place of a star's."[18]

During the years that followed, directors became sensitive to the way in which the configuration of their names could burnish their image. Like the names of actors, directors' names were frequently altered to erase signs of ethnicity; for example, John Ford was born John Feeney and Michael Curtiz was once Mihaly Kertesz.[19] Other modifications were made with an eye to creating an image of dignity and status. Many directors used a middle initial. Both Joseph Sternberg and Erich Stroheim added a "von." David Wark Griffith, who insisted on being addressed as "mister" by his coworkers, elected to use the chilly designation "D. W." rather than encourage the use of his given name. DeMille, who also insisted on being addressed as "mister," altered his famous surname (De Mille) in such a way as to forestall the possibility that the high-toned French "De" could be deleted. Today, directors are routinely identified in traditional authorial style, by means of surnames alone (Hitchcock or Spielberg). Such authorial names may, in turn, be converted to adjectives or common nouns ("Wellesian" or "Capracorn"). All of these strategies familiarized audiences with directors' names and raised their stature in the eyes of the public.

For Frank Capra, having his name prominently placed on screen was the key to asserting creative dominance over the productions he oversaw, as his autobiography, *The Name Above the Title*, proclaims. Capra's self-presentation in this book is filled with ruminations about the meaning of credits. "Marquee lights featured 'Frank Capra' above the title of the film and the names of the stars," he writes at one point, describing the opening of *Mr. Deeds Goes to Town*. "[I was] the first . . . director to wrest that distinction from the Hollywood Establishment."[20]

Capra was so fixated on credits that his obsession surfaced in other areas of his life as well. As a hobby, he collected first editions of important literary works and paid particular attention to the form in which a book's author was credited. His autobiography includes the following commentary on this practice:

> You probably have read Milton's *Paradise Lost* and loved it. But wouldn't you love it more if you knew that the first edition of this classic—with the title page reading *Paradise Lost* by JOHN

MILTON—was a complete failure? And that when the disgruntled publisher grudgingly printed a second edition, he lower-cased the author's name to *John Milton*? And that when the second edition moved as slowly as the first, the name on the third edition was further diminished to *J. Milton*—and to just *J. M.* on the fourth edition? But then the book began to sell. On the fifth edition the initials expanded back to *John Milton*, and by the sixth printing the author's name was restored to the upper-case glory of the first edition: JOHN MILTON.

If you yawn and ask *why* that bit of trivia should make you love *Paradise Lost* more than you do now—that's what makes us book collectors so snooty—nobody understands us.[21]

This passage reveals not just Capra's preoccupation with credits but also his association of this concern with the "snooty" high art tradition of epic poetry and book collecting. Notably, he refused to explain the reasons for his preoccupation with the evolving configurations of Milton's authorial credit, as though he were embarrassed by the seeming superficiality of this issue. Possibly he also felt that it would be unseemly to equate the way in which a canonical literary figure had been credited with the strategies he had applied to his own career, but the comparison is inescapable.

Capra was not alone in his belief that modes of credit attribution in traditional art forms are consequential. The signing of artworks is one such mode, a time-honored practice by which visual artists authenticate their work and ensure that it retains its aura.[22] In Hollywood, the symbolic meaning of signatures is tainted by its association with autograph hounds, but directors have nonetheless employed this strategy to their advantage.[23] When D. W. Griffith put his initials on the intertitles of all of his productions, he did so in the style that emulated a signature. For its fiftieth anniversary, in 1986, the DGA attempted to prompt the public to associate directors with such authorial signatures by selling Saul Bass–designed movie posters signed by directors of the films involved.[24] In 1992, the group mounted a similar event, this one a benefit auction featuring member donations of "signed artwork [and] signed scripts with handwritten favorite lines or anecdotes."[25]

The conventions of credit attribution have played a significant role in marginalizing women, who have historically been socialized to relinquish their names at marriage and to act as unsung helpmates to men.[26] Alma Reville is a well-known example of such a woman, content to work in the shadow of her famous husband, Alfred Hitchcock, during her lifetime.[27] In 1921, June Mathis, a writer and studio executive, directed the performance of her discovery, Rudolph Valentino, in *The Four Horsemen of the Apocalypse* and was on the set every day, but she received no directorial credit for her work. Nor does her name appear on drafts of many of the scripts she contributed to over the years. In 1930, Dorothy Arzner codirected two films with Robert Milton (*Behind the Makeup* and *Charming Sinners*) without receiving any on-screen recognition, and in 1937 she completed *The Last of Mrs. Cheyney* for Richard Boleslavsky without credit.[28] Lois Weber included a photograph of herself at the beginning of her first film, *Hypocrites* (1915), which was signed "Sincerely, Lois Weber." Instead of calling attention to her creative authorship, however, such a mark of identification aligned her with the female stars who sent autographed images of themselves to fans.[29]

Despite the advent of second wave feminism in the 1970s and 1980s, the situation remains largely unchanged. At the 1998 Cannes Film Festival, for example, the Scandinavia-based Dogme 95 group disseminated a manifesto entitled "Vow of Chastity." Among its declarations was a pledge to forego any directorial credit card. It is noteworthy that only the lone woman in the group, Suzanne Bier, complied with this directive; as of 2019, her 2002 film *Open Hearts* (*Elsker dig for evigt*, aka *Dogme 28*) remains the only Dogme film without a directorial credit.

THE DGA AND CREDIT CONFIGURATION

The DGA's first agreement with the studios, from 1939, insists on the director's "right to screen credits" and gives the Guild the right to assign these credits. Since that time, all signatories to the organization's Basic Agreement have been obliged to submit drafts of on-screen credits and promotional materials for Guild approval. Though A-list directors may bargain for special credit consideration above and beyond what is called for in the Basic Agreement, every Guild member is covered by the group's standard contract, which spells out in voluminous detail the minimum specifications governing all directorial credits. The agreement states that the directorial credit will be the last to appear on the screen during the front roll before principle photography begins, in both film and television productions. It must be of a given size and placed on a separate title card.[30] Thirty years later, provision was made for the credit crawl that appeared at the end of films; in such instances, the director's name must be placed first, and in the case of television programs, no commercials can intervene. At the Guild meeting where this last agreement was discussed, Mabel Walker Willebrandt, the DGA negotiator, commented that the producers were dragging their feet on this provision. "Keep that right in there," responded Capra.[31]

Placing the director's credit card at the end of a movie's front roll identifies him or her as the person who synthesizes and supersedes the work of the other creative personnel.[32] The practice of granting the final credit to the director is also designed to encourage audiences to make the closest possible connection between the director's name and the experience of the movie's interior world. Some films take this principle even further, setting the director credit apart from all the other creative participants by bleeding it into the action rather than featuring it against a title page–type background. A similar principle governs credits that appear at the end rather than the beginning of a film; in such cases, the director's name appears first, just after the narrative ends.

In a few instances, the Guild has waived its credit placement regulations to accommodate special circumstances. For example, Paul Newman was permitted to place his name at the end rather than the beginning of the final credit crawl of *Rachel, Rachel* (1968), which he had directed.[33] However, in 1981 the Guild denied a request from George Lucas, the producer of *Star Wars: Episode V—The Empire Strikes Back*, to put Irvin Kershner's directorial credit at the end rather than the beginning of the picture. Lucas ignored the ruling, and the DGA forced him to pay a $25,000 fine. Lucas subsequently resigned from the Guild.[34]

The DGA agreements also specify in which advertising contexts directors' names should appear and how they should be configured in both posters and paid ads. Before 1987, directors' names had to appear on all paid ads in which stars' names were mentioned. This form of recognition triggered a sense of entitlement among other moviemaking groups as well, so that by the mid-1980s credit information typically took up 20 percent of ad space, forcing poster designers to employ highly condensed typefaces to squeeze everything in. This practice prodded the Guild to reassess the situation. "We are getting too many complaints about the increasing diminution and camouflage of our credits in advertising when they are barely seen," stated a 1981 DGA press release. "[They are] buried in a cavalcade of names equal in size, but not in time spent or responsibility borne."[35] During the 1987 battle over residuals, the DGA pulled back on its requirement that its members always be mentioned alongside stars, stipulating that up to two actors could be named without triggering the name of the director.[36] But in 1993 the Guild further expanded the formats for directorial credits by winning the right to have directors' names appear on posters in thin boxes.[37] In 1995, DGA president Gene Reynolds stated, "Credit rules prevent our members from accepting a less favorable billing.... Our rules also provide that no other craft group (except actors) exceeds us in visibility."[38]

The 1948 DGA agreement addressed another aspect of the credit question by restricting the groups who have a right to call themselves directors, specifying that dance directors be credited as "choreographers" and dialogue directors be called "dialogue coaches."[39] "Everybody wanted a director credit," recalled former DGA executive secretary Joseph Youngerman in his autobiography, "so there was a 'sound director,' a 'costume director,' a 'musical director,' and on and on. We fought like hell to get rid of all 'director' credits. The only two we couldn't fight down were Art Directors, because they were in there before we were, and DP—Directors of Photography."[40] Youngerman was echoing a concern that had long troubled his colleagues. As early as 1924 an issue of the publication of the Motion Picture Directors Association complained,

> Originally, in the motion picture business, the word "director" applied only to one position. But because that position was important, dignified and powerful, persons of lesser importance conceived the idea of glorifying their humble jobs by appropriating the title and applying it to themselves. Thus, casting clerks became casting directors; architect, set dressers, and even property men

became Art Directors. Month by month the list grew until now we have Supervising Directors, Publicity Directors, Transportation Directors, Location Directors and Editorial Directors.

In another year, no doubt, many new hybrid titles will be invented and perhaps it will be found possible to equip every person in the industry with some kind of directorship.[41]

In 1954, the DGA agreement was challenged when Ray Heindorf, musical director for Warner Bros., insisted on keeping his title when he was recognized in movie credits, and the Guild became a party to a messy court case.[42] In 1983, DGA chief officer Michael Franklin wrote a letter to Guild members reinforcing the organization's position. The letter stated, "Employers will not grant to any individual, other than a director, any screen or paid advertising credits which includes the word 'Director,' 'Direction,' or any derivation thereof."[43]

ONE MAN, ONE FILM: KEEPING UP APPEARANCES

The most important aspect of screen credits, in the eyes of the Directors Guild, is their ability to project an image of directors as singular creative artists with total control over the films on which they work. Thus, though the credits on a Hollywood production may list several writers or producers, only in very rare cases is more than one director credited. The 1978 DGA Basic Agreement codified the Guild's accepted practice of crediting only one director for each film unless the Guild grants a specific waiver.[44] As Elliot Silverstein, chair of the DGA's Creative Rights Committee at the time, later recalled, "We did not want the Guild's members to be involved in a 'piece goods' profession, blurring individual vision, authority and credit."[45]

The single director credit obscures a more complicated reality, for directors often replace one another. A 1986 *Variety* chart prepared as part of the DGA Jubilee commemoration listed 179 films made between 1970 and 1986 that had been overseen by more than one director; an even longer list named directors who were replaced before filming began.[46] Furthermore, as is evident from examining the credit roles of any number of big budget productions, even though a single director may be designated as the director of record, much of the location work is supervised by second unit directors, and specialized sections like stunt sequences and montages may be handed over to others as well.

The Guild has denied directors the right to share credit on numerous occasions. One famous case involves *Gone with the Wind* (1939). Though the Guild ultimately decreed that Victor Fleming would get sole screen credit, he shot, at most, only 55 percent of the movie. David O. Selznick, who had produced the film, protested, asking the DGA to grant production designer William Cameron Menzies codirecting credit. In a letter he wrote to DGA president Frank Capra, Selznick noted, "Bill Menzies spent perhaps a year of his life in laying out camera angles, lighting effects, and other important directorial contributions to *Gone with the Wind*, a large number of which are in the picture just as he designed them a year before Victor Fleming came on the film. . . . In addition, there are a large number of scenes which he personally directed, including a most important part of the spectacle."[47]

William Wyler faced a similar problem dealing with Samuel Goldwyn on the production of *Come and Get It* (1936), which Howard Hawks had begun. Wyler later recalled,

> The best parts—the first half hour, were done by Hawks and the magnificent logger operations footage by second-unit director Richard Rosson. When I finished, Goldwyn still was sore at Hawks and wanted to take his name off the picture altogether and give me credit alone. I said, "Absolutely no" and we had another blowup. The Directors Guild was just being formed but was not yet recognized by the studios and there was no way of appealing or bringing to arbitration such a decision.
>
> Goldwyn finally agreed to a half measure—putting both our names on the screen, and I insisted that Hawks's name come first and that's how it appears."[48]

In 2004, Robert Rodriguez resigned from the Guild when the organization denied him a waiver to credit himself as codirector of *Sin City*, along with Frank Miller, and to list Quentin Tarantino as a guest director on the film. As a result of his action, Rodriguez was taken off his next project, *A Princess of Mars*, because the picture was to be cofinanced by Paramount, a signatory to the DGA contract, which required that the film's director be a Guild member.[49]

Despite its strict policy on shared credit, the Guild has increasingly faced the dilemma presented by directorial teams; it granted only ten waivers to such teams during the ten-year period from 1979 to 1989 but gave out sixty during a similar ten-year period from 2000 to 2009.[50] To determine whether a given pair of directors will qualify as a team, the Guild's credits committee looks for a history of cooperative activity. Under these guidelines, siblings like the Farrelly brothers and the Coen brothers are eligible for waivers, as are husband-and-wife teams like Nancy Meyers and Charles Shyer or Valerie Faris and Jonathan Dayton.[51] Absent a history of this sort, directorial teams may not be credited as such. Codirectors who split up duties rather than working in tandem also are denied waivers. "In that situation, the spirit of making a film is bifurcated," explains longtime DGA leader and spokesperson Gilbert Cates. "What it says is 'OK, there's going to be one voice speaking for the actor, and another voice speaking for the camera.' The best interpretation of music is made by a single conductor. The best painting is made by a single painter. And I think the best film is made by a single artist."[52]

ALLEN SMITHEE

The status of the director's credit as the signature of a single artist whose name speaks for the quality of a film was given a new twist in 1969 when the DGA created a fictional director named Allen Smithee to allow its members to avoid signing films they had directed with someone else or productions that had embarrassed them. The DGA specifies that directors who apply for the privilege of using the Allen Smithee credit must show evidence that their work has been "extremely brutalized," and they must agree not to speak of the matter to the press. John Rich, who was a member of the Guild's Directors' Council when the nom de plume originated, explained, "We didn't want to create a situation where it would be easy for directors to abdicate responsibility for their work."[53] The proximate cause of this policy was the production *Death of a Gunfighter* (1969). When the film's original director, Robert

Totten, was fired after clashing with star Richard Widmark, Don Siegel was brought in to finish the picture. Siegel, however, did not want to sign the film and appealed to DGA arbitration. The final credit on *Death of a Gunfighter* thus reads "Directed by Allen Smithee."[54]

As Genette has argued, creating false identities is itself a creative act and calls further attention to the person of the author, especially as the pseudonym and the reasons behind it become widely known.[55] The Allen Smithee pseudonym has functioned in this manner. Putatively devised to conceal the names of individual directors, it has added significantly to the fame and stature of directors as a group, functioning as a testament to directorial integrity. Journalists have found the practice an engaging topic for feature stories.[56] In 1997, writer Joe Eszterhas mounted a cinematic satire of the movie industry entitled *An Alan Smithee Film: Burn Hollywood Burn*. Helmed by Arthur Hiller, a onetime president of the DGA, the production denounced the commercial constraints placed on the film artist. In a bizarre irony, Eszterhas and Hiller clashed over creative control of the project and the movie itself was ultimately credited to Alan Smithee, thereby creating a literal meaning to its title that was not originally intended.[57] A few years later an anthology entitled *Directed by Allen Smithee* was published, complete with a forward by auteurist *éminence grise* Andrew Sarris.[58]

By 2003, anecdotes about Smithee had become staples on the Universal Studios tour. The DGA itself surrendered to the temptation to exploit the publicity surrounding its fictional auteur and published at least two stories about Smithee in its magazine.[59] Finally, after a highly publicized altercation between director Tony Kaye and actor Edward Norton over the film *American History X* (1998), Kaye requested an Allen Smithee credit, but the Guild denied it. The barrage of publicity that followed prompted the DGA to retire the name Smithee in 2000; it was replaced with the more anonymous-sounding Thomas Lee and other pseudonyms.[60]

THE DIRECTORS GUILD, THE WRITERS GUILD, AND THE CONTROVERSY OVER CREDITS

As we saw in the previous chapter, in the first days of cinema, writers were often thought of as the authors of films; thus, their names were typically privileged over those of directors in movie credits. As early as 1912, Horace J. Plimpton, manager of Edison's negative production department, stated that he planned to give screen credit for freelance scenarios. "The new policy is somewhat in the nature of an experiment," he stated, "intended to encourage the comparatively unknown writers who might otherwise be discouraged by the use now being made of copyrighted works of well-known authors."[61] Other companies soon followed suit. The press of the day quickly took note of this development. A 1911 article published in *Moving Picture World* claimed, "More [screenwriters] would enter the field if their names appeared on the films. The only companies to comply with their aspirations have been the Edison and the Paris studio of the Pathe Freres [sic]."[62] Another piece, published at around the same time, looked to the established art form of the theater for a model for crediting writers. "In the field of the spoken drama, the author of a piece is fully recognized on posters, programs and in its advertising, no matter how little known or obscure he may be at the time his play is produced," the article argued. "It is this policy that has given to the spoken drama some of its most brilliant authors. It would do the same thing for the picture play."[63]

Control over credits was a major factor spurring union organizing efforts not only by directors but also by writers. John Howard Lawson, the first president of the Writers Guild of America, commented, "A writer's name is his most cherished possession. It is his creative personality, the symbol of the whole body of his ideas and experience."[64] A joint statement by WGA, West president Frank Pierson and WGA, East president Herb Sargent in 1995 restates this principle: "The creative recognition of the contribution of the writer to the film was a founding principle of the Screenwriters Guild in 1933."[65] For many years, the WGA's newsletter featured a column entitled "Credit Watchdog," which flagged movie reviews that failed to mention screenwriters.

Writers' efforts to be properly credited were plagued by numerous setbacks over the years. To begin with, as we have seen, they had failed to establish a "one man, one film" principle as the directors had done. In 1934, an Academy of Motion Picture Arts and Sciences bulletin stated, "For many years the names of directors have been built into assets in selling pictures. Writers' names can be made equally valuable, but never as long as three or four names are used on the screen."[66] The difficulty created by the studio's practice of assigning multiple writers' credits was exacerbated by the inclination of producers to casually grant writing credits to their friends and relations.[67] Ever since it won the right to assign writers' credits, in its 1941 agreement, the Writers Guild has struggled mightily to overcome this handicap by limiting the number of writing credits on films, a policy that has resulted in numerous nasty and widely publicized battles among its members.[68]

The writers' credit dilemma was further exacerbated during the 1950s, when many who had been blacklisted were forced to hide behind pseudonyms. In 1956, Dalton Trumbo received an Oscar for writing *The Brave One* under the name of Robert Rich. The same year saw the release of *Friendly Persuasion*, a film that contained no screenwriting credit because Michael Wilson, who had written the script, had been blacklisted. The Academy of Motion Picture Arts and Sciences subsequently nominated the *Friendly Persuasion* screenplay for an Oscar and then withdrew the nomination when it could not resolve the issue of how to credit the recipient.[69]

Writers have long blamed directors for their compromised status. In a 1917 article in *Photoplay*, screenwriter Leslie Peacocke objected that directors "resented hotly any efforts that writers made to get credit for the work of their brains. They did all in their power to prevent the writers of original photoplays from getting 'name credit' as the authors of the stories on films and advertising matter."[70] In 1937, the studios made a deal with the Screen Playwrights group that allowed producers to grant directors the right to story credit. This development spurred the reactivation of the Writers Guild, which was then virtually moribund.[71] The reinvigorated WGA signed a pact with producers stipulating that directors must contribute at least 50 percent of the dialogue to a given screenplay to qualify for writing credit.[72]

A special source of friction between the directors and the writers is the growing popularity of possessory (or possessive) credits for directors.[73] Possessory credits can be expressed with apostrophes, as in "Francis Ford Coppola's *The Godfather*," or they can take the form of "A Film by...." In television, the customary locutions are "Created by..." or "Developed by...." This form of recognition, sometimes derisively termed a vanity credit, puts directors, who are the usual recipients, both first and last on the front credit role. To cite one example, Michael

Cimino's 1980 contract with United Artists for *Heaven's Gate* specified, "Mr. Cimino's presentation credit shall be in the form, 'Michael Cimino's *Heaven's Gate*' (or in such other form as [Cimino] may designate); Mr. Cimino's name in such credit shall be presented in the same size as the title, including all artwork titles and on a separate line above the title, and shall appear in the form just indicated on theater marquees."[74]

Even if a director can claim no established reputation coming into a given production, the producer, who typically wields final authority, is often willing to grant such a credit as compensation for offering a reduced director's fee. Producers also may give way in the expectation that the director's name—even if it is unknown—will carry more weight by the time the film is made available to ancillary markets, mimicking a practice long familiar in the literary world. As Genette has commented, "Magical thinking (act as if it were so, and you'll make it happen) occasionally leads the publisher [of a book] to engage in promotional practices that somewhat anticipate glory by mimicking its effect."[75]

A possessory credit connotes possession. If the final credit card connects the name of a lone individual with the narrative that follows, a possessory credit, by incorporating the form of possessive pronouns, implies that whoever receives this kind of recognition possesses—or owns—the film in which it appears. Of course, Hollywood directors do not actually own the productions they supervise; American work for hire copyright provisions designate the studios as the legal owners of most movies. But the popular mythology that sees works of art as the rightful property of the artists who create them supports the assumption that directors, who have long cultivated an image of themselves as individualistic creators, are best positioned to claim this form of credit. Since the advent of auteurism, many publications routinely mimic the form of the directorial possessory credit by referring to all films in a way (for instance, "Hitchcock's *Vertigo*") that implies that they are the property of their directors.[76]

Possessory credits have not always been the prerogative of directors. The name above the title has sometimes been that of the producer—as with Samuel Goldwyn's *The Best Years of Our Lives* (1946, directed by William Wyler) or *Andy Warhol's Dracula* (1974, directed by Paul Morrissey)—or of the writer of the original material—as with

Truman Capote's *In Cold Blood* (1967, directed by Richard Brooks), Stephen King's *Pet Sematary* (1989, directed by Mary Lambert), or *Bram Stoker's Dracula* (1992, directed by Francis Ford Coppola).[77] But possessory credits are ordinarily a perk reserved for directors. The first American director known to have taken it was D. W. Griffith, for *The Birth of a Nation* (1915).[78] During the 1960s, directors won the right to take this form of credit in film, while writers won it in television. In 1981, the DGA negotiated an agreement ensuring that such recognition, once granted, would appear on all billboards containing more than six personal credits.[79] From 1990 to 2016, three-fifths to three-quarters of all studio films contained a possessory credit, and in the vast majority of cases they named the director.[80]

As writers have repeatedly observed, a possessory credit goes the furthest in marginalizing the contribution of other creative hands. "The credit that says, 'a film by' makes it sound like one person, a director, is responsible for the film, and it denigrates the writer," screenwriter Cheryl Rhoden has commented.[81] Philip Dunne claimed that the practice of assigning such credits to directors has been abetted by the "pernicious" auteur theory, which has "focused on the director as the individual artist responsible for the whole.... The auteur theory enriches [the director] in prestige while it robs the writer of the credit he deserves."[82] As early as 1940, the WGA was working to limit directors' right to take a possessory credit. In 1955, the group raised an objection to Otto Preminger taking such a credit for *The Man with the Golden Arm*, which was based on a best-selling novel by Nelson Algren.[83]

At the end of 1966, passions erupted on both sides when it came to light that a WGA agreement with the Alliance of Motion Picture and Television Producers denied directors the right to take possessory credit and gave it to the writers instead. The agreement stated in part, "Producer shall not accord presentation credit in the form 'A Film (or Photoplay or Picture) of Sam Jones,' 'A Film (or Photoplay or Picture) by Sam Jones,' or in the following two forms: 'Sam Jones' *Hamlet*' or 'Sam Jones' Film,' unless the person so accorded credit is a writer entitled to credit on the screen or the author of source material.[84] "We were really quite stunned," said Delbert Mann, then the DGA's first vice president. "We had learned nothing of it until it was announced. It was a fait accompli.... It took a while for the meaning of it to really sink in. I think those big directors who had always received the possessory credit figured it out very quickly. In a little while the anger built in all directors."[85]

Beginning on January 4, 1967, the Guild began to send a series of threatening telegrams to the Alliance of Motion Picture and Television Producers and all the major studio heads, protesting the WGA pact. In response, the AMPTP, then chaired by industry titan Lew Wasserman, offered a number of compromises. The DGA rejected all of them, including a proposal to let the WGA adjudicate the granting of possessory credits only for those directors who had not received such recognition in the past, and another proposal to allow directors possessory credit provided that writers received equal billing. In April of the same year, Jack Valenti, representing the AMPTP, approached director Fred Zinnemann to attempt to resolve the issue. The Guild responded with a telegram to Valenti that read, "You misunderstand the fact that this is an official Guild position. This issue has been hanging fire for four months and nothing has been done. We can sit on it no longer. Our members insist on action now. Please do not underestimate the seriousness of this threat to an amicable relationship of long standing."[86]

In May 1967, the directors brought an injunction against the WGA. An article in the May–June issue of the DGA's magazine *Action* contrasted the situation with the prevailing conventions surrounding the auteurs of European art cinema. "Future *Blow-Up*s will be Antonioni's, future *8 1/2*s will be Fellini's, future *Persona*s will be Bergman's," the article stated, "but future *Psycho*s will not be Alfred Hitchcock's, and future *The Collector*s will not be William Wyler's, and future *Mickey One*s will not be Arthur Penn's."[87]

On May 16, 1967, fifty-three Guild members, including many top names, met at DGA headquarters to discuss the WGA policy. When the DGA threatened to take the case to court, Frank Capra, Alfred Hitchcock, King Vidor, and Fred Zinnemann all submitted affidavits in defense of the directors' position. Hitchcock's statement referred to the credit as a trademark and asserted, "If I am prevented from using this trademark identification in the future, I shall be deprived of my most valuable asset."[88] Vidor countered the writers' claims by stating, "Under no circumstance is the contribution of the single element of writing the screenplay sufficient to justify exploiting the [writer's] name, which in truth and in fact means nothing at the box office. On the other hand,... the motion picture public has a widespread understanding of the director's importance to the film."[89]

Though the DGA's suit was unsuccessful, the directors persisted in their efforts to thwart the new policy, threatening to strike over this issue after their own contact expired on April 30, 1968. In the meantime, they began negotiating agreements with independent producers—many of them members of the AMPTP—in defiance of the WGA pact. At last, on April 10, 1968, the DGA came to an understanding with the AMPTP. Their new agreement affirmed the right of anyone to negotiate for special credits and specifically granted directors the right to bargain for any form of screen credit after the WGA contract expired in 1970. The language of the agreement stated that, in the future, allowing directors to negotiate for possessory credit would be "recognized as an inalienable right which shall not be abridged in any manner."[90]

But the struggle between the two guilds over the possessory credit continued to fester, flaring up during negotiations in 1973, 1977, 1988, 1994, 1998, and 2001.[91] During the 2001 industry negotiations, a DGA spokesperson stated, "The WGA unfortunately disrupted what should have been unity between the guilds by attacking directors with their possessory credit and so-called creative rights proposals, eliminating any possibility that we would sit down with them at the bargaining table for any part of their negotiation."[92] At this time, the WGA estimated that directors took possessory credits on about 70 percent of all studio films. Though the 2001 WGA contract again reflected the fact that the writers had been forced to back down on the possessory credit issue, negotiators called for a forum on credits, in conjunction with the DGA, to be held before October 1 of that year. But this event never took place. The World Trade Center bombing that occurred on September 11 most likely figured in the postponement of the proposed forum; afterwards, however, no date was ever set.

By 2004, the DGA's stance had softened, and the Guild drafted a policy that limited the conditions under which directors could take a possessory credit. Directors were by then taking such a credit on fewer than 50 percent of major studio releases.[93] In a letter to DGA members, president Michael Apted wrote,

> The founders of the Guild and many of the greatest practitioners of the craft had a vision of the possessory that, frankly, has been diminished in this era of questionable credits.... The Guild should take some action to insure that the possessory credit continues to signify that what appears on the screen should be identified with its director.... The criteria should be whether the director has established a marketable name or a signature style of filmmaking, or received critical acclaim, or possesses a substantial body of work consisting of three or more films, or has received a possessory credit on a previous film.[94]

Apted later commented, "I felt we had to make a concession about the possessory credit, since I could understand why the Writers Guild was annoyed by it, so we introduced a rule where [first-time directors] could only take the possessory if [they] wrote the script, brought the film to the studio or had a major part in creating it."[95] But Apted's concession did not end the dispute. In 2007, European screenwriters entered the fray, producing a manifesto that called for writers to be recognized as film authors and labeling possessory credits "unacceptable."[96] The following year, the WGA attached a nonbinding preamble to its agreement that read in part, "Since its founding, the Writers Guild has opposed the use of the so-called 'possessory credit' on screen and in advertising and promotion when used to refer to a person who is not the sole author of the screenplay."[97]

Despite the DGA's aggressive stance on the issue of possessory credits, however, not all directors are convinced of its value. Steven Soderbergh has consistently refused it, as has Woody Allen, who called it "pretentious and unnecessary."[98] And Steve Martin lampooned the practice in a short piece he contributed to the screenwriters' online newsletter.

> "Directed by . . ." says I'm the guy who directs the actors, approves the sets and costumes, approves the script, and that's all.
> "A film by . . ." says much, much more. I'm more of a . . . how can I say it? A film personality, I guess. I'm a guy who makes films. I supply the aura.

What if someone watching in Oklahoma sees the film and there's no "A film by..." credit?

He sees the "Directed by..." credit and wonders, "Yes, but who made the film? Whose film is it in the existential sense?"

This could spoil the film experience for him.[99]

Though the dismissive attitudes of directors like Allen and Martin might lead one to believe that the possessory credit merely functions as a symbol of directors' grandiosity, such a credit plays an important role in the way in which directors are perceived. Like all the other forms of credit the DGA has fought for over the years, the possessory credit is weighted with symbolic meaning for both the industry and for the public at large. Though it is only letters on the screen, the placement, size, and position of directors' credits make up a discourse that sets directors apart from their colleagues and endorses their claim to be viewed as the singular artists who create Hollywood cinema.

CHAPTER FOUR

Politics

The DGA Stages HUAC

> Any historical narrative is a particular bundle of silences.
> —MICHEL-ROLPH TROUILLOT

> Historical facts do not ordain interpretations;
> only plot structures do that.
> —ALUN MUNSLOW

In 1941, two years after the Directors Guild of America signed its first agreement with the Hollywood studios, Preston Sturges's comedy *Sullivan's Travels* satirized a significant issue faced by the newly minted organization: What kind of artists did directors want to be? Sturges's protagonist, director John L Sullivan, or "Sully" as he is known, has built his reputation on mindless comedies. In the film's opening scene, Sully shows his producers a dramatic scene from a politically progressive film as an example of the kind of serious production he would like to undertake, a picture that is "something like Capra." In the spirit of Capra, the movie Sullivan wants to make, *O Brother, Where Art Thou?*, will combine mass market appeal and incisive social commentary. Sturges thus implies that Hollywood defines art as weighty subject matter as much as formal mastery.

Given the political climate of the day, Sturges could well have had the DGA in mind, for, like John L. Sullivan, the Guild was engaged in fostering an image of its members as artists driven by politically enlightened goals.[1] Yet, like the overprivileged Sullivan's inept attempts to live as a tramp in order to gather materials that will provide an authentic background for his production, the DGA's encounters with issues of social justice have often drawn the organization into uncharted waters and pulled its members in many directions. The most dramatic and highly publicized of these encounters occurred during a period when the House Un-American Activities Committee had turned its gaze on Hollywood. The climax came at a dramatic seven-hour membership meeting on Sunday, October 22, 1950, in the Crystal Room of the Beverly Hills Hotel. The melodramatic narrative that Guild members subsequently constructed out of this event enabled the organization to elaborate on its image as a haven for artists within the Hollywood industry by adding a motif of political commitment. In the process, the directors also reinforced their aura of charismatic masculinity. This underlying agenda is the focus of the following historiographic inquiry into the Guild's story of that night.

THE STORY

In numerous memoirs and interviews, various DGA members and associates have described the group's legendary conclave at the Beverly Hills Hotel, and this event has become the dramatic high point of the organization's history.[2] A latter-day chronicle of this traumatic moment, drawing on these sources, appeared in a special issue of the *DGA Magazine* published in 1996, on the occasion of the organization's sixtieth anniversary.[3] This account reads as follows:

> The most heated debate in Guild history exploded in 1950 after Cecil B. DeMille, the leader of the DGA's more conservative forces, set up the Foundation for Americanism, the chief function of which was to pass on information about communist sympathizers to the California Un-American Activities Committee. The infamous "Hollywood 10" had already been identified by the McCarthy era "witch-hunts," and included DGA member Edward Dmytryk, director of *Crossfire* (1947).[4] Joseph L. Mankiewicz, director of *All About Eve* (1950), was Guild president when DeMille and his supporters urged every member of the DGA to sign a loyalty oath and provide information on the political beliefs of all the actors and

Politics 87

technicians they employed as a condition for being allowed to work in Hollywood.[5] Mankiewicz opposed this move.

A petition was circulated to impeach Mankiewicz from the presidency.[6] Guild members rallied with a counter-petition and a meeting was organized at the Beverly Hills Hotel. More than 500 directors jammed the hotel on October 22, 1950.[7] For seven hours, DeMille and Albert S. Rogell, his main ally, stood firm as many directors assailed his motives and tactics. William Wyler threatened to clobber the next guy who accused him of Communism simply because he wouldn't sign DeMille's petition.

George Stevens implored DeMille to recall the petition. He refused. Rouben Mamoulian's disappointment showed in tears. Don Hartman vehemently asked DeMille to resign from the DGA board of directors. He refused again. Ford finally stood up, his characteristic baseball cap at a tilt. There was great apprehension as to what was on the master's mind.

"My name's John Ford," he said. "I make Westerns.[8] I don't think there is anyone in this room who knows more about what the public wants than Cecil B. DeMille—and he certainly knows how to give it to them. In that respect, I admire him." Then he leveled a stare at DeMille and said. "But I don't like you, C.B. I don't like what you stand for and I don't like what you've been saying here tonight."

Ford demanded an apology for Mankiewicz from DeMille and was refused. Then he announced that he had only one conclusion: that the board of directors resign and a new board be elected, with an executive committee made up of past presidents, including Mankiewicz, running the Guild in the interim.[9] The motions were cheered, seconded and carried by acclamation. One by one the board members resigned. The meeting was adjourned.

"It was such an exciting and suspenseful and intense and victorious meeting, and such a clear-cut victory for the more liberal forces in the Guild, that several of us—John Sturges, Mark Robson and myself—went to Chasen's and relived the evening over and over again," remembered Robert Wise, who was present at the meeting and served as Guild president two decades later, from 1971 to 1975.[10]

The melodramatic underpinnings of this version of events are obvious: an intensifying, emotion-laden conflict between forces coded as good and evil culminates in two of Hollywood's star directors facing off against each other in a climactic showdown, which is followed by a happy ending. John Ford's dramatic speech forms the climax. But this narrative, which has become the accepted version of the historic DGA meeting, tells only part of the story.[11]

THE BACKSTORY

Most scholarly accounts of the blacklist era focus on the havoc the House Un-American Activities Committee investigation wrought on lives and careers. Other versions stress the anti-Semitism that was mingled with the anticommunism of the period. Still others emphasize the way in which studio heads, working in collusion with conservative lawmakers, used the investigation as a tool to quash organized labor.[12] At the time all these events took place, however, issues of a different nature were at play as well. The DGA was then facing major challenges that weighed heavily on the mind of every Guild member. The massive reorganization of the studios brought about by the 1948 Paramount antitrust decree had transformed legions of full-time workers, including directors, into freelancers. Moreover, the postwar slump at the box office and a shift away from B movies meant fewer jobs.[13]

Most significantly, at the very moment when the second round of HUAC hearings was about to begin, the DGA was attempting to merge with the Radio and Television Directors Guild, a move that many DGA members felt was vital if their group was to survive.[14] The negotiations surrounding the merger were fractious, with the RTDG accusing the DGA of unfair labor practices while the DGA counterchanged that the New York group was Communist dominated. It was in this atmosphere of frustration and anxiety about the future of the Guild itself that the October 22 meeting at the Beverly Hills Hotel took place.

Allegations about Communist infiltration of film industry unions had been in the air since the early 1930s, but in the 1940s such allegations became more serious when the Conference of Studio Unions challenged the dominance of a rival union, the International Alliance of Theatrical Stage Employees, over Hollywood's craft workers. In the ensuing struggle, both the Conference of Studio Unions and its leader, Herbert Sorrell, were branded as Communist. In 1945, a series of militant strikes and the subsequent studio lockout of returning Conference of Studio Unions workers made national news, with headlines announcing dramatic acts of violence involving strikers and goons hired by the studios.[15]

The House Un-American Activities Committee had begun its most important set of hearings focused on Hollywood in 1947.[16] The committee had subpoenaed forty-five witnesses from the film community and subsequently branded nineteen as "unfriendly."[17] The unfriendly nineteen included five directors: Herbert Biberman, Edward Dmytryk, Lewis Milestone, Irving Pichel, and Robert Rossen. Two of these, Biberman and Dmytryk, were among the Hollywood Ten subsequently cited for contempt of Congress and jailed. John Huston, William Wyler, and screenwriter Philip Dunne had launched a protest against HUAC by organizing the Committee on the First Amendment, which sent a group to Washington in September to protest the hearings in person. The Committee on the First Amendment also sponsored two radio broadcasts featuring prominent Hollywood personalities who spoke out against HUAC's attack on the movie colony.[18]

Though most of the press coverage treated these early congressional hearings as a publicity grab on the part of Washington politicians, some of the stories, especially those published in the Hearst press, painted a dire picture of the threat posed to Americans by the Communists presumed to be rampant in Hollywood. In her column published in the *Los Angeles Times* on June 16, 1950, Hedda Hopper mused, "[Lewis] Milestone was born in Chisinau, Russia.... He has a beautiful home, in which he holds leftish rallies, is married to an American wife, and has made a fortune here. But still his heart seems to yearn for Russia. Wonder if Joe [Stalin] would take him back?"[19] H. R. Wilkerson's "Trade Views" column in the *Hollywood Reporter* a few days later gave voice to similar sentiments. "Wilder, Wyler and Henried are foreigners, came to this country, were given citizenships," he wrote. "For a naturalized citizen, particularly one who has been given such an elevation in our country as have the above three, to go out and virtually bite the hand that's been feeding them so well, is something we can't take."[20]

As David Prindle observed in his history of the Actors Guild, an image-oriented industry like moviemaking was particularly vulnerable to such smears.[21] At a meeting on November 20, 1947, the producers attempted to counter the bad publicity by persuading the three major talent guilds to forward to the studios the names of any members who were presumed to be Communist. All three guilds refused.[22] Then, on November 24 and 25, studio executives met at the Waldorf Astoria Hotel in New York City and signed a pledge not to hire production personnel known to belong to the Communist Party. This pledge, subsequently known as the Waldorf Statement, officially inaugurated the blacklist. [23]

Initially, the Directors Guild stood strong, entering an official protest against the committee's action.[24] The DGA registered another protest when director Sam Wood, one of the first witnesses who testified in Washington, suggested that left-leaning Guild members had tried to take over the organization.[25] Though he had little of substance to report, Wood offered such colorful descriptions of Hollywood radicals as "If you drop their rompers, you'll find the hammer and sickle on their rear ends."[26] A statement he gave to reporters before his testimony claimed that the Directors Guild was formed for the specific purpose of fighting communism and fascism.[27] In his official testimony, he further claimed, "There is a consistent effort [by Communists] to get control of the [Directors] Guild. . . . John Cromwell . . . with the assistance of three or four others, tried to steer us into the Red River. But we had a little too much weight for that."[28] Wood named the "others" as Edward Dmytryk, Irving Pichel, and Frank Tuttle.[29]

As the hearings wore on and were featured in the media, many DGA members became more supportive of HUAC's project. At a Guild meeting held on December 1, 1947, shortly after Wood's testimony and the publication of the Waldorf Statement, some directors booed Robert Rossen for speaking out in favor of Dmytryk, one of the Hollywood Ten.[30] Around the same time, Guild officers wrote an open letter to HUAC chairman J. Parnell Thomas describing their efforts to prevent Communist infiltration into the Guild.[31] Then, at a Guild meeting on August 18, 1950, while president Joseph L. Mankiewicz was abroad, Leo McCarey proposed that all members agree to sign a loyalty oath. His idea was approved by an open show of hands. Liberal director John Huston, who was present at the meeting, later stated, "I looked on in amazement as everyone in the room except Billy Wilder and me raised their hands in an affirmative vote."[32] Following this meeting, numbered ballots were mailed to the membership to solicit their approval of the new policy.[33] Two weeks later, on September 5, the DGA board further voted to send the names of any Guild members who refused to sign the proposed loyalty oath to producers, an action that, in effect, supported the studios' blacklisting plan.

When Mankiewicz returned to Los Angeles, he vehemently objected to what the board had done and called for a special meeting of director members to discuss the matter. Enraged by Mankiewicz's recalcitrance and his putatively unsupportive statements to the press, DeMille prodded the board to pass a vote of no confidence in their president.[34] Following this vote, on Friday, October 13, Vernon Keays, who was then serving as the DGA executive secretary, dispatched messengers on motorcycles to the homes and offices of Guild members thought to be opposed to Mankiewicz to get their signatures on a motion to recall him from the presidency.[35] The numbered ballots read, "This is a ballot to recall Joe Mankiewicz. Sign here—yes."[36]

Mankiewicz supporters quickly rallied to stop the recall, gathering at the Brown Derby restaurant that same evening to prepare a petition requesting a special membership meeting so that the recall movement and the issues surrounding it could be discussed.[37] Though the group of Mankiewicz supporters tried to get the addresses and phone numbers of members from the DGA headquarters the next day, they discovered that Keays had closed the offices.[38] Nonetheless, they managed to get the requisite twenty-five signatures on a petition. On Monday, October 16, the group published an ad in the trade press that urged fellow DGA members to attend the upcoming meeting and, in the meantime, to hold fire on the recall petition. The DGA board, alarmed at the outcry it had occasioned, reversed itself at a meeting hastily convened on Wednesday, October 18, passing a unanimous vote of confidence in Mankiewicz.[39] But despite the board's backtracking, DeMille was adamant about forcing a showdown. The meeting destined to become the most talked-about event in the Guild's history was held on the following Sunday, October 22.

Those most intimately involved in the events of the Guild's famous meeting, including Frank Capra, John Ford, John Huston, William Wyler, Elia Kazan, Cecil B. DeMille, and Guild president Joseph Mankiewicz, all found themselves in compromised positions during and after the struggle. Neither Capra nor DeMille make any mention of the meeting in their autobiographies, and many latter-day biographers of these major players find the vacillating behavior of their subjects incomprehensible. But the explanation for the silences, flip-flops, and incoherencies of these Guild leaders is simple enough: everyone wanted to save the Guild. For these men, who had fought so hard to establish the DGA as an institution that could advance their aspirations as artists and who had already won so much, this goal trumped all other considerations. Political convictions, intellectual coherence, and even personal integrity were cast aside when the Guild's very existence was threatened. George Sidney's remarks at the Beverly Hills Hotel meeting summed up what everyone was feeling. "This organization has come through a couple of rough years," he stated. "And now I think we should . . . just fight to keep our group together." William Wellman sounded a similar note when he implored the group to "get a wedding between Mr. DeMille and his very dear friends for the sake of the Guild and start worrying about why the Hell we can't take away the directorial credits from the director of cinematographers." Wellman's comments were greeted with applause.[40]

Of all the leading players in the drama that unfolded at the Beverly Hills Hotel that fateful evening, none played both sides more strenuously than Frank Capra. Though some of Capra's films were then under attack in the press for their "un-American" criticism of the government, the veteran director had long worked actively to banish Communist influence from the DGA.[41] In a letter written to John Ford in January 1951, three months after the famous meeting, Capra documents his political stance. Capra wanted at that time to travel to Russia, and he needed a letter of support from Ford so that he could get security clearance. "John, it would be impossible for me to ever be dis-loyal [sic] to America," he wrote. "It would also be impossible for me to ever be anything but violently anti-Communist. I believe you also know how I hate the bastards, and how anti-Red I've been in the Guild."[42]

As a member of the DGA board, Capra had voted to recall Mankiewicz as Guild president on October 13 because of Mankiewicz's opposition to the loyalty oath. Along with other board members who supported the recall, Capra had been alarmed by an October 11 story in *Variety* that he believed had been planted by Mankiewicz. The story, which reported on the Guild's recent board meetings in detail, stated that Mankiewicz was resolved to call an open meeting to consider the issue of the oath.[43] According to Capra, the DGA board had repeatedly tried to talk Mankiewicz out of calling such a meeting. "An open membership meeting called to discuss a loyalty oath after 90 percent of the members had voted for it could only result in a split in the guild," he protested.[44] Less than a week later, however, he signed a petition supporting Mankiewicz and resigned from the board.

Capra initially agreed to serve on the interim board set up at the Beverly Hills Hotel meeting of October 22, "on the basis of 'let's forget everything and get back to the welfare of the Guild.'"[45] By October 27, however, he had changed course again and wrote a letter resigning from the interim board. He subsequently attempted to justify his about-face by emphasizing his concern for the good of the Guild. "I became a member of a committee to recall Mr. Mankiewicz as president because I was convinced that Joe was to lead a revolt in the Guild against the loyalty oath by-law," he stated. "I thought such a revolt on such an issue would be fatal to the guild and a black eye to our whole industry. . . . I myself, along with other board members, was against the passing of a [mandatory oath]. But we bowed to the will of the great majority, realizing that to make an issue of such a red-hot potato when we were in a shooting war in Korea could only bring discredit to our guild and to our industry."[46] Capra remained embittered and disheartened by the HUAC affair for many years thereafter. He did not direct another feature film until 1959.

Like Capra, John Ford flip-flopped. In his response to Capra's 1951 request for security clearance, Ford wrote a letter of recommendation that read in part, "Frank Capra and I joined hands in our Guild some sixteen years ago when the 'Commies,' 'Fellow Travelers,' . . . 'Bleeding Hearts' or whatever you want to call them, tried to infiltrate the Motion Picture Directors Guild. Together with ninety-nine percent of our Guild members, we waged a very successful fight and kept them out." Ford went on to distinguish himself from Capra, however, by casting himself as a principled voice standing against the Hollywood Red scare. "Reference is made to the fact that Frank Capra, or Colonel Capra, as I prefer to call him, objected to the Congressional investigation of Hollywood Communists," Ford wrote. "If so, I never heard him mention it: I don't believe he did. Frankly, I objected to it loudly and vociferously. I'll now go on record and say I think it was a publicity stunt."[47]

Ford's bravado in this letter of support for his director colleague, however, was not of a piece with his behavior and attitudes on other occasions. During the 1940s, Ford was active in the Motion Picture Alliance for the Preservation of American Ideals, a conservative organization that openly invited HUAC to direct its attention to Hollywood.[48] And a few days after he had called out DeMille at the Beverly Hills Hotel meeting, Ford apologized to him. He amplified his contrition in a phone call he made to DeMille a short time later. "That meeting Sunday night was a disgusting thing to see—not a wolf pack, but [a] mice pack attacking you," Ford said at that time.

> That was your greatest performance. I just wish you could have seen yourself—a magnificent figure so far above that goddam pack of rats. I have recommended men for courage in battle, but I have never seen courage such as you displayed Sunday night. God bless you, you're a great man. I have talked to many men in Hollywood in the last two days, including Joseph Mankiewicz, and all agree you will emerge from this greater than ever.[49]

Just as Capra had done, Ford changed course out of a desire to save the Guild and protect the status of its members. He had said as much at a board meeting in early October—before the Beverly Hills Hotel gathering—when he was one of four board members who opposed sending to producers a list of those who had not signed the loyalty oath. To justify his stance, he stated, "This organization [exists] to better our own standing as directors."[50] In Ford's case, the specific goal was to placate DeMille, whose continued support he understood to be crucial if the organization was to survive. DeMille had been deeply affected by the Beverly Hills Hotel meeting, calling it "one of the worst nights in my entire life."[51] In his memoir, longtime Guild executive secretary Joseph

Youngerman takes credit for convincing Ford and other DGA leaders to patch things up with the Guild's disgruntled elder statesman. "The opposition to his point of view and his failure to have Mankiewicz removed as president made him so disenchanted that he wanted no more part of the Guild," Youngerman writes. "I convinced the board to woo him back again. He finally returned for some functions, but it took a lot of coaxing."[52] Ford himself also recognized the importance of DeMille's continued participation in the Guild in a comment he made at the October 22 meeting: "If Mr. DeMille is recalled, your guild is busted up."[53]

In the long run, three DGA members who were leaders of the anti-recall meeting at the Beverly Hills Hotel—John Huston, William Wyler, and Elia Kazan—also emerged as compromised figures. In 1952, members of the American Legion picketed Huston's film *Moulin Rouge*. Shortly thereafter, Roy Brewer, president of the anticommunist Motion Picture Alliance, persuaded the director to write a "clearance letter" that apologized for past activities and affiliations deemed to be subversive. Such a missive could be sent to studio heads so that they could feel comfortable continuing to hire the author of it.[54] Huston's letter read in part, "I am convinced that my duty to America and the free world requires me to increase my knowledge of the problem [of communism] and work to undo any aid that I might have unintentionally given them in the past.... I will start by making a study of the Communist forces in the motion picture unions, particularly in France and Italy."[55]

Brewer also pressured Huston to meet with actress Marsha Hunt, who had gone to Washington, D.C., with a group representing the Committee on the First Amendment to protest HUAC's actions. She had been resisting signing a clearance letter, but she relented when Huston told her that Communists had organized the First Amendment group.[56]

Huston's next production, *Beat the Devil* (1953), was shot in Italy with an all-American crew. As was reported at the time, "Huston deliberately decided that this film would be the first American motion picture to be made in Italy with a complete free labor crew—there would be no [Italian] Communist technicians or stars in it."[57] In his autobiography *An Open Book*, Huston claimed to have taken a defiant stance in his meeting with Brewer (whom he does not name), and he makes no mention of the clearance letter he signed or of his capitulation on the matter of foreign crew members. Shortly afterwards he moved to Ireland, and in 1964 he became an Irish citizen.

Wyler, too, was ultimately caught up in right-wing pressure. Following a series of critical pieces about him in the anticommunist publication *Counterattack*, and at the urging of his agent, Paul Kohner, he, too, wrote a clearance letter.[58] To convince his reluctant client, Kohner pointed to the disastrous rollout of Chaplin's *Limelight*: most American exhibitors refused to book the film after Chaplin was denied reentry into the United States because of his communist sympathies. Kohner advised Wyler to speak to John Huston, who had just written a clearance letter, and he also suggested that Wyler work with Arthur Jacobs, a press agent who specialized in composing such documents. After Wyler met with Roy Brewer, Brewer's associate Art Arthur sent him a series of published articles written by other liberals, in which they detailed the threats communism posed to the American way of life. Wyler then drafted a tortured fourteen-page letter in which he described at great length his activities and the liberal political views that had motivated them, before confessing to a change of heart about these left-leaning views. Wyler's letter read in part:

> Through the events of the last four years it has become clear to me that which was not clear at the time of the above activities, namely: that all over the world there exists a conspiracy with a view to eventually overthrowing by any means expedient to them all noncommunist societies, a way of life [characterized by] free and democratic institutions and government as we know it.... As with religions, I used to believe in a separate, peaceful co-existence of the two ideologies. These hopes have long since been shattered, and today one form of war seems inevitable.... Communist infiltration with its accompanying dangers has been far greater than I ever suspected at the time of the above activities, [which] were based on a completely wrong estimate of the number (and therefore influence) of communists or former communists in Hollywood.... Extremists of either side are the enemies of the Liberal. I believe that Communists and extreme nationalists are both a danger to civil liberties.[59]

Jacobs cut Wyler's letter down to three pages that began by referring to "the world-wide conflict between the Free World of the Democracies and the Slave States of the Soviet System."[60]

Elia Kazan's role in the effort to reinstate Mankeiwicz was still more compromised. Though Kazan was present at the dinner at Chasen's restaurant, where the Mankiewicz supporters planned their strategy, his name did not appear on the petition the group issued to stop the recall. Moreover, after he had helped Mankiewicz write the speech the embattled president gave at the Beverly Hills Hotel meeting, Kazan abandoned his fellow director at the door of the Crystal Room. "I need you," Mankiewicz pleaded in vain. "I need every vote. My career's on the line."[61] Kazan subsequently justified his actions by claiming that he had bailed out on Mankiewicz on that fateful night because he feared being publicly embarrassed by the DeMille faction. "My way of survival was to avoid a conflict," he admitted, "and come back when the smoke had cleared."[62]

Many years later, when preparing his autobiography, Kazan traveled to New England to visit Mankiewicz and interview him about the famous DGA meeting. Mankiewicz was then nearing eighty and had not seen Kazan in many years. According to Kazan's report of this interview in his autobiography, Mankiewicz supported his decision to avoid the meeting.[63]

Notwithstanding all their wavering and backpedaling, the Mankiewicz forces were cast as the heroes in the narrative of the Beverly Hills Hotel meeting that the DGA put together afterwards, while Cecil B. DeMille was relegated to the role of the heavy. But DeMille's powerful position made him a problematic adversary. Even though he had spoken strongly against the creation of the Guild in the beginning, this venerable Hollywood figure had dominated the organization throughout the 1940s. DeMille's papers confirm his role as the DGA's godfather during this period and show that much of his agenda for the organization was directed by MGM cinematographer Harold Rosson via his sister, DeMille's longtime secretary, Gladys Rosson. Known as the Guild's kingmaker, DeMille exerted a strong influence over many of those who became major figures in the organization, including Albert Rogell and George Marshall. Vernon Keays, who was DGA executive secretary during the time of the Mankiewicz dustup, and Joseph Youngerman, who replaced Keays afterwards, both began their careers with DeMille. And because DeMille had been the one to nominate Joseph Mankiewicz as president in May 1949, he may well have assumed that Mankiewicz would support his vision for the Guild.[64]

A rabid anticommunist, DeMille had been reporting to the Federal Bureau of Investigation on Communist rallies beginning in 1937.[65] As a delegate to Republican Conventions in 1936 and 1944, he supported right-to-work laws as well as various anticommunist measures. He had repeatedly lobbied Congress to pass the Taft–Hartley Act, which demanded that all union leaders sign a loyalty oath. The bill became law in 1947. During the heated debate over the issue of a similar oath to be signed by the rank-and-file DGA membership, in 1950, DeMille brought up the DGA–RTDG merger, telling his colleagues that thirty-four New York TV directors who belonged to the Radio and Television Directors Guild wanted to secede from their union and join the DGA. According to him, this group believed that the prospect of having to sign a loyalty oath would discourage the Communist-leaning members of the RTDG from joining the merger.[66]

The position of Mankiewicz himself was perhaps the least consistent of any of the evening's major players. Some of his actions were needlessly provocative. On September 19, 1950, after he had returned from Europe and had met with the DGA board to discuss the loyalty oath, he made a widely reported speech to the B'nai B'rith Foundation, which referred to liberals as a "new minority," oppressed by "an organized enemy as evil in practice and purposes—and indistinguishable from—the communist menace," sentiments that could hardly have failed to anger DeMille.[67] On Friday, October 27, five days after his victory at the legendary Beverly Hills Hotel meeting, the newly re-legitimatized DGA president published an open letter to all Guild members in the trade press. In this letter, as in other statements he made then and later, Mankiewicz emphatically denied that he had opposed the oath itself and said he had only objected to the decision not to employ a secret ballot to decide the matter.[68] The open letter reads in part:

> Some of us have always known and all of us know now, that the late and lamentable rift within our ranks had nothing whatsoever to do with the pros or cons of a loyalty oath. As I told you the other

night, no member has ever voiced to me his opposition to one. Certainly I have never opposed one. And most certainly it has occurred to you that throughout the seven hours of our meeting, the loyalty oath was at no time a subject of discussion.

And yet there exists a wicked and widespread misconception to the contrary—both within our industry and without. A misconception that continues to vilify and smear both our person and our Guild. It is essential that you help to remove that misconception.

My signing [the Guild's own oath] was a voluntary act since the Guild considered me already in compliance and had not submitted its oath to me.[69]

I ask you to do no less. I ask you, as a voluntary act in affirmation of the confidence in your Guild you so vigorously professed last Sunday night, to set aside whatever reservations you may have concerning any aspect of the oath or its method of adoption, and sign it now. . . .

And then let's get back to our proper concern: the Director. His rights and privileges, his welfare as a craftsman.[70]

Some of Mankiewicz's statements in this communication were most likely disingenuous, for in his October 27 letter to the DGA board, Capra charged that the DGA president had declared himself "in violent opposition to a loyalty oath for all members" at several board meetings immediately preceding the climactic October 22 assembly. "Mr. Mankiewicz's letter to the membership is not to me a sincere attempt to heal the rift," Capra wrote. "It is vindication and sanctification for himself and consignment to hell for the opposition."[71] Mankiewicz's son, Tom, later confessed to Scott Eyman that DGA members had pressured his father to soften his stance against the oath, stating, "He had to make some kind of unifying statement."[72] Whatever drove Mankiewicz to characterize the problem as he did in his open letter, the letter itself amounted to a capitulation to the DeMille forces. Individual Guild members would now be vulnerable to blacklisting.[73] Mankiewiecz, for his part, gave up the Guild presidency the following spring and moved to New York City

Shortly after the Beverly Hills Hotel meeting, the DGA's interim board appointed a unity committee. The committee's report made no mention of the recall or the famous meeting. Instead, it cast Albert

Rogell as the villain who had caused disunity in the Guild.[74] But rather than censuring Rogell for his role in the recall, it condemned his activities as the producer of a Guild-sponsored radio program, citing this issue as the source of disunity in the organization. In Capra's handwritten notes on the back of this undated report (which he appears to have used to compose a letter he subsequently sent to the DGA board), he objects that "the *unity* committee is a whitewash committee."[75] Capra further complains that his letter of October 27, which described the strenuous opposition to the loyalty oath that Mankiewicz had voiced at various board meetings, was not communicated to the board. Capra also scoffs at the committee's strategy of targeting Rogell and the radio program instead of dealing with the matter of the loyalty oath and the way in which the Guild hierarchy handled it. He adds, "the issue that split the guild was the loyalty oath and Mankiewicz's attitude toward it—not Rogell making a hell of a lot of money for the guild. . . . If the unity committee and Mankiewicz can shift heavies from Mankiewicz and the loyalty oath to Rogell and money, it will be the greatest trick of the year."

In his letter, Capra also questions the way in which the unity committee was formed, implicitly suggesting that Mankiewicz appointed friends who would avoid mentioning the questionable aspects of his activities. "Mankiewicz is not St. Joseph," Capra wrote. "He is a damn good politician who will use any means he can—including kicking and eye-gouging." Capra concluded his comments with a threat: "If this committee report is read to membership, I will be forced to read my letter of resignation with this present letter to the membership. I will do anything for unity except become a complete sucker and stooge."[76] If Capra's interpretation, which was never made public, is to be believed, there was a powerful agenda at play, in which everyone rallied around the newly reaffirmed president to reshape the past in whatever way they could to allow for this reconciliation and to make peace in the Guild.

THE GENRE

The story that the DGA subsequently created about its legendary conclave at the Beverly Hills Hotel reflected not simply what the group wished to repress but also what it wanted to celebrate. The congruity of the accounts constructed later by many of those who were there reflected a vision that was not merely sanitized but also narrativized. Drawing on the familiar formulas of melodrama to shape the events they had experienced allowed Guild members to transform the uncomfortable inconsistencies of the historical record into an uplifting, easy-to-understand story. All those present at the famous meeting told the same version of the story afterwards because it conformed to the image they had of themselves. This image was rooted in their claim to be artists who defined themselves as virile Americans.

Shaping a narrative of the past is not unique to the Directors Guild. As Hayden White has argued, all histories are stories, each one built around established genre conventions.[77] Building on White's taxonomy, many historians have observed that melodrama is the genre that most often supplies the tropes that drive popular discourses about historical events.[78] Richard Maltby has suggested that histories of the HUAC hearings, in particular, have been structured as variations of this form.[79] In a further refinement of this thesis Neal Gabler has proposed that Hollywood's understanding of the HUAC years has been powerfully influenced by the melodramatic movies of Frank Capra.[80] The DGA's history of its famous meeting follows a similar pattern. In true Hollywood tradition, this widely circulated account employs well-known conventions of melodrama, featuring heightened emotions, a clear-cut conflict between good and evil and, most crucially, a happy ending.[81] It is a tale built around themes of patriotism and masculinity that fit the group's idea about the kind of artistic identity its members wanted to claim.

The Guild's narrative centers on what came to be viewed as the evening's turning point: the showdown between John Ford and Cecil B. DeMille. Virtually every account of what occurred sees the moment that Ford rose to speak as the drama's climax and casts Ford as the story's hero. "It was John Ford that was the turning point of that meeting," assistant director Joseph Newman later recalled, "and John Ford was magnificent."[82]

The position of authority from which Ford addressed the crowd that night was unquestionable. A multiple Oscar winner, he was one of the Guild's founding members and had served as its first treasurer. All reports quote his first words: "My name's John Ford. I am a director of

Westerns." Of course, of the hundreds of directors present, Ford was probably least in need of an introduction, and even those in the far corners of the Crystal Room could easily identify him by his signature baseball cap. But Ford's self-identification as a director of Westerns, which usually occupied the second half of double bills of the day, represents more than simply false modesty, for it positioned him not as a star but as part of the rank and file.

Ford's introduction also served to remind his audience of his association with values that resonated with the Guild's sense of itself: Americanism and masculinity. The veteran director's very name, John Ford, reeked of homespun Americana and offered a striking contrast to the fussy, French-sounding surname of his adversary, Cecil B. DeMille. In a discussion that was centered on the validity of a loyalty oath to the United States government, such a self-naming on Ford's part resonated.[83] His baseball cap, linking him with a sport long associated with the United States, reinforced the impression. Ford's second sentence, "I am a director of Westerns," furthered the connection between the speaker and his adopted country. This statement, too, is sometimes seen as archly self-effacing, or at best redundant. According to some accounts, the remark got a laugh from the audience.[84] But if Westerns functioned as staples of the B movie assembly line of the day, they also could claim to be the most American of genres, drawing on the unique history and landscape of the country. Ford's self-characterization as a maker of Westerns thus resonated in an atmosphere in which patriotism had been brought to the fore.

In the 1920s, Hollywood directors had embraced a brand of nativist Americanism as an integral part of their identity when the Motion Picture Directors Association, precursor to the DGA, met to discuss the incursion of foreign filmmakers on their turf. "Time was when Hollywood was swamped with foreign directors," Albert Rogell later recalled. "If you had a foreign name, you got a job in Hollywood. . . . Everybody was worried about these foreign directors coming in and taking our jobs. So the association called a meeting to talk about it. Some directors wanted to ban the foreigners from the country."[85] The anti-immigrant rhetoric continued through the 1930s.[86]

At one point during the October 22, 1950, meeting, DeMille alluded to the foreign origins of some members of the antirecall group by

Politics 103

pronouncing their names with a strong Yiddish accent.[87] But Ford was not susceptible to such slurs, and he could point to his Westerns as further proof of his Americanism. As much as DeMille tried to wrap himself in the American flag, his own productions, which often took up themes focused on the exotic and culturally distant, made him seem less American than Ford.

If the Western was the most American of genres, it also was the most masculine of genres, and another of the attributes the Guild associated with artists like themselves was machismo. As a bastion of homosociality, the DGA followed the model of most other labor unions of the era, but directors, who had positioned themselves as charismatic leaders, had a special stake in promoting their profession as one characterized by an aura of assured masculine heterosexuality, whatever attitudes and practices individual directors may have harbored in their private lives.[88] As an unquestionably tough-minded American patriot who made adventure pictures featuring rugged male heroes, Ford held the moral high ground before he ever opened his mouth. DeMille, by contrast, was best known for crafting overblown biblical epics and frothy sex comedies, and he projected a persona that seemed both pompous and—given prevailing stereotypes of the day—slightly effeminate.[89] The melodramatic story of Ford's triumph over DeMille at the Beverly Hills Hotel meeting thus served to embellish the DGA's image of itself as a haven for the kind of artists who were also manly patriots.

THE DENOUEMENT

In 1951, the year following the fracas at the Beverly Hills Hotel, the DGA gave its award for best director of the year to Joseph Mankiewicz. The following year, the Guild bestowed its first lifetime achievement award on Cecil B. DeMille.[90] In 1952 and 1955, the group also awarded honorary memberships to Louis B. Mayer and Walt Disney, two studio chiefs whose friendly testimony before HUAC helped to validate the committee's agenda. Such gestures undoubtedly helped to mend fences and shore up the DGA's position as a formidable force in the industry at a vulnerable moment in its history, even as they undermined the liberal values with which most Guild members aligned themselves. As the first Hollywood guild to require its members to sign a loyalty oath, the DGA implicitly endorsed the studios' blacklist. On October 26, 1950, four days after the DGA's famous meeting, the Independent Motion Picture Producers Association endorsed the concept of an industry-wide oath as proposed by the Screen Actors Guild. The SAG finally enacted its own oath in 1953.[91] Subsequently, in the early 1950s, Charlie Chaplin was denied membership in the DGA because he refused to sign its oath.

It was not until 1965 that the Guild's loyalty oath came under attack. At this time, the New York–based Screen Directors International Guild was in the process of merging with the DGA. Some members of the New York group took the case to court in 1966, and the U.S. Supreme Court ultimately declared the oath unconstitutional.[92] Even after so many years had elapsed, some of the DGA heavyweights lobbied the International Guild to withdraw the suit, and the DGA itself appealed the initial decision so that the oath could be retained and the deep wounds that had scarred the DGA at the Beverly Hills Hotel meeting would not be reopened.[93] As Joseph Mankiewicz wrote to Gene Searchinger, one of the plaintiffs, the court's decision "would demonstrate that [the Guild] had been making a horse's ass of itself for some sixteen years."[94]

The foregoing account of the larger context surrounding the DGA's meeting at the Beverly Hills Hotel complicates the tidy melodramatic plot that has come down to us. What actually occurred was not a melodrama. It was not even a plot, but rather a hodgepodge of data such as one invariably confronts when examining the historical record. Nonetheless, conclusions do present themselves.

Ultimately, the famous conclave is best viewed not as an ideological battle but as a fight to save the Guild—whatever the cost to the political ideals and professional integrity of some of its most prominent members. However, this was not the story the directors wanted to tell. In the story they did tell, the organization and its membership were not compromised pragmatists protecting their turf but virile Americans with a socially enlightened agenda. While Preston Sturges ended *Sullivan's Travels* with a paean to the virtues of escapist Hollywood entertainment in a world rife with suffering and injustice, members of the DGA sought a different moral, one that had more in common with Sturges's hero John L. Sullivan than with Sturges himself. They saw themselves as progressively minded male artists who made films that were "something like Capra."

CHAPTER FIVE

Law

The DGA and Artists as Owners

> All the laws about movies were drafted at the beginning of the century, when movies were considered to be nothing more than attractions at the country fair—like dancing bears. Meanwhile, the movies have developed into the most important, most powerful genuine American art form of the twentieth century—and the laws are still for dancing bears.
> —MILOŠ FORMAN

> The thing which is *indivisible*, that is, which constitutes the essence of the cinema work, is *capital itself*, whose representative, the producer, is the sole author.
> —BERNARD EDELMAN

Beginning in the 1980s, the Directors Guild of America expanded the focus of its creative rights platform to encompass not just control over the creative process itself but also control over the fate of films after they had entered the marketplace. This initiative brought the directors into conflict with a distinctive feature of American jurisprudence, the centrality of property rights, a tradition that originated in the Lockean principles on which the country was founded and has since come to include rights to intellectual property as well as real property.[1] Unlike the organization's political struggles during the House Un-American Activities Committee era, however, the Guild's encounter with the law lacked a dramatic high point that could be shaped into a compelling narrative that affirmed the group's values; instead, it proved to be a frustrating project that ate up money and resources with little result. In the realm of property rights, the charismatic authority the directors brought to the table proved no match for the legal authority of the state. Notably, the series of articles chronicling the Guild's history published in the Winter 2006–2007 *DGA Quarterly* omits any mention of the members' long and expensive quest to assert ownership rights over the films they made.[2]

The question of whether directors have a right to be considered creative authors with jurisdiction over films after their release took center stage in the 1980s when colorization, a new technological process that added color to video copies of black-and-white movies, became widespread. The novelty of seeing old films on TV in newly colorized versions soon captured the interest of the public. But after a colorized version of the 1947 holiday favorite *Miracle on 34th Street* was broadcast to an unprecedentedly large audience in 1985, Gene Siskel and Roger Ebert's popular television show *At the Movies* aired an episode entitled "Colorization: Hollywood's New Vandalism," in which the pair attacked the process in the name of directors' rights. "The colorizers are appropriating someone else's work," Ebert declared. "Not a single movie director anywhere in the world is in favor of colorization."[3] Other interested parties quickly piled on with their own critiques. Ted Turner, the most visible of the would-be colorizers, responded with his own argument, which trumped all the others. "Last time I looked," he commented, "I owned these films. I can do what I like with them."[4]

The DGA quickly seized upon the colorization controversy as a news hook to rally support for larger creative rights goals for which its members had already been fighting.[5] Directors had long objected that their pictures were routinely disfigured for various purposes after leaving the studios. Television showings of old movies typically featured versions that were repeatedly interrupted by commercials, speeded up to make them fit into predetermined time frames, and resized using panning and scanning procedures so they could be squeezed into the square shape of TV screens. In 1965, both George Stevens and Otto Preminger had unsuccessfully sued TV stations to outlaw such practices.[6] Earlier, in 1955, the DGA itself had gone on record to oppose bowdlerization of films by state censorship boards.[7] As Guild members saw it, colorization was just the latest rationale that could be used to desecrate their creations.[8]

Law 107

In a 1986 letter to Directors Guild president Gilbert Cates, American Film Institute head George Stevens Jr advised the DGA to take action on the colorization issue.[9] Stevens also sent copies of this missive to several individual directors. Fred Zinnemann was among the first to respond.[10] In his position as honorary president of the Directors Guild of Great Britain, Zinnemann was in a position to sponsor initiatives that opposed alterations of films in the United Kingdom.[11] His efforts found support on the European continent, when directors Bertrand Tavernier and Ettore Scola became active in the cause and enlisted the support of organizations such as the Federation of European Film Directors and the Société des Auteurs et Compositeurs Dramatiques. Other European filmmakers joined the fight as well, and a conclave on creative rights for directors was held in Greece in 1988.

Back in England, Zinnemann continued to work with the Directors Guild of Great Britain and various other interested groups to find ways of protecting the integrity of films after their release, but they came up against a host of objections. Should such a principle apply to quickie exploitation pictures and program fillers such as the countless poverty row Westerns? What if the director were dead? What if the director needed the money to be gained from producing an altered version of his or her movie? What if the many creative talents who had contributed to the film disagreed about the proper course to be taken? What if directors themselves had already authorized various versions of one of their films?[12] Unable to craft satisfactory solutions to these questions, Zinnemann settled on calling for the creation of a list of canonical films that could be protected from tampering. Such films were to be selected by a committee of recognized authorities.[13]

As the colorization controversy took hold in America, Frank Capra again found himself in the eye of the storm. In 1985, the Hal Roach Studios, which had been purchased by Norman and Earl Glick, proposed to colorize Capra's 1946 production *It's a Wonderful Life*. Capra initially approved of the Glicks' plans, but, influenced by Elliot Silverstein, chair of the newly formed DGA Creative Rights Committee, he had a change of heart. "My integrity is in question," he stated. "I want no part of it."[14]

The DGA soon became active in Washington, lobbying an array of (mostly Democratic) lawmakers to sponsor laws that would ratify moviemakers' creative rights over films after their release.[15] The adversary thwarting the Guild's efforts to achieve its legislative goals was the Motion Picture Association of America, the lobbying arm of the studios, long represented in Washington by the popular and influential Jack Valenti. The press generally sized up the battle as one involving principled artists (directors) struggling against crass commercialism (the studios). *Variety*'s Todd McCarthy, for example, wrote that John Huston was "angered by Ted Turner's colorizing of his great first film *The Maltese Falcon*, which the director considered 'an eternal unjustified public humiliation.'"[16]

It was a propitious moment for the DGA to raise the issue of legal authorship in Congress, for the international community was at that time putting pressure on the United States to conform its intellectual property laws to those of other countries. An updated version of the Berne treaty, which was to set new international standards governing intellectual property rights, was in the process of being drafted, and the United States became a signatory in 1988. But to bring America into compliance with the treaty's guidelines proved a difficult matter because incompatible juridical traditions had to be accommodated: the European doctrine of moral rights and the Anglo-American doctrine of copyright.

Continental Europe is governed by a civil law tradition that grants certain rights to artists.[17] First developed in France during the nineteenth century, the so-called moral rights doctrine (*droit d'auteur*) was described by one French scholar as a law designed to secure "the intimate bond that exists between a literary or artistic work and its author's personality."[18] Under this system, an artist's moral rights include "(1) the right of paternity, i.e., the right to be identified as the author of the work; (2) the right of integrity, i.e., the right to object to derogatory treatments of the work; (3) the right of divulgation or of dissemination, i.e., the right to decide when and how a work should be made public (including the right to make it public); and (4) the right to withdraw the work from commerce."[19] Following the model of the European doctrine of artists' moral rights, Article 6*bis* of the Berne treaty specifies that "Independently of the author's economic rights, and even after the transfer of the said rights, the author shall have the right to claim authorship of the work and to object to any distortion, mutilation or other modification of, or other derogatory action in relation to, the said work, which would be prejudicial to his or her honor or reputation."[20]

Unlike the European moral rights doctrine, American judicial tradition grants total legal ownership to the copyright holder, and for this reason the United States excluded article 6*bis* from its Berne agreement contract.[21] In the case of a Hollywood movie, American law further defines such a production as "a work made for hire," which includes:

> a work specially ordered or commissioned for use as a contribution to a collective work, as a part of a motion picture or other audiovisual work, as a translation, as a supplementary work, as a compilation, as an instructional text, as a test, as answer material for a test, or as an atlas, if the parties expressly agree in a written instrument signed by them that the work shall be considered a work made for hire.[22]

The work made for hire category thus explicitly excludes creative authors from all ownership rights.

The value of the European principle of artists' moral rights for Hollywood directors was dramatized in 1988, when a series of decisions by French courts cited the moral rights doctrine as a justification for refusing to allow a colorized version of *The Asphalt Jungle* to be shown on French television without the approval of the estate of its deceased director John Huston.[23] Other similar cases in Europe were supported by the DGA as well, including one over a proposed showing of a colorized version of Ford's *They Were Expendable* on Danish TV.[24] The Guild also made much of court victories in the United States vindicating the rights of Orson Welles and Warren Beatty to veto changes being proposed for *Citizen Kane* and *Reds*, respectively—even though a provision in the original contracts of both directors explicitly granted them the right to prohibit alterations, making these court cases about the fulfillment of contractual rights, not authorial rights per se.[25] But the DGA's cause suffered a major setback in 1992, when European director Marcel Carné, citing economic reasons, agreed to sanction a colorized version of his classic film *Children of Paradise*, despite the pleas of Zinnemann and others.[26]

Having hired a lobbyist in Washington, the Guild sponsored several pieces of federal legislation designed to further its creative rights agenda, beginning with the Film Integrity Act, which Congressman Richard Gephardt proposed in 1987.[27] Inspired by the European moral rights doctrine, this piece of legislation sought to grant filmmakers the right to prevent any screening of their productions if the film in question had been changed in a way that was detrimental to the director's reputation. Gephardt's proposed law found little support among his congressional colleagues, however, and Gephardt himself was brought up short when studio heavyweight Lew Wasserman called his office to complain. "Why is the smartest young man in Congress running around worrying about who is colorizing films?" Wasserman asked. "Tell him if he doesn't like colorized films to go to every television in America and take the color knob off."[28] In 1990, Congress passed an amended form of Gephardt's legislation, the Film Disclosure Act, which called for labeling films that had been altered.[29]

During the war of words surrounding the Film Disclosure Act, Valenti accused directors of using Gephardt's film-labeling bill as a stalking horse to create a legislative wedge for the law they ultimately desired: the Visual Artists Rights Act, a version of moral rights legislation Congress was considering that sought to provide painters, photographers, and sculptors with legal protection if their work was modified after completion.[30] DGA president Arthur Hiller acknowledged as much when he commented that the DGA's goal was to pass moral rights "so that film artists might achieve the same legal protection now afforded painters and sculptors." Hiller confessed, however, that such protection for Hollywood directors "might be a long time coming in the United States."[31] His prognostication proved prescient; in 1990, a version of the act that specifically excluded audiovisual works—including films—was passed into law.

To provide conceptual support for their legislative aspirations, the DGA argued that Hollywood movies should be thought of as art rather than entertainment and that those who created them were therefore to be deemed artists. Sydney Pollack, one of many A-list directors who represented the DGA at the Washington hearings on the Berne treaty, asked, "Are motion pictures art?" and responded to his own question by

Law 111

stating, "There is no question but that the [Berne] treaty regards them as such. Then who, for heaven's sake, is the artist? Clearly [they] are those people whose choices define the shape and texture, the style and tone of what the art is."[32]

The DGA rhetoric that identified Hollywood movies as art was further embellished by the use of similes that equated film to painting or sculpture. In his comments about the controversy over the colorization of old films shown on television, DGA president Gilbert Cates stated, "It's like tearing down a landmark building or painting Michelangelo's *David* blue."[33] John Huston added his voice by comparing the colorization of his film *The Maltese Falcon* to "washing flesh tones on a da Vinci drawing."[34]

Senators Ted Kennedy and Alan Simpson, who supported the DGA's efforts in Washington, adopted comparable similes when they debated the issue of artistic ownership of Hollywood films on *Face Off*, a radio show put out by the Mutual Broadcasting System. In one exchange on the program, Simpson said, "If we're going to give artists the right to disclaim and sue on their altered works, then movie directors certainly are entitled to the same right." Kennedy then decried "the crass commercialization of famous black-and-white films by colorizing them for TV. It's wrong to tamper with great works of art. . . . You might as well put a jester's hat on the Mona Lisa or paint the Statue of Liberty red, white, and blue. Other countries protect their heritage by granting protection to painters and sculptors against mutilation of their works of art."[35]

Despite all the legal barriers they encountered, the directors persevered in their fight for moral rights. Supported by a $2 million grant from John Paul Getty, which Zinnemann had brokered, the DGA spun off a separate organization, the Artists Rights Foundation, dedicated to coordinating the efforts of various Hollywood talent groups in the cause of moral rights.[36] In April of 1990, the ARF became an independent nonprofit entity that was intended to serve the interests not just of directors but of all of Hollywood's creative community. "The more the merrier," asserted Elliot Silverstein, who served as president of the new organization.[37] Getty's official statement on the occasion of the grant stressed his commitment to the ideal of the freedom of artists. "It seems that in today's world, art is being turned rapidly into a commodity," the statement reads. "Artists must be allowed full expression of their thoughts and feelings, free from interference of any kind. It is their right. It is their form of free speech."[38] In a letter to DGA members on behalf of the foundation, directors George Lucas and Steven Spielberg defined the group's aim as "fighting to maintain the quality of our films and to protect the integrity of these works of art created by you, their authors. As film artists, we understand exactly what is at stake."[39]

The Artists Rights Foundation at one time claimed a membership of over three thousand. The organization took on three major initiatives: encouraging new legislation, educating the public and members of the film industry on the issue of artists' rights, and honoring those who had made noteworthy contributions in furthering the mission of the organization. To carry out the first of these goals, the ARF supported the 1998 Sonny Bono Copyright Term Extension Act, which enabled directors and others to extend the period during which they could collect residual payments.[40] To fulfill the second goal, the ARF produced three short educational films on the subject of directors' creative rights: *Now You See It, Now You Don't*, directed by Robert Wise; *Who Did That?*, directed by Joe Dante; and a video primer for high school students on the art of directing.[41] Beginning in 1994, the foundation addressed its third goal by mounting an annual symposium featuring directors, producers, cinematographers, actors, studio executives, and government officials debating the issue of who should control the right to colorize, reedit, reformat, or otherwise materially alter a movie after its initial release. The symposium was highlighted each year by the presentation of the John Huston Award to a Hollywood personage who has furthered the cause of artists' rights. Fred Zinnemann was the first recipient.[42]

The screenwriters embraced the ARF's moral rights mission enthusiastically. In 1999, an article in the Writers Guild of America publication *Written By* stated, "We need to reclaim the plain meaning of the word *author*. We must implement the Berne Convention, which establishes our moral rights as authors to protect the artistic integrity of what we write. And we must demand our economic rights, stemming from our copyright as inalienable personal 'rights for natural human beings' for us writers, not some Godzilla-suited multimedia company masquerading as an author."[43]

Yet, though writers, actors, cinematographers, editors, and producers served on the organization's board of directors and were slated as panelists at its symposiums, the ARF was dominated by the DGA. The group was housed in the Directors Guild building on Sunset Boulevard. Elliot Silverstein, the foundation's president, had, for twenty-seven years previously, chaired the DGA's Creative Rights Committee. The chairman of the organization was DGA president Arthur Hiller and its three vice presidents, George Lucas, Steven Spielberg, and Martin Scorsese, also were directors. In addition, all but one recipient of the ARF's John Huston Award, given to recognize work on behalf of moral rights legislation, were directors.

Though the ARF's charge was to interpret the artists' rights concept so as to further the cause of moral rights for all creative filmmaking personnel, it is hard to see how such an ecumenical orientation could be sustained if the organization were to be placed in a position in which it had to adjudicate among the claims of its various constituent groups. This dilemma was articulated in a 1989 report to the Judiciary Committee of the House of Representatives from the Copyright Office, which concluded that, if the European moral rights doctrine were adopted, it would have to apply not only to directors but also to other film "authors," such as cinematographers, editors, art directors, and actors. This complication was pointed out by an article in *Variety*. "The irony is that while the directors strive for federal 'moral rights' legislation to protect the work of director-members from 'desecration' by those above them on the totem pole of power," the article stated, "the directors still maintain *their* right to deny moral rights to those who they consider to be below them, a sort of moral elitism. The right of individual negotiation, which is available to DGA members, is unilaterally denied to others in the industry by the DGA contract."[44] In response to challenges like this, Steven Spielberg asserted that "art is not a democratic process."[45]

In short, beneath the highly visible legal conflict between the filmmakers and the Hollywood business interests lay more irreconcilable inconsistencies surrounding the competing claims of the array of artisanal groups that made up the Artists Rights Foundation itself. Deciding which groups of artisans to designate as authors presented the ARF with a knotty problem, for a wide array of guidelines designating shared authorship can be found among nations that are Berne signatories. France, for example, grants moral rights to directors and screenwriters; other countries give them to composers, cinematographers, and other creative personnel. Only Japan grants such rights to anyone involved in producing a work.[46]

In its attempt to craft language that could accommodate the authorship rights claimed by the studios, Silverstein distinguished between "artistic authors" and "economic authors," following models existing in other nations, and he further sought to limit the categories of artistic authors. In a letter written in 1996 to television producer Barney Rosenzweig, the ARF chief admitted the difficulties the limitations he was proposing had created. "If a large group of collaborators are acknowledged as authors," he wrote, "they would all have the keys to the courts and the court dockets would be clogged with the petitions of offended authors." He concluded, "We feel that the group of artistic authors should be as small as possible in order not to frighten Congress."[47] Following this logic, the ARF defined artistic authors as directors, writers, and cinematographers.[48]

Fred Zinnemann, who had spearheaded the fight for moral rights legislation on two continents, argued that directors alone should be considered creative authors, with others relegated to the rank of associate authors. "The director's vision is and has been an *indispensable reality* since the days of D. W. Griffith," he once wrote. "This central personal vision is what we are being paid for and we will not be defeated or 'rolled back' as long as the spirit of men such as King Vidor, John Ford, and Frank Capra is going to prevail."[49] In a letter to Elliot Silverstein, Zinnemann went further. "The main thing is that all of us are fighting together to defend and enhance the status of the director," he wrote.[50] In his private correspondence to DGA president Arthur Hiller, Zinnemann linked the right of directors to claim sole authorship to the existence of the DGA itself. "Unless this point is forcefully maintained and if any compromises are made, it will mean the end of our guild," he stated, "and the end of film as we know it."[51]

Ultimately, the DGA's fight over moral rights in the United States evolved into a push for film preservation, following the path Zinnemann had pioneered in the United Kingdom years before. Largely as a result of pressure from Hollywood moviemakers, Congress passed the National Film Preservation Act in 1988. The law authorized the creation of a National Film Preservation Board made up of recognized authorities who were to select twenty-five titles each year to be designated as "national treasures" and archived at the Library of Congress in their original form. In a victorious mood, Billy Wilder proclaimed, "Congress has acknowledged that motion picture making is an art."[52]

However, the DGA remained dissatisfied with this solution, claiming that more films should be singled out for protection. Their objections prompted Bill Patry, an attorney for the Copyright Office of the Library of Congress, which was charged with carrying out the new law, to ask, "What has the DGA done to preserve classic films? Does it do anything other than complain about what others are doing?"[53] The Library of Congress representative charged that the DGA was not so much concerned with film preservation as such as it was with the right of its director members to be publicly recognized as the authorities who should determine what could be done with "their" movies. In 2001, the DGA finally stepped up, donating $50,000 to the National Film Preservation Board and partnering with the Alliance of Motion Picture and Television Producers and UCLA to sponsor preservation projects.[54]

In June 2002, the DGA shut down the ARF and shifted its support to the Film Foundation, an organization Martin Scorsese and others had founded in 1992 to foster film preservation.[55] Yet the larger legal issues that the organization's moral rights campaign raised remained salient, and the DGA itself continued to fight for such legal protections. In 2005, they joined forces with other groups of English-speaking directors to fight film piracy. Their statement read, "Piracy affects both the director's economic rights (right to be remunerated) and their creative rights (rights of integrity)."[56] Over the years, the DGA has also raised repeated protests about the legal rights of companies like CleanFlicks and VidAngel to bowdlerize films released on video for family viewing. In 2002, the Guild's executive director, Jay Roth, commented, "This is not about an artist getting upset because someone dares to tamper with their masterpiece. This is fundamentally about artistic and creative rights and whether someone has the right to take an artist's work, change it and then sell it."[57]

In the end, the DGA had little to show for its decades-long efforts to extend its creative rights agenda into the legal arena. In its struggle to attain ownership rights to films its members had directed, the Guild came up against what is perhaps the most intractable obstacle it had ever encountered in its mission to secure a place for Hollywood directors as artists in the venerable tradition of the high arts: United States law. As the bedrock of a state's sovereign power, law supersedes all other forms of authority. American jurisprudence is founded on the country's commitment to a system of free enterprise that grants property rights to those who risk capital. The question the Guild posed when it tried to claim moral rights for its members thus remains unresolved: Can Hollywood movies ever hope to have an unambiguous status as art as long as they are embedded in a legal system that elevates the rights of property owners over those of creative authors?

Conclusion

This study of the Directors Guild of America has examined the way in which a powerful institution and some of the men who served as its leaders have worked on many fronts to position directors as the singular artists who create Hollywood cinema. To be sure, the Guild did not achieve this goal unaided; trends within the industry and in the culture at large supported its efforts. It is impossible to guess what the status of directors would be today were it not for the success of the DGA's "one man, one film" creative rights mission, but the Guild's agenda has undeniably been a key factor in enabling directors to attain the preeminent position they now occupy both within the film industry and in the eyes of the public. Thanks largely to the DGA's efforts, directors now enjoy unprecedented control over the filmmaking process, and their names dominate movie credits. These accomplishments involve complications: the image of directors as charismatic leaders, which the Guild has fostered, has led to friction with some of the directors' most important creative partners, especially writers, and it has worked against women who might wish to enter the profession

As history moves forward, the DGA's creative rights mission has met with increasingly problematic roadblocks. Even before the organization was founded, the legal system that anchors American capitalism stood in the way of directors' ambitions to endow themselves with ownership rights over their work. The technological advances that have emerged since that time have posed another set of tests of the Guild's creative rights objectives by opening up new questions about works of art as the unique products of single individuals.

Television, with a small-screen aesthetic that has favored groups of writers over lone directors, was just the beginning. The home movie market enabled by the introduction of videotapes in the late 1970s encouraged the phenomenon of the director's cut, which morphed into a practice that allowed multiple versions of a particular film to be labeled in this way so that the director's "original" intention was sometimes difficult to untangle. In the digital era, concepts like flow and convergence describe a media landscape in which a wide array of platforms, from home theaters to cell phones, support endless permutations of any given content, calling into question art's traditional aura of authenticity and inimitability. At the same time, the internet has undermined older conceptions of artists as singular individuals by inviting audiences to become content creators. The altered cultural sphere represented by such developments presents ambiguities that go to the heart of Capra's "one man, one film" principle, since they signal a shift in popular ideas about artists as originary geniuses and works of art as stable entities. Given this reality, the challenges that lie ahead for the DGA's creative rights mission appear daunting.

And yet... *Hollywood's Artists* has traced a history that has seen the Directors Guild of America play a major role in elevating Hollywood cinema into a recognized art form in which directors are honored as the artists who create it. The result was not foreordained, and the achievement is not insignificant.

APPENDIX A

Beyond Creative Rights

Throughout its history, the Directors Guild of America's creative rights program has remained central to its mission. But this quest has been pursued in concert with more traditional union projects.[1] Though other talent groups have taken the initiative in union-related matters, directors have consistently supported their efforts. Prominent among the Guild's concerns in this realm are policies dealing with finances, diversity, safety, and globalization. The Guild is unique among the Hollywood talent unions in its willingness to invest in research that could provide hard numbers for it to take into negotiations over such union-oriented topics. Over the years, the organization has carried out costly investigations into such salient issues as the employment of minorities in the industry, the costs incurred by runaway productions (films made outside of Hollywood), and anticipated revenues from new media.[2] In contrast to writers and actors, directors have customarily launched their negotiations with the studios well before their existing contracts expire, creating a less pressured, more deliberative atmosphere.

FINANCES

Like other unions both inside and outside of Hollywood, the Directors Guild establishes compensation policies for its members.[3] Along with the other talent groups, it collects residuals on behalf of its members and monitors producers' compliance.[4] Its only strike was called in 1987, over this issue.[5] In the complex financial arena in which modern global entertainment industries operate, collecting residuals constitutes a major benefit for Guild members. In addition, residual payments create an ownership stake for directors in the productions in which they participate (as they also do for writers and actors). Directors thus become something more than simply paid employees; they share the profits. The process of establishing and dispersing residual payments, together with the maintenance of health and pension funds, puts the Guild in a position that in many other fields lies in the domain of management.[6]

As a general rule, the movie industry's unionized labor force is generously compensated, giving rise to periodic rumblings by studio management about out-of-control labor costs. In view of Hollywood's notoriously impenetrable bookkeeping methods, it is difficult to draw reliable conclusions about the industry's business practices, but some observations about the fiscal context in which the DGA functions may help to clarify its role in the culture of mainstream cinema production. First, despite some hard times and bankruptcies, moviemaking has been a lucrative enterprise over the years for the big Hollywood studios, which increasingly dominate the global entertainment marketplace. Undeniably, making movies is a high-risk undertaking. However, in today's film business the risk is customarily spread among numerous entities, including studio partners, foreign distributors, and holders of video, new media, and tie-in rights. Moreover, franchises and sequels act as dependable tent poles.

Despite the publicity given to high-grossing blockbusters and the rich paydays enjoyed by executives and above-the-line talent, the money distributed to outside investors in the film industry tends to lag behind that of most other businesses, and returns on investments are notably unreliable.[7] The industry has been characterized by economist Richard Caves as "a crapshoot with weak controls on extravagance and none on quality."[8] Entertainment analyst Todd Juenger concurs, commenting, "In general, making movies is a crummy business with terrible structural dynamics."[9] Yet, possibly because of their glamour and their potential as synergistic partners for online enterprises and manufacturers of electronic hardware, movie companies remain attractive as stocks and as corporate takeover targets.

Moreover, though some of Hollywood's labor costs might be reckoned high, nonunionized entry-level employees, such as script readers and production assistants, are paid poorly. Some other workers, though unionized, nonetheless earn little income overall because their employment is spotty. The highest salaries go to studio top brass, a tradition that has distinguished the industry from the beginning. In 1937, Leo Rosten found that executive pay as a percentage of net profits in Hollywood was the second highest of any industry, and the situation has only become more pronounced over time.[10] Movie moguls are also customarily rewarded with lucrative stock options, luxury cars, private jets, and plush travel expense accounts. Such stratospheric remuneration can be linked to Hollywood's self-imposed project of modeling glamorous lifestyles.

Given this economic environment, it is not surprising that Hollywood's unionized labor force can bargain for generous compensation packages. Directors, in particular, have felt entitled to demand high minimum wages because they want to enjoy a status comparable to the stars they must supervise. As former DGA president Gilbert Cates once explained, directors need to negotiate for perks like first-class transportation because "if the star of a movie flies first class and the director flies economy, what does that mean for the relationship between the star and the director? How much respect will the star have for the director?"[11]

A further rationale for the high compensation directors receive is that the work they do is both emotionally stressful and physically demanding, characterized by long hours; frequent travel; split-second, high-stakes decision making; and challenging personnel management responsibilities. Though film directing is routinely held up as a dream job, in actuality, few people are either willing or able to carry out the duties directors take on. If film directing is taxing, television—especially when broadcast live—is even more so. "You had to have the guts of a blind burglar and the coordination of an athlete," Arthur Penn once commented, recalling his days directing live TV. "Quite a few guys got sick from it."[12]

The avalanche of technological innovations that hit the media industry as a result of the digital revolution that got under way during the 1970s has opened up myriad new challenges for the DGA. The implications of this technological revolution for the Guild's creative rights mission are addressed in chapters 1 and 2. But financial concerns are also at play. The studios have balked at sharing the significant profits accruing from the burgeoning market in DVDs and online streaming, repeatedly refusing to increase residual payments to the unions from these new revenue sources.[13] In 2000, the DGA became the first Hollywood guild to negotiate an agreement for web-based productions.[14]

Still, problems have persisted. By 2008, frustration on the part of Hollywood's three major talent groups sparked a protracted Writers Guild strike. After stalling their negotiations for several months out of sympathy for the writers' stand, the DGA ultimately entered into negotiations with the Alliance of Motion Picture and Television Producers while the writers' strike was still going on, emerging with a less favorable deal than the one the writers were demanding. "This was the toughest decision," DGA president Michael Apted later recalled. "We had a responsibility to negotiate for our own members ... We waited and waited, but [the writers] were stalled. We were prepared and had done the research."[15] Still, the DGA pact represented an improvement on past agreements, and the writers and actors unions quickly lined up behind it. The writers, nonetheless, remained disheartened by a strike that had proved costly for many of them yet resulted in what many considered to be minimal gains. As screenwriter Ross McCall put it, "We didn't so much get a foot in the door as we got a toe."[16]

DIVERSITY

Following the pattern of many other unions, the DGA began to admit people of color at the junior level. Its first Chicano member, Francisco "Chico" Day, was admitted as an assistant director in 1937; Wendell Franklin, also an assistant director, became the group's first African American member, in 1960. Until the success of the blaxploitation cycle during the 1970s prompted the Hollywood studios to turn to African American filmmakers, black directors such as Oscar Micheaux and Spencer Williams were relegated to the marginal production and distribution networks of race movies, where senior-level membership in the DGA was not a possibility.[17]

But the difficulties the Guild has wrestled with in the area of diversity also grow out of the kind of work directors do. First of all, in a business where personal relationships carry enormous weight, cronyism must necessarily be deeply entrenched. Moreover, in their role as executives who oversee large cadres of workers, directors have been habituated to dealing with people of color who occupy the lowest echelons of the labor force. In addition, movie directors have historically participated in the creation and dissemination of ethnic stereotypes such as mammies, Uncle Toms, and greasers.[18]

Rising above this compromised history, the DGA set a progressive agenda to address the issue of equity.[19] In the late 1970s, the organization instituted mentoring and networking programs for women and people of color, seminars addressing discrimination, and tributes to pioneers in the industry who came from disadvantaged groups.[20] The first Ethnic Minority Committee, composed solely of black directors, was formed in 1979; by 1994, the group had changed its name to the African American Steering Committee.[21] A Latino Committee was organized in 1990, and an Asian American Committee came into being soon afterwards.[22] By the turn of the twenty-first century, the Guild was routinely sponsoring mentoring programs and mixers in which directors of color could network with studio executives.[23]

The DGA also began collecting and publicizing data on the employment of women and directors of color, publishing statistics in its magazine and later on its website. As early as 1985, the Guild reported on hiring discrimination, finding that fewer directors from these groups had been employed in the industry in that year than had found work the year before and that various studios and networks had hired such personnel disproportionately in low-level positions in order to beef up their statistics.[24] The Guild also mounted legal battles against discrimination at the studios. By the turn of the century, however, these initiatives had produced little in the way of results; the number of Guild members employed as directors who came from disadvantaged groups continued to be negligible. Moreover, though the DGA made a deal with ABC television in 2004 to ensure that at least 20 percent of series episodes aired on the network would be directed by members of such groups, the agreement quickly fell apart when the network chose to simply ignore it.[25]

Though, since 1984, the DGA has awarded prizes to directors of commercials and TV shows who are people of color, and presented a special award to Oscar Micheaux at its fiftieth anniversary celebration in 1986, it was not until 2000 that the organization fully embraced diversity by awarding a Best Feature Film Director accolade to an Asian American member (Ang Lee, for *Crouching Tiger, Hidden Dragon*).[26] In 2013, Alfonso Cuarón, the director of *Gravity*, was the first Latino to win the top prize, and in the same year, the openly gay African American TV director Paris Barclay became the Guild's first president who was a person of color.

Unlike minorities, gay directors in the American movie industry are impossible to track with any degree of accuracy. At an informal level, Hollywood has always been notably open to gay lifestyles, a tradition evident not only in the number of gays employed in the industry but also in the broad participation in social networks centered around such popular gay Hollywood directors as Alla Nazimova, Edmund Goulding, and George Cukor.[27] From the beginning, many mainstream films have featured thinly veiled gay characters played by actors such as Franklin Pangborn, following a tradition made popular by the "nance" figures that had long been a staple of burlesque and vaudeville. Even socially conservative filmmakers like John Ford helmed productions such as *Three Bad Men* and *The Purple Eagle* (both released in 1927) that featured gay characters and subplots.[28] But while the Hollywood community had always accepted gay culture at this informal level, it suppressed any evidence of such unorthodox lifestyles in more official contexts. As Cukor was later to put it, "If you were not heterosexual, you were discreet."[29] Thus, gay directors have belonged to the DGA from its inception but, until after the turn of the twenty-first century, they never played prominent roles in the group's activities and leadership structure.

SAFETY

On the set, especially on shoots in far-flung locations, directors are charged with the well-being of others. For many years, the DGA took an interest in safety only insofar as it affected directors themselves, and the directors strongly opposed the right of the Screen Actors Guild to take initiative in this area—even though SAG members were those most at risk.[30] In the 1980s, however, the responsibilities of directors as supervisors of people who might be working under dangerous conditions became a controversial issue. A widely publicized accident that killed three actors during the filming of *The Twilight Zone* in 1982 resulted in the film's director, John Landis, and several crew members being charged with manslaughter. Following this disaster, SAG questioned the ability of directors to provide performers and others with a safe environment in which to work.[31] In response, the DGA sponsored a number of workshops on safety.[32] Not all were satisfied with the DGA's response. "We wondered sometimes what the hell was this whole thing about," Richard Brooks later mused, "Was it a cover-up? Did anybody intend to do anything about it?"[33] Brooks's critique gained credibility in 2015, when assistant camera operator Sarah Hones was killed in a train accident that occurred during filming of a biopic about pop music star Gregg Allmann, and the film's director Randall Miller served a year in prison for involuntary manslaughter.[34]

It was not just dangerous conditions but also long working hours that put actors and crew members at risk. In a dramatic incident in 1997, assistant cameraman Brent Hershman suffered a fatal accident after working for nineteen hours straight on *Pleasantville*.[35] Earlier, in the 1980s, the DGA had attempted to forestall similar tragedies by negotiating provisions by which producers were directed to hire a second assistant director to stagger the work day, and in 2002 the Guild's Basic Agreement empowered first assistant directors to call a meeting of the production staff when crew members worked more than sixteen hours at a stretch.[36]

GLOBALIZATION

Following World War II, the industry's search for cheap labor and exotic locations meant that more and more movies were being filmed outside of Hollywood. Many European countries fostered the trend by granting subsidies for films made within their borders. Though these incentives were designed to encourage homegrown filmmaking, they could be accessed by Hollywood studios, which were quick to set up "local" production companies, often taking advantage not just of the subsidies on offer but also of the cheap nonunionized labor available in many foreign locales.[37]

The directors' response to these so-called runaway productions has evolved over the years. In the early days of the industry, William Desmond Taylor, president of the Motion Picture Directors Association, protested, "Members of the Association would deplore exceedingly a situation wherein domestic producers would find it economically profitable to make pictures in Europe at lessened production costs and bring them to the United States for cutting, editing, and distribution, ostensibly as American products."[38] Later, however, directors were inclined to view such productions in a more positive light. A 1947 report to DGA members advised directors to shoot more Hollywood pictures abroad, which could embed the distinctive settings and personnel available in foreign countries into American-made pictures and create international goodwill toward the United States in the process. The report cited the example of Henry King, the so-called flying director, who piloted his own plane to scout locations around the world. King claimed that he was encouraging local populations to adopt a favorable attitude toward the United States by featuring images of their homelands in his Hollywood productions.

> We not only get backgrounds that are different," King stated, "but with such a picture as [his recent film] *Captain from Castile*, where we had to duplicate Spanish and Mexican environments and went to Mexico for that purpose, we achieved a more authentic quality. Because we put forth an effort to attain this finer reality, we gain an appreciation from the people whose lands we visit, and this promotes the spirit of good will.[39]

As productions filmed overseas continued to comprise an ever-larger portion of the studios' revenue streams, however, the DGA's stance changed. Movie location shoots around Los Angeles fell 64 percent from 1996 to 2010.[40] In response, the Guild sought to shore up the income streams of its membership through protectionist legislation, forming a political action committee to lobby Congress to pass bills supporting tax breaks for movies shot in the United States.[41] In 1999, the DGA and SAG released the Monitor report, which documented the impact of runaway productions on the American economy and American workers. By 2004, a DGA-sponsored political action committee, in concert with an interguild organization called the Runaway Production Alliance, had persuaded Washington lawmakers to pass legislation granting tax breaks to homegrown pictures.[42] The Guild also mounted an ongoing effort to encourage individual states to impose their own tax incentives.

At the same time the Guild has also recognized the reality of modern internationalized moviemaking practices, and it has sought to shore up the rights and privileges of directors everywhere by forming alliances with sister organizations around the world. As early as 1967, the DGA sponsored a roundtable in London with its British colleagues; topics discussed included residuals, assistant director exchanges, and the editing of films shown on television.[43] In 1971, the Guild launched an exchange program. The first activity involved sending Robert Wise, Robert Aldrich, and Ralph Nelson to meet colleagues and tour production facilities in the Soviet Union; a similar trek to China and Japan took place in 1984.[44] A 1991 conclave at the Guild's Los Angeles headquarters led to a pact between the DGA and directors' organizations in Canada and Great Britain to resist the trend toward runaway productions.[45] At the 1993 Venice Film Festival, a group of European and American marquee-name directors announced the birth of the International Filmmakers Union, a group dedicated to promoting cooperation among directors across national borders.[46] By 2003, the DGA had elected Michael Apted, who was British, as its new president. In the same year, the Guild joined with colleagues in Australia, Canada, Ireland, New Zealand, and the United Kingdom to form the International Association of English Speaking Directors Organizations, which issued a code of best practices that addressed the central role of directors in film and television.[47]

The DGA's efforts to enlist international cooperation have at times been hampered by the different institutional contexts in which directors work. Outside the United States, more often than not, governments, not studio honchos, pull the strings, dispensing funds and defining the regulatory environment in which moviemaking takes place. In addition, foreign directors often resent Hollywood's dominance over the global film marketplace, where non-American films are often pushed out of theaters to make room for the latest Hollywood blockbusters; they also bridle at U.S. policies like subtitling (as opposed to dubbing), which many believe marginalize foreign films on American screens.[48]

By 2018, the DGA had more than 15,000 members, 140 staffers, and over $2 billion in pension and health plan assets. Its membership included directors of movies, television, radio, and commercials, as well as unit managers, who were admitted in 1964. Though it has attained a position of unparalleled strength and complexity, the organization faces evolving conditions that will challenge its commitment not only to its creative rights agenda but also to its identity as a union. And it must meet these challenges in an environment increasingly inhospitable to workers: by 2018, union membership in the United States had dropped to 11 percent of the population, a seventy-year low, and the United States had become distinguished among industrialized countries as a union-unfriendly nation.[49]

APPENDIX B

Chronology of the Directors Guild of America

1890	Printers strike establishes tradition of open shop in Los Angeles.
1910	*Los Angeles Times* building bombed, allegedly by labor activists.
1912	Authors League of America formed, including screenwriters.
1914	Photoplay Authors League formed.
1915	Motion Picture Directors Association formed.
1916	American Federation of Labor begins efforts to unionize Hollywood labor.
1917	Motion Picture Directors Association sets up New York branch. Motion Picture Producers Association is formed. Open shop policy established in Hollywood.
1918	Studio technicians organize as a local of the International Alliance of Theatrical Stage Employees (IATSE).

1918–1921	Hollywood craftspeople call a series of strikes against the studios.
1919	Photoplay Authors League collapses.
1920	Screenwriters Guild formed. Actors Equity gains jurisdiction over all screen players.
1924	Alliance of Motion Picture Producers—later the Alliance of Motion Picture and Television Producers (AMPTP)—formed.
1926	Motion Picture Directors Association collapses. Studios sign agreement with IATSE, which includes most studio craft workers.
May 1927	Academy of Motion Picture Arts and Sciences (AMPAS) formed.
January 1931	King Vidor, Cecil B. DeMille, Frank Borzage, and Lewis Milestone sign the Directors Declaration of Independence and plan to produce independent films, but the plan is never carried out.
January 1933	Paramount and RKO go into receivership.
March 5–9, 1933	Bank holiday declared by President Roosevelt. Studios institute eight-week 25 to 50 percent across-the-board pay cuts. IATSE refuses to accept cuts and calls workers out on strike.
April 1933	Screen Writers Guild (SWG) reactivated; most writers resign from AMPAS.
June 1933	Screen Actors Guild (SAG) formed.
June 16, 1933	Roosevelt signs National Industrial Recovery Act into law, to be administered by the National Recovery Administration (NRA).

October 1933	NRA Motion Picture Code released, providing that no salary can exceed $100,000 per year.
	Most actors resign from AMPAS.
	SAG consolidated.
October 8, 1933	SAG and SWG send telegrams to President Roosevelt denouncing NRA Motion Picture Code of Acceptable Practices. Roosevelt subsequently agrees to amend the code with input from writers and actors.
1935	AMPAS releases report stating policies on writers' credits, giving ultimate authority to studios but limiting credit to two writers on each film (amended to three in 1936).
May 1935	The U. S. Supreme Court declares the NRA Codes unconstitutional.
July 5, 1935	President Roosevelt signs the National Labor Relations Act (Wagner Act) requiring employers to bargain with recognized unions; parts of the NRA Code are included.
November 1935	Paramount threatens to assign directors to films without consultation.
December 23, 1935	Screen Directors Guild (SDG) holds first meeting at the home of King Vidor; twelve directors attend.
1936	SAG joins the American Federation of Labor.
	SDG sets up office in Crossroads of the World complex at Sunset and Las Palmas in Hollywood.
January 2, 1936	IATSE negotiates closed shop agreement with major studios.
January 8, 1936	Directors hold second clandestine meeting.

January 13, 1936	SDG incorporates.
January 16, 1936	SDG holds first official meeting at the Hollywood Athletic Club to adopt bylaws, elect a board of directors, and install King Vidor as president; forty attend.
January 22, 1936	SDG organizational meeting; 125 attend.
January 23, 1936	SDG severs all ties to other guilds, fires attorney Laurence Beilenson, who also represents SWG and SAG.
May 9, 1936	Screenwriters form Screen Playwrights; most resign from SWG.
April 1937	The U.S. Supreme Court upholds Wagner Act. SDG adds assistant directors and unit managers, swelling its numbers from 90 to 550.
April 12, 1937	National Labor Relations Board (NLRB) rules that movie industry is engaged in interstate commerce and thus comes under federal jurisdiction.
April 19, 1937	Producers sign deal with Screen Playwrights granting directors the right to story credit; SWG reactivates.
May 15, 1937	SAG reaches agreement with producers, focused on wages and working conditions; includes 100 percent guild shop.
May 19, 1937	Assistant directors and unit managers admitted to SDG as junior members.
September 10, 1937	IATSE claims jurisdiction over all Hollywood workers, including directors, swelling membership from 90 to 550.
October 1937	SDG, SWG, and SAG form Inter-Talent Council to resist domination by IATSE.

October 4–23, 1937	NLRB holds hearing in Los Angeles to decide whether screenwriters can be unionized.
1938?	Assistant director Francisco "Chico" Day becomes first Latino member of SDG. The U.S. House of Representatives establishes House Un-American Activities Committee (HUAC), with Texas Democrat Martin Dies as chair. Dies begins investigating a few Hollywood figures but soon drops the investigation.
	SDG represents 95 percent of all directors and assistant directors in Hollywood; Dorothy Arzner becomes first female member of the organization.
	AMPAS officially withdraws itself from all labor negotiations.
	SAG recognized by studios.
January 1938	Studios hold conference on unemployment with delegates from twelve unions and guilds, including SDG.
March 1938	NLRB recommends that producers' contract with Screen Playwrights be invalidated.
May 1938	Additional NLRB hearing held on screenwriters.
June 1938	IATSE progressives host studio unemployment conference with delegates from twelve Hollywood unions and guilds, including SDG.
June 4, 1938	NLRB rules that directors are employees and can be unionized.
June 7, 1938	NLRB rules that screenwriters are employees and can be unionized.
August 6–7, 1938	SDG publishes attack on associate producers.
August 8, 1938	SWG recognized by National Labor Relations Board.

August 29, 1938	SDG begins hearings before the NLRB.
October 13, 1938	SDG–NLRB hearings close.
February 17, 1939	SDG reaches agreement with producers establishing 80 percent guild shop (signed retroactively in 1940). Assistant directors win minimum salaries and working conditions. Directors win preparation time; consultation on cutting, casting, and crew; last credit card; right to assign credits; and arbitration system. Unit managers form separate guild. Chicano director Gabriel Soria becomes second minority member of the Guild.
1940	SWG attempts to limit possessory credit use.
1941	SWG recognized by studios.
1942	Radio Directors Guild begins in New York City
May 1942	SWG signs pact with producers.
1943	SDG organizes the Hollywood Victory Canteen, a touring show to raise money for the war effort. The Guild invites film editors to join, but editors decline.
1944	SDG signs pact with producers on minimum salaries for directors (for 1942).
1945	Feud between IATSE and Conference of Studio Unions leads to two protracted, violent strikes and draws national attention to alleged Communist infiltration of Hollywood unions. SDG establishes Educational and Benevolent Foundation (name later changed to DGA Foundation) and opens office in Chicago.
September 1946	Studio lockout of returning craft strikers leads to more violence and, ultimately, the dissolution of the Conference of Studio Unions.

1947	Directors Guild of America (DGA) membership at 281 directors.
	The Taft–Hartley Act passes, requiring all union officers to swear loyalty oath to United States.
	Radio Directors Guild, later to be called the Radio and Television Directors Guild (RTDG), is formed in New York City; the new group subsequently affiliates with the American Federation of Labor.
	WGA begins program of awards for outstanding screenwriting achievements.
September 1947	House Un-American Activities Committee subpoenas forty-five from film industry; HUAC denounced by unfriendly nineteen, including five directors: Herbert Biberman, Robert Rossen, Edward Dmytryk, Irving Pichel, and Lewis Milestone.
October 1947	SDG lodges protest against HUAC.
October 20, 1947	HUAC hearings begin. Sam Wood denounces five fellow directors.
December 1947	Film executives meet at Waldorf-Astoria in New York and agree not to hire "Hollywood Ten"—including directors Herbert Biberman and Edward Dmytryk—cited by HUAC for contempt of Congress.
1948	SDG initiates Directors Award for features; Joseph L. Mankiewicz first winner.
	Radio Directors Guild adds TV, becoming Radio and Television Directors Guild, gets contract with CBS-TV covering New York City staff directors; similar contracts with ABC and NBC follow.
July 1948	SDG signs pact with producers guaranteeing 100 percent guild shop, credit size, limits on those who can use the term "director."

1950	SDG reaches agreement on first television film contract, including policies on residuals. Ida Lupino becomes second female member.
	Screen Producers Guild founded. Three staffers to serve nine hundred members, which include assistant directors as well as directors.
March 19, 1950	SDG announces its intention to represent all television directors.
April 6, 1950	SDG changes its name to SDGA.
May 31, 1950	Joseph Mankiewicz elected SDGA president.
June 1950	Vernon Keays replaces William Holman as SDGA executive secretary.
July 30, 1950	Los Angeles TV station signs contract with SDGA.
August 17, 1950	Mankiewicz sets sail from Europe to America.
August 18, 1950	SDGA board votes to require membership to sign loyalty oath and sends out numbered ballots to members.
August 24, 1950	Mankiewicz arrives in New York and makes statements to the press questioning the manner in which the SDGA board handled the loyalty oath issue.
September 5, 1950	Mankiewicz meets with the SDGA board.
September 14, 1950	Mankiewicz makes speech defending liberalism.
September 18, 1950	RTDG files complaint against SDGA accusing the rival group of unfair labor practices and of being dominated by Communists.
September 19, 1950	SDGA files counter complaint with the NLRB against the RTDG, stating that the rival union is Communist dominated.

October 9, 1950	SDGA board votes to publish names of members who fail to sign loyalty oath, over objections of its president, Mankiewicz, who labels this policy a blacklist.
October 13, 1950	Cecil B. DeMille institutes movement to recall Mankiewicz, supported by a majority on the SDGA board.
October 15, 1950	Mankiewicz re-signs SDGA loyalty oath he had previously signed when elected as president.
October 16, 1950	Twenty-five SDGA members file petition for special membership meeting to discuss Mankiewicz recall.
October 18, 1950	SDGA board passes vote of confidence in Mankiewicz.
October 19, 1950	Frank Capra resigns from the SDGA board.
October 22, 1950	Seven-hour SDGA special meeting attended by more than five hundred members forces board of directors to resign.
October 27, 1950	Mankiewicz publishes statement asking DGA members to support loyalty oath, making the DGA the first Hollywood guild to adopt this policy. Capra resigns from interim board.
November 1950	Board of directors reorganized; Vernon Keays forced to resign as SDGA executive secretary because of collusion with DeMille on loyalty oath issue.
November 25, 1950	SDGA Unity Committee report released.
December 1950	NLRB dismisses complaint of RTDG against SDGA, citing lack of evidence.

Appendix B

1951	SDGA assets total $67,000; only 37 percent of its members are working. Joseph Youngerman becomes executive secretary and pursues program emphasizing screen credits, television negotiations, pension plan, real estate acquisitions, and social events.
March 1951	Second round of HUAC hearings. DGA member Elia Kazan takes out advertisements in various trade and consumer publications defending his decision to inform on others.
1952	Assistant directors granted screen credit by majors. Charlie Chaplin applies to become a member of the SDGA but refuses to sign loyalty oath, thereby becoming the only person ever to be denied membership in the Guild for this reason. SDGA membership at 717, more than 10 percent of whom work in TV.
1953	SDGA initiates Directors Award for television and Critics' Award, establishes annual university scholarship. D. W. Griffith Award for Lifetime Achievement initiated; Cecil B. DeMille becomes the first recipient. Guild purchases property at Sunset and Hayworth for planned new building.
1954	SWG joins Radio Writers Guild of America to form Writers Guild of America. SDGA membership reaches 750, nearly 80 percent of whom are working; assets reach $238,000.
June 1955	First SDGA building opens at 7950 Sunset.
October 1955	SDG produces TV series *Screen Directors Playhouse* on NBC

1957	Longtime SDG counsel Mabel Walker Willebrandt steps down from her position.
1959	Television accounts for 70 percent of jobs held by SDGA members.
1960	DGA signs pact with producers with specifics on TV residuals; establishes pension plan, the first in the industry, with $780,000 from producers given in lieu of pre-1960s residual payments. Initiation fee set at $1,200.
January 1, 1960	SDGA, with 1,212 members, merges with 856-member Radio and Television Directors Guild after RTDG disengages from American Federation of Labor; in the process, SDGA acquires its first black member, Wendell Franklin.
	SDGA changes its name to Directors Guild of America.
1961	DGA wins right to deal memos, binding producers to follow through on oral promises of employment made to directors prior to signing official contracts; also wins rights to residuals for movies shown on free TV.
1962	DGA establishes industry experience roster.
1963	New York assistant directors break with the International Association of Theatrical and Stage Employees (IATSE) and join DGA.
	DGA president George Sidney complains to the Federal Communications Commission about films altered for TV.
	Creative Rights Committee formed, chaired by Elliot Silverstein.
1964	Unit managers rejoin DGA.
	DGA forms first Creative Rights Committee with Elliot Silverstein as chair.

	The DGA wins the right to make director's cuts on films, right to last credit appearing prior to principal photography, and right to credit on all paid advertising; signs first pay TV contract; establishes Los Angeles–based training program for assistant directors and unit production managers; establishes minimum weekly salary for directors of features at $744. Unit production managers merge with DGA.
1965	Screen Directors International Guild merges with DGA.
	Directors' Bill of Rights is drafted, designating preparation time, participation in the selection of all production elements, control of rehearsals and shooting, and supervision of editing and scoring.
1966	DGA loyalty oath declared unconstitutional by the Supreme Court. Screen Producers Guild merges with Television Producers Guild.
	DGA establishes a publications committee and initiates *Action*, a bimonthly magazine, along with an annual directory of members; pension plan assets exceed $10 million.
December 13, 1966	WGA signs pact with AMPTP denying directors the right to possessory credits.
1967	DGA buys building at 110 West Fifty-Seventh Street and establishes permanent New York office.
	Delbert Mann becomes first television director to be elected DGA president. Membership reaches 3,300.
January 4, 1967	DGA sends protest to AMPTP over WGA agreement on possessory credits.
1968	DGA signs pact with producers granting them the right to be consulted on special effects, to supervise postrecorded sound, and to attend preview screenings; the pact also denies choreographers and casting coaches the right to use the title "director" on credits.

DGA threatens to strike over writers' request for possessory credits.

The Guild establishes east coast-based assistant directors training program.

Residual payment for TV shows aired abroad is established.

1969 DGA establishes health plan for members; initiates policy of granting "Allen Smithee" pseudonym to directors of troubled productions.

1971 DGA establishes cultural exchange program with the Soviet Union's Association of Film Makers.

1972 DGA wins jurisdiction over U.S.-financed overseas film production; initiates program of retrospective screenings and seminars.

1973 DGA signs industry-wide pact on pay TV; wins right to be consulted on editing feature films for television and right to be consulted when directors who have completed 90 percent of principal photography are replaced. The Guild also negotiates a policy that bans any person initially assigned to a given picture to replace the director. Policy on possessory credit secures the right of any director to negotiate with the studios for this privilege. Directors of television movies win the right to be consulted when these are edited for foreign theatrical distribution.

New York assistant directors leave IATSE and join DGA.

1975 DGA negotiates first industry-wide live and tape television contract with independent production companies. Pension and health care assets reach $50 million; staff grows to a dozen people.

1976 U.S. Copyright Act sets out specific guidelines covering category of "works made for hire."

DGA establishes Educational and Benevolent Foundation.

WGA attempts to negotiate clause specifying that no one except writers can receive possessory credit.

June 12, 1976 DGA sets up Special Projects Committee, suggested by Elia Kazan and chaired by Robert Wise.

Committee initiates oral history project and public tributes to Clarence Brown and John Cromwell.

1977 In order to comply with the terms of the Taft–Hartley Act, the DGA declares a sixteen-month open period in which people with ninety days of nonunion experience are permitted to join; both membership and unemployment swell.

Directors win right to edit their feature films when shown on television, and right to binding arbitration on director disputes with their employers. Guaranteed work period for directors of features extended from ten to thirteen weeks. The guild also puts in place further limitations on when directors can be replaced.

DGA resigns from the Inter-Guild Council in a dispute over directors' right to rewrite scripts. DGA president Robert Aldrich hires Michael Franklin, former executive director of the WGA, to replace Joseph Youngerman as executive secretary of the DGA (now called executive director). Franklin adds new departments and services, expanding the staff of eighteen employees; additions include a legal department, credits department, residuals department, credit union, and other new facilities.

DGA-negotiated studio weekly minimum salary for directors of features budgeted over $1.5 million jumps from $1,575 to $3,500 per week; dues set at 1.2 percent of salary above $10,000 and under $150,000. Guild membership reaches 5,500.

July 1977	*Action* discontinued; replaced by *DGA News*.
1978	DGA signs pact with producers: one director per film; guaranteed private office for directors; guaranteed projection facilities on location; right of Guild to binding out-of-court arbitration of legal disputes. DGA special projects program sponsors first annual Workshop for Educators. Membership tops 6,000. Residuals total $12 million; pension and health fund assets top $100 million.
1979	DGA founds Women's Steering Committee and Ethnic Minorities Committee.
1980	SAG strikes briefly over residuals.
1981	WGA strikes. DGA signs pact with producers on affirmative action provisions for women and minorities. In negotiations with producers, directors win right to select their first assistant director; in addition, individuals with authority of final cut must be specified in directors' initial deal memos; Directors further gain postproduction supervision rights for those who complete at least 90 percent of principal photography as well as the right to supervise retakes for those who have completed 100 percent of principal photography. Annual residuals collection reaches $23 million; membership at 6,300, 725 (11 percent) of whom are women.
1983	DGA launches class action lawsuit against Columbia Pictures and Warner Bros. over discrimination in hiring practices (ultimately unsuccessful).
1984	DGA puts low-budget agreement in place to support members' work on independent films.

The Guild wins new privileges: directors of episodic television programs must be given shooting script prior to their designated preparation period; cutting time for preparation of directors' cuts is increased to ten weeks after completion of principal photography; stunt sequences may not be revised without director's consent.

A reverse discrimination suit brought against the DGA by two white male second assistant director members is dismissed.

Choreographers ask DGA to represent them in negotiations, but the AMPTP vetoes this plan.

1985 San Francisco office opens.

Warren Beatty wins DGA arbitration holding Paramount to its original contract with him, thereby preventing the studio from cutting the three-and-one-half-hour *Reds* for showing on ABC-TV.

DGA-negotiated low-budget feature film contract reduces minimum compensation; studio weekly minimum salary for directors of productions budgeted over $2.5 million set at $6,580.

First DGA/Scarecrow Press oral history (on Byron Haskin) is published.

1986 DGA celebrates its Golden Jubilee with wide-ranging public programs around the world celebrating the art of directors; collective bargaining agreement is forged with holdout HBO.

The President's Committee, chaired by Elliot Silverstein, is established to report on the colorization of black-and-white films; the DGA board subsequently votes to oppose the practice.

Membership tops 7,800, including 15 percent women, 4 percent minority members.

1987	DGA strikes briefly over the issue of residuals.
	Directors win right to participate in Motion Picture Association of America ratings appeals. Incomplete television movies screened for anyone not involved in postproduction must contain notices at both beginning and end that they are subject to revision. Director must be informed of any images or sounds transmitted electronically from stage or control booth during production and must be consulted if their films are to be colorized.
	DGA staff swells to 85, serving more than 8,000 members.
July 14, 1987	DGA strikes briefly over residuals.
1988	WGA strikes; DGA threatens to sue producers that agree to writers' demands on credits and creative rights, but then issues joint "creative rights understanding" with WGA pledging to draft a voluntary code of suggested practice and to refrain from making proposals that would undermine the creative prerogatives of other moviemaking groups.
	DGA lobbying in Washington on behalf of artists' moral rights legislation results in Film Preservation Act.
	Glenn Gumpel replaces Michael Franklin as DGA executive director.
April 22, 1989	The DGA dedicates its new building at 7920 Sunset; membership reaches 9,000.
1990	Employers barred from negotiating collective bargaining provisions with other guilds that infringe on DGA creative rights.
	DGA Student Academy Award is instituted; pension and health care assets reach $500 million.

April 8, 1990	The Getty Foundation gives $1 million to establish Artists Rights Foundation, supplemented by contributions from Steven Spielberg and Fred Zinnemann.
	Foundation sets up its offices in the DGA building the following year.
1991	Assistant directors, unit production managers, and women and minority DGA members create mentoring program.
	DGA lobbies for new immigration bill, forms Latino Committee.
	First Preston Sturges Award for outstanding achievements in writing/directing, cosponsored by the DGA and WGA, is presented to Billy Wilder.
1992	Chicago office opens.
	DGA inaugurates Feature Film Nominee Symposium, gets first foreign levies payment.
1993	Guild must be informed of time allotted for director's cut on theatrical and long-form television films.
	Video assist prohibited on theatrical or long-form films without director's consent.
	DGA organizes symposium " 'Auteur! Auteur!' Thirty Years of the Auteur Theory in America" at Lincoln Center in New York to honor Andrew Sarris.
1994	DGA opens office in Hollywood, Florida (subsequently moved to Orlando); creates assistant unit production manager designation; establishes African American Steering Committee
1995	DGA legal counsel Jay Roth replaces Glenn Gumpel as executive director. Roth sets up credits department, research department, and government affairs department to work with newly created DGA political action committee. Executive position for women and minority affairs is created. Guild institutes speakers roster.

DGA signs first contract covering interactive media and launches a website at www.dga.org.

WGA and Alliance of Motion Picture and Television Producers agree to swap writers' and producers' credit positions, thereby placing writers second to last, immediately before directors.

DGA Membership approaches ten thousand; annual residuals exceed $100 million, plus $7 million additional from foreign video revenues.

1996 DGA celebrates its sixtieth anniversary as the "Year of Diversity" by publishing its first creative rights handbook and inaugurating the Joseph C. Youngerman Building at 8436 West Third Street in West Hollywood to house its pension and health plan.

The Guild signs a three-year pact with producers, including rights for directors to edit films for airlines, cable television, video, and foreign releases; also includes a nonbinding Code of Preferred Practices that would delineate basic creative rights for directors.

DGA creates political action committee charged with supporting Guild positions on runaway productions, violence in media, and directors' economic and intellectual property rights.

An in-house publicity department headed by longtime Guild publicist Chuck Warn is launched.

Congress creates National Film Preservation Board in response to lobbying efforts by the Artists Rights Foundation.

Sundance Film Festival Directing Award and Los Angeles Independent Film Festival Directing Award established.

DGA News replaced with *DGA Magazine* (bimonthly).

Pension and health plan assets top $1 billion.

1997	A DGA-sponsored Diversity Summit brings together executives and directors to discuss employment opportunities for women and minorities. The Guild inaugurates a Diversity Award honoring employers who have established a record of hiring women and minorities.
	Herbert Biberman, who disappeared from the Guild rosters during the blacklist period, is posthumously reinstated.
1998	The DGA retires its D. W. Griffith Award, citing Griffith as someone who "helped foster intolerable racial stereotypes."
	Independent Directors Committee formed.
	DGA sponsors four-part series about directors on the Sundance Channel, opens the Robert E. Wise Library in Los Angeles headquarters.
1999	In partnership with SAG, DGA releases report on the economic impact of runaway productions.
	Independent Directors Committee sponsors Director's Finder, a screening series of unreleased independent films made under DGA agreements.
	Guild launches DGA Honors program in New York; first recipient is Martin Scorsese.
2000	Through its political action committee, the DGA cosponsors first legislative initiative dealing with runaway production.
	The Guild negotiates agreement covering films distributed on the internet; it is the first guild to do so.
	Task Force on Violence and Social Responsibility calls for an overhaul of the ratings system and a zero-tolerance policy by theater owners on underage admissions.

Jeremy Kagan becomes president of Special Projects Committee, sets up symposia for DGA award nominees, seminars on new technologies, global cinema screening series, annual Digital Day.

DGA Foundation underwrites creation of DGA–Motion Picture Industry Conservation Collection at UCLA.

Through prosecution of arbitration and court actions, the legal department collects $5.5 million; residuals top $165 million.

2001 DGA hosts international conference of directors guilds of Australia, Canada, Great Britain, Ireland, and New Zealand to address creative rights issues.

Membership reaches 12,200, 26.6 percent of whom are women and 12.6 percent minority members.

PGA merges with American Association of Producers.

WGA mounts another attempt to limit use of possessory credits.

2002 Martha Coolidge becomes the first woman president of the DGA but declines to run for reelection.

The Guild engages in a court battle with CleanFlicks over efforts to bowdlerize videos of Hollywood films.

New areas of negotiations: episodic TV, documentary movies for TV, commercials, soap operas, musical variety, news, sports, children's programming, reality TV, mobisodes (for viewing on mobile phones), and webisodes (for online viewing).

2004 The DGA-sponsored political action committee, in concert with the interguild Runaway Production Alliance, is instrumental in getting Congress to pass legislation to encourage moviemaking in the United States by providing tax incentives.

Appendix B 151

	DGA sponsors legislation to provide tax breaks for low-budget films.
	Guild strikes deal with ABC Television, which specifies twenty series episodes in 2005 will be directed by women; the deal is not renewed the following year.
	DGA sets guidelines restricting the use of possessory credits for first-time directors.
	DGA Magazine replaced by *DGA Monthly* and *DGA Quarterly*.
	Membership reaches 12,800.
2005	Residuals top $246 million. Membership reaches 13,000.
2006	DGA celebrates court victory over CleanFlix.
	Staff numbers 135; assistant director training program graduates more than five hundred; pension and health plan assets top $2.1 billion.
2008–2009	WGA stages a protracted strike over residuals for new media.
2009	Guild sets internet piracy as top priority.
2010	Kathryn Bigelow becomes first woman to win DGA award for features.
	Membership tops 14,500.
2013	Guild negotiates first agreement covering subscription video-on-demand services. Membership reaches 15,000.
2015	The American Civil Liberties Union calls for an Equal Employment Opportunity Commission investigation in the hiring of women directors, claiming that the DGA compiles secret lists of directors that it recommends to producers.
2016	The new DGA contract augments residuals for streaming, covering overseas as well as U.S. markets. Membership tops 16,000.

APPENDIX C

Officers of the Directors Guild of America

PRESIDENTS

1936–1938	King Vidor
1938–1941	Frank Capra
1941–1943	George Stevens
1943–1944	Mark Sandrich
1944–1946	John Cromwell
1946–1948	George Stevens
1948–1950	George Marshall
1950–1951	Joseph L. Mankiewicz
1951–1959	George Sidney
1960–1961	Frank Capra
1961–1967	George Sidney
1967–1971	Delbert Mann
1971–1975	Robert E. Wise
1975–1979	Robert Aldrich
1979–1981	George Schaefer
1981–1983	Jud Taylor
1983–1987	Gilbert Cates
1987–1989	Franklin J. Schaffner
1989–1993	Arthur Hiller
1993–1994	Gene Reynolds

1994–1996	Gilbert Cates
1996–2002	Jack Shea
2002–2004	Martha Coolidge
2004–2009	Michael Apted
2009–2013	Taylor Hackford
2013–2017	Paris Barklay
2017–	Thomas Schlamme

EXECUTIVE SECRETARIES
(LATER, EXECUTIVE DIRECTORS)

1936–1938	J. O. Donovan
1938	F. Herrick Herrick
1938–1950	J. P. McGowan
1950	William S. Holman
1950–1951	Vernon Keays (*pro tem*)
1951–1977	Joseph Youngerman
1977–1987	Michael Franklin
1988–1995	Glenn Gumpel
1995–2017	Jay P. Roth
2017–	Russell Hollander

APPENDIX D

Chronology of the Artists Rights Foundation

1710 The Statute of Anne establishes copyright tradition in Britain.

1789 The U.S. Constitution grants authors "the exclusive right to their writing."

1790 The United States passes first copyright legislation

1886 Berne Convention for the Protection of Literary and Artistic Works produces first international copyright treaty. Revised versions are drafted in 1908, 1928, 1948, and 1971.

1908 Berne revision brings movies into international legal framework as adaptations.

1909 Work-for-hire doctrine becomes law in the United States.

1916 Charlie Chaplin loses a lawsuit against Essanay Studios for control over the editing of *Chaplin's Burlesque on* Carmen.

1922 Douglas Fairbanks wins suit against Majestic Pictures, denying them the right to recut his films.

1934 Marcel L'Herbier wins lawsuit over rights to *Le bonheur*, establishing moral rights for films in France.

1948	Berne revision recognizes movies as independent works.
1952	Roy Rogers and Gene Autry win the right to halt the sale of their films to television because of damage to their careers caused by commercials.
1954	U.S.-led Universal Copyright Convention drafts new international copyright treaty with weak requirements.
1957	Author's Moral Rights legislation enacted in France.
1965	Author's Moral Rights legislation enacted in Germany.
	Otto Preminger and George Stevens mount court cases to prevent their films from being shortened and interrupted when shown on television. Both lost.
1970	Using a new process, the U.S. National Aeronautics and Space Administration colorizes footage from the Apollo moon mission to show to Congress.
1976	Congress passes legislation specifying conditions of work for hire as part of an updated copyright bill.
	The Monty Python group wins a suit against ABC for misrepresenting an edited version of one of its episodes.
1980	Fox sues Universal at the behest of George Lucas, charging that *Battlestar Galactica* plagiarized *Star Wars*.
1981	The Directors Guild of America (DGA) begins campaigning for creative rights clause in directors' contracts.
1983	The first colorization labs are set up.
1984	Color conversion of *Casablanca* begins.
1985	Television showings of colorized *It's a Wonderful Life*, *Topper*, and Laurel and Hardy's *Way Out West* are judged successful.
	Film critics Gene Siskel and Roger Ebert host a nationally broadcast television show on colorization entitled *Hollywood's New Vandalism*.

1986 DGA appoints special President's Committee, subsequently called the Artists Rights Foundation, chaired by Elliot Silverstein. The committee files a formal request with Library of Congress to refuse to copyright colorized films; the fight is taken up by other Hollywood guilds including the Writers Guild of America, West, the Screen Actors Guild, the American Society of Cinematographers, and the Costume Designers Guild.

A colorized version of *Miracle on 34th Street* plays in syndication to twice its usual audience.

Turner Entertainment announces plans to colorize many of the MGM, RKO, and Warner Bros. titles it owns.

John Huston denounces the colorization of *The Maltese Falcon*.

The Directors Guild of Great Britain, led by Honorary President Fred Zinnemann, issues a condemnation of colorization and is joined by the Federation of European Film Directors and the Société des Auteurs et Compositeurs Dramatiques, groups representing continental Europe. Zinnemann's coalition asks the U.S. government to protect selected classic films.

1987 Representative Richard Gephardt (D-Mo.) introduces the Film Integrity Act supported by the DGA and the Writers Guild of America (WGA). It fails to pass.

Senator Patrick Leahy (D-Vt.) heads hearings on colorization and the alteration of film art.

Representative Robert Kastenmeier (D-Wis.) presents a bill in Congress that would bring American law into conformity with international copyright guidelines drafted at the Berne Convention, but excluding artists employed under work for hire provisions.

The Library of Congress announces it will copyright colorized films as "separate works."

Both colorized and black-and-white versions of *Yankee Doodle Dandy* are aired on TV in Louisville, Kentucky, and viewer response runs two to one in favor of the colorized version.

1988 The Film Preservation Act creates the National Film Preservation Board to designate twenty-five films each year as "national treasures."

The WGA strikes, in part over creative rights for screenwriters.

The Library of Congress holds hearings on colorization.

The John Huston estate, in partnership with the French Directors Guild and the Société des Auteurs et Compositeurs Dramatiques, files suit against Turner Entertainment to halt a showing of the colorized *Asphalt Jungle* on French television.

WTBS broadcasts colorized versions of *Casablanca* and *Key Largo*, garnering poor ratings.

A conclave on moral rights is held in Greece.

Great Britain enacts legislation granting some moral rights to filmmakers.

George Lucas and Steven Spielberg testify before Congress about colorization, on behalf of the DGA.

1989 Turner Entertainment prepares to colorize *Citizen Kane* but cancels its plans out of concerns over the rights granted in Welles's original contract with RKO.

The United States becomes signatory to the Berne treaty, excluding artists moral rights.

The ARF is incorporated as part of the DGA.

The National Copyright Office report on colorization calls for Congress to enact a uniform federal system of moral rights for film creators, designating directors and screenwriters as deserving of such protections.

Turner declares colorization "a dead issue."

1990 Congress passes the Visual Artists Rights Act but excludes audiovisual media.

Robert Wise protests Turner Entertainment's plan to colorize *The Haunting*, citing a clause in his original contract.

Martin Scorsese launches the Film Foundation, a funding organization dedicated to film preservation.

April 1990 The Artists Rights Foundation is launched, with Elliot Silverstein as president. The ARF sets up offices in the DGA headquarters while establishing its legal status as separate entity. The supporting coalition eventually includes DGA; WGA, West; the International Photographers Guild; the American Society of Cinematographers; the Screen Actors Guild; the American Cinema Editors; the Costume Designers Guild; the Publicists Guild of America; the Society of Composers and Lyricists; and the Society of Motion Picture and Television Directors.

1992 The ARF hosts a benefit auction, sets up a speakers bureau, and organizes creative rights events at the DGA, WGA Women's Steering Committee, Stanford, the University of Southern California, and San Diego State University.

Howard Metzenbaum (D-Ohio) and Alan Simpson (R-Wyo.) introduce a Film Disclosure Act in the Senate, which requires labeling of films and videos that have been altered from their original version.

The ARF produces a short film advocating the importance of film preservation and film integrity.

In Europe, director Marcel Carné arranges to colorize his film *Children of Paradise*.

1993 The John Huston Award for Artists Rights is established.

An ARF-sponsored Declaration of Solidarity with European film artisans on the issue of artists' moral rights is published in *Le Monde* (Paris) and *El País* (Madrid).

Barney Frank (D-Mass.) presents the DGA-sponsored Film Disclosure Bill in the House of Representatives.

The ARF participates in an American Film Market forum on artists' moral rights.

A Council of Ministers directive harmonizes European laws on authors' rights, stating "the principal director of a cinematographic or audiovisual work shall be considered as its author."

1994 The French high court overturns lower court ruling on *Asphalt Jungle* case, which stated that films may not be colorized against the wishes of their original authors.

The ARF inaugurates an annual Artists Rights Symposium (first topic: the Berne treaty).

Fred Zinnemann gets the first Huston Award.

Turner Entertainment launches Turner Classic Movies on cable with an announced policy of showing older films unedited and uncolorized.

1995 Steven Spielberg gets the Huston Award and pledges the support of his DreamWorks Pictures for the Artists Rights Foundation, though he later backs down on this pledge.

The ARF initiates a legal defense fund, introduces the Film Disclosure Act of 1995 and the Theatrical Motion Picture Authorship Act of 1995. It holds its second symposium (topic: digital imaging).

1996 With the cooperation of the DGA, the International Photographers Guild, the American Society of Cinematographers, and the computer industry, the group Americans for Better Digital Television is formed to protest current standards for high-definition television.

Backed by the ARF and other organizations, Fred Zinnemann files a formal complaint protesting the showing of a colorized version of *The Seventh Cross* on Italian television.

The DGA signs a three-year pact with producers that includes a nonbinding code of preferred practices, which would delineate basic creative rights for directors.

Martin Scorsese receives the Huston Award.

1997 A Danish court rules that a pan and scan version of *Three Days of the Condor* can be shown on Danish television despite the protest of its director, Sydney Pollack.

An Italian television station again airs a colorized version of *The Seventh Cross*.

Miloš Forman gets the Huston Award and John Paul Getty receives a special Stewardship of the Creative Arts award.

ARF representatives meet with national policy makers to discuss artists rights, publishes One Los Angeles Declaration, which situates artists' rights as a part of human rights.

1998 The Sonny Bono Copyright Term Extension Act, supported by ARF, extends period of residual payments for directors.

DGA donates $50,000 to the National Film Preservation Board.

Tom Cruise receives the Huston Award.

1999 Tim Zinnemann, son of director Fred Zinnemann, files suit in Italy over the showing of the colorized version of his father's film *The Seventh Cross* on Italian television.

Michael Mann has his name removed from an altered version of *Heat* shown on American network TV.

The ARF begins a public awareness campaign, with monthly press releases documenting the amount of editing films shown on American network TV undergo.

Sydney Pollack gets Huston Award.

June 2002 ARF merges with Martin Scorsese's Film Foundation; Scorsese becomes chair of the new DGA-sponsored organization.

DGA sues CleanFlicks over bowdlerized videos of Hollywood films.

2006 DGA wins court victory over CleanFlicks.

2013 Judy Chu (D-Calif.) and Howard Coble (R-N.C.) form the Congressional Creative Rights Caucus in the U.S. House of Representatives.

Notes

ACKNOWLEDGMENTS

1. Sherry Ortner, "Studying Sideways: Ethnographic Access in Hollywood," in *Production Culture: Cultural Studies of Media Industries*, ed. Vicki Mayer, Miranda J. Banks, and John Thornton Caldwell (New York: Routledge, 2009), 175–89.

INTRODUCTION

The epigraphs to this chapter are from Pierre Bourdieu, *The Field of Cultural Production*, ed. Randal Johnson (New York: Columbia University Press, 1993), 259; André Bazin, "La politique des auteurs," trans. Peter Graham, Cahiers du Cinema: *The 1950s—Neo-Realism, Hollywood, New Wave*, ed. Jim Hillier (1957; Cambridge, Mass.: Harvard University Press, 1985), 251; and Jesse L. Lasky, in Ian Hamilton, *Writers in Hollywood, 1915–1951* (New York: HarperCollins, 1990), 17.

1. The organization originally called itself the Screen Directors Guild. In 1950, it changed its name to the Screen Directors Guild of America, and in 1960, when the group merged with the Radio and Television Directors Guild, it became the Directors Guild of America. To avoid confusion, I have used the current nomenclature throughout this volume.
2. The history of the Screen Writers Guild is recounted in Nancy Lynn Schwartz and Sheila Schwartz, *The Hollywood Writers' Wars* (New York: Knopf, 1982); and

Miranda Banks, *The Writers: A History of American Screenwriters and Their Guild* (New Brunswick, N.J.: Rutgers University Press, 2015). The Screen Actors Guild history is chronicled in David Prindle, *The Politics of Glamour: Ideology and Democracy in the Screen Actors Guild* (Madison: University of Wisconsin Press, 1988). For a contemporary description of all three Hollywood talent unions in their formative years, see Robert Joseph, "Re: Unions in Hollywood," *Films* 1, no. 3 (Summer 1940): 34–50.

3. See, for example, Steven J. Ross's characterization of the Directors Guild of America: "What they [the directors] got [by organizing] was a kind of standardization. Now there's governance over working conditions." S. Ross, "Workers of Hollywood Unite," *DGA Quarterly*, Winter 2011, http://www.dga.org/Craft/DGAQ/All-Articles/1004-Winter-2010-11/10-Questions-Steven-J-Ross.aspx. Murray Ross describes the guild as a manifestation of directors' altruistic concern for the plight of the assistant directors and unit managers. M. Ross, *Stars and Strikes: Unionization in Hollywood* (New York: Columbia University Press, 1941), 209. Louis B. Perry and Richard S. Perry express a similar view, stating that "although a number of directors made more money than some of the producers, they wanted to improve working conditions and remuneration for assistant director and production unit managers." Perry and Perry, *A History of the Los Angeles Labor Movement, 1911–1941* (Berkeley: University of California Press, 1963), 357.

Brief histories of the Directors Guild can be found in Frank Capra, introduction to *Directors in Action: Selections from Action, the Official Magazine of the Directors Guild*, ed. Bob Thomas (Indianapolis, Ind.: Bobbs-Merrill, 1973), vii–x; David Robb, "Directors Guild Born Out of Fear 50 Years Ago," *Daily Variety*, October 29, 1985, 21–50; Golden Jubilee pamphlet, Directors Guild of America Files, California State University, Northridge, 1986; Chuck Warn, Directors Guild of America press release, DGA files, 1986; Directors Guild of America, *Fifty Years of Action*, documentary film, 1986; Jerry Roberts, Ted Elrick, and Tom Carroll, "Sixty Years of Action: A History of the Directors Guild of America," *DGA Magazine*, November–December 1996, January–February 1997; and "70 Years of Milestones," in "70th Anniversary Issue," special issue, *DGA Quarterly*, Winter 2006, 56–77.

Historical material on the DGA is also included in various biographies of key figures in its development. See, for example, Kenneth Geist, *Pictures Will Talk: The Life and Films of Joseph L. Mankiewicz* (New York: Da Capo, 1978); Raymond Durgnat and Scott Simmon, *King Vidor, American* (Berkeley: University of California Press, 1988); Joseph McBride, *Frank Capra: The Catastrophe of Success* (New York: Simon and Schuster, 1992); Mark Spergel, *Reinventing Reality: The Art and Life of Rouben Mamoulian* (Metuchen, N.J.: Scarecrow

Press, 1993); and Joseph McBride, *Searching for John Ford: A Life* (New York: St. Martin's Griffin, 2001).
4. Michel Foucault, "What Is an Author?," trans. Josué V. Hatari, in *The Foucault Reader*, ed. Paul Rabinow (1979; New York: Pantheon, 1984), 101–20.
5. See Pierre Bourdieu, *Distinction*, trans. Richard Nice (Cambridge, Mass.: Harvard University Press, 1984); *The Rules of Art: Genesis and Structure of the Literary Field*, trans. Susan Emanuel (Stanford, Calif.: Stanford University Press, 1992); *Field of Cultural Production*; and *On Television*, trans. Priscilla Park Fergusson (New York: New Press, 1996).
6. Thomas Schatz, *The Genius of the System: Hollywood Filmmaking in the Studio Era* (New York: Pantheon, 1988); John Thornton Caldwell, *Production Culture* (Durham, N.C.: Duke University Press, 2008); and Jerome Christensen, *America's Corporate Art: The Studio Authorship of Hollywood Motion Pictures* (Stanford, Calif.: Stanford University Press, 2012).
7. Bourdieu, *Field of Cultural Production*, 76.
8. See M. H. Abrams, "Literature as a Revelation of Personality," in *The Mirror and the Lamp: Romantic Theory and the Literary Tradition* (New York: Oxford University Press, 1953), 226–62; Stephen Greenblatt, *Renaissance Self-Fashioning: From More to Shakespeare* (Chicago: University of Chicago Press, 2005); Rudolph Wittkower, *Sculpture: Process and Principles* (New York: Harper and Row, 1977); Svetlana Alpers, *Rembrandt: The Studio and the Market* (Chicago: University of Chicago Press, 1988); Martha Woodmansee, *The Author, Art, and the Market: Rereading the History of Aesthetics* (New York: Columbia University Press, 1994); and Mark Rose, *Authors and Owners: The Invention of Copyright* (Cambridge, Mass.: Harvard University Press, 1995).
9. Sherry Ortner, "Studying Sideways: Ethnographic Access in Hollywood," in *Production Culture: Cultural Studies of Media Industries*, ed. Vicki Mayer, Miranda J. Banks, and John Thornton Caldwell (New York: Routledge, 2009), 175–89.

1. DIRECTORS AS ARTISTS: THE DGA RIDES THE WAVE

The epigraphs to this chapter are from the following sources: Gilbert Cates, quoted in "Seventy Years of Milestones," in "70th Anniversary Issue," special issue, *DGA Quarterly*, Winter 2006, 68; and William Wordsworth, "Essay Supplementary to the Preface (1815)," preface to *Lyrical Ballads*, in *Prefaces and Prologues to Famous Books*, ed. Charles W. Eliot (New York: Cosimo Classics, 2009), 348.
1. Hortense Powdermaker, *Hollywood, The Dream Factory: An Anthropologist Looks at the Movie-Makers* (London: Seeker and Warburg, 1950), 202.

2. For information about medieval guilds, see Andrew Martindale, *The Rise of the Artist in the Middle Ages and Early Renaissance* (New York: McGraw-Hill, 1972).
3. For further background on nineteenth-century labor unions, see David Montgomery, *The Fall of the House of Labor* (New York: Cambridge University Press, 1987), 13, 45; and David Brody, *In Labor's Cause: Main Themes on the History of the American Worker* (New York: Oxford University Press, 1993), 3–42.
4. Ten Shen, "Reel Life: Directors Guild Celebrates Fifty Years of Calling the Shots," *Chicago Reader*, March 14, 1986, A7.
5. Typed draft of remarks by Fred Zinnemann, 1962. Fred Zinnemann Papers, Margaret Herrick Library, Academy of Motion Picture Arts and Sciences, Beverly Hills, Calif., box 120, folder 5, DGA 1962–67.
6. For discussions of Los Angeles labor history, see Louis B. Perry and Richard S. Perry, *A History of the Los Angeles Labor Movement, 1911–1941* (Berkeley: University of California Press, 1963); Gerald Horne, *Class Struggle in Hollywood, 1930–1950: Moguls, Mobsters, Stars, Reds, and Trade Unions* (Austin: University of Texas Press, 2001); and John H. M. Laslett, *Sunshine Was Never Enough: Los Angeles Workers, 1880–2010* (Berkeley: University of California Press, 2012).
7. For information about allegations concerning communism, see Federal Bureau of Investigation, "Communist Political Influence and Activities in the Motion Picture Business in Hollywood, California" (1943), in *Movies and American Society*, ed. Steven J. Ross (Malden, Mass: Blackwell, 2002), 213–17.
8. Histories of the Academy of Motion Picture Arts and Sciences can be found in Pierre Norman Sands, *A Historical Study of the Academy of Motion Picture Arts and Sciences* (New York: Arno, 1973); and Emanuel Levy, *And the Winner Is . . . : The History and Politics of the Academy Awards* (New York: Continuum, 1991).
9. For a discussion of Hollywood culture, see Allen J. Scott, *On Hollywood: The Place, the Industry* (Princeton, N.J.: Princeton University Press, 2005).
10. The organization was originally called the Screen Writers Guild. Today, it is composed of two subgroups, the Writers Guild of America, East and the Writers Guild of America, West. For the sake of clarity, I use the current name and the acronym WGA throughout.
11. For a commentary on the situation of directors during this period, see Steven J. Ross, "Workers of Hollywood Unite," *DGA Quarterly*, Winter 2011, https://www.dga.org/Craft/DGAQ/All-Articles/1004-Winter-2010–11/10-Questions-Steven-J-Ross.aspx. For a general history of directors in Hollywood, see Virginia Wright Wexman, ed., introduction to *Directing* (New Brunswick, N.J.: Rutgers University Press, 2017), 1–25, which is part of the Behind the Silver Screen series.
12. Anthony Slide, *The American Film Industry: A Historical Dictionary* (New York: Limelight, 1990), 220–21. For other histories of the Motion Picture

Directors Association, see Charles Giblin, "History of the Motion Picture Directors Association," *Exhibitors Trade Review*, June 1, 1918, 2113; J. Searle Dawley Collection, Margaret Herrick Library, box 1, folder 26; William Beaudine Papers, Margaret Herrick Library, folder 14; Joseph McBride, *Searching for John Ford: A Life* (New York: St. Martin's Griffin, 2001), 193; John Ford, unpublished introduction to an anthology of essays on the Guild, Directors Guild of America Files, California State University, Northridge, box 35; Bruce Long, *Taylorology: A Continuing Exploration into the Life and Death of William Desmond Taylor* 95 (November 2000), http://www.taylorology.com/issues/Taylor95.txt; Long, *William Desmond Taylor: A Dossier* (Metuchen, N.J.: Scarecrow Press, 2004); Lisa Mitchell, "Ties That Bind: Searching for the Motion Picture Directors Association," *DGA Magazine*, November 2001, 36–42; Steve Pond, "A Guild Is Born," in "70th Anniversary Issue," special issue, *DGA Quarterly*, Winter 2006, 50–52; and "Before the Guild," *DGA Quarterly*, Winter 2011, 50–52.

The MPDA founders were Alan Curtis, Joseph de Grassi, Murdock McQuarrie, and William Desmond Taylor. Presidents included Reginald Barker, William Beaudine Sr., Roy Clements, John Ford, David M. Hartford, Fred Niblo, Henry Otto, Daddy Turner, and King Vidor. Other notable members included Frank Borzage, Cecil B. DeMille, Thomas Ince, Rex Ingram, Henry King, and Maurice Tourneur. At its height, the organization had one hundred members in Los Angeles and forty in New York.

13. Pond, "Before the Guild, " 51. See also J. Searle Dawley, "Development of Film Art Chief Object of the MPDA," *Exhibitors Trade Review*, June 1, 1918, 2114.
14. "Motion Picture Directors Association Song," *Exhibitors Trade Review*, June 1, 1918, 2118. See also Ashley Miller, "Director Is Guiding Genius in Screen's Great Mission," *Exhibitors Trade Review*, June 1, 1918, 2115.
15. "MPDA Will Produce Sixteen Pictures Costing $100,000 Each—Two Specials," *Daily Variety*, May 28, 1924, 23; "The Motion Picture Directors' Association Announcement: The Coming of Blue Ribbon Pictures," *Film Daily*, June 8, 1924, 8–9.
16. "News at a Glance," *Film Daily*, June 8, 1924, 6.
17. Scott Eyman, *Empire of Dreams: The Epic Life of Cecil B. DeMille* (New York: Simon and Schuster, 2010), 278. See also Cecil B. DeMille, *The Autobiography of Cecil B. DeMille*, ed. Donald Hayne (Englewood Cliffs, N.J.: Prentice Hall, 1959), 302. For a contemporary account of this organization, see "New Associated Director Group for Unit Production is Proposed," *Motion Picture Herald*, June 27, 1931, 29.
18. "Industry to Test Unit Production, Improve Quality," *Motion Picture Herald*, August 1, 1931, 9.

19. Screen Directors Inc. anticipated later structural changes in the industry by seeking to defer directors' salaries in favor of profit participation. For a history of the group, see Raymond Durgnat and Scott Simmon, *King Vidor, American* (Berkeley: University of California Press, 1988), 173.
20. For more information about this period, see Tino Balio, *Grand Design* (New York: Scribner's, 1993).
21. For a discussion of the Paramount policy, see Thomas Schatz, *The Genius of the System: Hollywood Filmmaking in the Studio Era* (New York: Pantheon, 1988), 75.
22. The threat of a unit production system is mentioned in Caleb Madison, "Directors Organize!," *Daily Variety*, January 17, 1936, 1–2. It also is referred to in Joseph McBride, *Frank Capra: The Catastrophe of Success* (New York: Simon and Schuster, 1992), 335; and McBride, *Searching for John Ford*, 191. For further discussions of assembly line practices of the day, see Edward Buscombe, "Walsh and Warner Bros.," in *Raoul Walsh*, ed. Phil Hardy (Edinburgh: Vineyard, 1974), 51–63; and Martin Rubin, *Showstoppers: Busby Berkeley and the Tradition of Spectacle* (New York: Columbia University Press, 1993), chap. 6.
23. Quoted in Charles Champlin, "The Guild at 60: More Than Dollars, Cents, and Safety," *DGA Magazine*, November–December 1996, 56; see also Schatz, *Genius of the System*, 46. MGM always kept a top director on call, ready to fill in at a moment's notice for an errant or disabled colleague.
24. Schatz, *Genius*, 139.
25. "Aside from the News: Directors Guild," *Daily Variety*, January 20, 1936, 3. For other early statements on the Guild that confirm directors' preoccupation with creative control, see "What the Directors Want: Interview with William K. Howard," *Commentator*, January 2, 1936, 2; "Directors Form Guild," *Hollywood Reporter*, January 17, 1936, 1–2; "Directors Organize!," *Daily Variety*, January 17, 1936, 1–2; "Directors Go into a Guild, Quit Academy," *Motion Picture Daily*, January 18, 1936, 1; "Film Directors Form Guild, Quitting Academy," *Film Daily*, January 18, 1936, 1, 8; "H'd 100% Closed Shop? Film Directors Form Own Guild," *Weekly Variety*, January 22, 1936, 7; "What the Directors Want: Interview with William K. Howard," *Commentator*, February 1, 1936, 2; "First Directors Guild Delphi: Howard's Refusing to Work," *Daily Variety*, March 27, 1936, 1; Anonymous [Frank Capra], "An Incorporated Report," *New York Times*, August 7, 1938, 4; "Producers Open Case Against SDG Charges," *Daily Variety*, September 22, 1938, 7; "Zanuck, Wallis Tell Limits on Duties of Assistant Directors," *Daily Variety*, September 23, 1938, 1, 6; "Directors Guild Hies to Labor Board," *Daily Variety*, October 24, 1938, 235; "Directors Guild Threatens Strike if Terms for Assistants Aren't Met: Action Delayed After Meeting Producers," *Motion Picture Herald*, February 25, 1939, 32; "Agreement on SDG Pact: Last Kink Ironed

Out at Parley," *Daily Variety*, March 11, 1939, 1, 5; "Producers, SDG Put Okay on Basic Pact," *Hollywood Reporter*, March 11, 1939, 1, 2; "Unit Managers Set Outfit Separate From Directors," *Daily Variety*, March 16, 1939, 7; "Writer Case Back to NLRB: Directors' Contract Given OK," *Daily Variety*, March 30, 1939; 1, 13; "SDG Pact Reveals 1st Five-Day Week Move: Deal Oked Up to Vote of Guild," *Daily Variety*, May 6, 1939, 1, 8; "Directors' Best Break," *Daily Variety*, December 11, 1940, 1, 3.

26. McBride, *Searching*, 193.
27. Richard Glatzer and John Raeburn, eds., *Frank Capra: The Man and His Films* (Ann Arbor: University of Michigan Press, 1975), 15.
28. Newman states that Vidor "thought that the directors, rather than each stand alone, collectively they could [prevail]. . . . He came down to George Hill's office [at MGM], and Jack Conway, Pop Leonard, Robert Z. Leonard—who else was there? I think Hobart Henley . . . Sam Wood . . . there [were] about eight or ten directors, and then he eventually talked to directors at other studios." Douglas Bell, *An Oral History with Joseph Newman / Interviewed by Douglas Bell*, Academy of Motion Picture Arts and Sciences, Oral History Program, Beverly Hills, Calif., 1995, 177.

Tino Balio's history of Hollywood in the 1930s mistakenly identifies Capra as the DGA's first president (Balio, *Grand Design*, 77). But Capra was initially reluctant to join the Guild, having established a formidable power base in the Motion Picture Academy, where he served as president from 1935 to 1939. Not coincidentally, Capra's 1934 comedy *It Happened One Night* won several Oscars in 1935, becoming the first film from a minor studio ever to capture an award for best picture. Capra repeated this achievement in 1939, when *You Can't Take It with You* took the Academy's top prize. And Capra himself won three Oscars for directing during the four years he served as president of the Academy. For a more complete discussion of Capra's activities during this period, see McBride, *Frank Capra*, 254–55, 284–87.

29. For various versions of this event, see Frank Tuttle, *They Started Talking* (Boalsburg, Penn.: Bear Manor Media, 2005), 107; Pond, "Before the Guild," 51; David Thomson, "The Man Who Would Be King," *DGA Quarterly*, Winter 2011, https://www.dga.org/Craft/DGAQ/All-Articles/1004-Winter-2010-11/Interview-King-Vidor.aspx; and McBride, *Searching*, 191.
30. For contemporaneous accounts of this meeting, see "Directors Back Guild For Defense," *Daily Variety*, January 13, 1936, 1, 3; "Directors Form Guild: 40 Topnotchers Organize and Affiliate with Actors and Writers: Will Bolt Academy," *Hollywood Reporter*, January 17, 1936, 1–2; "Film Directors Form Guild: Quitting Academy," *Film Daily*, January 18, 1936, 1, 8; "Directors Go into a Guild, Quit Academy," *Motion Picture Daily*, January 18, 1936, 1, 4; "Labor

Council Looms! Film Unions Uniting Cheered by Directors," *Daily Variety*, January 20, 1936, 1, 3; "Aside From the News: Directors' Guild," *Daily Variety*, January 20, 1936, 2; "Guilds, Labor in Joint Conference to Cement Tie-Up," *Hollywood Reporter*, January 21, 1936, 1, 6; "Directors Join Movement for 'One Big Union' in Hollywood," *Motion Picture Herald*, January 25, 1936, 27; and "A Guild for Directors," *New York Times*, January 26, 1936.

The Guild's first slate of officers was King Vidor, president; Lewis Milestone, first vice president; Frank Tuttle, second vice president; William K. Howard, secretary; and John Ford, treasurer. The board of directors consisted of Frank Borzage, Clarence Brown, John Cromwell, Howard Hawks, H. Bruce Humberstone, Gregory La Cava, Rouben Mamoulian, Wesley Ruggles, Edward Sutherland, and William Wellman.

31. For histories of Mabel Walker Willebrandt's work with the Guild, see Amy Dawes, "Good Counsel," *DGA Quarterly*, Winter 2011, https://www.dga.org/Craft/DGAQ/All-Articles/1004-Winter-2010-11/Good-Counsel-Mabel-Willebrandt.aspx; and Dorothy M. Brown, *Mabel Walker Willebrandt: A Study of Power, Loyalty, and Law* (Knoxville: University of Tennessee Press, 1984).

32. For a statement from the DGA itself in reaction to this charge, see "SDG Committee Abandons Negotiations as Futile," *Daily Variety*, September 23, 1937, 4. A later account is offered in Todd McCarthy, *Howard Hawks: The Grey Fox of Hollywood* (New York: Grove, 2000), 249. The DGA negotiating committee at the time consisted of Howard Hawks (chair), John Ford, and Edward Sutherland. At a general meeting on August 30, 1938, DGA members had voted unanimously to support all of the committee's demands.

Even after it was formed, the DGA was faced with threats to its existence because of the managerial duties routinely assumed by its members. In 1951, the National Labor Relations Board ruled that art directors were supervisors, not laborers, prompting DGA legal counsel Mabel Willebrandt to write to the Guild board: "Unless [Representative Richard] Nixon secures an amendment in the present law, the DGA will, in the near future, be ruled as supervisory (just as the AD's [art directors'] guild has been). Employers not already bound to the Guild by long-term contracts are liable to use this [new precedent] as a means of refusing to bargain for directors, assistant directors and TV members of the Guild." Zinnemann Papers, box 120, folder 2. This threat came to naught when the NLRB backed away from its ruling on the art directors, allowing them to retain their union status. A similar issue emerged in 1983, when Cannon Productions went to the NLRB and Cannon executive Chris Pearce stated, "We believe the DGA is not a legal bargaining unit because their members are managers who have the right to hire and fire people." "DGA Pickets N.Y. Shoot vs. Cannon: No Pic Disruption," *Weekly Variety*, November 2, 1983, 37.

33. George Mansion, "Hollywood's $100,000 a Year Union," *New Theatre*, March 1936, 25.
34. McCarthy, *Howard Hawks*, 249. For contemporary accounts of the hearings, see "Producers Open Case Against DDG Charges," *Daily Variety*, September 22, 1938, 7; "Zanuck, Wallis Tell Limits on Duties of Assistant Directors," *Daily Variety*, September 23, 1938; and "NLRB Told Directors Do Unusual Work," *Daily Variety*, September 28, 1938, 1, 5.
35. Interview with Elliott Silverstein, December 16, 1996. The unit managers formed a separate guild in 1939 but were readmitted to the DGA in 1964.
36. John Ford Papers, Lilly Library, Indiana University Bloomington, box 9, folder 2, Addresses. The Lilly Library's penciled date on this document is 1933(?), a year repeated in numerous published accounts of it, but it is difficult to understand how this date could be accurate, since the DGA was not yet in existence in 1933 and Ford refers to himself in his remarks as treasurer of the organization. The curator of Ford's papers at the Lilly Library states that there is no hard evidence by which to date the existing draft of the talk. If it is read as an exhortation to include assistant directors and unit managers in the Guild, it seems most likely that Ford made the speech in early 1937.

    For references to the Guild as a gentlemen's club, see Mansion, "Hollywood's $100,000 a Year Union"; "Darr Smith," *Los Angeles Daily News*, September 10, 1949, in Directors Guild of America Clipping Files, Margaret Herrick Library, 1936–49; Philip Dunne, *Take Two: A Life in Movies and Politics*, updated ed. (New York: Limelight, 1992), 286; and McBride, *Frank Capra*, 378.
37. For the complete text of the DGA's first pact with producers, see "DGA Pact with Studios Reveals 1st 5-Day Week Move," *Daily Variety*, May 6, 1939, 1, 8–11. Other contemporary accounts of these developments can be found in "SDG, Producer Kinks Ironed Out Yesterday: Wrinkles Left," *Daily Variety*, March 9, 1939, 8; "Agreement on SDG Pact: Last Kink Ironed Out at Parley," *Daily Variety*, March 11, 1939, 1, 5; Producers, SDG Put Okay on Basic Pact," *Hollywood Reporter*, March 11, 1939, 1, 2; "Writer Cases Back to NLRB; Directors' Contract Given OK," *Daily Variety*, March 30, 1939, 1, 13; "Final SDG-Major Pact Completed," *Daily Variety*, April 17, 1939, 21; and "Directors Win Big Victory," *Daily Variety*, October 30, 1939, 285. For latter-day accounts, see Douglas Gomery, *The Hollywood Studio System: A History* (London: British Film Institute, 2005), 191–93; Amy Dawes, "The Studios Recognize the Guild," *DGA Quarterly*, Winter 2011, http://www.dga.org/Craft/DGAQ/All-Articles/1004-Winter-2010-11/Features-Studios-Recognize-the-Guild.aspx; Jeffrey Ressner, "The War Years," *DGA Quarterly*, Winter 2011, http://www.dga.org/Craft/DGAQ/All-Articles/1004-Winter-2010-11/Features-The-War-Years.aspx; and Mark Harris, *Five*

Came Back: A Story of Hollywood and the Second World War (New York: Penguin, 2014).
38. DGA Files, box 14.
39. DGA Files, box 56.
40. Colin Shindler, *Hollywood in Crisis: Cinema and American Society, 1929–39* (New York: Routledge, 1996), 570.
41. Pond, "A Guild Is Born," 52.
42. Eugene L. Miller and Edward T. Arnold, eds., *Robert Aldrich: Interviews* (Jackson: University Press of Mississippi, 2004), 156.
43. DGA Files, box 14.
44. John Caldwell reports that, in many cases, the director who helms the pilot of a given TV series sets the style. However, even in these instances, the harum-scarum environment that exists on most TV sets precludes the possibility that directors could assert the same level of control they customarily do on movie sets. For more on this issue, see John Thornton Caldwell, *Production Culture* (Durham, N.C.: Duke University Press, 2008), 227–31.
45. James Sterngold, "'X-Files': An Adventure for Directors," *New York Times*, March 10, 1998, B1.
46. Richard Koszarski, "Joseph Lerner and the Post-War Film Renaissance," in "Auteurism Revisited," special issue, *Film History* 7, no. 4 (Winter 1995): 476.
47. Amy Dawes, "A More Perfect Union," *DGA Quarterly*, Spring 2011, https://www.dga.org/Craft/DGAQ/All-Articles/1101-Spring-2011/Feature-RTDG-SDG-Merger.aspx.
48. See "Directors Move into Video," *Daily Variety*, March 20, 1950, 1, 8; "SDG Board to Map Action on Television, *Daily Variety*, March 21, 1950, 11; "Video Directors Fight SDG," *Daily Variety*, March 21, 1950, 1, 3; "KTDC Girds for Jurisdiction Battle with SDG over TV Directors, Producers," *Weekly Variety*, March 22, 1950, 33; "DeMille Battling for SDG in that Television Tiff," *Daily Variety*, April 4, 1950, 10; "Film Directors Guild Aiming to Add TV Men," *New York Times*, April 5, 1950, A50; "Stations Play It Cozy in TV Directing Scrap," *Daily Variety*, April 6, 1950, 1, 2; "SDG Has Control over Directors on Live, Filmed TV Shows," *Weekly Variety*, April 5, 1950, 2, 54; "KTTV Staff First to Ask SDG for Pact," *Daily Variety*, April 13, 1950, 1, 9; "KTLA Staffers Bolt Radio-TV Guild En Masse, Join Rival SDG," *Daily Variety*, April 18, 1950, 3; "SDG Will Demand Screen Credit for Newly Joined KTTV Directors," *Daily Variety*, April 19, 1950, 30; "KTTV's Breckner Helms TV Group within the SDG," *Daily Variety*, May 3, 1950, 9; "SDG Asks NLRB OK to Rep KTLA and KECA-TV," *Daily Variety*, June 29, 1950, 2; "Breach Widens Between New York and Hollywood Directors Guilds," *Daily Variety*. July 12, 1950, 3; "NLRB Dismisses Radio-TV Charges Against Screen Directors," *Daily Variety*, December 19, 1950, 1.

49. The DGA's legal counsel, Mabel Walker Willebrandt, charged the Radio and Television Directors Guild's former president, William M. Sweets, and two current members, Ben Myers and Betty Todd, with having Communist ties. See "SDG Non-Red Oath Is Aimed at Infiltration from East," *Hollywood Reporter*, August 28, 1950, n.p.; and "Communist Charge Enters Directors Guild Scuffle," *Daily Variety*, September 20, 1950, 3, 15.
50. In 1951, only 37 percent of Guild members were employed; by 1954, 80 percent had jobs and membership had swelled to 750. David Robb, "Directors Guild Born Out of Fear 50 Years Ago," *Daily Variety*, October 29, 1985, 21.
51. The East Coast guild resented its marginalized status, as board meetings continued to be held in Los Angeles, and the Eastern board members feared de facto disenfranchisement. See "DGA Moves to Drop Eastern National Boards," *Daily Variety*, May 14, 1962, 1, 10.
52. See "Directors Guild Not a Union; Won't Change as Demanded by Easterners," *Daily Variety*, May 10, 1962, 1, 4. One DGA member characterized the New York organization as "fundamentally controlled by assistant directors and stagehands" (4). See also "DGA Moves to Drop Eastern Nat'l Boards," *Daily Variety*, May 14, 1962, 1, 10.
53. Dawes, "A More Perfect Union." See also Val Adams, "Directors Guild to Discuss Split," *New York Times*, April 16, 1962, 46.
54. Typed draft of remarks by Fred Zinnemann, Zinnemann Papers, box 120, file 5, DGA 1962–67.
55. Letter to DGA members from President George Sidney on June 25, 1962. Zinnemann Papers, box 120, folder 5, DGA 1952–67. Sidney's letter vociferously contradicts the *Variety* report of friction between the two groups.

   The tensions between the East and West Coasters were further heightened in 1964 when the DGA absorbed another union-oriented New York labor organization, the Screen Directors International Guild, which was made up of about eight hundred directors of television commercials and documentaries The division between the Los Angeles and New York factions of the Guild was resolved in 1992 by creating a third office in Chicago; with three offices, it made sense to designate a single location, Los Angeles, as the group's hub. This strategy and the rationale behind it is spelled out in a letter from H. C. Potter to Frank Capra, October 19, 1965, Frank Capra Papers, Wesleyan University, Middletown, Conn., folder, Directors Guild 1965, box 4, Professional Organizations. For further information about the merger of the DGA and the Screen Directors International Guild, see "New York Directors Attack Merger of Hollywood Film, TV Meggers," *Hollywood Reporter*, October 20, 1959, 1–2; "Directors Guild Merger Vote Told," *Daily Variety*, December 24, 1959, 2; Amy Dawes, "New York State of Mind," *DGA Quarterly*, Spring 2011, http://www.dga.org/Craft/DGAQ/All

-Articles/1101-Spring-2011/Feature-RTDG-SDG-Merger.aspx; and Jeanne Dorin McDowell, "The New Frontier," *DGA Quarterly*, Spring 2011, http://www.dga.org/Craft/DGAQ/All-Articles/1101-Spring-2011/Television-Advent-of-TV.aspx.

In 1999, the Guild took a positive step to recognize the work of directors based in New York City by creating the DGA Honors program, which feted East Coast luminaries at a celebration held in Manhattan. For a description of this program, see "Seventy Years of Milestones," *DGA Quarterly*, Winter 2006, http://www.dga.org/Craft/DGAQ/All-Articles/0604-Winter2006-07/Features-70-Years-of-Milestones.aspx.

56. It was initially called the President's Committee. Original members of the group included Robert Altman, Richard Brooks, Milos Forman, Jeffrey Hayden, Robert Ellis Miller, George Shaeffer, Sidney Pollack, and Robert Wise. For press reports on the ongoing activities of the committee and its role in contract negotiations, see Scott Collins, "Directors Guild Reaches Tentative Pact," *Los Angeles Times*, May 3, 1996, n.p. Extensive material on the activities of this committee is available in the Lamont Johnson Papers, Margaret Herrick Library, box 15, folders 131, 134.

57. The Directors' Bill of Rights describes the director's role as follows: "[The director] translates a motion picture script, story, or idea into visual and aural terms and arranges the images and sounds in a relationship he considers proper."

The Bill of Rights subsequently evolved into the Creative Rights Handbook. For contemporaneous press coverage of the release of the DGA's Bill of Rights, see "Directors' Arty 'Bill of Rights,'" *Daily Variety*, February 24, 1964, 1, 11; Vance King, "Four-Year Agreement Calls for 10% Raise, Spells Out Directors' Bill of Rights," *Hollywood Reporter*, December 3, 1964, 1, 4. The Guild's own view of this document can be found in Ira Marvin, "The Directors' 'Bill of Rights,'" *Action*, September/October 1966, 20; "Directors' Creative Rights (Summary)," 1981, Martin Ritt Papers, Margaret Herrick Library; and Lyndon Stambler, "Director's Cut," *DGA Quarterly*, Spring 2011, http://www.dga.org/CreativeRightsBill.

58. Lawrence Levine, *Highbrow/Lowbrow: The Emergence of Cultural Hierarchy in America* (Cambridge, Mass.: Harvard University Press, 1990).

59. For overviews of the way in which Hollywood cinema became accepted as art, see Virginia Wright Wexman, "Film as Art and Filmmakers as Artists: One Hundred Years of Progress," *Arachnē* 2, no. 2 (1995): 265–78; Michael Patrick Allen and Anne E. Lincoln, "Critical Discourse and the Cultural Consecration of American Films," *Social Forces* 82, no. 3 (March 2004): 871–93; and Shyon Baumann, *Hollywood Highbrow: From Entertainment to Art* (Princeton, N.J.: Princeton University Press, 2007).

60. Jill Andresky Fraser, "What's in a Symbol? Not the Statue of Liberty," *New York Times*, January 17, 1993, sec. 2, 21.
61. According to Pierre Norman Sands, the idea for the Academy was hatched by Conrad Nagel at a dinner at Louis B. Mayer's house in 1926. Nagel, whose father was dean of a music school at a college in Iowa, suggested the name for the new organization as one that "would properly reflect the dignity and honor of the profession." Sands, *Historical Study*, 27. The idea of a film academy had been proposed earlier by members of the MPDA. As Searle Dawley wrote, "We believe our organization is a forerunner of such an inspiring institution as our American Academy of Design or even the French Academy." "Development of Film Art Chief Object of the MPDA," *Exhibitors Trade Review*, June 1, 1918, 2114.
62. The central role the Academy of Motion Picture Arts and Sciences has played in furthering the practice of awarding prizes in the modern economy is examined in James F. English, *The Economy of Prestige* (Cambridge, MA: Harvard University Press, 2005). Baumann, *Hollywood Highbrow* argues that the Academy Awards were instituted to provide Hollywood with an aura of respectability, not artistic excellence, but the award given to *Sunrise* during the inaugural ceremony suggests that aesthetic preoccupations were in play from the beginning.
63. For a discussion of the public's view of stars as the creative authors of their pictures during the silent era, see Richard deCordova, *Picture Personalities: The Emergence of the Star System in America* (Champagne: University of Illinois Press, 2001), 80.
64. Cecil B. DeMille, "Directorial Opportunities for the Future," *The Director* 1, no. 3 (August 1924): 20.
65. This definition of staging is broader than that used by some critics. David Bordwell, for example, employs a narrower definition of the term, which excludes performance. Bordwell, *Figures Traced in Light: On Cinematic Staging* (Berkeley: University of California Press, 2005).
66. Similar transformations of popular works into pieces of art as the result of a cultural shift that began to focus on personal style had occurred in other genres during the nineteenth century. Pierre Bourdieu examines the way in which novelists like Gustave Flaubert and painters like Édouard Manet came to the fore as the culture began to emphasize style over content. Bourdieu, *The Field of Cultural Production*, ed. Randal Johnson (New York: Columbia University Press, 1993). Jane Gaines has shown the way in which American law defines proprietary rights over photographs and, by extension, claims to creative authorship over such work, in terms of a distinguishable individual style. See Gaines, *Contested Culture: The Image, the Voice, and the Law* (Chapel Hill: North Carolina University Press, 1991).

67. Frank Capra, introduction to *Directors in Action: Selections from* Action, *the Official Magazine of the Directors Guild of America*, ed. Bob Thomas (Indianapolis, Ind.: Bobbs-Merrill, 1973), ix (emphasis in original). The range of approaches used by scholars to discuss directors is described in Virginia Wright Wexman, "Directors," Oxford Bibliographies, 2017, https://www.oxfordbibliographies.com.

68. Analyses of directors as film authors can be found in Virginia Wright Wexman, introduction to *Film and Authorship* (New Brunswick, N.J.: Rutgers University Press, 2003), 1–18. See also Barry Keith Grant, ed., *Auteurs and Authorship* (Malden, Mass.: Blackwell, 2008); C. Paul Sellors, *Film Authorship: Auteurs and Other Myths* (London: Wallflower, 2010); and Sarah Kozloff, *The Life of the Author* (Montreal: Caboose, 2014).

69. Rembrandt lighting (a system devised by DeMille's collaborators, production designer Wilfred Buckland and cinematographer Alvin Wyckoff) is discussed in Charlie Keil, "The Silent Screen, 1895–1927," in *Directing*, ed. Virginia Wright Wexman (New Brunswick, N.J.: Rutgers University Press, 2017), 39. The industry's promotion of the art backgrounds of Maurice Tourneur and Rex Ingram is explored in Kaveh Askari, *Making Movies into Art* (London: Palgrave/British Film Institute, 2014).

70. Henry Stephen Gordon, "The Story of David Wark Griffith," *Photoplay*, October 1916, 89.

71. For more information about the history of film studies in colleges and universities, see Dana Polan, *Scenes of Instruction: The Beginnings of the U.S. Study of Film* (Berkeley: University of California Press, 2009). The history of the Museum of Modern Art's engagement with film can be found in Haidee Wasson, *Museum Movies: The Museum of Modern Art and the Birth of Art Cinema* (Berkeley: University of California Press, 2005).

72. For a discussion of this phenomenon, see Barbara Wilinsky, *Sure Seaters: The Emergence of Art House Cinema* (Minneapolis: University of Minnesota Press, 2001). Wilinsky writes, "The image of prestige and culture associated with films by the art cinema industry, particularly art film theaters, helped elevate cinema to the level of an art form and encouraged people to think of it as something more than 'mere' entertainment" (5).

73. For an in-depth examination of film festivals, see Cindy Hing-Yuk Wong, *Film Festivals: Culture, People, and Power on the Global Screen* (New Brunswick, N.J.: Rutgers University Press, 2012).

74. Baumann, *Hollywood Highbrow*, 127. For a further discussion of the way in which film critics helped to reshape the image of movies from cheap amusements into legitimate art, see Raymond J. Haberski, *"It's Only a Movie": Film and Critics in American Culture* (Lexington: University of Kentucky Press, 2001); and David

Bordwell, *The Rhapsodes: How 1940s Critics Changed Film Culture* (Chicago: University of Chicago Press, 2016).

75. For a discussion of the significance of this ad, see Tom Gunning, *D. W. Griffith and the Origins of Narrative Film: The Early Years at Biograph* (Champaign: University of Illinois Press, 1991), 51.

76. Eileen Bowser, *Biograph Bulletins, 1908–1912* (New York: Farrar, Straus and Giroux, 1973), 464–65.

77. For an extended examination of Alfred Hitchcock's self-promotion, see Robert Kapsis, *Hitchcock: The Making of a Reputation* (Chicago: University of Chicago Press, 1992).

78. DGA Files, box 39.

79. Cecil B. DeMille Papers, Brigham Young University, Provo, Utah, box 942, folder 4. See also "Stevens Re-Named DGA Head; Public Relations Planned," *Hollywood Reporter*, May 22, 1947, 1, 3. Earlier, in 1938, a concrete benefit of publicizing DGA members had been demonstrated at a crucial moment, when an image of Frank Capra, who was then acting as chief negotiator for the directors in their talks with producers, appeared on the cover of *Time* magazine, providing a welcome boost to the Guild's leverage in these discussions.

80. DeMille Papers, box 958, folder 9.

81. Ted Johnson, "DGA Launches Publicity Unit," *Weekly Variety*, January 22–28, 1996, 18.

82. Darryl Hope and Rob Feld, "Celebrating Excellence," *DGA Quarterly*, Winter 2007–2008, https://www.dga.org/Craft/DGAQ/All-Articles/0704-Winter-2007-08/Celebrating-Excellence-DGA-Awards.aspx.

At first, the DGA awards were bestowed quarterly, with fifteen nominees, five finalists, and one winner each term, followed by a grand prize recipient at the end of the year. Later, this system was scaled down to its present form, in which a single winner is selected annually from five nominees, following the practice the Academy of Motion Picture Arts and Sciences had established for the annual Academy Awards and timed to exploit the publicity attendant on the run-up to the Oscars. For further information about the early years of the DGA awards, see "DGA Will Present Quarterly Awards for Best Direction," *Hollywood Reporter*, August 12, 1948, 1, 8; "First DGA Award Goes to Zinnemann," *Hollywood Reporter*, August 30, 1948, 1; "Zinnemann Wins First DGA Award," *Daily Variety*, August 30, 1948, 1; and Steve Pond, "First Awards," *DGA Quarterly*, Spring 2011.

The initial impetus for all of the guilds to give out awards was likely a result of their members being cut out of the Oscar process. In 1937, the Academy added guild members to its nominating and voting rosters as a strategy for broadening participation, but as soon as its own membership swelled, it began to sideline the guilds. Beginning in 1946, the guilds could nominate but not vote, and in 1966 the Academy restricted the entire process to its members only. When the Academy cut the director award presentation from the abbreviated broadcast shown abroad in 1969, the DGA mounted a spirited protest. The Guild similarly objected, on several occasions, to the relegation of directors as also-rans at the Emmys. See "Directors Guild Votes Emmy Boycott, Asks Its Members to Quit Academy," *Weekly Variety*, December 16, 1970, 49; "TV Academy Board Reverses Self on On-Air Nods," *Daily Variety*, July 13, 1981, 1, 106; Will Tusher, "On-Air Emmy Snub of Directors Spawns DGA WGA Boycott," *Weekly Variety*, December 10, 1981, 48; and letter from George Shaeffer to Michael Franklin, October 3, 1984, Martin Ritt Papers, Margaret Herrick Library, folder 546, Directors Guild. For a further discussion of the Academy's procedures in its early days, see Sands, *Historical Study*.

A complete list of DGA awards can be found at https://www.dga.org/Awards/History.aspx. For an extended history of the awards, see Hope and Feld, "Celebrating Excellence."

83. "Guild Establishes Foreign Award in Slap at Academy," *Hollywood Reporter*, May 28, 1957, 1; "Screen Directors Honored," *Los Angeles Examiner*, June 10, 1957, n.p.; "DGA Judges Imports Uniquely," *Los Angeles Times*, June 7, 1958, n.p.
84. Carl Post, memo, February 26, 1955, DGA Files, box 34.
85. Capra Papers, box 3, SDG Correspondence 1956–57.
86. DGA Files, box 34. The critics prize was withdrawn after two years, possibly because of adverse press reaction. One writer commented, "Some will consider it merely a blatant attempt to curry favor for the screen work of directors individually or as a class." "Playing with Fire," *Motion Picture Herald*, March 21, 1953, DGA Clipping Files, 1950–59. See also "DGA Asks Film Critics Submit Own 'Constructive' Reviews in Contest," *Daily Variety*, March 19, 1953, 6.

The DGA showed a less supportive attitude toward reviewers in 1961, when its representatives apparently threatened to withdraw $250,000 the Guild had pledged to UCLA, after the student newspaper there published a series of negative film reviews. For a contemporaneous report on this situation, see "UCLA Paper Says DGA Tried to Sway Reviews of Film," *Daily Variety*, February 13, 1961, 3.
87. "Report of First Year of Activities of Educational and Benevolent Foundation, 1977," DGA Files, box 38.
88. For a review of Robert Wise's contributions as chairman of the Special Projects Committee, see Lael Loewenstein, "Wise Work," *DGA Quarterly*, Summer 2011, http://www.dga.org/Craft/DGAQ/All-Articles/1102-Summer-2011/Robert-Wise-Appreciation.aspx. The weekend retreats resulted in two books of interviews with the directors honored there. See Jeremy Kagan, ed., *Directors Close*

Up (Boston: Focal, 2000); and *Directors Close Up 2* (Metuchen, N.J.: Scarecrow Press, 2012).

89. Announcement of exhibition of Contemporary Painting and Sculpture and Related Arts, DGA Clipping Files, 1936–49.
90. This project was subsequently aborted, probably because of the upheaval the DGA went through during the House Un-American Activities Committee hearings, after which the standing of DeMille and Albert Rogell was much diminished within the Guild. The artist later sued for the money owed to her. See "Artist Sues 15 Film Directors for $100,000," *Hollywood Citizen News*, October 16, 1952, 13.
91. David Robb, "Address Fiftieth Anniversary Plans at Final DGA Meeting of 1985," *Weekly Variety*, December 25, 1985, 6; Richard F. Shepard, "Going Out Guide," *New York Times*, September 15, 1986, C16.

    The DGA has produced other documentaries celebrating the achievements of its members, including *Precious Images* (Chuck Workman, 1986); "Moments in Time," a series of six short films (Michael Stevens, 2011); and *Director's Cut* (Chuck Workman, 2011). For descriptions of these films, see Rob Feld, "Pictures Tell the Story," *DGA Quarterly*, Fall 2011, http://www.dga.org/75thFilms.
92. For more on the UCLA course, see Jim Robbins, "DGA's Training Program Marks Lucky Few for Film Boot Camp; Grads Emerge as Assistant Directors," *Weekly Variety*, September 3, 1986, 81, 110.
93. Leon Whiteson, "Critique: Directors Guild Design Marches to Its Own Drum," *Los Angeles Times*, July 9, 1989, 6. For more background on the building see "DGA Proposes New $13 Mil H.Q. to Its Members," *Daily Variety*, April 23, 1985, 1, 15; Charles Champlin, "A New Home for Directors," *Los Angeles Times*, April 25, 1989, part 6, 1, 4; and "Vidor Sculpture to Stand at DGA," *Daily Variety*, June 9, 1985 (DGA Clipping Files, 1980–1990). An earlier version of the plan had called for a twenty-story tower; it is described in "You Can See It Now: The 20-Story Tower Proposed as DGA's New Hollywood Home," *Action*, May–June 1967, 8–9; Will Tusher, "DGA Activates Long-Dormant Plans to Construct Two-Block Creative Community Center," *Daily Variety*, October 3, 1978, 1, 10 (DGA Clipping Files, 1970–1980); Capital-Rich Directors Plot Whopper Edifice for Self, Other Guilds," *Weekly Variety*, October 4, 1978 (DGA Clipping Files, 1970–1980).
94. David Robb, "DGA Members OK New H.Q.," *Daily Variety*, May 29, 1985 (DGA Clipping Files, 1980–1990).
95. DGA Clipping Files, 1980–1990.
96. Whiteson, "Critique."
97. Interview with *Variety*'s Dave McNary, March 11, 2004.

98. "Weekend with Capra Reaps Rare Rewards," *DGA News*, May 1981, 103. Of course, Capra did not actually carry out all these functions himself, but at Columbia he wielded absolute authority over his collaborators. McBride's biography, *Frank Capra: The Catastrophe of Success*, argues that Capra frequently capitalized on the power he had been granted by taking credit for the contributions of his colleagues, especially of Robert Riskin, who wrote many of Capra's most notable films.
99. John McCallum discusses Conlon's agenda at length. McCallum, *Scooper: Authorized Story of Scoop Conlon's Motion Picture World* (Seattle: Wood and Reber, 1960), especially chap. 23. Conlon was the DGA's first publicist, and he also represented many directors, including Frank Borzage, William Dieterle, Edward Dmytryk, Howard Hawks, Erle Kenton, Henry Koster, Gregory La Cava, Fritz Lang, Rowland V. Lee, Frank Lloyd, Leo McCarey, Norman Z. McLeod, George Marshall, Lewis Milestone, Ralph Murphy, Elliott Nugent, Harry Pollard, Steven Roberts, Mark Sandrich, William Seiter, George Stevens, Edward Sutherland, Norman Taurog, Frank Tuttle, and King Vidor.
100. Press release, DGA Files, box 34. See also Anonymous [Capra], "An Incorporated Report."
101. Glatzer and Raeburn, *Frank Capra*, 21.
102. Frank Capra, *The Name Above the Title* (1971; New York: Da Capo, 1997), 186.
103. Glatzer and Raeburn, *Frank Capra*, 21.
104. Peter Burger, *Theory of the Avant-Garde*, trans. Michael Shaw (Minneapolis: University of Minnesota Press, 1984), 11. Scott Burnham, *Beethoven Hero* (Princeton, N.J.: Princeton University Press, 1995) draws on this conceptualization, placing the composer's genius within a cultural context in which the individual self became ever more highly valued: "Beethoven's music has consistently been judged to be expressive of the primary features of the modern Western concept of self, such as the self as a spiritual or moral entity, the constitutive autonomy of the self, the possibility of self-transcendence, and the fundamental condition of struggle" (113). Beethoven's art represents "a self struggling to create and fulfill its own destiny" (xviii). For a critique of this approach, see Paul Feyerabend, "Creativity: A Dangerous Myth," *Critical Inquiry* 13 (Summer 1987): 700–711.
105. As political scientists like Seymour Martin Lipset have pointed out, this value system has resulted in a weaker labor movement in the United States than elsewhere in the West. Lipset, *American Exceptionalism: A Double-Edged Sword* (New York: Norton, 1996). For a discussion of the socialist realist tradition in the arts, see Dubravka Juraga and M. Keith Booker, eds., *Socialist Cultures East and West: A Post-Cold War Reassessment* (New York: Praeger, 2010).
106. Anonymous [Frank Capra], "An Incorporated Report."

107. Pond, "A Guild Is Born," 48.
108. Gene Handsaker, "The Age of the Director," *Action*, March–April, 1968, 25.
109. Gideon Bachman, "An Interview with John Huston," in *Interviews with Film Directors*, ed. Andrew Sarris (New York: Avon, 1967), 258.
110. For David Bordwell's definition, see Bordwell, "Art Cinema Narration," in *Narration in the Fiction Film* (Madison: University of Wisconsin Press, 1985), 205–33. See also Steve Neale, "Art Cinema as Institution," *Screen* 22, no. 1 (May 1981): 11–39. For an analysis of the way in which this mode of film practice has been updated in the years since 1980, see Rosanna Maule, "De-Authoring the Auteur: Postmodern Politics of Interpellation in Contemporary European Cinema," in *Postmodernism in the Cinema*, ed. Cristina Degli-Esposti (New York: Oxford University Press, 1998), 113–30; and Maule, *Beyond Auteurism: New Directions in Authorial Film Practices in France, Italy, and Spain Since the 1980s* (Chicago: University of Chicago Press, 2008). Tatiana Heise and Andrew Tudor have compared the way in which the concept of art cinema has been mobilized in Britain and Brazil. Heise and Tudor, "Constructing (Film) Art: Bourdieu's Field Model in a Comparative Context," *Cultural Sociology* 1, no. 2 (2007): 165–87.
111. This phenomenon is explored in detail in Linda Haverty Rugg, *Self Projection: The Director's Image in Art Cinema* (Minneapolis: University of Minnesota Press, 2014). Lucy Fischer, *Body Double: The Author Incarnate in the Cinema* (New Brunswick, N.J.: Rutgers University Press, 2013) extends this idea to explore the way in which moviemakers in Hollywood as well as abroad have inserted author figures in their filmic texts.
112. Gaylyn Studlar discusses the way in which Erich von Stroheim's career evolved in the opposite direction to that of Cecil B. DeMille during this period. Initially, both men played crucial roles in establishing directors as marketable stars who produced artistic pictures designed to attract culturally minded middle-class audiences. However, during the 1920s, von Stroheim refused to conform to commercial constraints, thereby derailing his career while furthering his claim to be thought of as an uncompromising creative genius. DeMille, by contrast, sacrificed his claim to artistic distinction by opting to produce movies that were widely popular. See Studlar, "Erich von Stroheim and Cecil B. DeMille: Early Hollywood Cinema and the Discourses of Directorial 'Genius,'" in *The Wiley-Blackwell History of American Film*, ed. Cynthia Lucia, Roy Grundemann, and Art Simon (Oxford: Wiley-Blackwell, 2012), 293–312.
113. Kate Kelly, "The Endless Summer Movie," *Wall Street Journal*, July 21, 2006, W1, W4.
114. For a discussion of Steven Spielberg's efforts to identify *Schindler's List* with his Jewish heritage, see Molly Haskell, *Steven Spielberg: A Life in Films* (New Haven, CT: Yale University Press, 2017).

115. Bernard Weinraub, "Film: Steven Spielberg Faces the Holocaust," *New York Times*, December 12, 1993, sec. 2, 1.
116. Brian D. Johnson, "Films: Saints and Sinners," *Macleans*, December 20, 1993, 51.
117. A selection of the *Cahiers* articles is available in English in Jim Hillier, ed., Cahiers du Cinéma: *The 1950s—Neo-Realism, Hollywood, New Wave* (Cambridge, Mass.: Harvard University Press, 1985); and Hillier, ed., Cahiers du Cinéma: *The 1960s—New Wave, New Cinema, Reevaluating Hollywood* (Cambridge, Mass.: Harvard University Press, 1986). English translations of foundational *Cahiers* essays can be found in Peter Graham and Ginette Vincendeau, eds., *The French New Wave: Critical Landmarks* (London: British Film Institute, 2011). For more background on auteurism, see Eleni Palis and Timothy Corrigan, "Auteurism," Oxford Bibliographies, 2017, http://www.oxfordbibliographies.com.
118. Richard Koszarski, introduction, in "Auteurism Revisited," special issue, *Film History* 7, no. 4 (1995), 355.
119. For an extensive overview of French film culture during this era, see Richard Abel, *French Film Theory and Criticism: A History/Anthology, 1907–1939* (Princeton, N.J.: Princeton University Press, 1984); and *The Ciné Goes to Town: French Cinema 1896–1914*, updated and exp. ed. (Princeton, N.J.: Princeton University Press, 1998).
120. From its beginnings, numerous DGA members have served as presidents of the Cannes feature film jury, including Fritz Lang (1964), Joseph Losey (1972), Alan Pakula (1978), Milos Forman (1985), Sydney Pollack (1986), Bernardo Bertolucci (1990), Roman Polanski (1991), Clint Eastwood (1994), Francis Ford Coppola (1996), Martin Scorsese (1998), David Cronenberg (1999), David Lynch (2002), Quentin Tarantino (2004), Stephen Frears (2007), Tim Burton (2010), Steven Spielberg (2013), and Joel and Ethan Coen (2015). The mix of Hollywood stalwarts with European art film luminaries significantly raised the artistic profile of the Hollywood group. Also noteworthy is the fact that, although actors, who bring celebrity power to the festival, have sometimes presided over the jury, no screenwriter of any nationality has ever been given this honor.
121. Grant, introduction to *Auteurs and Authorship*, 3. Jean-Luc Godard's subsequent practice in partnering with Jean-Pierre Gorin to form the Dziga Vertov Group, and later with Anne-Marie Miéville, tacitly repudiated this view.
122. Grant, introduction to *Auteurs and Authorship*, 3.
123. "Mise-en-scène" refers to elements of a film such as cinematography, blocking, production design, editing, and sound design that are presumably under the control of the director.
124. Hillier, Cahiers du Cinéma: *The 1950s*, 9.
125. Eric Rohmer, *The Taste for Beauty*, trans. Carol Volk (New York: Cambridge University Press, 1989), 71. In a defense of the auteurist method, published in

2017, Barrett Hodsdon refers to such instances of stylistic bravado as "sublime moments." Hodson, *The Elusive Auteur: The Question of Film Authorship Throughout the Age of Cinema* (Jefferson, N.C.: McFarland, 2017), chap. 12.

126. Peter Wollen, *Signs and Meaning in the Cinema*, 3rd ed. (Bloomington: Indiana University Press, 1972), 104.

127. The director-driven American cinema that emerged in the 1970s has gone through a number of phases and has been subject to numerous labels and periodizations, including "auteur renaissance," "New Hollywood," and "post-studio era." For recent discussions of this trend, see, for example, Michael D. Newman, *Indie: An American Film Culture* (New York: Columbia University Press, 2011); Arved Ashby, ed., *Popular Music and the New Auteur: Visionary Filmmakers After MTV* (New York: Oxford University Press, 2013); Nicholas Godfrey, *The Limits of Auteurism: Case Studies in the Critically Constructed New Hollywood* (New Brunswick, N.J.: Rutgers University Press, 2018); and Jeff Menne, *Post-Fordist Cinema: Hollywood Auteurs and the Corporate Counterculture* (New York: Columbia University Press, 2019).

128. Sherry Ortner offers another kind of explanation of the indie film movement, emphasizing its connection with increased social inequality and the darker visions associated with this trend. See Ortner, *Not Hollywood: Independent Film at the Twilight of the American Dream* (Durham, N.C.: Duke University Press, 2013).

129. Gene Handmaster, "The Age of the Director," *Action*, March–April 1968, 24.

130. "Directors Meet Critics," *Action*, May–June 1968, 15–17.

131. For a report on the proceedings, see Michael Barson, "Auteur of Duty: Sarris 'Theory' 30 Years On," *DGA News*, April–May 1993, 10–11.

132. Daniel Frankel, "Fed's Big Tax Bill Pays for Indies," *Daily Variety*, January 28, 2005, A1, A4.

133. Mitchell Zuckoff, *Robert Altman: The Oral Biography* (New York: Random House, 2009), 417.

134. Brooks Barnes, "Blockbuster Battle Between Spielberg and Netflix Fizzles, *New York Times*, April 23, 2019, https://www.nytimes.com/2019/04/23/business/media/steven-spielberg-netflix-academy-awards.html?searchResultPosition=1. See also Libby Hill, "Cannes Shuts Out Netflix Films from Festival Competition," *Los Angeles Times*, March 26, 2018, https://www.latimes.com/entertainment/la-et-entertainment-news-updates-2018-cannes-shuts-out-netflix-films-from-1522091667-htmlstory.html. A French law requires films to play in theaters for three years before going to streaming. Manohla Dargis, "At Cannes, the Heartfelt and the Divisive," *New York Times*, May 27, 2019, C1.

135. Josh Rottenberg, "DGA Boosts Theater Releases," *Los Angeles Times*, June 27, 2019, E4.

2. CHARISMA AND COMPETITION: THE DGA STAKES ITS CLAIM

The epigraphs to this chapter are from the following sources: Lois Weber, quoted in Anthony Slide, *The Silent Feminists: America's First Women Directors* (Lanham, Md.: Scarecrow Press, 1996), 38; and Molly Nesbit, "What Was an Author?," in *Authorship: From Plato to the Postmodern*, ed. Sean Burke (Edinburgh: Edinburgh University Press, 1995), 260.

1. Hy Hollinger, "Directors Reaffirm Creative Rights," *Weekly Variety*, 3 September 1986, 110.
2. This comment was made in a speech Kazan delivered at Wesleyan University. Directors Guild of America Clipping Files, Margaret Herrick Library, Academy of Motion Picture Arts and Sciences, Beverly Hills, Calif.
3. "Writers vs. Directors, Take 2," *DGA Magazine*, October–November 1994, 6.
4. John Ford, unpublished introduction to an anthology of essays on the DGA, Directors Guild of America Files, California State University at Northridge, box 35, 10.
5. Walter Murch, "A Digital Cinema of the Mind? Could Be," *New York Times*, May 2, 1999, A35.
6. Orlando Patterson, *Freedom*, vol. 1, *Freedom in the Making of Western Culture* (New York: Basic Books, 1992), 3–4.
7. Max Weber, *Economy and Society*, ed. Guenther Roth and Claus Wittich (1925; Berkeley: University of California Press, 1978), 241.
8. Pierre Bourdieu, *The Rules of Art: Genesis and Structure of the Literary Field*, trans. Susan Emanuel (Stanford, Calif.: Stanford University Press, 1992), 167. Jerome Christensen assigns charismatic authority to Hollywood studios. Christensen, *America's Corporate Art: The Studio Authorship of Hollywood Motion Pictures* (Stanford, Calif.: Stanford University Press, 2012), 176.
9. A 1915 article on D. W. Griffith described him as "a commander of men [with] an affinity for his old straw sombrero. He clings to that old Mexican headgear as devotedly as Samson did to his hair. He is never seen directing except under his straw hat." Harry C. Carr, "Directors: The Men Who Make the Plays," *Photoplay*, June 1915, 80–81. The Guild's own newsletter once described a director as "the man with the puttees and a megaphone." "Growth of the Guild Reflected by Prexy George Sidney," *DGA Newsletter*, June 1965, 1.
10. Gary Cary, "More about *All About Eve*," in *Joseph L. Mankiewicz: Interviews*, ed. Brian Dauth (Jackson: University of Mississippi Press, 2008), 110.
11. Willard Manus, "A Director for All Seasons," *Daily Variety*, April 1994, 28.
12. Joseph Youngerman to Frank Capra, 1956, Frank Capra Papers, Wesleyan University, Middletown, Conn., box 3, SDG Correspondence 1956–57.

13. For discussions of Hollywood moviemaking that focus on collaboration, see Donald Chase, *Filmmaking: The Collaborative Art* (Boston: Little, Brown, 1975); Alain Silver and Elizabeth Ward, *The Film Director's Team* (Los Angeles: Silman-James, 1983); Thomas Schatz, *The Genius of the System: Hollywood Filmmaking in the Studio Era* (New York: Pantheon, 1988); Alan Lovell and Gianluca Sergi, *Making Films in Contemporary Hollywood* (London: Hodder Arnold, 2005); Berys Gault, "Film Authorship and Collaboration," in *Film Theory and Philosophy*, ed. Richard Allen and Murray Smith (New York: Oxford University Press, 2000), 149–72; Robert Carringer, "Collaboration and Concepts of Authorship," *PLMA* 116, no. 2 (March 2001): 370–79; Jane Gaines, "Of Cabbages and Authors," in *A Feminist Reader in Early Cinema*, ed. Jennifer Bean and Diane Negra (Durham, N.C.: Duke University Press, 2002), 88–118; and John Thornton Caldwell, *Production Culture* (Durham, N.C.: Duke University Press, 2008). A lively anecdotal survey of the responses of various groups of Hollywood filmmakers to the director's evolving position within the industry can be found in Mark Litwak, *Reel Power: The Struggle for Influence and Success in New Hollywood* (New York: William Morrow, 1986).

A number of useful studies from across the humanities have proposed models for such collaborative endeavors. Howard Becker's concept of the "art world," for example, codifies the ways in which many social forces interact in the production of any work of art, as does George Dickie's institutional theory of art. Howard Becker, *Art Worlds* (Berkeley: University of California Press, 1982); George Dickie, *Art and Value* (Malden, Mass.: Wiley-Blackwell, 2001). For more specialized studies, see Svetlana Alpers, *Rembrandt: The Studio and the Market* (Chicago: University of Chicago Press, 1988); Wayne Koestenbaum, *Double Talk: The Erotics of Male Literary Collaboration* (New York: Routledge, 1989); Jack Stillinger, *Multiple Authorship and the Myth of the Solitary Genius* (New York: Oxford University Press, 1991); Janet Wolff, *The Social Production of Art*, 2nd ed. (New York: New York University Press, 1993); Martha Woodmansee, *The Author, Art, and the Market: Rereading the History of Aesthetics* (New York: Columbia University Press, 1994); Jeffrey Masten, *Textual Intercourse: Collaboration, Authorship, and Sexualities in Renaissance Drama* (New York: Cambridge University Press, 1997); Carolyn A. Jones, *The Machine in the Studio: Constructing the Postwar American Artist* (Chicago: University of Chicago Press, 1998); Charles Green, *The Third Hand: Collaboration in Art from Conceptualism to Postmodernism* (Minneapolis: University of Minnesota Press, 2001); Brian Uzzi and Jarrett Spiro, "Collaboration and Creativity: The Small World Problem," *American Journal of Sociology* 111, no. 2 (September 2005): 447–504; Grant H. Kester, *The One and the Many: Contemporary Art in a Global Context* (Durham, N.C.: Duke University Press, 2011). For general studies of collaboration, see Vera John-Steiner, *Creative Collaboration* (New York: Oxford University Press, 2000); Andrew B. Hargadon and Beth A. Bechky, "When Collections of Creatives Become Creative Collectives: A Field Study of Problem Solving at Work," *Organization Science* 17, no. 4 (August 2006): 484–500; Keith Sawyer, *Group Genius: The Creative Power of Collaboration* (New York: Basic Books, 2007); and Mathijs de Vaan, David Stark, and Balazs Vedres, "Game Changer: The Topology of Creativity," *American Journal of Sociology* 120, no. 4 (January 2015): 1–51.

Marxist critics have tended to theorize creative activity carried out by groups as collective rather than collaborative. See, for example, Raymond Williams, *Marxism and Literature* (New York: Oxford University Press, 1977); Walter Benjamin, "The Author as Producer," in *Reflections: Essays, Aphorisms, Autobiographical Writings*, ed. and trans. Peter Demetz (1966; New York: Harcourt Brace Jovanovitch, 1978), 220–38; Pierre Macherery, *A Theory of Literary Production* (1966; New York: Routledge, 2006); and Frederic Jameson, "The Existence of Italy," in *Signatures of the Visible* (New York: Routledge, 1992), 155–230. A collective model of filmmaking was famously advocated by Fernando Solanas and Octavio Getino in their film *Hour of the Furnaces* (1968) and in Solanas and Getino, "Towards a Third Cinema: Notes and Experiences for the Development of a Cinema of Liberation in the Third World," in *The New Latin American Cinema*, ed. Michael T Martin (Detroit: Wayne State University Press, 1997), 33–58.

In other fields, too, collective models of authorship have emerged, as exemplified by such groups as the Glasgow School, the Architects Collaborative, and the Fluxus artists' collective. American law similarly differentiates between collaborative and collective authorship. Collaborative authorship grants specific authorial rights to various individuals involved in the creation of a given work, whereas in cases of collective authorship, all rights reside with the group itself. For lengthy discussions of the implications of this distinction, see Jay Dougherty, "Not a Spike Lee Joint? Issues in the Authorship of Motion Pictures Under U.S. Copyright Law," *UCLA Law Review* 49 (2001): 225–334; and Justin Hughes, "The Personality Interest of Artists and Inventors in Intellectual Property," *Cardozo Arts and Entertainment Journal* 16, no. 1 (1988): 81–182.

Jane Gaines, working from a theorization originally put forward by Raymond Williams, has also argued for the creative force exercised by genres, which evolve in response to social as opposed to individual forces. For a full elaboration of this approach, see Gaines, "The Genius of Genre and the Ingenuity of Women," in *Gender Meets Genre in Postwar Cinemas*, ed. Christine Gledhill (Urbana: University of Illinois Press, 2012), 15–28; and Raymond Williams, *Marxism and Literature* (New York: Oxford University Press, 1977).

14. The title "producer" may designate a range of responsibilities, from marshaling financial backing for a project (executive producer) to assembling the production personnel to overseeing day-to-day operations, budgeting, and scheduling (line producer, associate producer, unit production manager). During the classical studio era, producers were customarily part of the studios' executive ranks, but later they increasingly began to function as independent agents who conceive, put together, and oversee projects while the studios act as distributors.
15. Press release, DGA Files, box 34. See also "Text of the Directors Guild Attack on 'Inept' Associate Producers," *MPH*, August 6, 1938, 61–62; and "Text of Directors Guild Report on the Film Industry," *New York Times*, August 7, 1938, 4.
16. Joseph McBride, *Searching for John Ford: A Life* (New York: St. Martin's Griffin, 2001), 243.
17. Douglas W. Churchill, "Honor Without Peace in Hollywood," *New York Times*, April 5, 1936, X3.
18. Rudy Behlmer, ed., *Memo from David O. Selznick* (New York: Viking, 1972).
19. Nancy Dowd and David Shepard, *King Vidor* (Metuchen, N.J.: Scarecrow Press, 1988), 210–11.
20. "Warn Scribes on Hotair Promises by Producers," *Weekly Variety*, February 19, 1964, 6.
21. Hortense Powdermaker, *Hollywood, the Dream Factory: An Anthropologist Looks at the Movie-Makers* (London: Seeker and Warburg, 1950),190.
22. Robert W. Welkos, "Memo to Executives: Put a Lid on It: Directors Guild Seeks to Stem Tide of Production Notes on Film, TV Projects," *Los Angeles Times*, May 29, 1996, F9. See also Ted Johnson, "Directors' New Code: Works in Theory, But Will Need Practice," *Weekly Variety*, May 6, 1996, 23, 72.
23. The Alliance of Motion Picture and Television Producers was originally called the Alliance of Motion Picture Producers. To avoid confusion, I have used the current nomenclature throughout.
24. Information in this paragraph comes from telephone interviews with producers Mark Gordon, Mark Johnson, and Jerry Hellman, April 12–13, 1995.
25. Janet Staiger, "The Hollywood Mode of Production, 1930–60," in David Bordwell, Kristin Thompson, and Janet Staiger, *The Classical Hollywood Cinema: Film Style and Mode of Production to 1960* (New York: Columbia University Press, 1985), 334–35.
26. For further background on this issue, see Richard Caves, *Creative Industries* (Cambridge, Mass.: Harvard University Press, 2000), 115.
27. Leo Rosten, *Hollywood: The Movie Colony, the Movie Makers* (New York: Harcourt Brace, 1941), 283.
28. David Robb, "Directors Guild Born Out of Fear 50 Years Ago," *Daily Variety*, October 29, 1985, 154.

29. David F. Prindle, *The Politics of Glamour: Ideology and Democracy in the Screen Actors Guild* (Madison: University of Wisconsin Press, 1988), 11. By 2008, the actors' situation had become even more dire. The *New York Times* reported that two-thirds of the union membership earned less than $1,000 a year. Brooks Barnes, "Guild Chief for Actors Is No Pacifist," *New York Times*, April 16, 2008, 7.

   Job security for directors, too, is far from certain. In 1987, when he was DGA president, Gilbert Cates reported that 75 percent of Guild members earned less than $18,000 annually. "Producers 'Greedy,' Say Directors, Who Are Ready to Walk," *Philadelphia Enquirer*, July 4, 1987, DGA Clipping Files.

30. Anne Thompson, "A Film Studio Fires a Director, Raising Eyebrows in Hollywood," *New York Times*, August 24, 2004, 5.

31. Sondra Locke, *The Good, the Bad, and the Very Ugly* (New York: William Morrow, 1997), 140. For a lengthy history of the production of *The Outlaw Josey Wales*, see Patrick McGilligan, *Clint: The Life and Legend* (New York: St. Martin's, 1999), 256–70.

   A similar situation prevailed on the set of the 1976 version of *A Star Is Born*, when director Frank Pierson tangled with star Barbra Streisand and her producer partner, Jon Peters. Though Pierson was the titular director, Streisand was the one who called the shots. The situation became common knowledge when Pierson wrote a widely read article about the production, "My Battles with Barbra and Jon," *New West Magazine*, November 22, 1976. For a discussion of the fallout from this experience, see Anne Edwards, *Streisand: A Biography* (Boston: Little, Brown, 1997), 364.

32. "Replacement of a Director," Directors Guild of America Inc., Basic Agreement (1978), 7-1400-14-4, 35–37. See also Marlene Adler Marks, "The New DGA Contract: Let's Hear It for Creative Rights," *Action*, March–April 1978, 38. According to longtime Creative Rights Committee chair Elliot Silverstein, the Guild had worked on such a provision much earlier. Silverstein claimed that Paul Newman taking over *Sometimes a Great Notion* from director Richard Colla, in 1970, was the original motivation for the rule, which the DGA wrote into its 1973 Basic Agreement but which did not go into effect until 1979. Tom Carrol, "For Those Who Care: Elliot Silverstein on the Battle for Creative Rights," *DGA Newsletter*, June–July 1990, 8. Among the first instances in which the new rule was enforced was during filming of *The Hunter* (1980). After Peter Hyams was fired from the picture, star Steve McQueen attempted to take over as director, but when the DGA won the arbitration, Buzz Kulik was hired to finish the film. "Directors' Victory: Actor Can't Take Over After Director's Make-Ready," *Daily Variety*, May 22, 1980, 6, 41.

33. Lawrence Cohn, "Helmers Who Handed Over the Microphone," *Weekly Variety*, September 3, 1986, 82.

34. For studies of the screenwriter's art, see Richard Corliss, *Talking Pictures: Screenwriters in the American Cinema* (New York: Penguin, 1975); Tom Stempel, *Framework: A History of Screenwriting in the American Film* (New York: Continuum, 1991); Mark Norman, *What Happens Next: A History of Screenwriting* (New York: Three Rivers, 2008); Steven Maras, *Screenwriting: History, Theory, and Practice* (London: Wallflower, 2009); and Steven Price, *The Screenplay: Authorship, Theory, and Criticism* (New York: Palgrave Macmillan, 2010).
35. John Furia Jr., "We, the Authors," *Written By: The Magazine of the Writers Guild of America*, August 1999, 19.
36. Peter Bodganovich, *Allan Dwan: The Last Pioneer* (New York: Praeger, 1971), 103.
37. "Film Author! Film Author!," *Screen Writer*, May 1947, 25–26 (emphasis in original).
38. Diane Jacobs, *Christmas in July: The Life and Art of Preston Sturges* (Berkeley: University of California Press, 1992), 130, 461.
39. Philip Dunne, *Take Two: A Life in the Movies and Politics* (New York: Limelight, 1992), 98–99.
40. Maras, *Screenwriting*, 112.
41. Todd McCarthy, "Capra, Walker Star at Directors Guild Weekend," *Weekly Variety*, March 18, 1981, 84.
42. For more information on the importance of writers during this period, see Charlie Keil, *Early American Cinema in Transition* (Madison: University of Wisconsin Press, 2001), 36.
43. Ian Hamilton, *Writers in Hollywood* (New York: Harper and Row, 1990), 18.
44. For information about this class, see Peter Decherney, *Hollywood and the Culture Elite: How the Movies Became American* (New York: Columbia University Press, 2005), 144–45.
45. Gerald Horne, *Class Struggle in Hollywood, 1930–1950: Moguls, Mobsters, Stars, Reds, and Trade Unions* (Austin: University of Texas Press, 2001), 41.
46. Mark Eaton, "Classical Hollywood," in *Screenwriting*, ed. Andrew Horton and Julian Hoxter (New Brunswick, N.J.: Rutgers University Press, 2014), 41.
47. For a discussion of this trend, see David Bordwell, *On the History of Film Style* (Cambridge, Mass.: Harvard University Press, 1997), 76.
48. Janet Staiger, "The Hollywood Mode of Production to 1930," in David Bordwell, Janet Staiger, and Kristin Thompson, *The Classical Hollywood Cinema: Film Style and Mode of Production to 1960* (New York: Columbia University Press, 1985), 118.
49. Aljean Harmetz, *"Round Up the Usual Suspects": The Making of Casablanca* (New York: Hyperion, 1993), 56. See also Jaime Wolf, "The Blockbuster Script Factory," *New York Times Magazine*, August 23, 1998, 31–35.

50. Howard Koch, "The Playwright Looks at the 'Filmwright,'" in *The Film Studies Reader*, ed. Joanne Hollows, Peter Hutchings, and Mark Jancovich (London: Arnold, 2000), 57. For a lengthy description of the difference between playwrights and screenwriters, see Sean Mitchell, "Hereinafter Referred to as the Author," *Written By: The Magazine of the Writers Guild of America*, June 2000, 40–49.
51. Many of the writers quoted by Karl Schanzer and Thomas Lee Wright attest to such an attitude. Schanzer and Wright, *American Screenwriters: The Insiders' Look at the Art, the Craft, and the Business of Writing Movies* (New York: Avon, 1993).
52. For summaries of this era and its effect on screenwriters, see Patrick McGilligan and Paul Buhle, *Tender Comrades: A Backstory of the Hollywood Blacklist* (New York: St. Martin's, 1999).
53. "Showdown for Hollywood: Director Charges Leftists Tried to Take Over Unions," *Los Angeles Herald-Express*, October 20, 1947, 1; and Frank Rogers, "Film Moguls Split on Reds: Mayer, Wood at Odds on Writers' Politics: MGM Exec Wants Law on Communist Jobs; Warner Defends 'Mission,'" *Los Angeles Daily News*, October 20, 1947, 1.
54. Furia, "We, the Authors"; William Goldman, *Adventures in the Screen Trade* (New York: Warner Books, 1983), 100.
55. Ted Elrick, "Here They Go Again," *DGA Magazine*, November 1999, 25–31.
56. Rudolph Grey, *Nightmare of Ecstasy: The Life and Films of Edward D. Wood, Jr.* (Port Townsend, Wash.: Feral House, 1991). In 2009, a second book on Wood was published: Rob Craig, *Ed Wood, Mad Genius: A Critical Study of the Films* (Jefferson, N.C.: McFarland, 2009). The year 2013 saw the publication of another study of a famously incompetent director, Tommy Wiseau, which was, in turn, made into a popular film, *The Disaster Artist* (2017). Greg Sestero and Tom Bissell, *The Disaster Artist: My Life Inside* The Room, *the Greatest Bad Movie Ever Made* (New York: Simon and Schuster, 2013).
57. Elvis Mitchell, "Scott Alexander and Larry Karaszewski: Big Eyes," January 7, 2015, KCRW, *The Treatment*, https://www.kcrw.com/culture/shows/the-treatment/scott-alexander-and-larry-karaszewski-big-eyes.
58. For contemporaneous accounts of these events, see Dave Kaufman, "Proposals Covering Credits and Script Changes Elicit Wrath of Directors' Board," *Daily Variety*, December 21, 1976, 1, 11; Kaufman, "Action, in Protest Over WGA Contractual Demands, Leaves Only Shell of Original IGC," *Daily Variety*, January 7, 1977, 1; James Harwood, "Directors Call Writers 'Ego Mad': Writers Argue, 'We're Not Bad,'" *Daily Variety*, January 28, 1977, 36; Glenn Gumpel, "Open Letter to Independent Producers," *Daily Variety*, June 2, 1988, 9; Jeremy Girard, "Directors Warn Writers About Independent Pacts," *New York Times*,

June 4, 1988, sec. 1, 54; Robert Reinhold, "Screen Writers and Directors Reach Pact," *New York Times*, January 25, 1990, C20; Nina J. Easton, "WGA and DGA Agree on Creative Input," *Los Angeles Times*, January 25, 1990, F1, 10; David Robb, "Directors, Writers Guild Boards OK Understanding," *Daily Variety*, January 25, 1990, 1, 41; Gene Reynolds, "Letter to DGA Members," September 16, 1994, 2, Fred Zinnemann Papers, Margaret Herrick Library, folder, Moral Rights/Authorship, 1993–95; and Dan Cox, "Writers Guild Gains Ground with New Pact," *Weekly Variety*, February 13–19, 1995, 18.

59. For extensive discussions of this issue, see Horace Newcomb, *The Producer's Medium: Conversations with Creators of American TV* (New York: Oxford University Press), 1983; John Caughie, *Television Drama: Realism, Modernism, and British Culture* (New York: Oxford University Press, 2000); and John Fisk and John Hartley, *Reading Television* (London: Methuen, 2003). For a discussion of directors' duties in relation to a range of television formats, see Silver and Ward, *Film Director's Team*, 8.

60. Caldwell, *Production Culture*, 211.

61. Dave McNary, "Writers, Helmers Guilds Address Divisive Issues," *Daily Variety*, October 17, 2000, 23. For a discussion of the evolution of television writer-auteurs, see Michael Z. Newman and Elana Levine, *Legitimating Television* (New York: Routledge, 2012), 38–58; and Jason Mittell, *Complex TV: The Poetics of Contemporary Television Storytelling* (New York: New York University Press, 2015), 55–85.

62. John Thornton Caldwell, *Televisuality: Style, Crisis, and Authority in American Television* (New Brunswick, N.J.: Rutgers University Press, 1995), 16–18. The trend had begun earlier in Europe, with acclaimed director-driven TV miniseries such as Jean-Luc Godard and Ann-Marie Miéville's *Six fois deux/Sur et sous le communication* (1976) and Rainer Werner Fassbinder's *Berlin Alexanderplatz* (1980).

63. The walking and talking style was originally devised by director Rod Holcomb for *ER*.

64. Steve Johnson, "The Seat of Power," *Chicago Tribune*, March 3, 2002, sec. 7, 1, 14. See also Margy Rochlin, "One Director, One Vision," *DGA Quarterly*, Winter 2018, https://www.dga.org/Craft/DGAQ/All-Articles/1801-Winter-2018/One-Director-One-Vision.aspx.

65. Mary McNamara, "Is *Game of Thrones* TV's Greatest Show of All Time? Yes, It Is," *Los Angeles Times*, April 11, 2019, https://www.latimes.com/entertainment/tv/la-et-st-game-of-thrones-greatest-tv-show-ever-20190411-story.html.

66. Edward Dmytryk, "The Director and the Editor," *Action*, March–April 1969, 23–25; Anthony Wollner, letter to the editor, *Action*, May–June 1969, 22.

67. Cecil B. DeMille Papers, Brigham Young University, Provo, Utah, box 124, DGA report, 6–7. See also "SDG, Prods Agree on Issues," *Daily Variety*, June 30, 1948, 1, 11.
68. "DGA Asks More Than WGA: Substantial Increases in Minimums Demanded by Directors in New Pact," *Daily Variety*, May 21, 1973, 1, 2; Will Tusher, "DGA Contract Bolsters Editing Rights, TV Pay," *Hollywood Reporter*, October 5, 1973, 1; Tusher, "How DGA Guards Decision Making," *Hollywood Reporter*, December 19, 1973, 3, 4.
69. Aljean Harmetz, "Hollywood Film Directors Approve Contract," *New York Times*, December 31, 1977, 6.
70. Will Tusher, "DGA's Creative Rights Bill Revealed," *Hollywood Reporter*, December 18, 1973, 1.
71. Marks, "New DGA Contract," 39.
72. Edgar Burcksen, "The Psychology of the Cutting Room," *Cinemeditor Magazine* (2001), excerpt, http://www.norman-hollyn.com/535/handouts/CuttingRoom_Psychology.pdf.
73. Kate Kelly, "The Endless Summer Movie," *Wall Street Journal*, July 21, 2006, W4.
74. Kelly, "Endless Summer Movie."
75. "Directors' Arty 'Bill of Rights,'" *Daily Variety*, February 24, 1964, 1, 11. Directors had been negotiating for such a right at least since 1947. See "Directors Angle for More Say in Editing Films," *Daily Variety*, August 6, 1947, 7. The language describing the director's cut in the standard Guild contract was tightened in 1981, following a messy and protracted negotiation over the film *Wolfen*. See Aljean Harmetz, "*Wolfen*: A Case of Director's Rights," *New York Times*, August 4, 1981, C7. Other reports describe the way in which the policy of director's cuts has continued to figure in DGA contract negotiations; see, for example, Ted Johnson, "Directors' New Code: Works in Theory, But Will Need Practice," *Daily Variety*, May 6, 1996, 23, 41.

    For discussions of issues involved in the phenomenon of the director's cut, see Greg Solman, "Uncertain Glories," *Film Comment* 29, no. 3 (May–June 1993): 19–27; Geoff King, *New Hollywood Cinema: An Introduction* (New York: Columbia University Press, 2002), 111–15; Terrence Rafferty, "Everybody Gets a Cut," *New York Times Magazine*, May 4, 2003, 58; and Jonathan Rosenbaum, "Potential Perils of the Director's Cut," in *Goodbye Cinema, Hello Cinephilia* (Chicago: University of Chicago Press, 2010), 12–24.
76. Kelly, "Endless Summer Movie." In other cases, studios may tack on happy endings, as happened to *Brazil* (1985) and *Payback* (1995), or remove censorable or otherwise objectionable content, as with *The Professional* (1994).
77. The right to a director's cut also gives directors the option of requesting at least one advance screening of their version before an audience of at least

one hundred people; in such cases, the producers are required to make whatever effects and music are available to be incorporated into this preview print. Directors Guild of America Inc., Basic Agreement (1978), 7-505-509, 28–37.

78. For a discussion of the influence of this reissue, see Jason Bailey, "The Director's Cut Is Redefined Again," *Los Angeles Times*, November 28, 2018, C1, C8.
79. J. D. Conner has labeled the studio strategy driving such reissues "continuity marketing." See Conner, *The Studios After the Studios* (Stanford, Calif.: Stanford University Press, 2015), 209.
80. Daniel Cerone, "The Kindest Cut," *Los Angeles Times*, December 18, 1991, F1.
81. Scott Hettrick, "'Trek' Voyages to Special DVD," *Daily Variety*, August 20, 2001, 5.
82. For background on these reissues, see Peter M. Nichols, "The 'Alien' Series, Stretched to the Nines," *New York Times*, November 18, 2003, B1, B4; "Fincher Speaks," *Hollywood Reporter*, October 22, 2007, 3; and Diane Garrett, "Filmmakers Get One More Chance," *Daily Variety*, March 5, 2007, 12.
83. See Peter M. Nichols, "Home Video," *New York Times*, April 4, 1997, B26.
84. Scott Roxborough, "New Beat for *Tin Drum*," *Hollywood Reporter*, May 17, 2010, 3.
85. Cerone, "Kindest Cut."
86. For more on this phenomenon, see Jonah Weiner, "The Man Who Makes the World's Funniest People Even Funnier," *New York Times Magazine*, April 15, 2015, https://www.nytimes.com/2015/04/19/magazine/the-man-who-makes-the-worlds-funniest-people-even-funnier.html.
87. Hugh Hart, "A Bigger Bang," *DGA Quarterly*, Spring 2019, https://www.dga.org/Craft/DGAQ/All-Articles/1902-Spring-2019/VFX.aspx. For an overview of the way in which directors' work has been transformed in the twenty-first century, see J. D. Conner, "The Modern Entertainment Marketplace, 2000 to the Present: Revolutions at Every Scale," in *Directing*, ed. Virginia Wright Wexman (New Brunswick, N.J.: Rutgers University Press, 2017), 137–54.
88. See, for example, Robert J. Thompson and Gary Burns, eds., *Making Television: Authorship and the Production Process* (New York: Praeger, 1990); Walter Murch, "Digital Cinema"; Henry Jenkins, *Participatory Culture in a Networked Era* (New York: New York University Press, 2006); Louisa Stein and Kristina Buss, "Limit Play: Fan Authorship Between Source Text, Intertext, and Context," *Popular Communication* 7, no. 4 (2009): 192–207; Derek Kompare, "More 'Moments of Television': Online Cult Television Authorship," in *Flow TV: Television in the Age of Media Convergence*, ed. Michael Kackman et al. (New York: Routledge, 2011), 95–113; Henry Jenkins, Mizuko Ito, and danah boyd, *Participatory Culture in a Networked Era* (Cambridge, Mass.: Polity, 2016); and Lev

Manovich, "Who Is the Author?," http://manovich.net/index.php/projects/models-of-authorship-in-new-media.

89. Karen Ward Mahar, *Women Filmmakers in Early Hollywood* (Baltimore, Md.: Johns Hopkins University Press, 2006). For a discussion of the early efforts of figures like Cecil B. DeMille and Erich von Stroheim to cement this association though styles of dress and autocratic behavior, see 196–99.

For other accounts of women directors in early Hollywood and the process by which their numbers were radically diminished by the 1920s, see Nancy Dowd, "The Woman Director Through the Years," *Action*, July–August, 1973, 15–18; Mark Garrett Cooper, *Universal Women: Filmmaking and Institutional Change in Early Hollywood* (Urbana: University of Illinois Press, 2010); Janine Basinger, "Giving Credit," *DGA Quarterly*, Winter 2011, https://www.dga.org/Craft/DGAQ/All-Articles/1004-Winter-2010-11/Features-Giving-Credit.aspx; Shelley Stamp, *Lois Weber in Early Hollywood* (Berkeley: University of California Press, 2015); and Jane Gaines, *Pink-Slipped: What Happened to Women in the Silent Film Industries* (Urbana: University of Illinois Press, 2018).

For studies of the hegemonic masculinity, see R. W. Connell, *Masculinities*, 2nd ed. (Berkeley: University of California Press, 2005); Alice Kessler-Harris, *Gendering Labor History* (Urbana: University of Illinois Press, 2006), 259; C. J. Pascoe and Tristan Bridges, eds., *Exploring Masculinities: Identity, Inequality, Continuity, and Change* (New York: Oxford University Press, 2015); and James W. Messerschmidt, *Hegemonic Masculinity Formulation, Reformulation, and Amplification* (New York: Rowman and Littlefield, 2018).

As many feminist critics have observed, social formations that have historically held sway in the high arts have also functioned in complex and subtle ways to marginalize women practitioners. Traditional women's art forms such as quilting and pottery making have been associated with anonymity, popular culture, and collective endeavor and have been labeled with terms like "decorative" and "sentimental." For discussion of the gendered associations with the term "artist," see Rozsika Parker and Griselda Pollock, *Old Mistresses: Women, Art, and Ideology* (New York: Pantheon, 1981); Linda Nochlin, "Why Have There Been No Great Women Artists?," in *Women, Art, and Power, and Other Essays* (New York: Harper and Row, 1988), 145–78; Christine Battersby, *Gender and Genius: Towards a Feminist Aesthetics* (Bloomington: Indiana University Press, 1989); Françoise Meltzer, *Hot Property: The Stakes and Claims of Literary Originality* (Chicago: University of Chicago Press, 1993); and Whitney Chadwick, *Women, Art, and Society*, 5th ed. (London: Thames and Hudson, 2012). As Andreas Huyssen has pointed out, the popular association of artists with masculinity has long been complemented by a linkage between mass culture and femininity. Huyssen, "Mass Culture as Woman: Modernism's Other," in *After *the Great Divide: Modernism, Mass Culture, Postmodernism* (Bloomington: Indiana University Press, 1986), 44–62.

90. Lillian Gish is quoted in Amy Unterberger, ed., *The St. James Women Filmmakers Encyclopedia* (Canton, Mich.: Visible Ink Press, 1999), 149. Dorothy Arzner is quoted in Lillian Faderman and Stuart Timmons, *Gay L.A.: A History of Sexual Outlaws, Power Politics, and Lipstick Lesbians* (New York: Basic Books, 2006), 62–63.
91. Dennis McLellan, "Actress Was Feisty Laverne Before Directing Hit Movies," *Los Angeles Times*, December 29, 2018, A7.
92. Ida Lupino, "Me, Mother Directress," *Action*, March–April 1967, 14.
93. For a discussion of the association of women with collaboration, see Carol Gilligan's classic study *In Another Voice: Psychological Theory and Women's Development* (Cambridge, Mass.: Harvard University Press, 1982).
94. For discussions of these partnerships, see Alison McMahan, *Alice Guy Blaché: Lost Visionary of the Cinema* (London: Bloomsbury, 2003); Kay Armatage, *The Girl from God's Country: Nell Shipman and the Silent Cinema* (Toronto: University of Toronto Press, 2003); Joan Simon, ed., *Alice Guy Blaché: Cinema Pioneer* (New Haven, Conn.: Yale University Press, 2009); and Shelly Stamp, *Lois Weber in Early Hollywood* (Berkeley: University of California Press, 2015). For studies of such partnerships in the contemporary art world, see Whitney Chadwick and Isabelle de Courtivron, eds., *Significant Others: Creativity and Intimate Partnership* (London: Thames and Hudson, 1993). In the twenty-first century, women artists like architect Denise Scott Brown and painter Lee Krasner, who have served as unsung marital and creative partners to lauded male colleagues (Robert Venturi and Jackson Pollock, respectively), have come to be better recognized. On Denise Scott Brown's role as a collaborator on her husband's architectural works, see Robin Pogrebin, "Partner Without the Prize," *New York Times*, April 18, 2013, C1, C4; on Lee Krasner, see Ellen G. Landau, *Jackson Pollock* (New York: M. H. Abrams, 2010).
95. David Robb, "Martha Coolidge: Blaming DGA for Lack of Female Directors Is 'Dangerous Side-Path,'" *Deadline*, May 22, 2015, http://deadline.com/2015/05/directors-guild-aclu-investigation-female-directors-martha-coolidge-1201430374. By contrast, within Hollywood's executive ranks, where women are less likely to be thrust into such misogynistic surroundings, they have made greater strides. For more information about female executives in Hollywood, see J. E. Smyth, *Nobody's Girl Friday: The Women Who Ran Hollywood* (New York: Oxford University Press, 2018).
96. Gendered labor patterns in Hollywood during the studio era are analyzed in Erin Hill, *Never Done: A History of Women's Work in Media Production* (New Brunswick, N.J.: Rutgers University Press, 2016).

97. The women were Ida May Park, Lottie Pickford, Lynn Reynolds, and Lois Weber. An article published in *Motion Picture News* on March 24, 1917, announced that the first dinner of the Motion Picture Director's Association was held in honor of Weber. Bruce Long, *Taylorology: A Continuing Exploration into the Life and Death of William Desmond Taylor* 95 (November 2000), http://www.taylorology.com/issues/Taylor95.txt. When Lois Weber was admitted as an honorary member in 1917, the organization resolved that "no other of the gentler sex will be admitted to membership" (Mahar, *Women Filmmakers*, 181).
98. Amy Dawes, "John Rich: A Lifetime of Service," in "70th Anniversary Issue," special issue, *DGA Quarterly*, Winter 2006, 60.
99. David Robb, "Directors Fought Long, Hard for Guild," *Weekly Variety*, September 3, 1986, 98. This short-lived policy revived a tradition first established in medieval guilds.
100. *DGA Newsletter*, 30th Anniversary Issue, June 1965, 14.
101. Frank Capra Papers, Wesleyan University, Middletown, Conn., box PO-4.
102. Louella Parsons and Harriet Parsons, "Ida Lupino: Rarest of the Rare," *New York Journal American*, December 5, 1965, in Ida Lupino Clipping File, Margaret Herrick Library.
103. The committee reported that, between 1949 and 1979, women had directed only 19 percent of all feature films made in Hollywood. Members of the original Women's Steering Committee were Susan Bay, Nell Cox, Joelle Dobrow, Dolores Ferraro, Victoria Hochberg, and Lynn Littman (the "Original Six"). For contemporary accounts of the progress of women within the DGA and in the film and television industry generally during the 1970s, see Aljean Harmetz, "Report Shows a Bleak Outlook for Female Directors," *New York Times*, June 20, 1980, C31; Sally Ogle, "The Struggle of Women Directors," *New York Times Magazine*, January 11, 1981, sec. 6, 94; and "Directors Concede Women Members Are at a Standstill," *Weekly Variety*, June 13, 1981, 7. Overviews of the situation can be found in Miranda J. Banks, "Gender Inequalities and Precarious Diversity in the 1970s U.S. Television Industry," *Feminist Media Histories* 4, no. 4 (Fall 2018): 109–29; and Maya Montañez Smukler, *Liberating Hollywood: Women Directors and the Feminist Reform of 1970s American Cinema* (New Brunswick, N.J.: Rutgers University Press, 2019).
104. Dale Pollock, "Directors Back ERA: Boycott Urged," *Los Angeles Times*, October 23, 1981, sec. 5, 1, 7; "States Refusing to Ratify ERA Will Be Boycotted by Directors," *Weekly Variety*, October 28, 1981, 2, 76. After the amendment failed, the boycott was rescinded.
105. Paul Brownfield, "Women Collaborate to Form Their Own Solutions," *Variety*, November 6, 1997, http://variety.com/1997/biz/news/women-collaborate-to-form-their-own-solutions-111660756. In 1992, the DGA and the Screen Actors

Guild cosponsored a symposium on sexual harassment. Marilyn Zeitlin, "DGA, SAG Combat Sexual Harassment," *DGA News*, August–September 1992, 7.

106. For accounts of the progress of this suit, which was initially set in motion in 1981 and originally targeted a number of media companies, see Gail Williams, "DGA Files Sex Discrimination Suit vs. Networks, Production Companies," *Hollywood Reporter*, February 25, 1981, 1, 21; Aljean Harmetz, "Suit to Allege Sex Bias by TV and Film Makers," *New York Times*, February 25, 1981, C24; "DGA Files Mass Gripes vs. 'Sex Bias Patterns' in Helmer Hiring as Talks Fail; Hit Majors, Webs," *Daily Variety*, May 25, 1981, 5, 34; David Robb, "DGA Gets EEOC Nod to File Class Action Discrimination Suit Against Webs, Majors, Indies," *Weekly Variety*, May 18, 1983, 4, 31; "DGA Readies Suit on WB Hiring of Women, Minorities," *Daily Variety*, July 20, 1983, 3, 32; "DGA Hits Warners with 'Discrimination Hiring' Class Action," *Weekly Variety*, July 27, 1983, 3, 6; "Warners Countersues DGA, Sez Directors 'Roster' Discriminates," *Weekly Variety*, October 5, 1983, 5, 32; David Robb, "DGA and Columbia Lock Horns Over Affirmative Action," *Daily Variety*, November 9, 1983, 6, 22; David Robb, "DGA Sues Columbia Over Hiring," *Daily Variety*, December 22, 1983, 1, 26; "Judge Will Mull DGA Suit Against Studios," *Daily Variety*, February 13, 1985, 3, 41; David Robb, "Rule Against DGA as Minority Rep Class Action Suit," *Weekly Variety*, March 13, 1985, 2, 125; David Robb, "Directors Guild Nixed as Plaintiff in Studio Discrimination Lawsuit," *Weekly Variety*, September 25, 1985, 4, 22. It is also described in the documentary *This Changes Everything* (2019), directed by Avi Lewis. A detailed account of the suit can be found in Smukler, *Liberating Hollywood*, 260–77.

107. "Discrimination Suit Against DGA Nixed by Federal Judge," *Daily Variety*, April 18, 1984, n.p.

108. For histories of the group's efforts, see Pamm Higgins, "What It Takes for Women to Reach the Top," *DGA Newsletter* 14, no. 4 (September–October 1989), 3–4; and Lyndon Stambler, "The Good Fight," *DGA Quarterly* (Fall 2011), http://www.dga.org/Craft/DGAQ/All-Articles/1103-Fall-2011/History-Guild-Diversity-Committees.aspx. For more extensive discussion of this issue, see Kim Masters, "Are Things Better? You Might Not Like the Answer," *Hollywood Reporter*, December 9, 2011, 13–14; Maureen Dowd, "Misdirection," *New York Times Magazine*, November 22, 2014, 40; Yvonne Villarreal, "DGA Urges More Diversity," *Los Angeles Times*, September 11, 2015, C5; Ryan Faughnder, "Hollywood Assailed on Diversity," *Los Angeles Times*, February 23, 2016, C1, C5; and Mike McPhate, "Hollywood's Inclusion Problem Extends Beyond the Oscars," *New York Times*, February 23, 2016, C1, C6. The DGA compiles its own statistics, which showed some progress in rookie hires for TV shows; from 2009 to 2017, the number of women hired tripled and the number of ethnic

minorities doubled. David Ng, "More Minority Directors Hired," *Los Angeles Times*, September 28, 2017, C3. Yet feature film statistics continued to lag: by 2017, women had directed only five of the top one hundred top-grossing productions, and female membership in the Guild itself was just 15.1 percent. Stacy L. Smith et al., *Inequality in 1,100 Popular Films: Examining Portrayals of Gender, Race/Ethnicity, LGBT & Disability from 2007 to 2017*, Annenberg Inclusion Initiative, 2018, http://assets.uscannenberg.org/docs/inequality-in-1100-popular-films.pdf. In 2019, female membership in the Guild at the director level stood at 16.4 percent. Directors Guild of America, "DGA Diversity: Frequently Asked Questions," https://www.dga.org/The-Guild/Diversity/Diversity-FAQ.aspx. The few women who did helm Hollywood movies seldom got a chance to repeat their success; from 2007 to 2017, 84 percent of first-time women directors never got another chance, compared to 55.3 percent of tyro male directors. Meg James and Meredith Blake, "'Boys' Club' Endures in Hollywood," *Los Angeles Times*, October 30, 2017, A1, A11. See also Rebecca Keegan, "Deeper Bias Probe in TV, Film," *Los Angeles Times*, May 12, 2016, E1, E2; Nell Scovell, "Who You Gonna Call to Direct?," *New York Times*, July 17, 2016, SR10; Meg James, "Low Marks for Film Diversity," *Los Angeles Times*, January 5, 2018, C3; Meg James, "Women's Behind-Camera Struggle," *Los Angeles Times*, January 11, 2018, C8; and Meredith Blake and Yvonne Villareal, "Show of Force," *Los Angeles Times*, March 11, 2018, E1, 4–5.

Beginning in 1981, the DGA includes in its Basic Agreement with the major television studios a clause that charges them to promote diversity in the directorial ranks. For updates on the DGA's reports on their ongoing activities around this issue, see their website, www.dga.org.

109. By 2019, the Guild had nominated a total of eight women for feature film awards: Lina Wertmuller (*Seven Beauties*, 1975), Randa Haines (*Children of a Lesser God*, 1986), Barbra Streisand (*The Prince of Tides*, 1991), Jane Campion (*The Piano*, 1993), Sofia Coppola (*Lost in Translation*, 2003), Valerie Faris (*Little Miss Sunshine*, 2006; with Jonathan Dayton), Kathryn Bigelow (*The Hurt Locker*, 2008, and *Zero Dark Thirty*, 2012), and Greta Gerwig (*Ladybird*, 2017).

110. Maane Khatchatourian, "Hollywood's 'Biased' Hiring Practices Against Women Subject of ACLU Inquiry," *Variety*, May 12, 2015, http://variety.com/2015/biz/news/hollywoods-biased-hiring-practices-against-women-subject-of-a-c-l-u-inquiry-1201493101; Rebecca Keegan, "Female Directors Are on the Outside Looking In," *Los Angeles Times*, May 13, 2015, A1, A8; Cara Buckley, "ACLU Pushes for Inquiry into Bias Against Female Directors," *New York Times*, May 13, 2015, C1, C5; David Robb, "Martha Coolidge"; Maureen Ryan, "Breaking the Old Boy Network," *Variety Ultimate*, November 10, 2015, 45–47; Rebecca Keegan, "Hollywood Takes on 'Bad Business' of Gender Bias," *Los Angeles Times*,

December 2, 2015, A1, A8; and Ryan Faughnder, "Hollywood Assailed on Diversity," *Los Angeles Times*, February 23, 2016, C1, C5. For the letter itself, see "ACLU Letter on the Exclusion of Women Directors," *New York Times*, May 12, 2015, http://www.nytimes.com/interactive/2015/05/12/movies/document-13filmwomen.html.

For a description of the Guild's subsequent activities in this area, focusing on the leading role that DGA president Martha Coolidge played in shepherding them forward, see Judith I. Brennan, "Fearless Leaders," *DGA Quarterly*, Fall 2011, https://www.dga.org/Craft/DGAQ/All-Articles/1103-Fall-2011/History-Guild-Presidents.aspx.

111. Gillian Thomas and Melissa Goodman, "Women Directors Might Just Get the Hollywood Ending They Have Been Hoping For," ACLU, February 18, 2017, https://www.aclu.org/blog/womens-rights/womens-rights-workplace/women-directors-might-just-get-hollywood-ending-they-have.
112. David Ng, "Weinstein Quits Directors Guild," *Los Angeles Times*, November 28, 2017, C2. On February 1, 2018, the Guild posted on its website sexual harassment policy guidelines for directors. David Ng, "Guild Addresses Sex Harassment," *Los Angeles Times*, February 2, 2018, C3.

3. RECOGNITION: THE DGA TAKES CREDIT

The epigraph to this chapter is from Joseph Youngerman, *My Seventy Years at Paramount and the Directors Guild of America* (Los Angeles: Directors Guild of America, 1995), 92.

1. Dan Ford, *Pappy: The Life of John Ford* (Englewood Cliffs, N.J.: Prentice-Hall, 1979), 211.
2. Bernard Weinraub, "Writers Claw Their Way Past Producers," *New York Times*, March 2, 1995, C13.
3. Schuyler M. Moore, *The Biz: The Basic Business, Legal, and Financial Aspects of the Film Industry* (Los Angeles: Silman-James, 2000), 173.
4. By the turn of the century, the proliferation of credits (known in the business as "credit creep") had reached gargantuan proportions, with the final credits of *The Lord of the Rings: The Fellowship of the Ring* (2001), for example, running over nine minutes. For a discussion of this phenomenon, see "Film Credits Stir Debate," *New York Times*, December 28, 1983, C17; Randy Kennedy, "Who *Was* That Food Stylist? Film Credits Roll On," *New York Times*, January 11, 2004, 1, 20; and Mekado Murphy, "Waiting for the Credits to End?," *New York Times*, May 28, 2017, AR15. Murphy notes Hollywood's attempt to enliven lengthy end credits by inserting "buttons," or brief additional scenes, into the sequence.

For a history of Hollywood credits, see James Crawford, "Film Credits" (PhD diss., University of Southern California, 2013), ProQuest 14349.

5. For a discussion of the relation of credits to residuals, see Alan Paul and Archie Kleingartner, "The Transformation of Industrial Relations in the Motion Picture and Television Industries: Talent Sectors," in *Under the Stars: Essays on Labor Relations in Arts and Entertainment*, ed. Lois S. Gray and Ronald L. Seeber (Ithaca, N.Y.: Cornell University Press, 1996), 169–70.

6. See Richard Caves, *Creative Industries* (Cambridge, Mass.: Harvard University Press, 2000), 126. Producers have had special difficulties with the proliferation of their credits, given the nebulous nature of the job. Over the years, the Producers Guild has attempted to sort out the situation, but with little success. For a discussion of this issue, see Michael Cieply, "Producers Guild Pushes for Clear Film Credits," *New York Times*, October 13, 2010, http://www.nytimes.com/2010/10/14/business/media/14producer.html.

7. Gérard Genette, "The Name of the Author," in *Paratexts: Thresholds of Interpretation*, trans. Jane Lewin (1987; New York: Cambridge University Press, 1997), 39.

8. Michel Foucault, "What Is an Author?," trans. Josué V. Hatari, in *The Foucault Reader*, ed. Paul Rabinow (New York: Pantheon, 1984), 101–20.

9. Jeremy Braddock has noted "the department store's assumption that display windows should be 'signed,' since the necessity of having a name to place on the decorative work presumes that the work in some sense originates from an author or artist." Braddock, "Smithee's Incorporation," in *Directed by Allen Smithee*, ed. Jeremy Braddock and Stephen Hock (Minneapolis: University of Minnesota Press, 2001), 149.

10. For a discussion of modern media forms that do not assign authorship, see Catherine Fisk, *Writing for Hire* (Cambridge, Mass.: Harvard University Press, 2016), 34–35.

11. For discussions of this tradition, see Eileen Bowser, *The Transformation of Cinema: 1907–1915* (Berkeley: University of California Press, 1990), 105; Tom Gunning, *D. W. Griffith and the Origins of Narrative Film: The Early Years at Biograph* (Champaign: University of Illinois Press, 1991), 45; and Jane Gaines, "Anonymity: Uncredited and Unknown in Early Cinema," in *A Companion to Early Cinema*, ed. André Gaudreault, Nicolas Dulac, and Santiago Hidalgo (Malden, Mass.: Wiley-Blackwell, 2012), 443–59.

12. Eileen Bowser, *Biograph Bulletins, 1908–1912* (New York: Farrar, Straus and Giroux, 1973), 105.

13. Bowser, *Transformation*, 118.

14. James R. Quirk, "Stars and Directors Whose Names Bring in the Public," *Photoplay*, May 1924, 44–45, 109; Terry Ramsaye, "What Makes a Director?," *Photoplay*, December 1925, 50. Quirk's article purports to be based on a survey of

five thousand exhibitors. The other directors he names are Cecil B. DeMille, D. W. Griffith, Rex Ingram, Allan Dwan, Marshall Neilan, William DeMille, James Cruz, and George Fitzmaurice.

15. For a discussion of the way in which directors came to the fore in the theater, see Helen Krich Chinoy. "The Emergence of the Director," in *Directors on Directing: A Source Book for the Modern Theater*, ed. Toby Cole and Helen Krich Chinoy (New York: Macmillan, 1963), 1–78.

16. Gunning, *D. W. Griffith*, 56. Especially in view of the confused nomenclature that prevailed in the early years, whether it is meaningful to speak of a single individual as the "first" movie director is debatable. Griffith laid the most well-publicized claim to this title, but others have also styled themselves as the first American director. Thomas Ince was hired as a director by Carl Laemmle in 1910; J. Searle Dawley states that he was hired by the Edison Manufacturing Company to direct *The Nine Lives of a Cabin* in 1907. For a review of Ince's claim, see J. Madison Davis, "Machine to Screen: The Evolution Towards Stars," in *Screenwriting*, ed. Andrew Horton and Julian Hoxter (New Brunswick, N.J.: Rutgers University Press, 2014), 26. Dawley's claim is noted in Steve Pond, "Before the Guild," *DGA Quarterly*, Winter 2011, 52. Anthony Slide argues that it was Frenchwoman Alice Guy-Blaché who "virtually single-handedly established the concept of the director as a separate entity in the filmmaking process." Slide, *The Silent Feminists: America's First Women Directors* (Lanham, Md.: Scarecrow Press, 1996), 15.

17. Sumiko Higashi, *Cecil B. DeMille and American Culture: The Silent Era* (Berkeley: University of California Press), 1994, 11. See also Charlie Keil, "The Silent Screen, 1895–1927: Cecil B. DeMille Shapes the Director's Role," in *Directing*, ed. Virginia Wright Wexman (New Brunswick, N.J.: Rutgers University Press, 2017), 25–47. DeMille also briefly took on the title of "director general" to designate his position as the production chief of the studio.

18. Higashi, *Cecil B. DeMille*, 19.

19. For a discussion of this phenomenon, see Laura Parigi, "Fake Americans of the Italian Cinema," in *Directed by Allen Smithee*, ed. Jeremy Braddock and Stephen Hock (Minneapolis: University of Minnesota Press, 2001), 209–28. From time to time, directors of foreign films have also Anglicized their names as a way of positioning their productions more advantageously in the global marketplace. Examples include Yimou Zhang (for Zhang Yimou), Apichatpong "Joe" Weerasethakul, and Alejandro G. Iñarritu (for Alejandro Gonzales Iñarritu).

20. Frank Capra, *The Name Above the Title* (New York: Macmillan, 1971), 266.

21. Capra, *Name Above the Title*, 240.

22. Literary scholar Peggy Kamuf has discussed the significance of authorial signatures. See Kamuf, *Signature Pieces: On the Institution of Authorship* (Ithaca,

N.Y.: Cornell University Press, 1988), viii–ix. Drawing on various writings by Jacques Derrida, especially *Glas*, Kamuf's discussion focuses in part on artists' handwritten signatures, which cannot be legitimately reproduced by anyone else.

23. For a discussion of the relationship of authorial signatures to Hollywood films, see Christian Keathley, "Signaturism and the Case of Allen Smithee," in *Directed by Allen Smithee*, ed. Jeremy Braddock and Stephen Hock (Minneapolis: University of Minnesota Press, 2001), 121–42.

24. Letter from Joseph Mankiewicz to David Shepard, August 22, 1986; minutes of the Golden Jubilee Committee meeting, January 3, 1986, Joseph L. Mankiewicz Papers, Margaret Herrick Library, Beverly Hills, Calif., folder, DGA Fiftieth Anniversary.

25. Letter to DGA members from Guild president Arthur Hiller, dated September 10, 1992, Directors Guild of America Files, California State University at Northridge, box 38.

26. In general, the rise of the emphasis on artists' names is associated with a shift in the gender of cultural workers, with women commonly producing anonymous creative works such as quilts and pottery. The distinctive values associated with such traditional arts is acknowledged in Mirra Bank's study of quilt making when she comments, "To rescue women folk artists from their anonymity is not exclusively a matter of discovering names and assigning dates. Such facts alone provide little insight into the significance of self-expression in lives consecrated to duty and domestic industry." Bank, *Anonymous Was a Woman* (New York: St. Martin's, 1979), 9. For a discussion of this phenomenon in early cinema, see Jane Gaines, "Anonymity: Uncredited and Unknown in Early Cinema," in *A Companion to Early Cinema*, ed. André Gaudreault, Nicolas Dulac, and Santiago Hidalgo (Malden, Mass.: Wiley-Blackwell, 2012), 443–59.

27. In 2012, Reville was the subject of a retrospective at the Il Cinema Ritrovato festival in Bologna, Italy; the same year saw two Hollywood releases that focused on Reville and Hitchcock's collaborative relationship: *The Girl* and *Hitchcock*.

28. Judith Mayne, *Directed by Dorothy Arzner* (Bloomington: Indiana University Press, 1994), 54–55, 183.

29. For an in-depth discussion of Weber's image and career, see Shelley Stamp, *Lois Weber in Early Hollywood* (Berkeley: University of California Press, 2015), 8.

30. For example, the 1968 Basic Agreement states in part, "In no event shall the director's credit be less than the minimum credit required to be accorded to any other person under the collective bargaining agreement entered into by the employer covering such person." Directors Guild of America Inc., Basic Agreement (1968), DGA Files, box 13.

31. DGA Files, box 34. For a description of the credit provisions in the DGA Basic Agreement, see Dina Appleton and Danel Yankelevits, *Hollywood Dealmaking*, 3rd ed. (New York: Allworth, 2018), 136–57.
32. In the days before the DGA gained jurisdiction, the names of producers like David O. Selznick often appeared in this position.
33. "Directors Guild Waiver Lets Paul Newman Retain Billing at End of 'Rachel,'" *Daily Variety*, September 16, 1968, 1, 4.
34. Jim Harwood, "Lucas Severs Last Hollywood Ties," *Daily Variety*, May 5, 1981, 1, 2; and Dale Pollack, *Skywalking: The Life and Films of George Lucas* (New York: Harmony, 1983), 248–49. Lucas later renewed his DGA membership and became active in the Artists Rights Foundation, a satellite organization.
35. "Some of the Opening Statements by DGA Representatives at Negotiations," DGA press release, April 21, 1981, 5, DGA Files, box 34.
36. Aljean Harmetz, "Directors Accept Pact as Producers Yield on Rollbacks," *New York Times*, July 15, 1987, C19.
37. "The New Status Credit," *Details*, August 1993, 133. For other discussions of director credit requirements on advertising, see "DGA Asks More Than WGA," *Daily Variety*, May 21, 1973, 1, 2; and Dale Pollock, "Two Key Arbitration Rulings Effectively Narrow Definition of Film Teaser Advertising," *Daily Variety*, August 31, 1979, 1, 5.
38. Gene Reynolds, "Credits Where Credits Are Due," *DGA News*, December–January 1995, 5.
39. For reports on the DGA's efforts to limit director credits, see the minutes of the DGA board meeting of June 4, 1946, DGA Files, box 34; "SDG and SAG Ironing Out Pact Kinks," *Daily Variety*, June 25, 1948, 1, 3; "SDG to Submit 5-Point Plan to Major Studios Tonight—Wants Exclusion on Term 'Director,'" *Hollywood Reporter*, February 8, 1949, 4; Louella O. Parsons, "Fight On Over Directors' Screen Credits," *Los Angeles Examiner*, June 26, 1950, sec. 1, 8; and Erskine Johnson, "Stage and Screen," *New York Daily News*, June 14, 1954, 27.
40. Youngerman, *My Seventy Years*, 92. In 1987, casting directors were subjected to similar pressure to change their titles. See David Robb, "Directors Push to Protect Their Films," *Weekly Variety*, May 27, 1987, 5, 37.
41. "A New Title Needed," *The Director* 1, no. 3 (August 1924): 4.
42. Correspondence related to this case is found in Fred Zinnemann Papers, Margaret Herrick Library, box 150, folder 2032. For press reports on the case, see "Ray Heindorf Loses Suit Over 'Director's Credit," *Hollywood Reporter*, August 27, 1956, Directors Guild of America Clipping Files, Margaret Herrick Library, 1950–59; Thomas M. Pryor, "Music Chief Sues Directors Guild," *New York Times*, October 20, 1954, sec. Amusements, 33.

43. DGA Files, box 23.
44. Directors Guild of America Inc., Basic Agreement (1978), 7-203, 25.
45. Ted Elrick, "A Film By," *DGA Magazine*, June/July 1998, 39–43.
46. Lawrence Cohn, "Helmers Who Handed Over the Megaphone," *Weekly Variety*, September 3, 1986, 92. See also Tim Grierson, "Films Where Credits Are a Puzzle," *Los Angeles Times*, November 12, 2018, E1, E3.
47. Aljean Harmetz, *On the Road to Tara: The Making of* Gone with the Wind (New York: N. H. Abrams, 1996), 158, 198. See also "DGA's One Director-Per-Pic Pact Provision Getting a Workout," *Daily Variety*, June 21, 1979, 1, 13.
48. Axel Madsen, *William Wyler* (New York: Thomas Y. Crowell, 1973), 154. Other well-known cases of this kind include *Duel in the Sun* (1946; King Vidor credited, William Dieterle and Joseph von Sternberg uncredited), and *Porgy and Bess* (1958; Otto Preminger credited and Rouben Mamoulian uncredited). For information about *Duel in the Sun*, see Raymond Durgnat and Scott Simmon, *King Vidor, American* (Berkeley: University of California Press, 1988), 238–41. On *Porgy and Bess*, see DGA Files, box 23; "Directors Boycott Goldwyn," *Hollywood Reporter*, August 4, 1958, 1; "SDG Board Votes OK for Preminger to Direct *Porgy*," *Daily Variety*, August 8, 1958, 1, 11; Joe Schoenfeld, "Time and Place," *Daily Variety*, August 8, 1958, 3; Thomas M. Pryor, "Hollywood Views; 'Porgy' Controversy Hurts Directors Guild Prestige—Other Matters," *New York Times*, August 17, 1958, X5; and Mark Spergel, *Reinventing Reality: The Art and Life of Rouben Mamoulian* (Metuchen, N.J.: Scarecrow Press, 1993).
49. Dave McNary, "Double Vision Hits DGA: Co-Helming Rule Jeopardizes Par's Mission to 'Mars,'" *Weekly Variety*, April 12–18, 2004, 5; Daniel Engber, "Why Not Quit the Directors Guild? What Robert Rodriguez Can and Can't Do," *Slate*, April 8, 2005, http://www.slate.com/articles/news_and_politics/explainer/2005/04/why_not_quit_the_directors_guild.html.
50. Ted Elrick, "Singularity of Vision," *DGA Quarterly*, May 2004, http://www.dga.org/Craft/DGAQ/All-Articles/0405-May-2004/Singularity-of-Vision.aspx. For post-2000 statistics, I am grateful to J. D. Connor, who has compiled a database of nearly two thousand films made during this period.
51. The Coen brothers were not granted such a waiver until 2004.
52. Elrick, "A Film By."
53. "It was going to be Allen Smith," John Rich has said. "I added the "ee" at the end to make it more unusual sounding." Nick Redman, "Allen Smithee Exposed," *DGA Magazine*, August–September 1992, 23. The first name has been variously spelled as Allen and Alan. Jeremy Braddock and Stephen Hock have speculated that the name Smithee could have been taken from Orson Welles's *Mr. Arkadin*, which includes the following exchange:

GUY: You don't have any memory of what happened to you before '27, right? So what makes you so sure your name is Arkadin?
ARKADIN: Hmm?
GUY: Well, maybe it's Arkadine, or Arkadini, or Arkapopoulos—or Smithee!
ARKADIN: Don't be a fool. I know my own name.

Braddock and Hock, "The Specter of Illegitimacy in an Age of Dissolution and Crisis," in *Directed by Allen Smithee* (Minneapolis: University of Minnesota Press, 2001), 4.

54. For more information about the production of *Death of a Gunfighter*, see Stuart Kaminsky, *Don Siegel: Director* (New York: Curtis Books, 1974).
55. Genette, "Name of the Author," 46–54. A similar phenomenon, though differently motivated, surfaced in the art world a few years later. The Neoist movement, which seeks to promote the anonymity of the artists, has produced the noms de plume Monty Cantsin and Karen Eliot, which have been used by various individual artists. For discussions of this phenomenon, see Clive Phillpot, "Artists' Magazines: News of the Art Strike, Monty Cantsin and Karen Eliot," *Art Documentation* (Fall 1992): 137–38.
56. See, for example, Irv Slivkin, "Allen Anon," *Entertainment Weekly*, October 10, 1997, 13; and Benjamin Svetkey, "X Marks the Spat," *Entertainment Weekly*, October 23, 1998, 28–36.
57. Joe Eszterhas has written at some length about his experience with the film. Eszterhas, *Hollywood Animal* (New York: Knopf, 2004), 641–62. See also Christine Spines, "Alan Smithee Skewers Hollywood," *Premiere*, March 1997, 32, 34; and Michael Fleming, "'Smithee' by Smithee," *Daily Variety*, May 6, 1997, 1, 17.
58. Andrew Sarris, "Foreword: Allen Smithee Redux," in *Directed by Allen Smithee*, ed. Jeremy Braddock and Stephen Hock (Minneapolis: University of Minnesota Press, 2001), vii–xvii.
59. See William Stetz, "Allen Smithee Exposed," *DGA News*, August–September 1992, 23; and Nick Redman, "The Well-Known, the Not-So-Known, and the Virtually Unknown," *DGA News*, August–September 1992, 13–15, 22–24.
60. See Braddock and Hock, "Specter of Illegitimacy," 22–23; and Andrew Gumpel, "Hollywood Decides to Kill the Man Who Never Was," *Independent*, January 16, 2000, 19. The feud over the director credit for *American History X* is explored at length in the documentary *Directed by Alan Smithee* (2002), directed by Lesli Klainberg.
61. "Credits for Scenarios," *Edison Kinetogram* 6, no. 1 (February 1, 1912), 15.
62. Charlie Keil, *Early American Cinema in Transition: Story, Style, and Filmmaking, 1907–1913* (Madison: University of Wisconsin Press, 2001), 37.

63. Keil, *Early American Cinema*, 37.
64. Affidavit of John Howard Lawson in Nedrick Young v. Motion Picture Association of America, Inc., 299 F.2d 119 (D.C. Cir. 1962), 95, in Miranda Banks, *The Writers: A History of American Screenwriters and Their Guild* (New Brunswick, N.J.: Rutgers University Press, 2015), 112. For discussions of writers in Hollywood that focus on issues of credit, see Maurice Rapf, "Credit Arbitration Isn't Simple," *Screen Writer* 1, no. 2 (July 1945): 31–36; Allen Rivkin, "Screen Writers: The Rocky Road to Recognition," *Daily Variety*, 41st Anniversary Issue, October 29, 1974, 16 (Rivkin was the public relations director of the Writers Guild of America at the time of this article); and Jorja Prover, *No One Knows Their Names: Screenwriting in Hollywood* (Bowling Green, Ohio: Bowling Green University Press, 1994).
65. WGA, West press release, March 29, 1995, collection of the author. See also Jonathan Cutler, "To Have and Have Not: Solving the Mysteries of the WGA Credits System," *WGA Magazine*, May 1999, 36–95.
66. "Screen Authorship Records," *Academy of Motion Picture Arts and Sciences Bulletin* 8 (July 1934). Letter signed by Waldemar Young, chair; Sidney Buchman; Robert Riskin; Jack Cunningham; Richard Schayer; Carey Wilson; and Howard J. Green, acting chairman.
67. By the turn of the twenty-first century, the Producers Guild was trying to reduce the number of producer credits as well. Anita M. Bush and Ted Johnson, "Panel Demands Credit, But Only for Producers Who Earn It," *Variety*, June 26, 1997; Dave McNary, "Producer Orgs Merg," *Daily Variety*, March 5, 2001, 2, 26; and Rick Lyman, "Produced by . . . Well, Just About Everybody," *New York Times*, May 21, 2001, B1, B3.

    A testimony to the waning power of producers vis-à-vis writers can be seen in the 1995 flare-up between the two groups over a pact between the WGA and the Alliance of Motion Picture and Television Producers that granted writers the next-to-last credit position, just before that of directors. Dave Cox, "Writers Guild Gains Ground with New Pact," *Weekly Variety*, February 13–19, 1995, 18; "Producers Piqued," *Weekly Variety*, February 27–March 6, 1995, 7, 9; and Dave McNary, "Writers, Producers Reach Deal," *Variety*, May 2001.
68. For further background on these altercations, see Hortense Powdermaker, *Hollywood: The Dream Factory* (Boston: Little, Brown, 1950), 154–55; WGA newsletter, June 1968, DGA Files, box 34; Nancy Lynn Schwartz and Sheila Schwartz, *The Hollywood Writers' Wars* (New York: Knopf, 1982); Tad Friend, "Credit Grab," *New Yorker*, October 20, 2003, 160–69; and Banks, *The Writers*.
69. For a discussion of this issue, see Banks, *The Writers*, 112–13.
70. Captain Leslie T. Peacocke, "The Scenario Writer and the Director," *Photoplay*, May 1917, 111.

71. Schwartz and Schwartz, *Hollywood Writers' Wars*, 99.
72. Richard Corliss, *Talking Pictures: Screenwriters in the American Cinema* (New York: Penguin, 1975), xxiii.
73. For overviews of this controversy from the WGA's perspective, see Banks, *The Writers*, 159–65; and Fisk, *Writing for Hire*, 83–84. On the other side of the coin was the less rancorous but still hot-button issue of the writers' near monopoly on the coveted "Created by" credit on television. See, for example, Steve Johnson, "The Seat of Power," *Chicago Tribune*, March 3, 2002, sec. 7, 1, 14.
74. Steven Bach, *Final Cut: Art, Money, and Ego in the Making of Heaven's Gate, the Film that Sank United Artists*, updated ed. (New York: Newmarket, 1999), 208.
75. Genette, "Name of the Author," 39.
76. This practice follows the possessory formula that prevails in the high arts, which conceptualizes authorship as emanating from a single source, as by referring to "Shakespeare's *Macbeth*."
77. In 1968, director Richard Brooks stated, "I put Truman Capote's name first on *In Cold Blood* because he was the star. Got hell from the Directors Guild, too." Kevin Thomas, "Hollywood Directors Rise to Power Position," *Los Angeles Times*, August 11, 1968, Calendar, 12.
78. For the Guild's own history of this practice, see "70 Years of Milestones," *DGA Quarterly*, Winter 2006, http://www.dga.org/Craft/DGAQ/All-Articles/0604-Winter2006-07/Features-70-Years-of-Milestones.aspx.
79. "Possessory Credits Timeline," *DGA Magazine*, February 2004, 9.
80. Cited in Fisk, *Writing for Hire*, 84.
81. Mark Caro, "Filmmakers and Writers Get Possessive About Lines of Credit," *Chicago Tribune*, November 19. 2000, sec. 7, 16.
82. Philip Dunne, *Take Two: A Life in Movies and Politics*, updated ed. (New York: Limelight, 1992), 46–47.
83. Fisk, *Writing for Hire*, 83.
84. William Wyler Papers, Margaret Herrick Library, folder 599, Directors Guild of America. The agreement was initiated by WGA executive director Michael Franklin in 1963, but the clause in the writers' contract went unnoticed by the directors until 1967. See Crawford, "Film Credits," 241. When President Robert Aldrich appointed Franklin as executive director at the DGA in 1977, he met with strong resistance from his board members, who regarded Franklin with considerable hostility because of his role in forging the 1963 WGA contract. The text of the DGA lawsuit can be found in the Alliance of Motion Picture and Television Producers records, Special Collections, Margaret Herrick Library. For a further discussion of the events surrounding the controversy, see Youngerman, *My Seventy Years*, 111; "Writers Guild Demand: 'Screen Credit for Writers Shall Precede That for Director,'" *Daily Variety*, January 12, 1973, 19;

"Writers Out-Fox Directors: DGA Awakes to 'No Top Credit,'" *Daily Variety*, May 3, 1967, 3; "'Presenter Status' Stirs Suit by DGA," *Hollywood Reporter*, May 10, 1967, 1, 4; A. D. Murphy, "DGA Sues to Nip Writers' Pact," *Daily Variety*, May 10, 1967, 1; William Tusher, "Writers Claim Early Round in Bout with Directors on Credits," *Film Daily*, May 11, 1967, 1; "Directors Guild Feels Suit Against Scribes' Pact Won't Jar Own Negotiations," *Daily Variety*, May 12, 1967, 1; "Writers Guild Files Court Denial of Directors' Charges," *Daily Variety*, May 17, 1967, 1, 10; A. D. Murphy, "DGA Loses 1st Court Round with Writers," *Daily Variety*, May 19, 1967, 1, 4; "Directors Lose Suit on Movie Credits," *Los Angeles Herald Examiner*, May 19, 1967, A9; Vance King, "Writers, Producers Win Round," *Daily Variety*, May 19, 1967, 1; "Directors Give AMPTP the Brush," *Daily Variety*, May 29, 1967, 1, 4; "The Great Giveaway," *Action*, May/June 1967, 11; "DGA to Speed Up Film Credits Suit," *Hollywood Reporter*, June 6, 1967, 1; "Directors Press for Trial of Suit vs. Writers, Producers," *Daily Variety*, June 6, 1967, 1; William Tusher, "Producers Firm Against DGA," *Film Daily*, February 5, 1968, 1; Harry Bernstein, "Battle Over Apostrophe May Cause Film Directors' Strike," *Los Angeles Times*, February 5, 1968, 3, 22; Thomas M. Pryor, "Directors' Drive to Upset Writers' Credits Gain Could Rack Industry," *Daily Variety*, February 14, 1968, 1, 15; Dave Kaufman, "First Directors' Strike Looms," *Daily Variety*, April 1, 1968, 1, 18; "Nationwide Film, TV Director Strike Seen," *Hollywood Citizen-News*, April 2, 1968, DGA Clipping Files, 1960–69; Dave Kaufman, "Writers Guild Says Directors' Tactic Illegal," *Daily Variety*, April 2, 1968, 1, 14; Harry Bernstein, "Directors' Strike May Close Film Industry," *Los Angeles Times*, April 2, 1968, part 1, 20; Thomas M. Pryor, "Press Reports Upset AMPTP and DGA: Like News Blackout," *Daily Variety*, April 8, 1968, 1, 6; Lew Wasserman, Jack Valenti, and Charles Boren, "Let's Set the Record Straight," paid advertisement, *Daily Variety*, April 8, 1968, Wyler Papers, folder 599, Directors Guild of America; "Directors Strike Called Off," *Hollywood Reporter*, April 10, 1968, 1; Dave Kaufman, "Directors End Strike Threat," *Daily Variety*, April 10, 1968; 1; "Mann Analyzes Director Problem," *Motion Picture Daily*, June 6, 1968, 6.
85. Wyler Papers, folder 599, Directors Guild of America.
86. John Huston Papers, Margaret Herrick Library, folder 599, DGA 1966–68.
87. "The Great Giveaway," 11.
88. Jack Shea, ed., *In Their Own Words: The Battle Over the Possessory Credit, 1966–1968* (Los Angeles: Directors Guild of America, 1970).
89. Shea, *In Their Own Words*.
90. "Possessory Credits Timeline," *DGA Magazine*, February 2004, 9. See also A. D. Murphy, "DGA Sues to Nip Writers Pact," *Daily Variety*, May 10, 1967, 1; Dave Kaufmann, "1st Directors Strike Looms," *Daily Variety*, April 1, 1968, 1, 18;

"Directors Strike Called Off: Lift April 30 Deadline as Result," *Hollywood Reporter*, April 10, 1968, 1; Harry Bernstein, "Directors' Strike May Close Film Industry: April 30 Set for Walkout Date in Dispute Over Writers Guild Claim to Credit in Billing," *Los Angeles Times*, April 20, 1968, 1, 20; Tom Gray, "The Controversy Over Possessive Credits," *Motion Picture Herald*, July 10, 1968, 1.

91. Considerable journalistic ink has been spilled over this issue. See, for example, Dave Kaufman, "Proposals Covering Credits and Script Changes Elicit Wrath of Directors' Board," *Daily Variety*, December 21, 1976, 1, 11; Dave Kaufman, "DGA, Convinced Writers Will Hit the Bricks, Met Sunday to Determine Strike Policy," *Daily Variety*, January 13, 1977, 1, 32; Gerry Levin, "DGA Threatens to Strike If Producers Accede to WGA's Contract Proposals," *Hollywood Reporter*, January 20, 1977, 1, 33; James Harwood, "Directors Call Writers 'Ego Mad': Writers Argue, 'We're Not Bad': Who Will Cross Picket Lines?," *Weekly Variety*, January 26, 1977, 1, 2; Dave Kaufman, "Won't Press Point of Money for Actors, Directors Who Polish Scripts on the Set," *Daily Variety*, February 3, 1977, 1, 2; Joseph McBride, "DGA Hyphenates Get Work Orders—Even If WG Strikes," *Daily Variety*, February 28, 1977, 1, 4; Ray Lloyd, "Writers' Two Concessions to Management Reaffirm Bond with Directors," *Hollywood Reporter*, April 2, 1981, 1, 4; David Robb, "DGA vs. WGA: 21 Year Credits Feud," *Daily Variety*, June 1, 1988, 1, 19; "DGA Open Letter to WGA," *Daily Variety*, June 1, 1988, 5; "DGA Open Letter to Independent Production Companies," *Daily Variety*, June 2, 1988, 9; David Robb, "DGA Threatens Suit Over Indies Pacting with WG," *Daily Variety*, June 2, 1988, 1, 20; David Robb, "Directors Threatening Action vs. Producers Signing WGA Contract," *Weekly Variety*, June 8, 1988, 1; Nina J. Easton, "WGA and DGA Agree on Creative Input," *Los Angeles Times*, January 25, 1990, F1, F10; "Writers Guild, DGA in Clash Over Credits," *Hollywood Reporter*, September 20, 1994, 1, 94; Dan Cox, "Writers Guild Gains Ground with New Pact," *Weekly Variety*, February 13–19, 1995, 16; "Producers Piqued," *Weekly Variety*, February 27–March 5, 1995, 8–9; Bernard Weinraub, "Writers Claw"; WGA press release, April 13, 1995; Virginia Wright Wexman, "Success Has Many Fathers; So Do Films," *New York Times*, May 23, 1995, B2; Jack Shea, letter to the editor, *Weekly Variety*, August 17, 1998, 49; Ted Elrick, "Here They Go Again," *DGA Magazine*, November 1999, 25–31; David Robb, "A Dispute by WGA and DGA Over Film Credit," *Daily Variety*, August 2, 1999, 1; Bernard Weinraub, "Strike Fears Grip Hollywood as Unions Flex New Muscle," *New York Times*, October 1, 2000, 1, 26; Dave McNary, "Scribe Solidarity, WGA Members Back Aggressive Strategy," *Daily Variety*, October 25, 2000, 8; David Robb, "DGA Says WGA Demands Will 'Wreak Havoc,'" *Hollywood Reporter*, January 10, 2001, 62; Dave McNary, "Writers Bloc," *Daily Variety*, January 16, 2001, 1, 46; Bernard Weinraub, "Screenwriters May Walk Out Over Film Credits and Respect," *New York Times*,

January 16, 2001, A1, C10; Dave McNary, "WGA Talks: Some Hope in Week 5," *Daily Variety*, February 2, 2001, 5, 27; Dave McNary, "WGA Eyes Rights, Files Unfair Labor Complaint," *Daily Variety*, February 9, 2001, 5, 27; Rick Lyman, "Writers Strike May Not Be Inevitable," *New York Times*, February 19, 2001, sec. C, 1, 8; David Robb, "DGA Won't Support WGA Stance on 'Film by' Credit," *Hollywood Reporter*, March 2, 2001, 28; Dave McNary, "DGA Counters Credits Plan," *Daily Variety*, March 21, 2001, 6, 16; David Robb, "Directors Relax 'Film by' Stance," *Hollywood Reporter*, March 30, 2001, 1, 44; Rick Lyman, "Hollywood Lives Its Own Cliffhanger," *New York Times*, April 30, 2001, B1, B6; Rick Lyman, "Writers Settle with Big Studios," *New York Times*, May 5, 2001, B1, B2; Dave McNary, "WGA Legacy: Relief but Also Consternation," *Daily Variety*, May 7, 2001, 1, 17; Peter Bart, "Peace Is Hell in Hollywood," *Weekly Variety*, May 14–20, 2001, 4; Dave McNary, "Scribes Seal Deal with Studios, Nets," *Daily Variety*, June 5, 2001; Dave McNary, "DGA Shows Shea the Way to 3," *Daily Variety*, June 25, 2001, 4, 13; Dave McNary, "Scribe Vibes OK with Shea," *Daily Variety*, September 3, 2001, 1, 18; and Michael Cieply, "Creative Tensions: The WGA-DGA Divide," *Los Angeles Times*, September 22, 2001, M3.
92. McNary, "WGA Talks," 27.
93. Dave McNary, "Where Credit May Be Due," *Weekly Variety*, April 14–20, 2003, 8, 43.
94. Michael Apted, "Special Notice on Possessory Credit," *DGA News*, February 2004, 7.
95. Gregg Kilday, "Michael Apted, Union Advocate," *Hollywood Reporter*, February 8, 2013, 77.
96. John Hazelton, "Writers' Rights," *Screen International*, June 29, 2007, 18.
97. "Preamble Regarding So-Called 'Possessive Credits,'" WGA Minimum Basic Agreement, 2008, 1–2, in Crawford, "Film Credits," 239.
98. Bernard Weinraub, "Screenwriters May Walk Out," C10.
99. From Steve Martin, "A Film by Steve Martin," quoted in Talent Development Resources, "Filmmaking" p. 3, http://talentdevelop.com/filmmaking3.html. Of course, as hyphenates, both Woody Allen and Martin undoubtedly feel less invested in this form of credit, since the authorship of films they both write and direct (not to mention star in) is unlikely to be questioned, even without such an on-screen mark of recognition.

4. POLITICS: THE DGA STAGES HUAC

The epigraphs to this chapter are from Michel-Rolph Trouillot, *Silencing the Past: Power and the Production of History*, 2nd ed. (Boston: Beacon, 2015), 27; and Alun Munslow, *Deconstructing History* (London: Routledge, 1997), 149.

1. For a commentary on Preston Sturges's movie as a critique of contemporary ideas about directors as creative authors, see Virginia Wright Wexman, "Preston Sturges, *Sullivan's Travels*, and Film Authorship in Hollywood, 1941," in *ReFocus: The Films of Preston Sturges*, ed. Jeff Jaekle and Sarah Kozloff (Edinburgh: Edinburgh University Press, 2015), 46–65. Sturges was one of the few major Hollywood directors who refused to join the Directors Guild.
2. See, for example, Robert Parrish, *Growing Up in Hollywood* (Boston: Little, Brown: 1976), 201–10; Fred Zinnemann, *Fred Zinnemann: An Autobiography* (London: Bloomsbury, 1992), 97–98; Douglas Bell, *An Oral History with Joseph Newman / Interviewed by Douglas Bell*, 3 vols. (Beverly Hills, Calif.: Academy of Motion Picture Arts and Sciences Oral History Program, 1995); Richard Fleischer, *Just Tell Me When to Cry: A Memoir* (New York: Carroll and Graf, 1993); and Edward Dmytryk, *Odd Man Out: A Memoir of the Hollywood Ten* (Carbondale: University of Southern Illinois Press, 1996), 143–49. The meeting is also recalled by various participants in the documentary *George Stevens: A Filmmaker's Journey* (1984), directed by George Stevens Jr. In 1987, Richard Brooks was engaged in talks with Columbia Pictures to make a movie (never realized) about the event. For information on this project, see Michael Ciepley, "The Night They Dumped DeMille," *Los Angeles Times*, June 4, 1987, part 6, 1, 6. Transcripts of the minutes of the meeting can be found in the Richard Brooks Papers, Margaret Herrick Library, Beverly Hills, Calif., folder 60–61; and in the Joseph L. Mankiewicz Papers, Margaret Herrick Library, folder DeMille/SDG, 10/22/50, no. 2. The most extended summary of the meeting itself can be found in Kevin Brianton, *Hollywood Divided: The 1950 Screen Directors Guild Meeting and the Impact of the Blacklist* (Lexington: University of Kentucky Press, 2016), 43–73.
3. The quoted account is from "The Communist Scare," *DGA Magazine*, November–December 1996, 62. I have appended a few notes to clarify certain details; these are not part of the original.
4. The Hollywood Ten also included director Herbert Biberman, who was subsequently dropped from the Guild. "SDG Demands Biberman Answer the $64 Question Before Readmitting Him," *Daily Variety*, October 3, 1952, 1, 4. Biberman was later reinstated, on the occasion of the Academy of Motion Picture Arts and Sciences 1997 symposium "Hollywood Remembers the Blacklist." Dan Margolis, "SDG's Day of Reckoning: Blacklisted Director Herbert Biberman Finally Reinstated," *Daily Variety*, October 24, 1997, 1.
5. The template for an oath of loyalty to the American government had been set by President Harry Truman's Executive Order 9835, issued in 1947; it included a pledge that the signatory was not a member of any organization deemed to be subversive, including the Nazi Party, the Ku Klux Klan, and the Communist Party.

6. The petition actually directed that Joseph Mankiewicz be recalled, not impeached.
7. This number includes both 240 senior members with voting privileges and many nonvoting junior members, including assistant directors and television directors, who were seated in the balcony.
8. John Ford actually said, "I am a director of Westerns." The rest of Ford's remarks, as reported here and elsewhere, represent a mash-up of several statements he made throughout the evening.
9. Those who were asked to resign were Claude Binyon, Frank Borzage, Clarence Brown, David Butler, Merian C. Cooper, Cecil B. DeMille, John Ford, Tay Garnett, Fritz Lang, Frank McDonald, Mark Robson, Albert Rogell, George Seiter, Richard Wallace, and John Waters. Board members representing the assistant and television directors were not asked to resign.
10. "The Communist Scare," *DGA Magazine*, November–December 1996, 62. See also Steve Pond, "A Guild Divided," in "70th Anniversary Issue," special issue, *DGA Quarterly*, Winter 2006, 92–99.
11. Brianton, *Hollywood Divided*, an extensively documented version of the meeting's context, focuses on its relationship to the latter-day reputations of Mankiewicz, Ford, and DeMille, ascribing subsequent distortions and embellishments of the record to Mankiewicz's efforts to enhance his reputation and to critics' desire to elevate the stature of Ford and diminish that of DeMille.
12. Joseph Litvak and Sarah Kozloff stress the anti-Semitism of the era, while Jon Lewis and Gerald Horne emphasize the setbacks for labor. See Joseph Litvak, *The Un-Americans: Jews, the Blacklist, and Stoolpigeon Culture* (Durham, N.C.: Duke University Press, 2009); Sarah Kozloff, "Wyler's Wars," *Film History* 20, no. 4 (2008): 456–73; Jon Lewis, "'We Do Not Ask You to Condone This . . .': How the Blacklist Saved Hollywood," *Cinema Journal* 39, no. 2 (2000): 3–30; and Gerald Horne, *Class Struggle in Hollywood, 1930–1950: Moguls, Mobsters, Stars, Reds, and Trade Unions* (Austin: University of Texas Press, 2001).

    For contemporaneous accounts of the meeting and the events surrounding it, see "DGA Calls for Loyalty Oath from Members, Applicants," *Hollywood Reporter*, August 21, 1950, 1; "SDG Non-Red Oath Disclaimed," *Daily Variety*, August 25, 1950, 1, 8; Thomas F. Brady, "Loyalty Oath Issue Raised in Hollywood," *New York Times*, August 27, 1950, X5; Thomas F. Brady, "Hollywood Divided by Loyalty Pledge Issue," *New York Times*, October 22, 1950, sec. 2, 5; "SDG's Recall of Mank Debated Far into the Night," *Hollywood Reporter*, October 23, 1950, 1; "Mankiewicz Wins: SDG Board Out: Membership Refutes DeMille, Orders Probe of Recall," *Daily Variety*, October 24, 1950, 1, 5; "Mank Group to Draft Plans for New SDG Board," *Hollywood Reporter*, October 24, 1950, 1, 8; "Mank Meets with SDG Leaders," *Hollywood Reporter*, October 26,

1950, 2; "Mank in Plea for Action on Oath," *Hollywood Reporter*, October 27, 1950, 1, 6; "Choose Temporary SDG Board and Officers," *Daily Variety*, October 27, 1950, 3; Thomas F. Brady, "Hollywood Turmoil," *New York Times*, October 29, 1950, X2; "Pro-Tem Board to Hold First Meet," *Hollywood Reporter*, November 1, 1950, 1; "SDG to Complete Reorganization," *Hollywood Reporter*, November 15, 1950, 1. Extensive records of press coverage of the House Un-American Activities Committee hearings can be found in the Jack Warner Papers, University of Southern California, Los Angeles; and the Mankiewicz Papers.

13. For a lengthy discussion of this shift, see Thomas Schatz, *Boom and Bust: American Cinema in the 1940s* (Berkeley: University of California Press, 1999).
14. The merger of the Directors Guild of America with the Radio and Television Directors Guild is described in detail in chapter 1.
15. For discussions of the Conference of Studio Unions, see Mike Nielsen and Gene Mailes, *Hollywood's Other Blacklist: Union Struggles in the Studio System* (London: British Film Institute, 1995); Lloyd Billingsley, *Hollywood Party: How Communism Seduced the American Film Industry in the 1930s and 1940s* (Roseville, Calif.: Forum, 2000); Ronald Radosh and Allis Radosh, *Red Stars over Hollywood: The Film Colony's Long Romance with the Left* (San Francisco: Encounter, 2005); and John H. M. Laslett, *Sunshine Was Never Enough: Los Angeles Workers, 1880–2010* (Berkeley: University of California Press, 2012), 210–14.
16. An earlier incarnation of the committee, under the chairmanship of Martin Dies (D-Tex.), was active from 1938 to 1944. In 1941, a Senate-led investigation into Hollywood's "warmongering" was cochaired by Gerald Nye (R-N.D.) and Bennett Champ Clark (D-Mo.); this committee ascribed the problem to a Jewish conspiracy promulgated by moviemakers who had been born abroad. Thomas Doherty offers an extensive analysis of this period. Doherty, *Show Trial: Hollywood, HUAC, and the Birth of the Blacklist* (New York: Columbia University Press, 2018).
17. Though membership in the Communist Party was at no time a crime in itself, HUAC's unfriendly witnesses could be cited for contempt of Congress if they refused to name others who were Communist Party members. Moreover, because party membership was not a crime, witnesses who wished to remain silent were not covered by Fifth Amendment protections against self-incrimination.
18. Other directors who belonged to the thirty-five-member Committee on the First Amendment included Richard Brooks, Melvin Frank, Anatole Litvak, Norman Krasna, and Billy Wilder.
19. William Wyler Papers, Margaret Herrick Library, box 46, folder 686, Political Clippings.

20. "Trade Views," *Hollywood Reporter*, July 25, 1950, 1. In 2012, the *Hollywood Reporter* ran a spate of articles that apologized for the leading role played by its one-time editor W. R. Wilkerson in stirring up the HUAC controversy, beginning in July of 1946. Gary Baum and Daniel Miller, "The Most Sinful Period in Hollywood History," *Hollywood Reporter*, November 30, 2012, 49–57, 67.
21. David Prindle, *The Politics of Glamour* (Madison: University of Wisconsin Press, 1988).
22. A report on this meeting, by Sheridan Gibney, is included in Wyler Papers, box 46, folder 590.
23. Association of Motion Picture Producers, "The Waldorf Statement" (December 3, 1947), in Steven Ross, *Movies and American Society* (Malden, Mass.: Blackwell, 2002), 217–18. Although the studios had hoped the Waldorf Statement would quiet public suspicions about Hollywood's putatively subversive culture, a second round of HUAC hearings targeting the film industry began in 1951 and continued until 1954.
24. The DGA committee that recommended this step included George Stevens, Merian C. Cooper, John Huston, George Sidney, and William Wyler. John Ford was chair. A copy of the committee's report can be found in the Directors Guild of America Files, California State University, Northridge, box 9, folder 1. See also "Johnson's Statement on Reds Blasted by SDG," *Los Angeles Examiner*, December 23, 1947, 1; "Screen Directors Rap Anti-Red Statement," *Los Angeles Herald-Express*, December 23, 1947, A2, Mankiewicz Papers, box 44, folder 84, L.A. Papers, December 23, 1947.
25. Reports of the DGA's response to Sam Wood's testimony can be found in "Wood's Red Probe Charges Denied by Directors Guild," *Daily Variety*, October 23, 1947, 10; and Scott Eyman, *Print the Legend: The Life and Times of John Ford* (New York: Simon and Schuster, 1999), 374–77.
26. "Cards on the Table," *Daily Variety*, October 21, 1947, 3.
27. "Reds Tried to Infiltrate Directors Guild, Probe Told," *Atlanta Journal*, October 20, 1941, 1.
28. A transcript of Wood's testimony can be found in DGA Files, box 9, folder 1; and in the John Huston Papers, Margaret Herrick Library, box 1688, SDG. Wood was the first president of the Motion Picture Alliance for the Preservation of American Ideals, a conservative organization dedicated to fighting communism, founded in 1944, in which C. B. DeMille was also active.
29. In a telegram Wood later sent to the committee, he added the name of Lewis Milestone. "Reds Have Hollywood Inside," *Daily Variety*, October 23, 1947, 8.
30. Larry Ceplair and Steven Englund, *The Inquisition in Hollywood: Politics in the Film Community, 1930–60* (Urbana: University of Illinois Press, 2003), 339; Alan Casty, *Robert Rossen* (Jefferson, N.C.: McFarland, 2013), 125; Herbert Biberman,

"Memoir: In Defense of America," in Herbert Biberman Papers, Wisconsin Historical Society, Madison, box 21, folder 12.

31. The Guild's letter to J. Parnell Thomas is cited in the clearance letter William Wyler later wrote to disassociate himself from the communist cause. Wyler Papers, box 46, folder 688, Personal and Political. The Guild also publicized its policy of disallowing Communists from serving as officers. "Directors Fite Commies, Bar Them as Officers," *Daily Variety*, December 4, 1947, 1, 9.

32. John Huston, *An Open Book* (New York: Da Capo, 1980), 135. The proposed oath stated, "I am not a member of the Communist Party or affiliated with such party, and I do not believe in, and I am not a member of nor do I support any organization that believes in or teaches the overthrow of the United States Government by force or by any illegal or unconstitutional methods." Huston Papers, Folder 1699, SDG 1950.

33. The numbered ballots enabled the ballots to be traced back to their recipients, thus negating the anonymity of the voting process.

34. Several board members abstained from the no confidence vote, including Frank Borzage, Claude Binyon, Merian C. Cooper, John Ford, Walter Lang, Mark Robson, and George Sidney. Frank Capra was among those who voted against Mankiewicz. See telegram to Fred Zinnemann from members of the SDG board, October 13, 1950, Fred Zinnemann Papers, Margaret Herrick Library, box 120, folder 2, SDG 1949–51.

35. There is reason to suspect that DeMille had maneuvered to install Vernon Keays in this post as part of his overall strategy for enabling quick action on the loyalty oath. The DGA's former executive secretary, William Holman, had been summarily fired just four months earlier, and Keays, a former DeMille employee, was installed in his place. Holman voiced strong objections to the Guild's treatment of him, and board member George Stevens resisted signing Holman's letter of termination, presumably out of concern over the propriety of this action. George Stevens Papers, Margaret Herrick Library, box 17, folder 1. See also "Holman Sues SDG, Claims $9,800 Due Him on Dismissal," *Daily Variety*, July 26, 1950, 3. Mankiewicz was later to recall, "The Guild had been run for months out of C. B. DeMille's office." "When the Red Scare Gripped the Directors Guild," *DGA Newsletter*, June 1955, 4.

36. A copy of one of these ballots, along with other documents relating to the DGA's proposed loyalty oath, are reproduced in Zinnemann, *Fred Zinnemann*, 250–52. Many more of the key documents related to this fracas can be found in Zinnemann Papers, box 120, folder 2, SDG 1949–51; and Wyler Papers, box 46, folder 599. Zinnemann himself objected vehemently to the voting procedure at the time. "I am bitterly opposed to the undemocratic method you have adopted in trying to pass this measure," he stated in an undated letter to the Guild. "You

have required a signed vote rather than a secret ballot." Zinnemann Papers, box 120, folder 2, SDG 1949–51.

37. Among those who signed the petition were Richard Brooks, John Farrow, Richard Fleischer, Michael Gordon, Don Hartman, John Huston, Joseph Losey, Andrew Marton, Jean Negulesco, Robert Parrish, Nicholas Ray, Mark Robson, George Seaton, John Sturges, Charles Vidor, King Vidor, Billy Wilder, Robert Wise, William Wyler, and Fred Zinnemann. For a contemporaneous report on this development, see "Mank Recall Move Opposed by 25 Directors," *Film Daily*, October 17, 1950, 2.

38. Though the Guild's office was not officially open on Saturdays, there had always been workers present there before. When George Stevens questioned the staff, they reported that Keays had instructed them to stay home on that particular Saturday. Mankiewicz Papers, box, DGA Meeting 10/22/50, folder, DeMille/SDG, October 22, 1950, no. 2.

39. For a contemporaneous report on the Board's about-face, see "SDG Board Calls Special Meet: Factions on Mank Issue Conferring Tonight: SDG Board Rejects Oath," *Hollywood Reporter*, October 18, 1950, 1, 4; "Armistice Over Mank: SDG Board Factions Give Prexy Confidence Vote: Okay Proxies for Mtg," *Hollywood Reporter*, October 19, 1950, 1, 5; and "SDG Votes Confidence in Mark," *Film Daily*, October 24, 1950, 2.

40. Transcript of DGA meeting, Brooks Papers, folders 60, 72.

41. For an example of journalistic attacks on the political slant of Capra's films, see Hedda Hopper, "Looking at Hollywood," *Chicago Tribune/New York News Syndicate*, Warner Papers, box 45, folder 177, Industry Clips, 1947.

42. Letter from Frank Capra to John Ford, December 19, 1951, in John Ford Papers, Lilly Library, Indiana University Bloomington, box 3, folder 6.

43. "DGA Schism on Blacklist: Mankiewicz Will Not Sign Oath," *Daily Variety*, October 11, 1950, 1, 5. Capra later claimed that the *Variety* article "blew [the DGA board] to pieces." He charged that only someone on the board itself could have leaked the story, given the level of detail it contained. Frank Capra, letter to board of directors, October 27, 1950, 7, in Frank Capra Papers, Wesleyan University, Middletown, Conn., box 3, Professional Organizations. Kenneth Geist claims that the leak had come from the DeMille faction, but given *Variety*'s consistent tone of bias toward Mankiewicz, this conclusion is difficult to accept. Geist, *Pictures Will Talk: The Life and Films of Joseph L. Mankiewicz* (New York: Da Capo, 1978), 181.

44. Capra, letter to board of directors, October 27, 1950, 2–3. Having resigned from the board in mid-October, Capra was not present at the Beverly Hills Hotel meeting.

45. Capra, letter to board of directors, October 27, 1950, 5.

46. Capra, letter to board of directors, October 27, 1950, 5.
47. Letter from John Ford to Army, Navy, and Air Force Personnel Security Board, December 1951, in Ford Papers, box 3, folder 6.
48. Other prominent directors who belonged to the Motion Picture Alliance included Clarence Brown, Cecil B. DeMille, Victor Fleming, Leo McCarey, Fred Niblo, Norman Taurog, King Vidor, and Sam Wood.

    On October 21, the day before the Beverly Hills Hotel meeting, DeMille sent a telegram to Clarence Brown stating, "John Ford is with us." Cecil B. DeMille Papers, Brigham Young University, Provo, Utah, box 42, folder 4. Yet Ford had declined to join the recall committee. Ford's increasingly conservative political stance throughout the 1940s and 1950s is described in Joseph McBride, *Searching for John Ford: A Life* (New York: St. Martin's Griffin, 2001).
49. Notes on a telephone call from John Ford to Cecil B. DeMille, DeMille Papers, box 421, folder 5.
50. Draft of minutes of board of directors meeting, September 5, 1950, Mankiewicz Papers, folder Demille/SDG. The others who were opposed were Capra, Clarence Brown, and Mark Robson.
51. Scott Eyman, *Empire of Dreams: The Epic Life of Cecil B. DeMille* (New York: Simon and Schuster, 2010), 410.
52. Joseph Youngerman, *My Seventy Years at Paramount and the Directors Guild of America* (Los Angeles: Directors Guild of America, 1995), 91.
53. Geist, *Pictures Will Talk*, 203.
54. Roy Brewer had formerly headed the International Alliance of Theatrical and State Employees, a conservative union that had vied with the Conference of Studio Unions for control of Hollywood's below-the-line workers during the 1930s.
55. Wyler Papers, box 46, folder 688, Personal and Political.
56. Marsha Hunt describes her meeting with Huston in *Marsha Hunt's Sweet Adversity* (2015), a documentary about her life, directed by Roger Memo.
57. Victor Riesel, "U.S. Movie Director to Fight Reds on Propaganda Front," *Daily Oklahoman*, March 18, 1953, 18, Wyler Papers, box 46, folder 688, Personal.
58. Wyler Papers, box 46, folder 688, Personal. For discussions of this incident in the context of William Wyler's ongoing political struggles in Hollywood, see Gabriel Miller, *William Wyler* (Lexington: University Press of Kentucky, 2013), 315–17; and Kozloff, "Wyler's Wars."
59. Wyler Papers, box 46, folder 688, Personal and Political.
60. Wyler Papers, box 46, folder 688, Personal and Political.
61. Geist, *Pictures Will Talk*, 191. See also Greg Mitchell, *Tricky Dick and the Pink Lady: Richard Nixon vs. Helen Gahagan Douglas—Sexual Politics and the Red Scare, 1950* (New York: Random House, 1998), 218.

62. Elia Kazan, *A Life* (New York: Alfred A. Knopf, 1988), 393.
63. Kazan, *A Life*, 393.
64. Geist, *Pictures Will Talk*, 173.
65. From as early as April 1937, DeMille was engaged in collecting information on Herbert Biberman, Irving Pichel, Vincent Sherman, and Frank Tuttle. Letter to Gladys Rosson from John W. Milner, public relations representative, DeMille Foundation for Political Freedom, April 20, 1947, DeMille Papers, box 124.
66. Geist, *Pictures Will Talk*, 179. A draft copy of DeMille's speech can be found in DeMille Papers, box 942, folder 4. This draft also contains a proposal by DeMille to withdraw the recall petition, though he never put this forward.
67. "Mankiewicz Pleads the Cause of the Liberal in U.S.," *Daily Variety*, September 15, 1950, 6; "Mankiewicz on 'The New Minority,'" *Weekly Variety*, September 20, 1950, 22.
68. An earlier statement Mankiewicz published in *Variety* on October 19, 1950, attested to his focus on the matter of a secret ballot. "As long as I am president of the Screen Directors Guild of America," this statement read, in part, "I will continue to fight for the right of every member to open discussion and a closed ballot" (4).
69. The Taft–Hartley Act required all union leaders to sign such an oath.
70. Geist, *Pictures Will Talk*, 205.
71. Capra, letter to board of directors, October 27, 1950, 2, 7. By "the opposition," Capra meant those board members, including himself, along with DeMille and others, who had supported the recall.
72. Eyman, *Empire*, 411.
73. Whether the oath was to be mandatory or voluntary was a distinction without a difference, since DGA members who refused to sign would be vulnerable to blacklisting in either case. Despite Mankiewicz's capitulation on the question of the loyalty oath, the conservatives in the DGA were not pacified. The following May, they circulated an anonymous letter to selected members that urged those sympathetic to the cause to pack the incoming board with a preselected slate of men "whose personal character, patriotism and loyalty to the guild cannot be questioned." Capra's name appeared as part of this slate. Zinnemann Papers, box 120, folder 2, SDG 1949–51; DeMille Papers, box 950, folder 3.
74. Unity Committee report, Capra Papers, box 3, Professional Organizations.
75. Unity Committee report, Capra Papers, box 3, Professional Organizations. In a letter to Capra on November 1, 1950, Mankiewicz states, "After consulting with George Stevens, George Sidney and King Vidor, it was unanimously decided not to read your letter to the Board." Mankiewicz Papers, box DeMille/SDG.
76. Unity Committee report, Capra Papers, box 3, Professional Organizations.

77. Hayden White, *The Content of the Form: Narrative Discourse and Historical Representation* (Baltimore, Md.: Johns Hopkins University Press, 1987). For more recent elaborations and critiques of White's approach, see Mark Poster, *Cultural History and Postmodernity* (New York: Columbia University Press, 1997); Alun Munslow, *Narrative and History* (New York: Palgrave Macmillan, 2007); and Sarah Maza, *Thinking About History* (Chicago: University of Chicago Press, 2017).
78. For a summary of these approaches, see Rohan McWilliam, "Melodrama and the Historians," *Radical History Review* 78 (2000): 57–84.
79. Richard Maltby, "Made for Each Other: The Melodrama of Hollywood and the House Committee on Un-American Activities, 1947," in *Cinema, Politics, and Society in America*, ed. Philip Davies and Brian Neve (New York: St. Martin's, 1981), 76–96.
80. Neal Gabler, "Why the Drama Never Ends," *Los Angeles Times*, March 21, 1999, M1, M6. In a presentation at the WGA Theater in Beverly Hills on October 27, 2017, as part of a program commemorating the seventieth anniversary of the blacklist, Ben Mankiewicz, grandnephew of Joseph Mankiewicz, likened the DGA's meeting to a Western, culminating in a symbolic shootout between Ford and DeMille.
81. Both Maltby and Gabler use, somewhat loosely, the term "melodrama," which has since become a fraught concept in media studies. In what follows, I employ a traditional definition of this mode, which derives from its formal features, and avoid the more recent controversies over contested terms such as "excess," "muteness," and "classical." For recent definitions and debates around the term, see Linda Williams, "Melodrama," Oxford Bibliographies, 2011, http://www.oxfordbibliographies.com; and Christine Gledhill and Linda Williams, eds., *Melodrama Unbound: Across History, Media, and National Cultures* (New York: Columbia University Press, 2018).
82. Bell, *Oral History*, 701.
83. Early in the evening, Mankiewicz asked that all speakers identify themselves for the benefit of the stenographer, but most did not bother to do so. Ford's self-naming was thus a choice.
84. As Douglas Sirk later recalled, "People were so surprised that the great John Ford had chosen to categorize himself like that." McBride, *Searching*, 416.
85. Darr Smith, "Darr Smith," *Los Angeles Daily News*, January 24, 1949, Albert Rogell Clipping Files, Margaret Herrick Library.
86. Among many examples is a letter to Frank Capra from DGA executive secretary F. Herrick Herrick, dated July 7, 1938: "Dick Wallace called my attention to the fact that there are many aliens here who are making pictures . . . who

probably should not be here at all." Capra Papers, box 2, Correspondence 1938, July–Sept.

87. Both Eyman and Brianton note that the offensive portion of DeMille's remarks at the Beverly Hills Hotel meeting does not appear in the official minutes and suggest that it was a story later concocted to smear him. However, the minutes do record that, later in the meeting, both Fritz Lang and Rouben Mamoulian made rueful statements about their accents. Moreover, in a 1985 interview with Joseph McBride, Mamoulian recalled DeMille taunting him about his foreign background. McBride, *Searching*, 482. See also McBride, *Frank Capra: The Catastrophe of Success* (New York: Simon and Schuster, 1992), 578. Moreover, several of those present later recalled that DeMille referred to the foreign origins of some signers of the meeting petition and spoke their names with a foreign accent. Parrish, *Growing Up*, 208; Ed Sikov, *On Sunset Boulevard: The Life and Times of Billy Wilder* (New York: Hyperion, 1998), 332. In addition, Mankiewicz refers to DeMille's caricature of a Yiddish accent in George Stevens Jr.'s documentary *George Stevens*. However, such a reference does not appear in the transcript of the meeting itself. The most likely explanation is that the minutes were subsequently redacted to remove DeMille's ethnic slurs (possibly at his own request) in order to avoid embarrassing him.

88. At the time of the meeting, Ida Lupino was the only woman who was a senior member of the DGA. She attended the Beverly Hills Hotel meeting but did not speak. For a discussion of the low profile kept by gay members of the Guild, see appendix A.

89. According to Mankiewicz, DeMille had arranged for the Crystal Room to be fitted with a flattering pink spotlight, which was to be trained on him during the October 22 meeting. Geist, *Pictures Will Talk*, 193. Though presumably flattering, such a self-presentation would not have added to DeMille's aura of masculinity.

90. George Sidney stated that the award was initiated specifically to placate DeMille. See "DGA 60 Years," *DGA Magazine*, November–December 1962, 62.

91. "IMPPA Endorses SAG-Style Oath," *Daily Variety*, October 27, 1950, 5. For a discussion of the circumstances surrounding the actors' capitulation to this test of patriotism, see K. Kevyne Baar, "'What Has My Union Done For Me?': The Screen Actors Guild, the American Federation of Television and Radio Artists, and Actors' Equity Association Respond to McCarthy-Era Blacklisting," *Film History* 20, no. 4 (2008): 437–55. For accounts about the loyalty oath issue in the trade press of the day, see "Spark All Ind Loyalty Oath: Pattern Set by Producers, Directors," *Daily Variety*, October 3, 1950; "MPIC Details Its Proposed 3-Part Loyalty Oath," *Daily Variety*, October 11, 1950, 7; "Vote 'Blacklist' for Non-Signers of DGA Loyalty Oath," *Weekly Variety*, October 11, 1950, 3, 61;

"Producers Guild vs. MPIC Oath," *Hollywood Reporter,* October 13, 1950, 1; "Proposed Loyalty Oath Referred to 19-Member Committee," *Daily Variety,* October 19, 1950, 1, 19; "Screen Guild Backing Given Mankiewicz," *Los Angeles Times,* October 24, 1950, 13; and "MPA Walks Out of MPIC Talks, Renewing Drive on Hollywood Reds," *Daily Variety,* December 4, 1950, 1, 3.

92. The DGA loyalty oath was challenged in court by Screen Directors International Guild members Leo Hurwitz, Lee Bobker, Robert Braverman, Gene Searchinger, Darrell Random, and Hilary T. Harris. For accounts of the case, see "Loyalty Oath Goes with Wedding, but East's Directors Detest Proviso," *Weekly Variety,* February 10, 1965, 15; Peter Bart, "Directors Query Oath Statement," *New York Times,* October 19, 1965, 50; Sidney E. Zion, "U.S. Court Voids a Loyalty Oath," *New York Times,* July 15, 1966, 36; "Directors Guild Denied Encore," *Civil Liberties,* December 1966, 6; and "Directors Guild Is Ordered to Drop Oath Requirement," *New York Times,* January 28, 1967, 17.
93. For a description of the resistance mounted by DGA members, see Leo Hurwitz, "Response to Fred Zinnemann," *DGA Newsletter,* November 1986, 4.
94. Letter from Joseph Mankiewicz to Gene Searchinger, February 11, 1967, 2, in Mankiewicz Papers, folder DeMille, SDG/Misc.

5. LAW: THE DGA AND ARTISTS AS OWNERS

The epigraphs to this chapter are from the following sources: Miloš Forman, quoted in Chuck Crisafulli, "Rights and Wrongs," *Hollywood Reporter,* April 1, 1997, S4; Bernard Edelman, *Ownership of the Image: Elements for a Marxist Theory of Law* (London: Routledge and Kegan Paul, 1979), 51.

1. For a discussion of the centrality of property rights in American law, see David Schultz, *Property, Power, and American Democracy* (New Brunswick, N.J.: Transaction, 1992).
2. "70 Years of Milestones," in "70th Anniversary Issue," special issue, *DGA Quarterly,* Winter 2006, 56–77. http://www.dga.org/Craft/DGAQ/All-Articles/0604-Winter2006-07/Features-70-Years-of-Milestones.aspx
3. *Siskel & Ebert & the Movies—Colorization, Hollywood's New Vandalism (1 of 4),* video, 8:23, March 5, 2011, https://www.youtube.com/watch?v=YpT1DkBOnq0.
4. Leslie Bennetts, "Colorization: A Boon or a Bane," *New York Times,* August 5, 1986, A1. For other contemporanous reports on the colorization controversy, see Philip Elmer-DeWitt, "Play It Again, This Time in Color," *Time,* October 8, 1984, 83; Todd McCarthy, "Color Institute B & W When It Comes to Vintage Films," *Daily Variety,* October 2, 1986, 28; Robert Osborne, "Rambling Reporter," *Hollywood Reporter,* October 7, 1986, 2; David Robb, "ASC Joins Opposition to B & W Coloring," *Daily Variety,* October 8, 1986, 1; Richard Corliss, "Raiders of

the Lost Art," *Time*, October 20, 1986, 98; Vincent Canby, "'Colorization' Is Defacing Black and White Film Classics," *New York Times*, November 2, 1986, 1, 21; Michael Dempsey, "Colorization," *Film Quarterly* 40, no. 2 (Winter 1986–87): 2–3; David Robb, "Huston's Cup Overfloweth with Harsh Words for B & W Colorizing and Ted Turner," *Daily Variety*, November 14, 1986, 28; Aljean Harmetz, "Huston Protests Coloring of 'Falcon,'" *New York Times*, November 14, 1986, C36; Roger L Mayer, "Colorization: The Arguments For," *Journal of Arts Management and Law* 17, no. 3 (Fall 1987): 64–78; Woody Allen et al., "Colorization: The Arguments Against," *Journal of Arts and Management* 17, no. 3 (Fall 1987): 79–93; Roger L. Mayer, "Colorization: It's the People's Choice," *Video Review*, 116 (Fred Zinnemann Papers, Margaret Herrick Library, Beverly Hills, Calif., box 121, folder 1, Directors Guild of America, 1987–1988; and Stephen Farber, "The Man Hollywood Loves to Hate," *Los Angeles Times Magazine*, April 30, 1989, 9–20, 39. Overviews of the controversy can be found in Stuart Klawans, "Rose-Tinted Spectacles," in *Seeing Through Movies*, ed. Mark Crispin Miller (New York: Pantheon, 1990), 150–85; and Anthony Slide, *Nitrate Won't Wait: A History of Film Preservation* (Jefferson, N.C.: McFarland, 1992), 122–33.

5. Both Gary Edgerton and Carolyn Frick have argued that the DGA became active on the colorization issue to gain the moral high ground in a dispute the Guild was engaged in with the studios over residuals. Gary Edgerton, "The Germans Wore Gray, You Wore Blue," *Journal of Popular Film and Television* 27, no. 4 (Winter 2000), 24–32; Carolyn Frick, *Saving Cinema: The Politics of Preservation* (New York: Oxford University Press, 2011). However, this view does not take into account the group's long-standing focus on creative rights.

6. "Blurb Belches in Pix on TV Disturb DGA," *Daily Variety*, November 12, 1965, 1, 4.

7. Thomas M. Pryor, "Film Code Upheld by Directors Unit," *New York Times*, June 14, 1955, 26.

8. For a histories of moviemakers' attempts to assert ownership rights to their films, see Peter Decherney, *Hollywood's Copyright Wars: From Edison to the Internet* (New York: Columbia University Press, 2012); and Douglas Gomery, *Shared Pleasures: A History of Movie Presentation in the United States* (Madison: University of Wisconsin Press, 1992), 257–62. Laura Wittern-Keller describes the way in which the directors' efforts dovetailed with the legal wrangling over whether the film could be considered art and thus protected as such, from the Mutual decision in 1915 (which held that movies were a business) to the *Miracle* decision in 1952 (which recognized film as a form of artistic expression and thus entitled to protection under the First Amendment). Keller, *Freedom of the Screen: Legal Challenges to State Film Censorship, 1915–1981* (Lexington: University of Kentucky Press, 2008).

The legal wrangling over the issue of authorial ownership (and the accompanying rights that ownership implies) has a long history in the literary arena. For discussions of this history, see Martha Woodmansee, *The Author, Art, and the Market: Rereading the History of Aesthetics* (New York: Columbia University Press, 1994); Roger Chartier, *The Order of Books: Readers, Authors, and Libraries in Europe Between the Fourteenth and Eighteenth Centuries*, trans. Lydia G. Cochrane (Stanford, Calif.: Stanford University Press, 1994); Roger Chartier, "Figures of the Author," in *Of Authors and Origins: Essays on Copyright Law*, ed. Brad Sherman and Alan Strowell (New York: Oxford University Press, 1994), 7–22; Mark Rose, *Authors and Owners: The Invention of Copyright* (Cambridge, Mass.: Harvard University Press, 1995); Grantland S. Rice, *The Transformation of Authorship in America* (Chicago: University of Chicago Press, 1997); and Siva Vaidhyanathan, *Copyrights and Copywrongs: The Rise of Intellectual Property and How It Threatens Creativity* (New York: New York University Press, 2001).

9. Zinnemann Papers, box 117, folder 3, Colorization 1986, April–August. For press reports on the American Film Institute's public response, see Cliff Rothman, "AFI Blasts Colorization, Sets Forum to Resolve Controversy," *Hollywood Reporter*, October 2, 1986, 1, 8; Jack Mathews, "A Sneak Preview of the Colorization Wars," *Los Angeles Times*, October 2, 1986, 1, 3; and Todd McCarthy, "Color Institute Black and White When It Comes to Vintage Films," *Daily Variety*, October 2, 1986, 1, 28.

10. Other DGA members who sent letters to the DGA asking the organization to take action in response to George Stevens Jr.'s alert included Woody Allen, John Huston, and Elia Kazan. Zinnemann Papers, box 117, folder 3, Colorization 1986, April–August. David T. Friendly reports on a DGA press conference in which the group protested the practice of airing colorized films on television. Friendly, "War Against Colorization Joined by John Huston," *Los Angeles Times*, November 14, 1986, Calendar, 1, 15. See also Chuck Ross, "Mayer Speaks for Film Colorization," *Hollywood Reporter*, November 13, 1986, 1, 17; and Ross, "Huston Urges Product Boycott by Public to Fight Colorization," *Hollywood Reporter*, November 14, 1986, 1, 4.

11. Terry Ilot, "U.K. Directors Guild Launches Anti-Colorization Campaign," *Screen International*, September 9, 1986, 4; "Fred Zinnemann Sees Red Over Colorizing Classics," *Daily Variety*, September 10, 1986, 8; Quentin Falk, "Black and White and Bright All Over," *London Sunday Telegraph*, November 16, 1986, 57–58; Mike Downer, "Copyright: A Time to Act," *Direct*, September–October 1987, 10. A DGA report on Zinnemann's activities in the United Kingdom can be found in the *DGA Newsletter*, September 1986, 1, 2, Joseph L. Mankiewicz Papers, Margaret Herrick Library, folder, DGA Newsletters.

12. This last possibility became a more problematic issue when rereleases of films labeled as director's cuts became popular in the 1990s, as described in chapter 2.
13. Letter to George Stevens, May 16, 1986, Zinnemann Papers, box 117, folder 3, Colorization 1986, April–August. See also Fred Zinnemann, "Colorization Is Not a Black and White Issue," *Daily Variety*, March 17, 1989, 42, 52. Zinnemann continued to be deeply concerned about this matter until his death in 1997, and his papers contain voluminous records of his activities.
14. Cliff Rothman, "Colorized Classics Raise Capra's Ire," *Hollywood Reporter*, March 15, 1985, 1. Rothman reports that there were various versions of the events surrounding this negotiation. One version has it that the Glicks first approached Capra, believing that he owned the copyright to *It's a Wonderful Life*. When they eventually discovered that the film was in the public domain, they cut the director out of the deal. Capra himself tells a different story. In a letter to Dorothy Shrader of the U.S. Copyright Office, he claimed that he initially believed that the Glicks held the copyright and had backed out of the deal himself when he discovered that the rights were not the Glicks to give. Letter from Frank Capra to Dorothy Shrader, December 13, 1984, Zinnemann Papers, box 117, folder 3: Colorization, 1986, April–August.

    Capra did own copyright to many of his other films, as did many other directors of the day, including Charlie Chaplin, Alfred Hitchcock, Otto Preminger, and George Stevens. Elliot Forbes and David Pierce, "Who Owns the Movies?," *Film Comment* 30, no. 6 (1994): 49.

    The Creative Rights Committee was originally called the President's Committee.
15. The lawmakers who worked to further the DGA's interests in Washington included senators Edward Kennedy (D-Mass.) and Patrick Leahy (D-Vt.), and congressmen Thomas Downey (D-N.Y.), Barney Frank (D-Mass.), Richard Gephardt (D-Mo.), Robert Kastenmeier (D-Wis.), Robert Mrazek (D-N.Y.), Alan Simpson (R-Wyo.), and Sidney Yates (D-Ill.). Mrazek, in particular, became very active on these issues. He and his wife were close friends of Zinnemann's and great admirers of his films. In 1999, Mrazek arranged for Zinnemann to receive a Congressional Gold Medal, along with Frank Capra and James Stewart, who had also been active in the colorization battle on Capitol Hill.

    For reports on the DGA's activities in Washington around colorization, see Thomas M. Pryor, "Senate to Explore Merits of Colorizing Film Classics—as Defined by Whom?," *Daily Variety*, April 14, 1987, 1; "Morning Report," *Los Angeles Times*, April 14, 1987, part 6; Teresa McMasters, "Directors Denounce Colorizing 'Butchers' in Plea to Congress," *Hollywood Reporter*, May 13, 1987, 1, 4; Paul Harris, "Cinematic Art vs. Technology," *Daily Variety*, May 13, 1987, 1,

14; Penny Pagano, "Colorization Gets a Senate Hearing," *Los Angeles Times*, May 13, 1987, part 4, 1, 4; "Pic Coloring Political Grist," *Daily Variety*, May 14, 1987, 1, 8; Teresa McMasters, "Gephart Proposes Anti-Coloring Bill," *Hollywood Reporter*, May 14, 1987, 1, 8; David Robb, "DGA Sings 'My Way' for Studios: Ban on Colorizing Heads Directors Guild List of Creative Rights," *Daily Variety*, May 26, 1987, 1–3; David Robb, "Directors Push to Protect Their Films," *Daily Variety*, May 27, 1987, 5, 37; Chuck Warn, DGA Press Release on Colorization, June 26, 1987, Artists Rights Foundation Clipping File, Margaret Herrick Library; "Final Say Over Films at Issue," *New York Times*, March 4, 1988, in ARF Clipping File; Don Shannon, "Angry Movie Personalities Go to Washington," *Los Angeles Times*, March 16, 1988, ARF Clipping File; "Guild Takes Moral Right Cause to U.S. Capital," *DGA Newsletter*, April 1988, 4, 7; David Robb, "Colorizing Hearings to Spice Up Capital," *Daily Variety*, May 26, 1988, 1, 21; Michael Martinez, "DGA, WGA Reps Play Berne Push for Moral Rights," *Hollywood Reporter*, June 27, 1990, 1, 5; and Andrew F. Yarrow, "Action But No Consensus on Film Coloring," *New York Times*, August 2, 1988, C13, C16.
16. Todd McCarthy, "Directing His Life to a Principle," *Daily Variety*, April 27, 1990, 22.
17. For discussions of the differences between moral rights and copyright doctrine, see Vincent Porter, "Film Copyright: Film Culture," *Screen* 19, no. 1 (Spring 1978): 90–108; Justin Hughes, "The Personality Interest of Artists and Inventors in Intellectual Property," *Cardozo Arts and Entertainment Journal* 16, no. 1 (1988): 81–182; Jane Ginsburg, "A Tale of Two Copyrights: Literary Property in Revolutionary France and America," *Tulane Law Review* 64 (1990): 991–1031; David Saunders, *Authorship and Copyright* (New York: Routledge, 1992); Marjut Salokannel, "Film Authorship in a Changing Audio-Visual Environment," in *Of Authors and Origins: Essays on Copyright Law*, ed. Brad Sherman and Alan Strowell (New York: Oxford University Press, 1994), 58–77; Jane Ginsburg, "The Concept of Authorship in Comparative Copyright Law," *DePaul Law Review* 52, no. 4 (Summer 2003): 1063–92; and Paul Goldstein, "The Two Cultures of Copyright," in *Copyright's Highway: From Gutenberg to the Celestial Jukebox*, rev. ed. (Stanford, Calif.: Stanford University Press, 2003), 135–62. Robert Davenport discusses this difference as it relates to screen credits. Davenport, "Screen Credit in the Entertainment Industries," *Loyola Entertainment Law Journal* 10, no. 1 (1990): 129–61.
18. Goldstein, "Two Cultures," 136.
19. Pacal Kamina, *Film Copyright in the European Union* (Cambridge, Mass.: Cambridge University Press, 2002), 285.
20. "Berne Convention for the Protection of Literary and Artistic Works (Paris Text 1971)," Article 6*bis*, Legal Information Institute, Cornell Law School,

https://www.law.cornell.edu/treaties/berne/6bis.html. For a report on the DGA's intervention in the deliberations taking place in Geneva around the Berne treaty, see Amy Dawes, "DGA to Push Moral Rights Fight at Geneva Meeting," *Daily Variety*, June 27, 1990, 27.

The moral rights issue had actually emerged in the United States earlier, during congressional hearings on colorization in the mid-1980s and in the 1987 contract talks between the DGA and the Alliance of Motion Picture and Television Producers.

21. Lee May, "Reagan Authorizes Copyright Expansion," *Los Angeles Times*, November 1, 1988, ARF Clipping File. At the time the Berne treaty was being negotiated, Congress invoked American laws dealing with slander and libel to claim that the United States conformed in a minimal way with the language of the treaty, thus enabling the American representatives to sign the document without compromising the Anglo-American copyright tradition. The legal protocols governing moral rights and copyright remain far apart.

22. Henry Campbell Black et al., *Black's Law Dictionary* (St. Paul, Minn.: West Publishing, 1990), 1606. The history of the work-for-hire doctrine is traced in Catherine Fisk, "Authors at Work: The Origins of the Work-for-Hire Doctrine," *Yale Journal of Law and the Humanities* 15, no. 1 (2003): 32–70; and Fisk, *Writing for Hire: Unions, Hollywood, and Madison Avenue* (Cambridge, Mass.: Harvard University Press, 2016). The media industry's ongoing struggles with this judicial tradition are explored in Matt Stahl, "Privilege and Distinction in Production Worlds: Copyright, Collective Bargaining, and Working Conditions in Media," in *Production Culture: Cultural Studies of Media Industries*, ed. Vicki Mayer, Miranda J. Banks, and John Thornton Caldwell (New York: Routledge, 2009), 54–68.

For a discussion of the distinction between a work made for hire and other forms of copyright protection, see Jonathan Kirsch, *Kirsch's Handbook of Publishing Law* (Los Angeles: Acrobat, 1995), 36–37. Peter Jaszi has pointed out that, historically, the many legal battles around this issue in the literary world, though carried out in the name of authors, primarily benefited publishers and booksellers. Jaszi, "On the Author Effect: Contemporary Copyright and Collective Creativity," in *The Construction of Authorship: Textual Appropriation in Law and Literature*, ed. Martha Woodmansee and Peter Jaszi (Durham, N.C.: Duke University Press, 1994), 29–56.

23. See James Ulmer, "DGA Hails French Colorizing Ban," *Hollywood Reporter*, November 20, 1988, 3, 22; Jane Galbraith, "Huston Heirs Lose Fight vs. Tinted 'Jungle,'" *Daily Variety*, July 7, 1989, 1, 38; Jane Galbraith, "Huston Heirs to Appeal Tint Ruling," *Daily Variety*, July 11, 1989, 1, 10; "French Court Hears Arguments in Film Colorization Dispute," *BNA's Patent, Trademark and Copyright*

Journal 38 (1990): 126–27; David Robb, "DGA Hails French 'Asphalt' Ruling," *Daily Variety*, June 3, 1991, 1, 12; and Alan Riding, "Film Makers Are Victors in a Lawsuit on Coloring," *New York Times*, August 25, 1991, sec. 1, 60. Besides Huston's heirs, the plaintiffs included screenwriter Ben Maddow. After many appeals, the French high court ultimately confirmed the initial court ruling, in 1994.

24. Joseph McBride, "Colorized Pic Is Dane Bane," *Daily Variety*, April 12, 1990, 3, 31.
25. Will Tusher, "DGA Picks Up Editing Gauntlet," *Daily Variety*, April 23, 1985, 1, 15; *DGA Newsletter*, January 1986, 3, ARF Clipping File; Morrie Gelman, "DGA Wins One: Kane Staying in the Black," *Daily Variety*, February 15, 1989, 1, 25; Jack Mathews, "How 'Kane' Triumphed Over Turner in Black and White," *Los Angeles Times*, February 26, 1989, part 6, 26–27. In the case of *Citizen Kane*, the original contract appears to have been lost, but according to Elliot Silverstein (pers. comm., December 16, 1996), the DGA managed to bluff the Turner Organization, which held the rights, by suggesting that, if the contract were unearthed, it would be found to contain the clause in question.

    A similar case came to trial in the United States in 1998, after TriStar shortened *Thunderheart* by almost thirty minutes for a TV showing without consulting film's director, Michael Apted. Apted, whose contract gave him the right to object, brought suit and was supported by the DGA. The California Court of Appeals subsequently ruled in support of Apted's claim. Nick Madigan, "Judge Upholds DGA–Apted Ruling," *Daily Variety*, June 16, 1998, 1, 19.
26. Philip French, "Bananas Leave a Nasty Taste," *London Observer*, May 12, 1992, Zinnemann Papers, box 157, folder 2112, Moral Rights of Authorship-Correspondence 1992. Zinnemann's papers include considerable correspondence about this case.
27. A letter from DGA lobbyist Larry Chernikoff to Executive Director Jay Roth, dated November 19, 1986, states the group's major issues (copyright, moral rights, and government support of the arts) and strategy (to lobby Patrick Leahy, chair of the Senate Subcommittee on Patents, Copyright, and Trademark). Zinnemann Papers, box 148, folder 2017, Colorization 1986.
28. Ronald Brownstein, *The Power and the Glitter: The Hollywood–Washington Connection* (New York: Vintage, 1992), 218.
29. Dennis Wharton, "Boxer Dukes It Out with Valenti Over Labeling Bill," *Variety*, August 21, 1995, https://variety.com/1995/film/features/boxer-dukes-it-out-with-valenti-over-labeling-bill-99129704. The Guild's suggestion for language on the labels evolved over time, from "This is not the version originally released. It has been panned and scanned. The director and cinematographer object because this alteration removes visual information and changes the composition

of the images" to "This is a colorized [or materially altered] version of a film originally marketed and distributed to the public [in black and white]. It has been altered without the participation of the principal director, screenwriter, and other creators of the original film." The National Film Preservation Board recommended that "material alteration" be interpreted as "any change in the original theatrically released film other than to conform to network standards or for commercials or public service announcements." The Motion Picture Association of America's suggested language for such labels, which ultimately was adopted, was much milder: "This film has been formatted for home viewing so that it may be viewed on a TV screen." "The National Film Registry," *DGA Newsletter*, June–July 1990, 8.

30. Jack Valenti, "National Film Preservation Board Is a Dangerous Chink in Show Biz Armor," *Daily Variety*, August 2, 1988, ARF Clipping File; Paul Harris, "Congress Probes Hard Realities of Authors' Rights vs. Technologies," *Daily Variety*, September 14, 1988, 2, 95.

31. Dennis Wharton, "DGA Cool to Valenti Labeling Plan," *Daily Variety*, February 2, 1993, 1, 22.

32. Paul Harris, "WGA and DGA Reps Push Berne Treaty in D.C.," *Daily Variety*, October 1, 1987, 1. Note the shift from singular to plural in Sydney Pollack's statement.

   Other filmmakers who testified in Washington on the moral rights issue before the Senate Judiciary Committee, which had adjudicatory power in the matter, included Elliot Silverstein, George Lucas, Ginger Rogers, and Steven Spielberg. In addition, the DGA arranged for congressional leaders to meet privately with numerous Hollywood personalities, including Robert Wise, Fred Zinnemann, Peter Bogdanovich, James Goldstone, Ronald Neame, James Stewart, Burt Lancaster, Katharine Hepburn, and Clint Eastwood. The legislators on the judiciary committee included Jim Wright, Joseph Biden, Edward Kennedy, Alan Cranston, Claiborne Pell, Dennis DeConcini, Richard Gephardt, and Sidney Yates. Larry Chernikoff, "Briefing Materials for Elliot Silverstein: Washington, D.C., May 11–13, 1987," Zinnemann Papers, box 120, folder 8, Directors Guild of America 1987.

33. Hi Hollinger, "Directors Reaffirm Creative Rights," *Weekly Variety*, September 3, 1986, 81.

34. "Guild Opposes Coloring of Black-and-White Films," *DGA Newsletter*, November 1986, 1, 6, Mankiewicz Papers, folder, DGA Newsletters.

35. Zinnemann Papers, box 148, folder 2019, Colorization 1987.

36. David J. Fox, "Power Play for Artists' Rights: Movies: Spielberg, Lucas and Ovitz Are Among the Creative Community Heavyweights to Launch a Foundation to Protect Filmmakers' Work," *Los Angeles Times*, December 6, 1991,

http://articles.latimes.com/1991-12-06/entertainment/ca-576_1_creative-community. See also "$100,000 Getty Grant Helps Launch Artists' Right Organization," *Weekly Variety*, April 18, 1990, 1; David Robb, "Artists' Rights Organization Established," *Daily Variety*, June 3, 1991, 1, 12; David Robb, "Lucas, Spielberg Join Call for Protecting Moral Rights," *Daily Variety*, December 6, 1991, 5, 57; Braden Phillips, "Regal Eagles Press Moral Rights," *Daily Variety*, December 8, 2000, A2; and "Artists Rights Organization in a Nutshell," *Daily Variety*, December 8, 2000, A12.

Other major contributors to the organization included Stephen Spielberg, who gave more than $200,000, and the Writers Guild, which gave $10,000. A chronology of events relevant to the Artists Rights Foundation can be found in appendix D.

37. Kristine Andersen, "A Moral Fixation: The Artists Rights Digital Technology Symposium," *DGA Magazine*, May–June 1996, 16.
38. Robb, "Artists' Rights Organization Established," 1.
39. ARF Clipping File.
40. See "House OK's 'Bono' Bill on Copyright Extension, *Daily Variety*, March 26, 1998, ARF Clipping File.
41. Jon Healy, "Focus on Filmmaking," *Los Angeles Times*, March 15, 2001, http://articles.latimes.com/2001/mar/15/news/tt-37920.
42. For descriptions of these events, see Dan Cox, "H'wood Plugs Rights," *Daily Variety*, April 14, 1994, 1, 13; Robert Levine, "Fighting to Keep Movies as Their Makers Intended," *Los Angeles Times*, April 26, 1994, http://articles.latimes.com/1994-04-26/entertainment/ca-50584_1_film-alteration; Gregory Solman, "Artists Rights Given Forum," *Millimeter*, June 1994, 23; "Artists Rights Foundation: Summary of Achievements," October 1996, ARF Clipping File; Joseph Hanania, "Battle Over Film Rights Swells with the Internet," *Los Angeles Times*, April 17, 1997, http://articles.latimes.com/print/1997–04–17/entertainment/ca-49430_1_film-artists; Robert Koehler, "Artists Rights Honors: Where Integrity Counts," *Daily Variety*, April 16, 1998, A1, A8; and "Artists Rights Foundation Timeline," *Daily Variety*, December 8, 2000, A2.
43. John Furia Jr., "We, the Authors," *Written By*, August 1999, 19.
44. Jim Danforth, "DGA's Position on 'Moral Rights,'" *Daily Variety*, August 8, 1988, 12. Danforth was president of Effects Association Inc. See also Danforth, letter to the editor, *Daily Variety*, February 26, 1988, 39, 75; and Jack Mathews, "Colorization: Debate Takes on New Hue," *Los Angeles Times*, March 16, 1989, 1, 9. As early as 1945, an essay by the Writers Guild of America's legal counsel cited moral rights doctrine to advance the writers' claim to authorship. See Morris Cohn, "The Author's Moral Rights," *Hollywood Quarterly* 1, no. 1 (1945): 69–79.
45. Decherney, *Hollywood's Copyright Wars*, 321.

46. Letter from Elliot Silverstein to Barney Rosenzweig, December 11, 1996, 5, Zinnemann Papers, box 158, folder 2116, Moral Rights of Authorship—Correspondence 1996. See also Paul Goldstein, *International Copyright: Principles, Law, and Practice* (New York: Oxford University Press, 2001), 212–13. A more recent development organized around file sharing practices on the internet proposes granting rights of authorship to consumers as well.
47. Silverstein to Rosenzweig, December 11, 1996, 4–6. See also letter to Robert Mrazak from John M. Kernochan, Columbia Law School, March 13, 1989: "The basic notion of moral rights reflects an individualistic concept of creation in which the work of the author is seen as a reflection of his or her personality.... The impact of individualistic moral rights theory must be fairly and carefully worked out where *collaborative* endeavor is the basis for producing protected works of the mind.... Reconciliation of the rights of creators with the possibly conflicting rights and interests of other creators or the owners of the works created or the rights and interests of persons portrayed in such works may not be a simple matter." Zinnemann Papers, box 156, folder 2110, Colorization—Directors Guild of America, 2–3.
48. An argument for this position can be found in Toby Miller et al., *Global Hollywood* (London: British Film Institute, 2001), 202–10. See also Craig A. Wagner, "Motion Picture Colorization, Authenticity, and the Elusive Moral Right," *N.Y.U. Law Review* 64 (1989), 628, 658 note 174.
49. Letter from Fred Zinnemann to David Russell, April 10, 1988, Zinnemann Papers, box 156, folder 2110, Moral Rights of Authorship 1988–91.
50. Zinnemann Papers, box 157, folder 2112, Moral Rights of Authorship—Correspondence 1992.
51. Zinnemann Papers, box 157, folder 2114: Moral Rights of Authorship—Correspondence 1993–95.
52. "National Film Registry," 8. See also Thomas M. Pryor, "Two Wrongs Don't Make a Right," *Daily Variety*, August 22, 1989, 6; and Joseph McBride, "Eight Form Preservation Board," *Daily Variety*, May 2, 1990, 1, 8. The Pryor article notes the absence of producers and cinematographers on the thirteen-member National Film Preservation Board; only directors, screenwriters, and actors were represented.
53. Paul Harris, "DGA Comes Up Short on Colorizing Talks," *Daily Variety*, September 9, 1988, 12. For further information about the DGA's activities around film preservation, see William J. Eaton, "House Panel OK's Film Commission," *Los Angeles Times*, June 17, 1988, ARF Clipping File; DGA President's Committee, "Open Letter to Jack Valenti," *Daily Variety*, August 1, 1988, 14, 17; Nina J. Easton, "Valenti Refuses His Vote in Pushing Campaign Against Film Preservation Board," *Los Angeles Times*, July 21, 1989, part 6, 10; Nina J. Easton, "'Moral

Rights' Issue Pits Directors Guild Against Valenti," *Los Angeles Times*, August 31, 1989, part 6, 10; David Robb, "Rights Battle Linked to Pix," *Daily Variety*, September 20, 1989, 1, 10; Dennis Wharton, "D.C. Has Preservation Reservations," *Daily Variety*, June 13, 1991, 1, 30; David Kelly, "DGA Makes Case to Preserve Label System, More Classic Pix," *Hollywood Reporter*, June 13, 1991, 1, 28; Dennis Wharton, "Moral Right on Hold, as Congress Begins Talks on Preservation," *Weekly Variety*, June 17, 1991, 1, 13; and Dick Madigan, "DGA Aids Film Preservation," *Daily Variety*, June 30, 1998, 19.

54. David Robb, "DGA and AMPTP in Preservation Mode," *Hollywood Reporter*, March 15, 2001, 1, 47; David McNary, "DGA, Studios Set Pic Preservation Backup," *Daily Variety*, March 15, 2001, 3.

55. "Press Release: The Film Foundation and Artists Rights Foundation Consolidate Under the Film Foundation, Inc.," Film Foundation, June 25, 2002, http://www.film-foundation.org/the-film-foundation-and-artists-rights-foundation-consolidate#sthash.7DKwG9Ir.dpuf; Dave McNary, "Orgs Take on New Shape at DGA," *Daily Variety*, May 29, 2002, ARF Clipping File.

56. Dave McNary, "English Lingo Orgs Wave Piracy Plaint," *Daily Variety*, November 16, 2004, 6. See also "The Piracy Showdown," *Hollywood Reporter*, December 16, 2001, 30, 32; Dave McNary, "Filtering Fight," *Weekly Variety*, January 28, 2005, A4; and Andrew Keen, "Losing Independence," *DGA Quarterly*, Spring 2011, https://www.dga.org/Craft/DGAQ/All-Articles/1101-Spring-2011/Internet-Theft-Losing-Independence.aspx.

57. Rick Lyman, "Hollywood Balks at High-Tech Sanitizers," *New York Times*, September 19, 2002, B1. See also Dave McNary, "House Group to Hear DGA Copyright Issues," *Daily Variety*, May 18, 2004, 2, 10; Ryan Faughnder, "Cleaned-Up Films Draw Hollywood's Ire," *Los Angeles Times*, September 15, 2015, C1; and Josh Rottenberg, "Judd Apatow and the Directors Guild Blast Sony Plan to Release 'Clean' Versions of Films," *Los Angeles Times*, June 1, 2017, http://www.latimes.com/entertainment/la-et-entertainment-news-updates-june-judd-apatow-and-the-directors-guild-1497461838-htmlstory.html.

APPENDIX A: BEYOND CREATIVE RIGHTS

1. For general background on the twentieth-century labor movement, see Steven Greenhouse, *Beaten Down, Worked Up: The Past, Present, and Future of American Labor* (New York: Knopf, 2019). The continuing strength of Hollywood's unionized labor force runs counter to the long decline in the power of labor unions nationwide. See David Ng, "Hollywood Guilds Flex Their Muscles," *Los Angeles Times*, May 9, 2017, C1, C4; and "The Wind at Labor's Back," editorial, *New York Times*, August 9, 2018, A20.

2. The Directors Guild of America's research program was instituted by Executive Director Jay Roth in 1995. For further information, see Dave McNary, "Methodical Man: Ready for Action," *Weekly Variety*, January 29, 2010, A7–A8; and Jeffrey Ressner, "To Serve and Protect," *DGA Quarterly*, Summer 2011, http://www.dga.org/Craft/DGAQ/All-Articles/1102-Summer-2011/DGA-Interview-Gil-Cates.aspx.

3. For descriptions of the financial policies of the Hollywood talent unions, see Susan Christopherson, "Flexibility and Adaptation in Industrial Relations: The Exceptional Case of the U.S. Media," in *Under the Stars: Essays on Labor Relations in Arts and Entertainment*, ed. Lois S. Gray and Ronald L. Seeber (Ithaca, N.Y.: Cornell University Press, 1996), 86–112; Alan Paul and Archie Kleingartner, "The Transformation of Industrial Relations in the Motion Picture and Television Industries: Talent Sectors," in Gray and Seeber, *Under the Stars*, 156–80; and "70 Years of Milestones," in "70th Anniversary Issue," special issue, *DGA Quarterly*, Winter 2006, http://www.dga.org/Craft/DGAQ/All-Articles/0604-Winter2006–07/Features-70-Years-of-Milestones.aspx.

Dates and details of the major DGA financial benefits are documented in appendix B.

4. Notably, in discussions of these matters, the name of the DGA is rarely mentioned. Business historians Alan Paul and Archie Kleingartner have concluded, "Although [the historical record] suggests that SAG [Screen Actors Guild] has been the leader in extending residuals to new markets, the WGA [Writers Guild of America] holds that its rhetoric gives shape to the residual struggles, and SAG's strike power provides the muscle." Paul and Kleingartner, "Transformation of Industrial Relations," 168.

5. The strike was a brief one, lasting only five minutes on the West Coast and three hours in the East. For reports on this event, see David Robb, "Producers Reject Residuals Proposal, DGA Set to Walk," *Daily Variety*, July 1, 1987, 1, 15; David Robb, "Directors Guild Strike Is Over as It Starts," *Weekly Variety*, July 15, 1987, 1, 52; Aljean Harmetz, "Directors Accept Pact as Producers Yield on Rollbacks," *New York Times*, July 15, 1987, C19; and Aljean Harmetz, "The Strike That Never Was," *New York Times*, August 9, 1987, F6.

Between 1952 and 1990, residuals figured as a major factor in strikes by talent guilds in eighteen out of twenty-one cases. Paul and Kleingartner, "Transformation of Industrial Relations," 172.

6. The entire organized labor force began to see their unions institute health and pension benefits during the 1950s; by the last years of the decade, more than half of all unionized employees were covered. David Brody, *Workers in Industrial America: Essays on the 20th Century Struggle*, 2nd ed. (New York: Oxford University Press, 1993), 158. The DGA's pension plan is the only one within the

film industry with a "Robin Hood" policy, which makes wealthier members contribute more. See "DGA Inaugurates Retirement Plan," *Hollywood Reporter*, May 27, 1959, n.p.; and John Rich, *Warm Up the Snake: A Hollywood Memoir* (Ann Arbor: University of Michigan Press, 2006), 88–91.

7. Over the long haul, stockholders are unlikely to realize anything more than modest gains on a notably volatile investment option. But studio executives have devised myriad Byzantine accounting practices involving stratospheric fees and add-ons to ensure that they themselves will reap lavish rewards in most situations.

8. Richard Caves, *Media Industries* (Cambridge, Mass.: Harvard University Press, 2000), 142.

9. Brooks Barnes, "Former Warner Executive to Head Disney Studio," *New York Times*, June 1, 2012, B2.

10. Leo Rosten, *Hollywood: The Movie Colony, the Movie Makers* (New York: Harcourt Brace, 1941), 86. Some of the most well-publicized tales of Hollywood's extravagant executive rewards surfaced in the 1990s, with the costly buyouts of Jon Peters from his position as co-production chief at Columbia Pictures in 1991 ($80 million) and of Michael Ovitz from a similar job at Disney in 1997 ($140 million). For an account of the Peters deal, see Nancy Griffin and Kim Masters, *Hit and Run* (New York: Simon and Schuster, 1997). Ovitz's situation is discussed in James Stewart, *Disney War* (New York: Simon and Schuster, 2005).

It is also worth noting that the highest-paid executive in the United States during the 1930s was Louis B. Mayer; during the 1980s it was Disney's Michael Eisner. In 2005, the three chief executives at Viacom each got more than $50 million in salary and benefits, which compensation analyst Brian Foley called "beyond breathtaking." Geraldine Fabricant, "While Shares Fell, Viacom Paid Three $160 Million," *New York Times*, April 16, 2005, B1. In 2012, though no movie studios ranked in the top twenty corporations in terms of net worth, their top executives took in an average of $10 million more than their peers in other industries. David Carr, "For Media Moguls, Paydays That Stand Out," *New York Times*, May 6, 2013, C1. The tradition was carried forward in 2015. An article on executive pay found Viacom's Philippe Dauman, CBS chief Leslie Moonves, and Disney's Robert Iger to be among the top ten best paid CEOs, prompting Michael Price-Jones of the corporate watchdog group CW Investment to comment, "Media executives have perpetuated the myth that there is something so unique about success in this industry that CEOs cannot be judged or paid by conventional standards." David Gelles, "It's (Still) Their Party," *New York Times*, May 17, 2015, BU4. See also Meg James, "Media Executives' Pay Packages Are Still in Stratosphere," *Los Angeles Times*, April 11, 2015, C1, C5. There were similarly rich compensation packages in 2017, with CBS's Leslie Moonves ranked at number four among top earners and Time-Warner's Jeff Bewkes at number eight. "CEO Pay: The Rankings," *New York Times*, May 27, 2018, B6–B7. See also Matthew Goldstein, "Executive Pay: Race to the Top," *New York Times*, May 28, 2017, BU1. In 2018, Disney's Robert Iger ranked as the third most highly paid executive in the country on Equilar's list of CEO pay at the largest U.S. companies.

In 2004, Disney shareholders took the company's former studio chief, Michael Ovitz, to court to recoup part of the rich payout he received when Disney fired him after nine months on the job. "I took one million a year in salary," Ovitz testified at his trial, "which, in this country, is a lot of money. In the entertainment business it's not even a base salary for anybody." Laura M. Holson, "There Really Is No Business Like Show Business," *New York Times*, November 7, 2004, BU3.

11. Gilbert Cates, pers. comm., March 12, 2004.
12. Jeanne Dorin McDowell, "The New Frontier," *DGA Quarterly*, Spring 2011, https://www.dga.org/Craft/DGAQ/All-Articles/1101-Spring-2011/Television-Advent-of-TV.aspx.
13. Michael Cieply and Brooks Barnes, "Directors Reach Accord with Hollywood Studios," *New York Times*, January 18, 2008, http://www.nytimes.com/2008/01/18/arts/18directorscnd.html.
14. Dave McNary, "DGA OKs Agreement for 'Net Productions," *Variety*, April 7, 2000, http://variety.com/2000/digital/news/dga-oks-agreements-for-net-productions-1117780312; McNary, "No-Nonsense Artisans," *Variety*, March 3, 2001, http://variety.com/2001/film/awards/no-nonsense-artisans-1117795020.
15. Judith I. Brennan, "Fearless Leaders," *DGA Quarterly*, Fall 2011, 70–75. For contemporaneous accounts of the DGA's role in the WGA strike, see Dave McNary, "DGA's Roth Key to Guild Accords for Writers, Thesps as Talks Loom," *Weekly Variety*, August 30–September 5, 2004, 11; "Good DGA Buzz Brings Focus to Guild Picture," *Weekly Variety*, September 13–19, 2004; Dave McNary, "H'd in Strike Zone," *Weekly Variety*, December 5–11, 2005, 8, 67; Dave McNary, "H'wood's Fog of War," *Weekly Variety*, August 13–19, 2007, 1, 56; Carl DiOrio, "Directors Line Up Shots," *Hollywood Reporter*, September 21–23, 2007, 1, 49; Michael Cieply, "Behind the Screenwriters' Strike: A Bigger Slice of a Half-Eaten Pie," *New York Times*, November 12, 2007, B1, B5; Michael Cieply, "Directors' Pact Nears End, Adding More Intrigue to Strikes," *New York Times*, December 8, 2007, B3; Michael Cieply, "Directors Offer Talks, Compounding Writers' Plight," *New York Times*, December 14, 2007, C4; David Carr, "A Warning From Behind the Curtain," *New York Times*, December 17, 2007, B1, B5; Kevin Morris and Glenn C. Altschuler, "Curtains for the Guilds," *Los Angeles*

Times, December 20, 2007, A33; Richard Verrier and Claudia Eller, "Writers Have a Lot Riding on a Director," *Los Angeles Times*, December 25, 2007, C1, C7; Carl DiOrio, "Studios Taking Director Approach," *Hollywood Reporter*, January 4–6, 2008, 1, 77; Cynthia Littleton, "Striking a Chord," *Weekly Variety*, January 7–13, 2008, 7, 50; Michael Cieply, "Directors and Producers to Hold Talks," *New York Times*, January 12, 2008, B3; Michael Cieply and Brooks Barnes, "In Tentative Deal, Directors Send Message," *New York Times*, January 18, 2008, B1, B5; and Carl DiOrio, "Directors' Deal: It's a Wrap," *Hollywood Reporter*, January 18–20, 2008, 1, 37.

16. Miranda J. Banks, *The Writers: A History of American Screenwriters and Their Guild* (New Brunswick, N.J.: Rutgers University Press, 2015), 227.
17. For more information on black directors in the first half of the twentieth century, see Pearl Bowser, Jane Marie Gaines, and Charles Musser, eds., *Oscar Micheaux and His Circle: African-American Filmmaking and Race Cinema of the Silent Era* (Bloomington: Indiana University Press, 2001); and Jacqueline Stewart, *Migrating to the Movies: Cinema and Black Urban Modernity* (Berkeley: University of California Press, 2005).
18. At the same time, it was also true that many DGA members helmed films that complicated such portrayals or called them into question. Examples include *Cimarron* (Wesley Ruggles, 1931), *Imitation of Life* (John M. Stahl, 1934), *High Noon* (Fred Zinnemann, 1950), and *Broken Arrow* (Delmer Daves, 1950).
19. For the Guild's own history of its efforts on behalf of disadvantaged groups among its membership, see "70 Years of Milestones."
20. The special issues presented by women directors are addressed in chapter 2.
21. The group's first members were William Crane, Ivan Dixon, Jamaa Fanaka, Wendell Franklin, and Reuben Watt. Subsequently, Fanaka mounted a class action suit against the Guild, the studios, and the Motion Picture Export Association of America, charging them with discriminatory hiring practices. For a discussion of Fanaka's relations with the DGA, see Jan-Christopher Horak, "Tough Enough: Blaxploitation and the L.A. Rebellion," in *L. A. Rebellion: Creating a New Black Cinema*, ed. Allyson Nadia Field, Jan-Christopher Horak, and Jacqueline Najuma Stewart (Berkeley: University of California Press, 2015), 124–25.

    SAG's ethnic minority and women's committees both were formed in 1972. An Equal Employment Opportunity Committee investigation in the 1960s had found racial discrimination in the film industry, but enforcement petered out.
22. Founding members of the Latino Committee were Sylvia Morales, Edward James Olmos, Luis Ruiz, Jesus Trevino, Luis Valdez, and Frank Zegna.
23. Nick Madigan, "Minority Programs Try to Keep Hollywood Honest," *Daily Variety*, March 9, 2001, 1, 7.

24. "Directors Guild: Hiring of Women and Minorities Down for First Quarter," *Daily Variety*, July 3, 1985, 1, 86.
25. Michael Schneider, "Diversity Directives: Touchstone, ABC, DGA Tout Hiring Effort," *Daily Variety*, March 31, 2004, 5; and Desa Philadelphia, "1980s: Road to Diversity," in "70th Anniversary Issue," special issue, *DGA Quarterly*, Winter 2006, 70–71.
26. Subsequent winners of color are Ang Lee (*Brokeback Mountain*, 2005), Alfonso Cuarón, (*Gravity*, 2013), Alejandro Gonzáles Iñárritu (*Birdman*, 2014; *The Revenant*, 2015), and Guillermo Del Toro (*The Shape of Water*, 2017). Feature film nominees from such groups are Lee (*Sense and Sensibility*, 1995; *Life of Pi*, 2012), M. Night Shyamalan (*The Sixth Sense*, 1999), Iñárritu (*Babel*, 2006), Lee Daniels (*Precious*, 2009), Steve McQueen (*12 Years a Slave*, 2013), Barry Jenkins (*Moonlight*, 2016), Jordan Peele (*Get Out*, 2017), and Spike Lee (*BlacKkKlansman*, 2018).
27. For discussions of the role played by gays in Hollywood culture, see David Ehrenstein, *Open Secret: Gay Hollywood, 1928–1998* (New York: Morrow, 1998); William S. Mann, *Behind the Screen: How Gays and Lesbians Shaped Hollywood* (New York: Penguin, 2001); Lillian Faderman and Stuart Timmons, *Gay L.A.: A History of Sexual Outlaws, Power Politics, and Lipstick Lesbians* (New York: Basic Books, 2006), 39–71 and elsewhere; and David Thomson, *Sleeping with Strangers: How the Movies Shaped Desire* (New York: Knopf, 2019).
28. The contemporary trade press was well aware of such practices. For example, in 1933, *Variety* reported that movie producers were "going heavy on the panz stuff." Faderman and Timmons, *Gay L.A.*, 42.
29. Richard Lippe, "Authorship and Cukor: A Reappraisal," in "Rethinking Authorship," special issue, *CineAction!* 21–22 (Summer/Fall 1990): 27.
30. For early discussions of this issue, see "The Dangers of Directing," *Action*, September–October 1973, 10–13; and Joseph McBride, "Directors: Pay Our Aides More: Will Concede, with Some 'Ifs' on Certain Working Rules," *Weekly Variety*, May 25, 1977, 39.
31. The fire department report on the incident attributed the crash to the "careless attitude" and "poor judgment" of those in charge, but the case was later settled out of court. For accounts of the catastrophe and subsequent trial, see Stuart Black, "Danger on the Film Set," *New York Times Magazine*, December 4, 1983, sec. 6, 122; "Film Deaths Witness Says He Warned of Danger," *New York Times*, October 19, 1986, sec. 1, 38; Stephen Farber and Marc Green, *Outrageous Conduct: Art, Ego, and the Twilight Zone Case* (New York: Arbor House/Morrow, 1988); and Jerome Christensen, *America's Corporate Art: The Studio Authorship of Hollywood Motion Pictures* (Stanford, Calif.: Stanford University Press, 2012), 324–25.

32. "Directors Guild to Hold a Symposium on Film Safety," *Weekly Variety*, November 24, 1982, 27; David Robb, "DGA Adopts Safety Ethics Code, Eyes Booze and Drug Use," *Weekly Variety*, February 2, 1983, 4, 41; Gilbert Cates, letter to the editor, *New York Times*, January 29, 1984, sec. 6, 70. For the Guild's continuing interest in this issue, see David Robb, "Landis, Allingham, Cohn Cited for 'Zone' Conduct," *Daily Variety*, January 19, 1988, 1, 54; "Safety Passport Training Class," Directors Guild of America, October 11, 2003, https://www.dga.org/Events/2003/10-October/Safety-Passport-Training-Class.aspx.

33. Farber and Green, *Outrageous Conduct*, 213.

34. For more information on the case, see David Zucchino and Richard Verrier, "Hollywood on Notice About Film Set Safety," *Los Angeles Times*, March 10, 2015, A1, A8.

35. For reports on this tragedy, see Claudia Puig, "A Call for Industry to Reconsider Time Limits," *Los Angeles Times*, April 16, 1997, https://www.latimes.com/archives/la-xpm-1997-04-16-ca-49080-story.html; and Ted Johnson, "Cameraman Killed in Car Crash," March 10, 1997, *Variety*, https://variety.com/1997/scene/vpage/cameraman-killed-in-car-crash-1117342715.

36. Daniel Frankel, "Clock Work," *DGA Quarterly*, Summer 2010, 46–49.

37. For general discussions of this trend, see Thomas Guback, "Hollywood's International Market," in *The American Film Industry*, rev. ed., ed. Tino Balio (Madison: University of Wisconsin Press, 1985), 463–86; and Greg Elmer and Mike Gasher, eds., "Introduction: Catching Up to Runaway Production," in *Contracting Out Hollywood: Runaway Productions and Foreign Location Shooting* (New York: Rowman and Littlefield, 2005), 1–18.

38. Lisa Mitchell, "Ties that Bind: Searching for the Motion Picture Directors Association," *DGA Magazine*, November 2001, 39.

39. "Past, Present and Future," report to DGA members 1947, 4, Cecil B. DeMille Papers, Brigham Young University, Provo, Utah, box 124. See also John Huston Papers, Margaret Herrick Library, Beverly Hills, Calif., folder 1688, SDG,1946–47.

40. Michael Cieply, "For Hollywood, Stand-Ins Play Hollywood's Part," *New York Times*, February 5, 2010, A1, A3.

41. "DGA PAC Report," *DGA Newsletter*, September 2003; "Seventy Years of Milestones."

42. Susan Crabtree, "Runaways Pique Pol," *Daily Variety*, May 8, 2003, 6, 27.

43. "A Historic Occasion," *Action*, July–August 1967, 10–11. For accounts of subsequent, similar activities, see "If DGA Strikes, Helmers in U.K, Canada to Resist 'Runaways,'" *Daily Variety*, April 15, 1981, 3; "Accord Reached by 3 Nations' Directors," *DGA Newsletter*, May 1981, 1; "DGA, Canada, and U.K. Helmers Affiliate to Further Like Goals," *Weekly Variety*, September 7, 1983, 33; "U.S., Canada Helmers Agree on Support," *Weekly Variety*, April 15, 1987, 5. The DGA's

efforts to forge ties with its counterparts in other countries was part of a broader trend among unions. See Matt Bai, "The New Boss," *New York Times Magazine*, January 20, 2005, 38–45.

44. See "Wise, Aldrich, Nelson on USSR Exchange Visit," *Hollywood Reporter*, April 22, 1971; and "DGA Delegation Heads for China," *Weekly Variety*, March 21, 1984, 2.
45. See "Accord Reached by 3 Nations' Directors," 1.
46. Deborah Young, "Venice Fest Session Seeks to Bridge U.S., Europe Gap," *Variety*, September 7, 1993, http://variety.com/1993/film/markets-festivals/venice-fest-session-seeks-to-bridge-u-s-europe-gap-110288.
47. Dave McNary, "Helmers Set up Intern'l Body," *Variety*, September 21, 2003, http://variety.com/2003/film/news/helmers-set-up-int-l-body-1117892794/; and Dave McNary, "Guild Targets Global Goals," *Daily Variety*, February 6, 2004, A12.
48. For a discussion of these differences, see Michael Gubbins, "Lights, Camera, Action," *Screen International*, June 27, 2008, 6.
49. U.S. Department of Labor, Bureau of Labor Statistics, "Union Members Summary," Economic News Release, January 18, 2019, https://www.bls.gov/news.release/union2.nro.htm.

Bibliography

ARCHIVES

Alliance of Motion Picture and Television Producers records, Special Collections, Margaret Herrick Library, Academy of Motion Picture Arts and Sciences, Beverly Hills, Calif.

Argosy Pictures Papers, Brigham Young University, Provo, Utah.

Cecil B. DeMille Papers, Brigham Young University, Provo, Utah.

Directors Guild of America Clipping Files, Margaret Herrick Library, Academy of Motion Picture Arts and Sciences, Beverly Hills, Calif.

Directors Guild of America Files, Oviatt Library, Special Collections, California State University, Northridge.

Directors Guild of America Inc., Basic Agreements (1968, 1978, 1984, 1990, 1993, 2002), Margaret Herrick Library, Academy of Motion Picture Arts and Sciences, Beverly Hills, Calif.

Frank Capra Papers, Wesleyan University, Middletown, Conn.

Fred Zinnemann Papers, Margaret Herrick Library, Academy of Motion Picture Arts and Sciences, Beverly Hills, Calif.

George Marshall Clipping File, Margaret Herrick Library, Academy of Motion Picture Arts and Sciences, Beverly Hills, Calif.

George Stevens Papers, Margaret Herrick Library, Academy of Motion Picture Arts and Sciences, Beverly Hills, Calif.

Herbert Biberman Papers, Wisconsin Historical Society, Madison.

Ida Lupino Clipping File, Margaret Herrick Library, Academy of Motion Picture Arts and Sciences, Beverly Hills, Calif.
Jack Warner Papers, University of Southern California, Los Angeles.
John Ford Papers, Lilly Library, Indiana University Bloomington.
John Huston Papers, Margaret Herrick Library, Academy of Motion Picture Arts and Sciences, Beverly Hills, Calif.
Joseph L. Mankeiwicz Papers, Margaret Herrick Library, Academy of Motion Picture Arts and Sciences, Beverly Hills, Calif.
J. Searle Dawley Collection, Margaret Herrick Library, Academy of Motion Picture Arts and Sciences, Beverly Hills, Calif.
King Vidor Papers, University of Southern California, Los Angeles.
Lamont Johnson Papers, Margaret Herrick Library, Academy of Motion Picture Arts and Sciences, Beverly Hills, Calif.
Martin Ritt Papers, Margaret Herrick Library, Academy of Motion Picture Arts and Sciences, Beverly Hills, Calif.
Richard Brooks Papers, Margaret Herrick Library, Academy of Motion Picture Arts and Sciences, Beverly Hills, Calif.
Vincente Minnelli Papers, Margaret Herrick Library, Academy of Motion Picture Arts and Sciences, Beverly Hills, Calif.
William Beaudine Papers, Margaret Herrick Library, Academy of Motion Picture Arts and Sciences, Beverly Hills, Calif.
William Wyler Papers, Margaret Herrick Library, Academy of Motion Picture Arts and Sciences, Beverly Hills, Calif.

NEWSPAPERS AND PERIODICALS

Daily Variety
Film Daily
Hollywood Citizen-News
Hollywood Reporter
Los Angeles Daily News
Los Angeles Times
Motion Picture Daily
Motion Picture Herald
New York Times
Screen International
Variety
Weekly Variety

BOOKS AND JOURNAL ARTICLES

"70 Years of Milestones." In "70th Anniversary Issue," special issue, *DGA Quarterly*, Winter 2006, 56–77.

Abel, Richard. *The Ciné Goes to Town: French Cinema, 1896–1914*. Updated and exp. ed. Princeton, N.J.: Princeton University Press, 1998.

——. *French Film Theory and Criticism: A History/Anthology, 1907–1939*. Princeton, N.J.: Princeton University Press, 1984.

Abrams, M. H. "Literature as a Revelation of Personality." In *The Mirror and the Lamp: Romantic Theory and the Critical Tradition*, 226–62. New York: Oxford University Press, 1953.

Adorno, Theodor, and Max Horkheimer. *The Dialectic of Enlightenment*. Ed. Gunzelin Schmid, trans. Noerr Edmund Jephcott. Stanford, Calif.: Stanford University Press, 2007. Originally published 1944.

Allen, Jeanne. "Copyright Protection in Theater, Vaudeville, and Early Cinema." In *Screen Histories: A Screen Reader*, ed. Annette Kuhn and Jackie Stacey, 115–28. London: Oxford University Press, 1998.

Allen, Michael Patrick, and Anne E. Lincoln. "Critical Discourse and the Cultural Consecration of American Films." *Social Forces* 82, no. 3 (March 2004): 871–93.

Allen, Richard, and Murray Smith, eds. *Film Theory and Philosophy*. New York: Oxford University Press, 1997.

Alpers, Svetlana. *Rembrandt's Enterprise: The Studio and the Market*. Chicago: University of Chicago Press, 1988.

Anderson, Benedict. *Imagined Communities: Reflections on the Origin and Spread of Nationalism*. New York: Verso, 1998.

Andrew, Dudley. *Film in the Aura of Art*. Princeton, N.J.: Princeton University Press, 1984.

——. "The Unauthorized Auteur Today." In *Film Theory Goes to the Movies*, ed. Jim Collins, Hilary Radner, and Ava Preacher Collins, 77–85. New York: Routledge, 1993.

Appleton, Dina, and Daniel Yankelevits. *Hollywood Dealmaking*. 3rd ed. New York: Allworth, 2018.

Armatage, Kay. *The Girl from God's Country: Nell Shipman and the Silent Cinema*. Toronto: University of Toronto Press, 2003.

Arnheim, Rudolf. "Who Is the Author of a Film?" In *Film Essays and Criticism*, 62–69. Madison: University of Wisconsin Press, 1997.

Arnold, Edward T., and Eugene L. Miller Jr. *The Films and Career of Robert Aldrich*. Knoxville: University of Tennessee Press, 1986.

Ashby, Arved, ed. *Popular Music and the New Auteur: Visionary Filmmakers After MTV*. New York: Oxford University Press, 2013.

Askari, Kaveh. *Making Movies into Art*. London: Palgrave/British Film Institute, 2014.
Association of Motion Picture Producers. "The Waldorf Statement." In *Movies and American Society*, ed. Steven J. Ross, 217–18. Malden, Mass.: Blackwell, 2002. Originally issued December 3, 1947.
Astruc, Alexandre. "The Birth of a New Avant-Garde; la Caméra-Styló," trans. Peter Graham. In *The French New Wave: Critical Landmarks*, ed. Peter Graham with Ginette Vincendeau, 17–23. London: British Film Institute, 2009. Originally published 1948.
"Auteurism Revisited." Special issue, *Film History* 7, no. 4 (1995).
Azlant, Edward. "The Theory, History, and Practice of Screenwriting, 1897–1920." PhD diss., University of Wisconsin, 1980.
Baar, K. Kevyne. "'What Has My Union Done For Me?': The Screen Actors Guild, the American Federation of Television and Radio Artists, and Actors' Equity Association Respond to McCarthy-Era Blacklisting," *Film History* 20, no. 4 (2008): 437–55.
Bach, Steven. *Final Cut: Art, Money, and Ego in the Making of* Heaven's Gate, *the Film that Sank United Artists*. Updated ed. New York: Newmarket, 1999.
Bachman, Gideon. "An Interview with John Huston." In *Interviews with Film Directors*, ed. Andrew Sarris, 253–73. New York: Avon, 1967.
Bakhtin, M. M. *The Dialogic Imagination: Four Essays*. Ed. Michael Holquist, trans. Caryl Emerson and Michael Holquist. Austin: University of Texas Press, 1981.
Balio, Tino, ed. *The American Film Industry*. Rev. ed. Madison: University of Wisconsin Press, 1985.
———. *Grand Design*. New York: Scribner's, 1993.
———, ed. *Hollywood in the Age of Television*. Boston: Unwin Hyman, 1990.
Bank, Mirra. *Anonymous Was a Woman*. New York: St. Martin's, 1979.
Banks, Miranda J. "Gender Inequalities and Precarious Diversity in the 1970s U.S. Television Industry." *Feminist Media Histories* 4, no. 4 (Fall 2018): 109–29.
———. *The Writers: A History of American Screenwriters and Their Guild*. New Brunswick, N.J.: Rutgers University Press, 2015.
Barnett, Rosalind C., and Caryl Rivers. *The New Soft War on Women: How the Myth of Female Ascendance Is Hurting Women, Men*. New York: Tarcher, 2013.
Bart, Peter. *Boffo: How I Learned to Love the Blockbuster and Fear the Bomb*. New York: Miramax Books, 2007.
———. *Infamous Players: A Tale of Movies, the Mob (and Sex)*. New York: Weinstein, 2011.
Barthes, Roland. "The Death of the Author." In *Image–Music–Text*, ed. and trans. Stephen Heath, 142–48. New York: Hill and Wang, 1977.
———. *Sade, Fourier, Loyola*. Trans. Richard Miller. New York: Hill and Wang, 1976.

Barzman, Norma. *The Red and the Blacklist*. New York: Nation Books, 2003.
Basinger, Jeanine. "Giving Credit." *DGA Quarterly*, Winter 2011, 52–56.
Battersby, Christine. *Gender and Genius: Towards a Feminist Aesthetics*. Bloomington: Indiana University Press, 1989.
Baumann, Shyon. *Hollywood Highbrow: From Entertainment to Art*. Princeton, N.J.: Princeton University Press, 2007.
Baxanall, Michael. *Painting and Experience in Fifteenth-Century Italy*. New York: Oxford University Press, 1988.
Bazin, André. "La politique des auteurs." Trans. Peter Graham. In *Cahiers du Cinéma: The 1950s—Neo-Realism, Hollywood, New Wave*, ed. Jim Hillier, 248–59. Cambridge, Mass.: Harvard University Press, 1985. Originally published 1957.
Beach, Christopher. *A Hidden History of Film Style: Cinematographers, Directors, and the Collaborative Process*. Berkeley: University of California Press, 2015.
Bean, Jennifer, and Diane Negra, eds. *A Feminist Reader in Early Cinema*. Durham, N.C.: Duke University Press, 2002.
Beardsley, Monroe. *Aesthetics: Problems in the Philosophy of Criticism*. 2nd ed. Indianapolis, Ind.: Hackett, 1981.
Beauchamp, Cari. *Without Lying Down: Frances Marion and the Powerful Women of Early Hollywood*. Berkeley: University of California Press, 1997.
Becker, Howard. *Art Worlds*. Berkeley: University of California Press, 1982.
Behlmer, Rudy, ed. *Memo from David O. Selznick*. New York: Viking, 1972.
Bell, Douglas. *An Oral History with Joseph Newman / Interviewed by Douglas Bell*. 3 vols. Beverly Hills, Calif.: Academy of Motion Picture Arts and Sciences, Oral History Program, 1995.
Benjamin, Walter. "The Author as Producer." In *Reflections: Essays, Aphorisms, Autobiographical Writings*, ed. and trans. Peter Demetz, 220–38. New York: Harcourt Brace Jovanovich, 1978. Originally published 1966.
——. *The Work of Art in the Age of Mechanical Reproduction*. San Bernardino, Calif.: Prism Key, 2010.
Bennett, Andrew. *The Author*. New York: Routledge, 2005.
Bickerton, Emilie. *A Short History of Cahiers du Cinéma*. London. Verso, 2009.
Billingsley, Lloyd. *Hollywood Party: How Communism Seduced the American Film Industry in the 1930s and 1940s*. Roseville, Calif.: Forum, 2000.
Birchard, Robert. *Cecil B. DeMille's Hollywood*. Lexington: University Press of Kentucky, 2004.
Biriotti, Maurice, and Nicola Miller, eds. *What Is an Author?* Manchester: Manchester University Press, 1993.
Biskind, Peter. *Easy Riders, Raging Bulls: How the Sex-Drugs-and-Rock 'n' Roll Generation Saved Hollywood*. New York: Simon and Schuster, 1998.

Bitzer, Billy. *His Story: The Autobiography of D. W. Griffith's Master Cameraman*. New York: Farrar, Straus and Giroux, 1973.

Black, Henry Campbell, et al. *Black's Law Dictionary*. St. Paul, Minn.: West Publishing, 1990.

Blanke, David. *Cecil B. DeMille, Classical Hollywood, and Modern American Mass Culture: 1910–1960*. New York: Palgrave Macmillan, 2018.

Bloom, Harold. *The Anxiety of Influence: A Theory of Poetry*. New York: Oxford University Press, 1973.

Bogdanovich, Peter. *Allan Dwan: The Last Pioneer*. New York: Praeger, 1971.

———. *John Ford*. Berkeley: University of California Press, 1978.

Bordwell, David. *Figures Traced in Light: On Cinematic Staging*. Berkeley: University of California Press, 2005.

———. *The Films of Carl-Theodor Dreyer*. Berkeley: University of California Press, 1981.

———. *Making Meaning: Inference and Rhetoric in the Interpretation of Cinema*. Cambridge, Mass.: Harvard University Press, 1989.

———. *Narration in the Fiction Film*. Madison: University of Wisconsin Press, 1985.

———. *On the History of Film Style*. Cambridge, Mass.: Harvard University Press, 1997.

———. *Ozu: The Poetics of Cinema*. Princeton, N.J.: Princeton University Press, 1988.

———. *The Rhapsodes: How 1940s Critics Changed Film Culture*. Chicago: University of Chicago Press, 2016.

Bordwell, David, Janet Staiger, and Kristin Thompson. *The Classical Hollywood Cinema: Film Style and Mode of Production to 1960*. New York: Columbia University Press, 1985.

Born, Georgina. "Making Time: Temporality, History, and the Cultural Object." *New Literary History* 46, no. 3 (Summer 2015): 361–86.

Bourdieu, Pierre. *Distinction*. Trans. Richard Nice. Cambridge, Mass.: Harvard University Press, 1984.

———. *The Field of Cultural Production*. Ed. Randal Johnson. New York: Columbia University Press, 1993.

———. *On Television*. Trans. Priscilla Park Fergusson. New York: New Press, 1996.

———. *The Rules of Art: Genesis and Structure of the Literary Field*. Trans. Susan Emanuel. Stanford, Calif.: Stanford University Press, 1992.

Bowser, Eileen. *Biograph Bulletins, 1908–1912*. New York: Farrar, Straus and Giroux, 1973.

———. *The Transformation of Cinema: 1907–1915*. Berkeley: University of California Press, 1990.

Bowser, Pearl, Jane Marie Gaines, and Charles Musser, eds. *Oscar Micheaux and His Circle: African-American Filmmaking and Race Cinema of the Silent Era*. Bloomington: Indiana University Press, 2001.

Braddock, Jeremy, and Stephen Hock, eds. *Directed by Allen Smithee*. Minneapolis: University of Minnesota Press, 2001.

———. "The Specter of Illegitimacy in an Age of Dissolution and Crisis." In *Directed by Allen Smithee*, ed. Jeremy Braddock and Stephen Hock, 3–28. Minneapolis: University of Minnesota Press, 2001.

Branigan, Edward. "Diegesis and Authorship in Film." *Iris* 7 (1986): 37–54.

Braudy, Leo. *The Frenzy of Renown: Fame and Its History*. New York: Oxford University Press, 1986.

Brecht, Bertolt. *Brecht on Theatre: The Development of an Aesthetic*. Ed. and trans. John Willett. New York: Hill and Wang, 1994. Originally published 1957.

Brennan, Judith I. "Fearless Leaders," *DGA Quarterly*, Fall 2011, 70–75.

Brianton, Kevin. *Hollywood Divided: The 1950 Screen Directors Guild Meeting and the Impact of the Blacklist*. Lexington: University of Kentucky Press, 2016.

Brody, David. *In Labor's Cause: Main Themes on the History of the American Worker*. New York: Oxford University Press, 1993.

———. *Workers in Industrial America: Essays on the 20th Century Struggle*. 2nd ed. New York: Oxford University Press, 1993.

Brown, Dorothy M. *Mabel Walker Willebrandt: A Study of Power, Loyalty, and Law*. Knoxville: University of Tennessee Press, 1984.

Browne, Nick, ed. *Cahiers du Cinéma: The 1970s*. Cambridge, Mass.: Harvard University Press, 1990.

Brownstein, Ronald. *The Power and the Glitter: The Hollywood–Washington Connection*. New York: Vintage, 1992.

Buhle, Paul, and Dave Wagner. *Hide in Plain Sight: The Hollywood Blacklistees in Film and Television, 1950–2002*. New York: Palgrave Macmillan, 2005

———. *Radical Hollywood: The Untold Story Behind America's Favorite Movies*. New York: New Press, 2002.

———. *A Very Dangerous Citizen: Abraham Lincoln Polonsky and the Hollywood Left*. Berkeley: University of California Press, 2001.

Bukatman, Scott. *Terminal Identity: The Virtual Subject in Postmodern Science Fiction*. Durham N.C.: Duke University Press, 1993.

Burger, Peter. *Theory of the Avant-Garde*. Trans. Michael Shaw. Minneapolis: University of Minnesota Press, 1984.

Burke, Sean, ed. *Authorship: From Plato to the Postmodern*. Edinburgh: Edinburgh University Press, 1995.

———. *The Death and Return of the Author: Criticism and Subjectivity in Barthes, Foucault, and Derrida*. Edinburgh: Edinburgh University Press, 1992.

Burnham, Scott. *Beethoven Hero*. Princeton, N.J.: Princeton University Press, 1995.

Buscombe, Edward. "Ideas of Authorship." In *Theories of Authorship*, ed. John Caughie, 22–34. London: British Film Institute, 1981.
——. "Walsh and Warner Bros." In *Raoul Walsh*, ed. Phil Hardy, 51–63. Edinburgh: Vineyard, 1974.
Cahiers du cinéma editors. "John Ford's *Young Mr. Lincoln*," trans. Helen Lackner and Diana Matias. *Screen* 13, no. 3 (Autumn 1972): 5–44.
Caldwell, John Thornton. *Production Culture*. Durham, N.C.: Duke University Press, 2008.
——. *Televisuality: Style, Crisis, and Authority in American Television*. New Brunswick, N.J.: Rutgers University Press, 1995.
Capra, Frank. Introduction to *Directors in Action: Selections from* Action, *the Official Magazine of the Directors Guild*, ed. Bob Thomas, vii–x. Indianapolis, Ind.: Bobbs-Merrill, 1973.
——. *The Name Above the Title*. New York: Macmillan, 1971.
Carringer, Robert. "Collaboration and Concepts of Authorship." *PLMA* 116, no. 2 (March 2001): 370–79.
——. "Designing Los Angeles: An Interview with Richard Sylbert." *Wide Angle* 20, no. 3 (1998): 101–102.
——. *The Making of* Citizen Kane. Berkeley: University of California Press, 1996.
Cary, Gary. "More About *All About Eve*." In *Joseph L. Mankiewicz: Interviews*, ed. Brian Dauth, 46–124. Jackson: University of Mississippi Press, 2008.
Casty, Alan. *Communism in Hollywood*. Lanham, Mass.: Scarecrow Press, 2009.
——. *Robert Rossen*. Jefferson, N.C.: McFarland, 2013.
Cattani, Gino, Simone Ferriani, and Paul D. Allison. "Insiders, Outsiders, and the Struggle for Consecration in Cultural Fields: A Core-Periphery Perspective." *American Sociological Review* 79, no. 1 (April 2014): 1–24.
Caughie, John. *Television Drama: Realism, Modernism, and British Culture*. New York: Oxford University Press, 2000.
——, ed. *Theories of Authorship*. London: British Film Institute, 1981.
Cavellero, Jonathan J. "Written Out of the Story: Issues of Television Authorship, Reception, and Ethnicity in NBC's 'Marty.'" *Cinema Journal* 56, no. 3 (Spring 2017): 24–46.
Caves, Richard. *Creative Industries*. Cambridge, Mass.: Harvard University Press, 2000.
Ceplair, Larry, and Steven Englund. *The Inquisition in Hollywood: Politics in the Film Community, 1930–60*. Urbana: University of Illinois Press, 2003.
Chadwick, Whitney. *Women, Art, and Society*. 5th ed. London: Thames and Hudson, 2012.
Chadwick, Whitney, and Isabelle de Courtivron, eds. *Significant Others: Creativity and Intimate Partnership*. London: Thames and Hudson, 1993.

Chartier, Roger. "Figures of the Author." In *Of Authors and Origins: Essays on Copyright Law*, ed. Brad Sherman and Alan Strowell, 7–22. New York: Oxford University Press, 1994.

———. *The Order of Books: Readers, Authors, and Libraries in Europe Between the Fourteenth and Eighteenth Centuries*. Trans. Lydia G. Cochrane. Stanford, Calif.: Stanford University Press, 1994.

Chase, Donald. *Filmmaking: The Collaborative Art*. Boston: Little, Brown, 1975.

Chinoy, Helen Krich. "The Emergence of the Director." In *Directors on Directing: A Source Book for the Modern Theater*, ed. Toby Cole and Helen Krich Chinoy, 1–78. New York: Macmillan, 1963.

Chris, Cynthia, and David Gerstner, eds. *Media Authorship*. New York: Routledge, 2013.

Christensen, Jerome. *America's Corporate Art: The Studio Authorship of Hollywood Motion Pictures*. Stanford, Calif.: Stanford University Press, 2012.

Christopherson, Susan. "Flexibility and Adaptation in Industrial Relations: The Exceptional Case of the U.S. Media." In *Under the Stars: Essays on Labor Relations in Arts and Entertainment*, ed. Lois S. Gray and Ronald L. Seeber, 86–112. Ithaca, N.Y.: Cornell University Press, 1996.

———. "Labor: The Effects of Media Concentration on the Film and Television Workforce." In *The Contemporary Hollywood Film Industry*, ed. Paul McDonald and Janet Wasko, 155–66. Malden, Mass.: Wiley-Blackwell, 2008.

Clark, Danae. *Negotiating Hollywood: The Cultural Politics of Actors' Labor*. Minneapolis: University of Minnesota Press, 1995.

Clayton, Sue, and Jonathan Curling. "On Authorship." *Screen* 2, no. 1 (Spring 1979): 35–61.

Clover, Carol J. "Dancin' in the Rain." *Critical Inquiry* 21, no. 4 (Summer 1995): 722–47.

Coates, Paul. *Film at the Intersection of High and Mass Culture*. New York: Cambridge University Press, 1994.

Cogley, John. *Report on Blacklisting*. Vol. 1, *Movies*. New York: Fund for the Republic, 1956.

Cole, Toby, and Helen Krich Chinoy, eds. *Directors on Directing: A Source Book for the Modern Theater*. New York: Macmillan, 1963.

Collier, Peter, and Helga Geyer-Ryan, eds. *Literary Theory Today*. Ithaca, N.Y.: Cornell University Press, 1990.

Cones, John W. *Film Finance and Distribution: A Dictionary of Terms*. Los Angeles: Silman-James Press, 1992.

Connell, R. W. *Masculinities*. 2nd ed. Berkeley: University of California Press, 2005.

Conner, J. D., *The Studios After the Studios*. Stanford, Calif.: Stanford University Press, 2015.

Cook, David. "Auteur Cinema and the 'Film Generation' in Hollywood." In *The New American Cinema*, ed. Jon Lewis, 11–37. Durham, N.C.: Duke University Press, 1998.

———. *Lost Illusions: American Cinema in the Shadow of Vietnam and Watergate.* Berkeley: University of California Press, 2000.

Cook, Pam, Nöel King, and Toby Miller. "Authorship and Cinema." In *The Cinema Book*, 2nd ed., ed. Pam Cook and Mieke Bernink, 235–318. London: British Film Institute, 1999.

Coombe, Rosemary J. *The Cultural Life of Intellectual Property: Authorship, Appropriation, and the Law.* Durham, N.C.: Duke University Press, 1998.

Cooper, Mark Garrett. *Love Rules: Silent Hollywood and the Rise of the Managerial Class.* Minneapolis: University of Minnesota Press, 2003.

———. *Universal Women: Filmmaking and Institutional Change in Early Hollywood.* Urbana: University of Illinois Press, 2010.

Corliss, Richard. *Talking Pictures: Screenwriters in the American Cinema.* New York: Penguin, 1975.

Corrigan, Timothy. "The Commerce of Auteurism: Coppola, Klug, Ruiz." In *A Cinema Without Walls: Movies and Culture After Vietnam*, 10–36. New Brunswick, N.J.: Rutgers University Press, 1991.

Craig, Rob. *Ed Wood, Mad Genius: A Critical Study of the Films.* Jefferson, N.C.: McFarland, 2009.

Crawford, James. "Film Credit." PhD diss., University of Southern California, 2013. ProQuest 14349.

Critchlow, Donald T. *When Hollywood Was Right.* New York: Cambridge University Press, 2013.

Crofts, Stephen. "Authorship and Hollywood." In *The Oxford Guide to Film Studies*, ed. John Hill and Pamela Church Gibson, 310–24. New York: Oxford University Press, 1998.

Csikszentmihalyi, Mihaly. *Creativity: Flow and the Psychology of Discovery and Invention.* New York: Harper, 1997.

Curtin, Michael, and Kevin Sanson, eds. *Voices of Labor: Creativity, Craft, and Conflict in Global Hollywood.* Berkeley: University of California Press, 2017.

Cutler, Jonathan. "To Have and Have Not: Solving the Mysteries of the WGA Credits System." *Written By* 3, no. 5 (May 1999): 36–45.

Daniel, Douglas K. *Tough as Nails: The Life and Films of Richard Brooks.* Madison: University of Wisconsin Press, 2011.

D'Arc, James, and Sumiko Higashi, eds. *Register of the Cecil B. DeMille Archives.* Provo, Utah: Brigham Young University, 1991.

Darke, Chris. "Why *Cahiers* Still Matters." *Film Comment* 37, no. 5 (September–October 2001): 37.

Dauth, Brian, ed. *Joseph L. Mankiewicz Interviews*. Jackson: University Press of Mississippi, 2008.

Davenport, Robert. "Screen Credit in the Entertainment Industries." *Loyola Entertainment Law Journal* 10, no. 1 (1990): 129–61.

Davies, Philip, and Brian Neve, eds. *Cinema, Politics, and Society in America*. New York: St. Martin's, 1981.

Davis, J. Madison. "Machine to Screen: The Evolution toward Story." In *Screenwriting*, ed. Andrew Horton and Julian Hoxter, 11–35. New Brunswick, N.J.: Rutgers University Press, 2014.

Davis, Ronald L. *John Ford: Hollywood's Old Master*. Norman: University of Oklahoma Press, 1995.

Dawes, Amy. "Good Counsel," *DGA Quarterly*, Winter 2011, https://www.dga.org/Craft/DGAQ/All-Articles/1004-Winter-2010-11/Good-Counsel-Mabel-Willebrandt.aspx.

———. "The Studios Recognize the Guild." *DGA Quarterly*, Winter 2011, http://www.dga.org/Craft/DGAQ/All-Articles/1004-Winter-2010-11/Features-Studios-Recognize-the-Guild.aspx.

Decherney, Peter. "Auteurism on Trial: Moral Rights and Films on Television." *Wisconsin Law Review* (2011): 273–331.

———. *Hollywood and the Culture Elite: How the Movies Became American*. New York: Columbia University Press, 2005.

———. *Hollywood's Copyright Wars: From Edison to the Internet*. New York: Columbia University Press, 2012.

deCordova, Richard. *Picture Personalities: The Emergence of the Star System in America*. Champagne: University of Illinois Press, 2001.

Degli-Esposti, Cristina, ed. *Postmodernism in the Cinema*. New York: Oxford University Press, 1998.

de Lauretis, Teresa, ed. *Feminist Studies/Critical Studies*. Bloomington: Indiana University Press, 1986.

DeMille, Cecil B. *The Autobiography of Cecil B. DeMille*. Ed. Donald Hayne. Englewood Cliffs, N.J.: Prentice Hall, 1959.

———. "Motion Picture Directing." In *The DeMille Legacy*, ed. Paolo Cherchi Usai and Lorenzo Codelli, 218–20. Pordenone: Edizioni Biblioteca dell'Immagine.

Dempsey, Michael. "Colorization." *Film Quarterly* 40, no. 2 (Winter 1986–1987): 2–3.

de Vaan, Mathijs, David Stark, and Balazs Vedres. "Game Changer: The Topology of Creativity," *American Journal of Sociology* 120, no. 4 (January 2015), 1–51.

De Vany, Arthur. *Hollywood Economics: How Extreme Uncertainty Shapes the Film Industry*. New York: Routledge, 2003.

DeVeaux, Scott, and Gary Giddens. *Jazz*. New York: Norton, 2009.

Dickie, George. *Art and Value*. Malden, Mass.: Wiley-Blackwell, 2001.

DiMaggio, Paul. "Cultural Boundaries and Structural Change: The Extension of the High Culture Model to Theater, Opera, and the Dance, 1900–1940." In *Cultivating Difference: Symbolic Boundaries and the Making of Inequality*, ed. Michéle Lamont and Marcel Fournier, 21–57. Chicago: University of Chicago Press, 1992.

Dmytryk, Edward. *Odd Man Out: A Memoir of the Hollywood Ten*. Carbondale: University of Southern Illinois Press, 1996.

Doherty, Thomas. *Hollywood's Censor: Joseph I. Breen and the Production Code Administration*. New York: Columbia University Press, 2007.

———. *Show Trial: Hollywood, HUAC, and the Birth of the Blacklist*. New York: Columbia University Press, 2018.

Doty, Alexander. "Whose Text Is It, Anyway? Queer Cultures, Queer Auteurs, and Queer Authorship." In *Making Things Perfectly Queer: Interpreting Mass Culture*, 17–38. Minneapolis: University of Minnesota Press, 1993.

Dougherty, Jay. "Not a Spike Lee Joint? Issues in the Authorship of Motion Pictures under U.S. Copyright Law." *UCLA Law Review* 49 (2001): 225–334.

Dowd, Nancy, and David Shepard. *King Vidor*. Metuchen, N.J.: Scarecrow Press, 1988.

Dulles, Foster Rhea, and Melvyn Dubofsky. *Labor in America: A History*. 4th ed. Arlington Heights, IL: Harlan Davidson, 1984.

Dunaway, Faye. *Looking for Gatsby*. New York: Simon and Schuster, 1995.

Dunne, Philip. *Take Two: A Life in Movies and Politics*. Updated ed. New York: Limelight, 1992.

Durgnat, Raymond, and Scott Simmon. *King Vidor, American*. Berkeley: University of California Press, 1988.

Dyer, Richard. "Believing in Fairies: The Author and the Homosexual." In *Inside/Out: Lesbian Theories, Gay Theories*, ed. Diana Fuss, 185–201. New York: Routledge, 1991.

———. *Only Entertainment*. New York: Routledge, 1992.

Eco, Umberto. "*Casablanca*: Cult Movies and Intertextual Collage." In *Faith in Fakes: Travels in Hyperreality*, 197–212. New York: Vintage, 1995.

Ede, Lisa, and Andrea Lunsford. "Collaboration and Concepts of Authorship." *PMLA* 116, no. 2 (March 2001): 354–69.

Edelman, Bernard. *Ownership of the Image: Elements for a Marxist Theory of Law*. Trans. Elizabeth Kingdom. London: Routledge and Kegan Paul, 1979.

Edgerton, Gary. "The Germans Wore Gray, You Wore Blue." *Journal of Popular Film and Television* 27, no. 4 (Winter 2000): 24–32.

Edwards, Anne. *Streisand: A Biography*. Boston: Little, Brown, 1997.

Ehrenstein, David. *Open Secret: Gay Hollywood, 1928–1998*. New York: Morrow, 1998.

Eliot, Marc. *American Rebel: The Life of Clint Eastwood*. New York: Three Rivers, 2009.
Elmer, Greg, and Mike Gasher, eds. "Introduction: Catching Up to Runaway Production." In *Contracting Out Hollywood: Runaway Productions and Foreign Location Shooting*, 1–18. New York: Rowman and Littlefield, 2005.
Elrick, Ted. "A Film By." *DGA Magazine*, June/July 1998, 39–43.
——. "Here They Go Again." *DGA Magazine*, November 1999, 25–31.
——. "Singularity of Vision." *DGA Magazine*, May 2004.
Elsaesser, Thomas. "*Chinatown*: The Poetics of Production." In *Studying Contemporary Film: A Guide to Movie Analysis*, Thomas Elsaesser and Warren Buckland, 131–33. London: Arnold, 2002.
——. *The Persistence of Hollywood*. New York: Routledge, 2011.
——. "Two Decades in Another Country: Hollywood and the Cinephiles." In *European Cinema: Face to Face with Hollywood*, 233–50. Amsterdam: Amsterdam University Press, 2005. Originally published 1975.
English, James F. *The Economy of Prestige: Prizes, Awards, and the Circulation of Cultural Value*. Cambridge, Mass.: Harvard University Press, 2005.
Epstein, Edward Jay. *The Big Picture: Money and Power in Hollywood*. New York: Random House, 2006.
——. *The Hollywood Economist: The Hidden Financial Reality Behind the Movies*. Brooklyn, N.Y.: Melville House, 2010.
Eszterhas, Joe. *Hollywood Animal*. New York: Knopf, 2004.
Evans, Robert. *The Kid Stays in the Picture*. New York: Hyperion, 1994.
Eyman, Scott. *Empire of Dreams: The Epic Life of Cecil B. DeMille*. New York: Simon and Schuster, 2010.
——. *Print the Legend: The Life and Times of John Ford*. New York: Simon and Schuster, 1999.
Eysenck, H. J. *Genius: The Natural History of Creativity*. New York: Cambridge University Press, 1995.
Faderman, Lillian, and Stuart Timmons. *Gay L.A.: A History of Sexual Outlaws, Power Politics, and Lipstick Lesbians*. New York: Basic Books, 2006.
Farber, Stephen, and Marc Green. *Outrageous Conduct: Art, Ego, and the* Twilight Zone *Case*. New York: Arbor House/Morrow, 1988.
Faulkner, Robert R., and Andy B. Anderson. "Short-Term Projects and Emergent Careers: Evidence from Hollywood." *American Journal of Sociology* 92, no. 4 (January 1987): 879–909.
Federal Bureau of Investigation. "Communist Political Influence and Activities in the Motion Picture Business in Hollywood, California." In *Movies and American Society*, ed. Steven J. Ross, 213–17. Malden, Mass.: Blackwell, 2002.
Feyerabend, Paul. "Creativity: A Dangerous Myth." *Critical Inquiry* 13 (Summer 1987): 700–711.

Field, Allyson Nadia, Jan-Christopher Horak, and Jacqueline Najuma Stewart, eds. *L.A. Rebellion: Creating a New Black Cinema*, Berkeley: University of California Press, 2015.

Field, Syd. *Screenplay: The Foundations of Screenwriting*. Rev. ed. New York: Bantam Dell, 2005.

"Film Authorship." Special issue, *Film Criticism* 19, no. 3 (Spring 1995).

Fine, Richard. *Hollywood and the Profession of Authorship, 1928–1940*. Ann Arbor, Mich.: UMI Research Press, 1985.

———. *West of Eden: Writers in Hollywood, 1928–1940*. Washington, D.C.: Smithsonian Institution Press, 1993.

Fink, Leon. *American Labor History*. Washington, D.C.: American Historical Association, 1997.

Fischer, David Hackett. *Liberty and Freedom: A Visual History of America's Founding Ideas*. New York: Oxford University Press, 2004.

Fischer, Ernst. *The Necessity of Art*. Trans Anna Bostock. New York: Verso, 2010. First published 1971.

Fischer, Lucy. *Body Double: The Author Incarnate in the Cinema*. New Brunswick, N.J.: Rutgers University Press, 2013.

Fisk, Catherine. "Authors at Work: The Origins of the Work-for-Hire Doctrine." *Yale Journal of Law and the Humanities* 15, no. 1 (2003): 32–70.

———. "The Role of Private Intellectual Property Rights in Markets for Labor and Ideas: Screen Credit and the Writers Guild of America, 1938–2000." *Berkeley Journal of Employment and Labor Law* 32, no. 2 (2011): 215–78.

———. *Writing for Hire: Unions, Hollywood, and Madison Avenue*. Cambridge, Mass.: Harvard University Press, 2016.

Fisk, John, and John Hartley. *Reading Television*. London: Methuen, 2003.

Fleischer, Richard. *Just Tell Me When to Cry: A Memoir*. New York: Carroll and Graf, 1993.

Forbes, Elliot, and David Pierce. "Who Owns the Movies?" *Film Comment* 30, no. 6 (1994): 43–50.

Ford, Dan. *Pappy: The Life of John Ford*. Englewood Cliffs, N.J.: Prentice Hall, 1979.

Foucault, Michel. "What Is an Author?," trans. Josué V. Hatari. In *The Foucault Reader*, ed. Paul Rabinow, 101–20. New York: Pantheon, 1984.

Frankel, Glenn. *High Noon: The Hollywood Blacklist and the Making of an American Classic*. New York: Bloomsbury, 2017.

Frick, Carolyn. *Saving Cinema: The Politics of Preservation*. New York: Oxford University Press, 2011.

Fried, Richard M. *Nightmare in Red: The McCarthy Era in Perspective*. New York: Oxford University Press, 1990.

Fukuyama, Francis. *Political Order and Political Decay: From the French Revolution to the Globalization of Democracy*. New York: Farrar, Straus and Giroux, 2015.

Gaines, Jane M. "Anonymity: Uncredited and Unknown in Early Cinema." In *A Companion to Early Cinema*, ed. André Gaudreault, Nicolas Dulac, and Santiago Hidalgo, 443–59. Malden, Mass.: Wiley-Blackwell, 2012.

——. *Contested Culture: The Image, the Voice, and the Law*. Chapel Hill: University of North Carolina Press, 1991.

——. "Early Cinema's Heyday of Copying." *Cultural Studies* 20 (2006): 2–3.

——. "The Genius of Genre and the Ingenuity of Women." In *Gender Meets Genre in Postwar Cinemas*, ed. Christine Gledhill, 15–28. Urbana: University of Illinois Press, 2012.

——. "Of Cabbages and Authors." In *A Feminist Reader in Early Cinema*, ed. Jennifer Bean and Diane Negra, 88–188. Durham, N.C.: Duke University Press, 2002.

——. *Pink-Slipped: What Happened to Women in the Silent Film Industries*. Urbana: University of Illinois Press, 2018.

Gallagher, Tag. *John Ford: The Man and His Films*. Berkeley: University of California Press, 1986.

——. "Reading, Culture, and Auteurs." *Screening the Past* 12. http://www.screeningthepast.com/2014/12/reading-culture-and-auteurs.

Gallop, Jane. *The Deaths of the Author: Reading and Writing in Time*. Durham, N.C.: Duke University Press, 2011.

Gault, Berys. "Film Authorship and Collaboration." In *Film Theory and Philosophy*, ed. Richard Allen and Murray Smith, 149–72. New York: Oxford University Press, 1997.

Geertz, Clifford. "Art as a Cultural System." In *Local Knowledge: Further Essays in Interpretive Anthropology*, 94–120. New York: Basic Books, 1983.

——. "History and Anthropology." *New Literary History* 21, no. 1 (Winter 1990): 321–35.

Geist, Kenneth. *Pictures Will Talk: The Life and Films of Joseph L. Mankiewicz*. New York: Da Capo, 1978.

Genette, Gérard. "The Name of the Author." In *Paratexts: Thresholds of Interpretation*, trans. Jane Lewin. New York: Cambridge University Press, 1997. Originally published 1987.

Gilbert, Sandra, and Susan Gubar. *The Madwoman in the Attic*. 2nd ed. New Haven, Conn.: Yale University Press, 2000.

Gilligan, Carol. *In Another Voice: Psychological Theory and Women's Development*. Cambridge, Mass.: Harvard University Press, 1982.

Ginsburg, Jane. "The Concept of Authorship in Comparative Copyright Law." *DePaul Law Review* 52, no. 4 (Summer 2003): 1063–92.

———. "A Tale of Two Copyrights: Literary Property in Revolutionary France and America." *Tulane Law Review* 64 (1990): 991–1031.

Glatzer, Richard, and John Raeburn, eds. *Frank Capra: The Man and His Films*. Ann Arbor: University of Michigan Press, 1975.

Gledhill, Christine, ed. *Gender Meets Genre in Postwar Cinemas*. Urbana: University of Illinois Press, 2012.

Gledhill, Christine, and Linda Williams, eds. *Melodrama Unbound: Across History, Media, and National Cultures*. New York: Columbia University Press, 2018.

———, eds. *Reinventing Film Studies*. New York: Oxford University Press, 2000.

Godfrey, Nicholas. *The Limits of Auteurism: Case Studies in the Critically Constructed New Hollywood*. New Brunswick, N.J.: Rutgers University Press, 2018.

Goldman, William. *Adventures in the Screen Trade*. New York: Warner Books, 1983.

Goldstein, Paul. *Copyright's Highway: From Gutenberg to the Celestial Jukebox*. Rev. ed. Stanford, Calif.: Stanford University Press, 2003.

———. *International Copyright: Principles, Law, and Practice*. New York: Oxford University Press, 2001.

Gomery, Douglas. *The Hollywood Studio System: A History*. London: British Film Institute, 2005.

———. *Shared Pleasures: A History of Movie Presentation in the United States*. Madison: University of Wisconsin Press, 1992.

Goodridge, Mike. *Film Craft: Director*. New York: Focal, 2012.

Gordon, Bernard. *Hollywood Exile, or How I Learned to Love the Blacklist*. Austin: University of Texas Press, 1998.

Gottesmann, Ronald, ed. *Perspectives on* Citizen Kane. Boston: G. K. Hall, 1995.

Graham, Peter, and Ginette Vincendeau, eds. *The French New Wave: Critical Landmarks*. London: British Film Institute, 2011.

Grant, Barry Keith, ed. *Auteurs and Authorship*. Malden, Mass.: Blackwell, 2008.

Grant, Catherine. "www.auteur.com?" *Screen* 41, no. 1 (Spring 2000): 101–108.

Gray, Jonathan, and Derek Johnson, eds. *A Companion to Media Authorship*. Malden, Mass.: Wiley-Blackwell, 2013.

Gray, Lois S., and Ronald L. Seeber, eds. *Under the Stars: Essays on Labor Relations in Arts and Entertainment*. Ithaca, N.Y.: Cornell University Press, 1996.

Green, Charles. *The Third Hand: Collaboration in Art from Conceptualism to Postmodernism*. Minneapolis: University of Minnesota Press, 2001.

Green, James R. *The World of the Worker: Labor in Twentieth Century America*. New York: Hill and Wang, 1980.

Greenblatt, Stephen. *Renaissance Self-Fashioning: From More to Shakespeare*. Chicago: University of Chicago Press, 2005.

Greenhouse, Steven. *Beaten Down, Worked Up: The Past, Present, and Future of American Labor*. New York: Knopf, 2019.

Grey, Rudolph. *Nightmare of Ecstasy: The Life and Films of Edward D. Wood, Jr.* Port Townsend, Wash.: Feral House, 1991.

Gridley, Mark C. *Jazz Styles*. 10th ed. Upper Saddle River, N.J.: Prentice Hall, 2009.

Griffin, Nancy, and Kim Masters. *Hit and Run: How Jon Peters and Peter Guber Took Sony for a Ride in Hollywood*. New York: Simon and Schuster, 1997.

Grodal, Torben, Bente Larsen, and Iben Thorving Laursen, eds. *Visual Authorship: Creativity and Intentionality in Media*. Copenhagen: Museum Tusculanum Press, 2005.

Guback, Thomas. "Hollywood's International Market." In *The American Film Industry*, rev. ed., ed. Tino Balio, 463–86. Madison: University of Wisconsin Press, 1985.

Gunning, Tom. *D. W. Griffith and the Origins of Narrative Film: The Early Years at Biograph*. Champaign: University of Illinois Press, 1991.

Habermas, Jürgen. "An Alternative Way Out of the Philosophy of the Subject: Communicative Versus Subject-Centered Reason." In *The Philosophical Discourse of Modernity*, trans. Frederick Lawrence, 294–326. Cambridge, Mass.: MIT Press, 1987.

Haberski, Raymond J. *"It's Only a Movie": Films and Critics in American Culture*. Lexington: University of Kentucky Press, 2001.

Hadjinicolaou, Nicos. *Art History and Class Struggle*. Trans. Louise Asmal. London: Pluto Press, 1979.

Hamilton, Ian. *Writers in Hollywood, 1915–1951*. New York: HarperCollins, 1990.

Hampton, Benjamin B. *History of the American Film Industry: From Its Beginnings to 1931*. New York: Dover, 1970. Originally published 1931.

Hardy, Phil, ed. *Raoul Walsh*. Colchester: Vineyard, 1974.

Hargadon, Andrew B., and Beth A. Bechky. "When Collections of Creatives Become Creative Collectives: A Field Study of Problem Solving at Work." *Organization Science* 17, no. 4 (August 2006): 484–500.

Harmetz, Aljean. *The Making of* The Wizard of Oz. New York: Hyperion, 1998.

——. *On the Road to Tara: The Making of* Gone with the Wind. New York: N. H. Abrams, 1996.

——. *"Round Up the Usual Suspects": The Making of* Casablanca. New York: Hyperion, 1993.

Harris, Mark. *Five Came Back: A Story of Hollywood and the Second World War*. New York: Penguin, 2014.

Harrison, Charles, and Paul Wood. *Art in Theory*. Malden, Mass.: Blackwell, 1992.

Hartley, John, ed. *Creative Industries*. Malden, Mass.: Blackwell, 2005.

Haskell, Molly. *Steven Spielberg: A Life in Films*. New Haven, Conn.: Yale University Press, 2017.

Hastie, Amelie. *Cupboards of Curiosity*. Durham, N.C.: Duke University Press, 2007.

———. "Filmakers: The Troubles with Authorship." In *The Bigamist*, 16–27. London: Palgrave Macmillan/British Film Institute, 2009.

Hauser, Arnold. *The Social History of Art*. Vol. 4. New York: Routledge, 1999. Originally published 1951.

Heath, Stephen. "Comment on 'The Idea of Authorship.'" *Screen* 14, no. 3 (Autumn 1973).

Heise, Tatiana, and Andrew Tudor. "Constructing (Film) Art: Bourdieu's Field Model in a Comparative Context." *Cultural Sociology* 1, no. 2 (2007): 165–87.

Henderson, Felicia D. "The Writers Room." In *Production Culture: Cultural Studies of Media Industries*, ed. Vicki Mayer, Miranda J. Banks, and John Thornton Caldwell, 224–31. New York: Routledge, 2009.

Hess, John. "*La politique des auteurs* (part 1): World View as Aesthetics." *Jump Cut* 1 (May/June 1974): 19–22.

———. "*La politique des auteurs* (part 2): Truffaut's Manifesto." *Jump Cut* 2 (July/August 1974): 20–22.

Hesse, Carla. "Enlightenment Epistemology and the Laws of Authorship in Revolutionary France, 1777–1793." *Representations* 30 (1990): 109–37.

Heuman, Josh. "'Independence,' Industrial Authorship, and Professional Entrepreneurship: Representing and Reorganizing Television Writing in the FCC Media Ownership Reviews." *Cinema Journal* 52, no. 3 (Spring 2013): 99–119.

Higashi, Sumiko. *Cecil B. DeMille and American Culture: The Silent Era*. Berkeley: University of California Press, 1994.

Higham, Charles. *Merchant of Dreams: Louis B. Mayer*. New York: E. P. Dutton, 1993.

Hill, Erin. *Never Done: A History of Women's Work in Media Production*. New Brunswick, N.J.: Rutgers University Press, 2016.

Hill, John, and Pamela Church Gibson, eds. *The Oxford Guide to Film Studies*. New York: Oxford University Press, 1998.

Hillier, Jim, ed. Cahiers du Cinéma: *The 1950s—Neo-Realism, Hollywood, New Wave*. Cambridge, Mass.: Harvard University Press, 1985.

———, ed. Cahiers du Cinéma: *The 1960s—New Wave, New Cinema, Reevaluating Hollywood*. Cambridge, Mass.: Harvard University Press, 1986.

Hock, Stephen. "Smithee's Incorporation." In *Directed by Allen Smithee*, ed. Jeremy Braddock and Stephen Hock, 143–74. Minneapolis: University of Minnesota Press, 2001.

Hodsdon, Barrett. *The Elusive Auteur: The Question of Film Authorship Throughout the Age of Cinema*. Jefferson, N.C.: McFarland, 2017.
Hollins, Joanne, and Mark Jancovich, eds. *Approaches to Popular Film*. Manchester: Manchester University Press, 1995.
Hollows, Joanne, Peter Hutchings, and Mark Jancovich, eds. *The Film Studies Reader*. London: Arnold, 2000.
Home, Stewart. *Neoist Manifestos*. Chico, Calif.: A.K. Press, 1991.
Horak, Jan-Christopher. "Tough Enough: Blaxploitation and the L.A. Rebellion." In *L.A. Rebellion: Creating a New Black Cinema*, ed. Allyson Nadia Field, Jan-Christopher Horak, and Jacqueline Najuma Stewart, 124–25. Berkeley: University of California Press, 2015.
Horne, Gerald. *Class Struggle in Hollywood, 1930–1950: Moguls, Mobsters, Stars, Reds, and Trade Unions*. Austin: University of Texas Press, 2001.
———. *The Final Victim of the Blacklist: John Howard Lawson, the Dean of the Hollywood Ten*. Berkeley: University of California Press, 2006
Hubner, Laura, ed. *Valuing Films: Shifting Perceptions of Worth*. New York: Palgrave Macmillan, 2011.
Hughes, Justin. "The Personality Interest of Artists and Inventors in Intellectual Property." *Cardozo Arts and Entertainment Journal* 16, no. 1 (1988): 81–182.
Humphries, Reynold. *Hollywood's Blacklists: A Political and Cultural History*. Edinburgh: Edinburgh University Press, 2010.
Huston, John. *An Open Book*. New York: Da Capo, 1980.
Huyssen, Andreas. *After the Great Divide: Modernism, Mass Culture, Postmodernism*. Bloomington: Indiana University Press, 1986.
Inge, M. Thomas. "Collaboration and Concepts of Authorship." *PMLA* 116, no. 3 (May 2001): 623–30.
Jacobs, Diane. *Christmas in July: The Life and Times of Preston Sturges*. Berkeley: University of California Press, 1992.
James, David E. "The Producer as Author." In *Andy Warhol's Film Factory*, ed. Michael O'Pray, 136–45. London: British Film Institute, 1989.
Jameson, Frederic. "The Existence of Italy." In *Signatures of the Visible*, 155–230. New York: Routledge, 1992.
Jaszi, Peter. "On the Author Effect: Contemporary Copyright and Collective Creativity." In *The Construction of Authorship: Textual Appropriation in Law and Literature*, ed. Martha Woodmansee and Peter Jaszi, 29–56. Durham, N.C.: Duke University Press, 1994.
Jaszi, Peter, and Martha Woodmansee. "The Ethical Reaches of Authorship." *South Atlantic Quarterly* 95, no. 4 (Fall 1996): 947–78.
Jenkins, Henry. *Convergence Culture*. New York: New York University Press, 2006.

Jenkins, Henry, Mizuko Ito, and danah boyd. *Participatory Culture in a Networked Era*. Cambridge, Mass.: Polity, 2016.

Jeter, Ida B. "The Collapse of the Federated Motion Picture Crafts: A Case Study of Class Collaboration in the Motion Picture Industry." In *The Hollywood Film Industry: A Reader*, ed. Paul Kerr, 78–96. London: Routledge and Kegan Paul, 1986.

Jewell, Richard. "Orson Welles and the Studio System: The RKO Context." In *Perspectives on* Citizen Kane, ed. Ronald Gottesmann. Boston: G. K. Hall, 1995.

John-Steiner, Vera. *Creative Collaboration*. New York: Oxford University Press, 2000.

Jones, Carolyn A. *The Machine in the Studio: Constructing the Postwar American Artist*. Chicago: University of Chicago Press, 1998.

Joseph, Robert. "Re: Unions in Hollywood." *Films* 1, no. 3 (Summer 1940): 34–50.

Juraga, Dubravka, and M. Keith Booker, eds. *Socialist Cultures East and West: A Post-Cold War Reassessment*. New York: Praeger, 2010.

Kackman, Michael, Marnie Binfield, Matthew Thomas Payne, Allison Perlman, and Bryan Sebok, eds. *Flow TV: Television in the Age of Media Convergence*. New York: Routledge, 2011.

Kagan, Jeremy, ed. *Directors Close Up*. Boston: Focal, 2000.

———. *Directors Close Up 2*. Metuchen, N.J.: Scarecrow Press, 2012.

Kahn, Gordon. *Hollywood on Trial: The Story of the Ten Who Were Indicted*. New York: Boni and Gaer, 1948.

Kamina, Pascal. *Film Copyright in the European Union*. New York: Cambridge University Press, 2002.

Kaminsky, Stuart. *Don Siegel: Director*. New York: Curtis Books, 1974.

Kamuf, Peggy. *Signature Pieces: On the Institution of Authorship*. Ithaca, N.Y.: Cornell University Press, 1988.

Kanfer, Stefan. *A Journal of the Plague Years: A Devastating Chronicle of the Era of the Blacklist*. New York: Atheneum, 1973.

Kaplan, E. Ann, ed. *Feminism and Film*. New York: Oxford University Press, 2000.

Kapsis, Robert. *Hitchcock: The Making of a Reputation*. Chicago: University of Chicago Press, 1992.

Kaufman, Scott Barry, and Carolyn Gregoire. *Wired to Create: Unraveling the Mysteries of the Creative Mind*. New York: Penguin, 2016.

Kazan, Elia. *A Life*. New York: Alfred A. Knopf, 1988.

Keathley, Christian. "Signateurism and the Case of Allen Smithee." In *Directed by Allen Smithee*, ed. Jeremy Braddock and Stephen Hock, 121–42. Minneapolis: University of Minnesota Press, 2001.

Kehr, Dave. "*Cahiers du Cinéma*," *Film Comment* 37, no. 5 (September–October 2001): 30–36.

Keil, Charlie. *Early American Cinema in Transition: Story, Style, and Filmmaking, 1907–1913*. Madison: University of Wisconsin Press, 2001.

Kemper, Tom. *Hidden Talent: The Emergence of Hollywood Agents*. Berkeley: University of California Press, 2010.

Kempers, Bram. *Painting, Power, and Patronage: The Rise of the Professional Artist in Renaissance Italy*. New York: Penguin, 1987.

Kerr, Paul, ed. *The Hollywood Film Industry: A Reader*. London: Routledge and Kegan Paul, 1986.

———. "My Name Is Joseph H. Lewis." In *The Studio System*, ed. Janet Staiger, 50–73. New Brunswick, N.J.: Rutgers University Press, 1994.

Kessler-Harris, Alice. *Gendering Labor History*. Urbana: University of Illinois Press, 2006.

Kester, Grant H. *The One and the Many: Contemporary Art in a Global Context*. Durham, N.C.: Duke University Press, 2011.

King, Geoff. *New Hollywood Cinema: An Introduction*. New York: Columbia University Press, 2002.

Kirsch, Jonathan. *Kirsch's Handbook of Publishing Law*. Los Angeles: Acrobat, 1995.

Kirshner, Jonathan. *Hollywood's Last Golden Age: Politics, Society, and the Seventies Film in America*. Ithaca, N.Y.: Cornell University Press, 2012.

Klaiber, Isabell. "Multiple Implied Authors: How Many Can a Text Have?" In "Implied Author: Back from the Grave or Simply Dead Again?," ed. Brian Richardson, special issue, *Style* 45, no. 1 (Spring 2011): 138–52.

Klawans, Stuart. "The Politics of Authorship." In *Film Follies: The Cinema Out of Order*, 41–68. London: Wellington House, 1999.

———. "Rose-Tinted Spectacles." In *Seeing Through Movies*, ed. Mark Crispin Miller, 150–85. New York: Pantheon, 1990.

Klinger, Barbara. *Melodrama and Meaning: History, Culture, and the Films of Douglas Sirk*. Bloomington: Indiana University Press, 1994.

Knapp, Steven, and Walter Benn Michaels. "Against Theory." *Critical Inquiry* 8 (Summer 1982): 723–42.

Knox, Donald. *The Magic Factory: How MGM Made* An American in Paris. New York: Praeger, 1973.

Koch, Howard. "The Playwright Looks at the 'Filmwright.'" In *The Film Studies Reader*, ed. Joanne Hollows, Peter Hutchings, and Mark Jancovich. London: Arnold, 2000.

Koestenbaum, Wayne. *Double Talk: The Erotics of Male Literary Collaboration*. New York: Routledge, 1989.

Kompare, Derek. "More 'Moments of Television': Online Cult Television Authorship." In *Flow TV: Television in the Age of Media Convergence*, ed. Michael Kackman, Marnie Binfield, Matthew Thomas Payne, Allison Perlman, and Bryan Sebok, 95–113. New York: Routledge, 2011.

Koszarski, Richard. Introduction. In "Auteurism Revisited," special issue, *Film History* 7, no. 4 (Winter 1995): 355–56.

———. "Joseph Lerner and the Post-War New York Film Renaissance." In "Auteurism Revisited," special issue, *Film History* 7, no. 4 (1995): 456–76.
Koury, Phil. *Yes, Mr. DeMille: A Humorous and Candid Appraisal of an Extraordinary Showman*. New York: Putnam, 1957.
Kozloff, Sarah. *The Life of the Author*. Montreal: Caboose, 2014.
———. "Wyler's Wars." *Film History* 20, no. 4 (2008): 456–473.
Krutnik, Frank, Steve Neale, Brian Neve, and Peter Stanfield, eds. *"Un-American": Hollywood Politics in the Blacklist Era*. New Brunswick, N.J.: Rutgers University Press, 2007.
Kuhn, Annette, and Guy Westwell. *The Oxford Dictionary of Film Studies*. New York: Oxford University Press, 2012.
Landau, Ellen G. *Jackson Pollock*. New York: M. H. Abrams, 2010.
Lapsley, Robert, and Michael Westlake. *Film Theory: An Introduction*. Manchester: Manchester University Press, 1988.
Lardner, Ring, Jr. *I'd Hate Myself in the Morning: A Memoir*. New York: Thunder's Mouth, 2000.
Laslett, John H. M. *Sunshine Was Never Enough: Los Angeles Workers, 1880–2010*. Berkeley: University of California Press, 2012.
Lauzen, Martha M. *The Celluloid Ceiling: Behind-the-Scenes Employment of Women on the Top 250 Films of 2011*. San Diego State University, Center for the Study of Women in Television and Film, 2012. http://womenintvfilm.sdsu.edu/files/2011_Celluloid_Ceiling_Exec_Summ.pdf.
Lentricchia, Frank, and Thomas McLaughlin, eds. *Critical Terms for Literary Study*. Chicago: University of Chicago Press, 1990.
Leonard, James S. *Authority and Textuality: Current Views of Collaborative Writing*. West Cornwall: Locust Hill, 1994.
Levine, Lawrence. *Highbrow/Lowbrow: The Emergence of Cultural Hierarchy in America*. Cambridge, Mass.: Harvard University Press, 1990.
Levy, Emanuel. *All About Oscar*. New York: Continuum, 2003.
———. *And the Winner Is . . . : The History and Politics of the Academy Awards*. New York: Continuum, 1991.
———. *Cinema of Outsiders: The Rise of American Independent Film*. New York: New York University Press, 1999.
———, ed. *Citizen Sarris, American Film Critic: Essays in Honor of Andrew Sarris*. Lanham, Md.: Scarecrow Press, 2001.
Lewis, Jon. *Hollywood v. Hard Core: How Censorship Saved the Film Industry*. New York: New York University Press, 2002.
———, ed. *The New American Cinema*. Durham, N.C.: Duke University Press, 1998.
———. "'We Do Not Ask You to Condone This . . .': How the Blacklist Saved Hollywood." *Cinema Journal* 39, no. 2 (2000): 3–30.

———. *Whom God Wishes to Destroy: Francis Coppola and the New Hollywood*. Durham, N.C.: Duke University Press, 1995.

Lippe, Richard. "Authorship and Cukor: A Reappraisal." In "Rethinking Authorship," special issue, *CineAction!* nos. 21–22 (Summer/Fall 1990): 21–34.

Lipset, Seymour Martin. *American Exceptionalism: A Double-Edged Sword*. New York: Norton, 1996.

Littleton, Cynthia. *TV on Strike: Why Hollywood Went to War Over the Internet*. Syracuse, N.Y.: Syracuse University Press, 2013.

Litvak, Joseph. *The Un-Americans: Jews, the Blacklist, and Stoolpigeon Culture*. Durham, N.C.: Duke University Press, 2009.

Litwak, Mark. *Reel Power: The Struggle for Influence and Success in New Hollywood*. New York: William Morrow, 1986.

Livingston, Paisley. *Cinema, Philosophy, Bergman: On Film as Philosophy*. New York: Oxford University Press, 2009.

———. "Cinematic Authorship." In *Film Theory and Philosophy*, ed. Richard Allen and Murray Smith, 132–48. New York: Oxford University Press, 1997.

Locke, Sondra. *The Good, the Bad, and the Very Ugly*. New York: William Morrow, 1997.

Long, Bruce. *Taylorology: A Continuing Exploration into the Life and Death of William Desmond Taylor* 95 (November 2000). http://www.taylorology.com/issues/Taylor95.txt.

———. *William Desmond Taylor: A Dossier*. Metuchen, N.J.: Scarecrow Press, 2004.

Louvish, Simon. *Cecil B. DeMille: A Life in Art*. New York: St. Martin's, 2006.

Love, Harold. *Attributing Authorship: An Introduction*. New York: Cambridge University Press, 2002.

Lovell, Alan, and Gianluca Sergi. *Making Films in Contemporary Hollywood*. London: Hodder Arnold, 2005.

Lower, Cheryl Bray, and R. Barton Palmer, eds. *Joseph L. Mankiewicz*. Jefferson, N.C.: McFarland, 2001

Lukacs, Georg. *The Meaning of Contemporary Realism*. London: Merlin, 1963.

Lumet, Sidney. *Making Movies*. New York: Random House, 1995.

Lunsford, Andrea, and Lisa Ede. *Singular Texts/Plural Authors: Perspectives on Collaborative Writing*. Carbondale: Southern Illinois University Press, 1990.

Macherery, Pierre. *A Theory of Literary Production*. New York: Routledge, 2006. Originally published 1966.

Mackendrick, Alexander. *On Film-Making: An Introduction to the Craft of the Director*, ed. Paul Cronin. New York: Faber and Faber, 2004.

Madsen, Axel. *William Wyler*. New York: Thomas Y. Crowell, 1973.

Mahar, Karen Ward. *Women Filmmakers in Early Hollywood*. Baltimore, Md.: Johns Hopkins University Press, 2006.

Malham, Joseph. *John Ford: Poet in the Desert*. Chicago: Lake Street, 2013.

Maltby, Richard. *Hollywood Cinema*. 2nd ed. Cambridge, Mass.: Blackwell, 2003.

———. "Made for Each Other: The Melodrama of Hollywood and the House Committee on Un-American Activities, 1947." In *Cinema, Politics, and Society in America*, ed. Philip Davies and Brian Neve, 76–96. New York: St. Martin's, 1981.

Mann, William S. *Behind the Screen: How Gays and Lesbians Shaped Hollywood*. New York: Penguin, 2001.

Manovich, Lev. "Who Is the Author? Sampling/Remixing/Open Source." *Manovich*, 2002. http://manovich.net/index.php/projects/models-of-authorship-in-new-media.

Maras, Steven. *Screenwriting: History, Theory, and Practice*. London: Wallflower, 2009.

Martin, Adrian. "Sign Your Name Across My Heart, or: 'I Want to Write About Delbert Mann.'" *Screening the Past* 12. http://www.screeningthepast.com/2014/12/sign-your-name-across-my-heart-or-i-want-to-write-about-delbert-mann.

Martin, Michael T., ed. *The New Latin American Cinema*. Detroit, Mich.: Wayne State University Press, 1997.

Martin, Roger L. *Fixing the Game: Bubbles, Crashes, and What Capitalism Can Learn from the NFL*. Boston: Harvard Business Review Press, 2011.

Martindale, Andrew. *The Rise of the Artist in the Middle Ages and Early Renaissance*. New York: McGraw-Hill, 1972.

Mastin, Jeffrey. *Textual Intercourse: Collaboration, Authorship, and Sexualities in Renaissance Drama*. New York: Cambridge University Press, 1997.

Matejka, Ladislav, and Krystyna Pomorska, eds. *Readings in Russian Poetics*. Cambridge, Mass.: MIT Press, 1971.

Maule, Rosanna. *Beyond Auteurism: New Directions in Authorial Film Practices in France, Italy, and Spain since the 1980s*. Chicago: University of Chicago Press, 2008.

———. "De-Authoring the Auteur: Postmodern Politics of Interpellation in Contemporary European Cinema." In *Postmodernism in the Cinema*, ed. Cristina Degli-Esposti, 113–30. New York: Oxford University Press, 1998.

Mayer, Vicki, Miranda J. Banks, and John Thornton Caldwell, eds. *Production Culture: Cultural Studies of Media Industries*. New York: Routledge, 2009.

Mayne, Judith. *Directed by Dorothy Arzner*. Bloomington: Indiana University Press, 1994.

———. "Lesbian Looks: Dorothy Arzner and Female Authorship." In *Feminism and Film*, ed. E. Ann Kaplan, 159–80. New York: Oxford University Press, 2000.

———. *The Woman at the Keyhole: Feminism and Women's Cinema*. Bloomington: Indiana University Press, 1990.

Maza, Sarah. *Thinking About History*. Chicago: University of Chicago Press, 2017.

McBride, Joseph. *Frank Capra: The Catastrophe of Success*. New York: Simon and Schuster, 1992.

——. "Riskinesque." *Written By* 3, no. 1 (December–January 2001): 47–53.

——. *Searching for John Ford: A Life*. New York: St. Martin's Griffin, 2001.

——. *Steven Spielberg: A Biography*. New York: Simon and Schuster, 1997.

McCabe, Colin. "The Revenge of the Author." *Critical Quarterly* 31–32 (1989): 3–15.

McCallum, John. *Scooper: Authorized Story of Scoop Conlon's Motion Picture World*. Seattle: Wood and Reber, 1960.

McCarthy, Todd. *Howard Hawks: The Grey Fox of Hollywood*. New York: Grove, 2000.

McDonald, Paul, and Janet Wasko, eds. *The Contemporary Hollywood Film Industry*. Malden, Mass.: Wiley-Blackwell, 2008.

McGill, Meredith L., ed. *Taking Liberties with the Author: Selected Essays from the English Institute*. Cambridge, Mass.: English Institute, in collaboration with the American Council of Learned Societies, 2013. https://hdl.handle.net/2027/heb.90058.0001.001.

McGilligan, Patrick. *Clint: The Life and Legend*. New York: St. Martin's, 1999.

——. *Robert Altman: Jumping off the Cliff*. New York: St. Martin's, 1989.

McGilligan, Patrick, and Paul Buhle. *Tender Comrades: A Backstory of the Hollywood Blacklist*. New York: St. Martin's, 1999.

McGowan, John J. *J. P. McGowan: Biography of a Hollywood Pioneer*. Jefferson, N.C.: McFarland, 2005.

McMahan, Alison. *Alice Guy Blaché: Lost Visionary of the Cinema*. London: Bloomsbury, 2003.

McWilliam, Rohan. "Melodrama and the Historians." *Radical History Review* 78 (2000): 57–84.

Menne, Jeff. *Post-Fordist Cinema: Hollywood Auteurs and the Corporate Counterculture*. New York: Columbia University Press, 2019.

Meyers, Jeffrey. *John Huston: Courage and Art*. New York: Crown, 2011.

Miège, Bernard. *The Capitalization of Cultural Production*. New York: International General, 1989.

Mekas, Jonas. *Movie Journal: The Rise of a New American Cinema, 1959–1971*. 2nd ed. New York: Columbia University Press, 2016.

Meltzer, Françoise. *Hot Property: The Stakes and Claims of Literary Originality*. Chicago: University of Chicago Press, 1994.

Messerschmidt, James W. *Hegemonic Masculinity: Formulation, Reformulation, and Amplification*. New York: Rowman and Littlefield, 2018.

Miller, Eugene L, and Edward T. Arnold, eds. *Robert Aldrich: Interviews*. Jackson: University Press of Mississippi, 2004.

Miller, Gabriel. *Fred Zinnemann: Interviews*. Jackson: University Press of Mississippi, 2005.

———. *William Wyler*. Lexington: University Press of Kentucky, 2013.

———. *William Wyler: Interviews*. Jackson: University Press of Mississippi, 2009.

Miller, Jacqueline T. *Poetic License: Authority and Authorship in Medieval and Renaissance Contexts*. New York: Oxford University Press, 1986.

Miller, Mark Crispin, ed. *Seeing Through Movies*. New York: Pantheon, 1990.

Miller, Nancy K. "Changing the Subject: Authorship, Writing, and the Reader." In *Feminist Studies/Critical Studies*, ed. Teresa de Lauretis, 102–20. Bloomington: Indiana University Press, 1986.

Miller, Toby, and Robert Stam, eds. *A Companion to Film Theory*. Malden, Mass.: Blackwell, 2004.

Miller, Toby, Nitin Govil, John McMurria, and Richard Maxwell. *Global Hollywood*. London: British Film Institute, 2001.

Minnelli, Vincente. *I Remember It Well*. New York: Samuel French, 1974.

Mitchell, Greg. *Tricky Dick and the Pink Lady: Richard Nixon vs. Helen Gahagan Douglas—Sexual Politics and the Red Scare, 1950*. New York: Random House, 1998.

Mittell, Jason. *Complex TV: The Poetics of Contemporary Television Storytelling*. New York: New York University Press, 2015.

Montgomery, David. *The Fall of the House of Labor*. New York: Cambridge University Press, 1987.

———. *Workers' Control in America*. New York: Cambridge University Press, 1979.

Moore, Schuyler M. *The Biz: The Basic Business, Legal, and Financial Aspects of the Film Industry*. Los Angeles: Silman-James, 2000.

Mukerjee, Chandra, and Michael Schudson. "Introduction: Rethinking Popular Culture." In *Rethinking Popular Culture: Contemporary Perspectives on Cultural Studies*, ed. Chandra Mukerjee and Michael Schudson, 1–62. Berkeley: University of California Press, 1991.

Munslow, Alun. *Deconstructing History*. London: Routledge, 1997.

———. *A History of History*. London: Routledge, 2012.

———. *Narrative and History*. New York: Palgrave Macmillan, 2007.

———. *The New History*. London: Routledge, 2003.

Murray, Janet. *Hamlet on the Holodeck: The Future of Narrative in Cyberspace*. Cambridge, Mass.: MIT Press, 1997.

Musser, Charles. "Pre-Classical American Cinema: Its Changing Modes of Production." *Persistence of Vision* 9 (1991): 46–65.

Myer, Clive, ed. *Critical Cinema: Beyond the Theory of Practice*. New York: Wallflower, 2011.

Naremore, James. "Authorship." In *A Companion to Film Theory*, ed. Toby Miller and Robert Stam, 9–24. Malden, Mass.: Blackwell, 2004.

——. "Authorship and the Cultural Politics of Film Criticism." *Film Quarterly* 44, no. 1 (1980): 14–22.

——. *More Than Night: Film Noir in Its Contexts.* Updated and expanded ed. Berkeley: University of California Press, 2008.

——. *Sweet Smell of Success.* London: Palgrave Macmillan/British Film Institute, 2010.

Naumberg, Nancy, ed. *We Make the Movies.* New York: Norton, 1937.

Navasky, Victor. *Naming Names.* New York: Viking, 1980.

Neale, Steve. "Art Cinema as Institution." *Screen* 22, no. 1 (May 1981): 11–39.

Nesbitt, Molly. "What Was an Author?" In *Authorship: From Plato to the Postmodern*, ed. Sean Burke, 247–62. Edinburgh: Edinburgh University Press, 1995.

Newberry, Michael. *Figuring Authorship in Antebellum America.* Stanford, Calif.: Stanford University Press, 1997.

Newcomb, Horace. *The Producer's Medium: Conversations with Creators of American TV.* New York: Oxford University Press, 1983.

Newman, Michael D. *Indie: An American Film Culture.* New York: Columbia University Press, 2011.

——. *Video Revolutions: On the History of a Medium.* New York: Columbia University Press, 2014.

Newman, Michael D., and Elana Levine, eds. *Legitimating Television.* New York: Routledge, 2012.

Nielsen, Mike, and Gene Mailes. *Hollywood's Other Blacklist: Union Struggles in the Studio System.* London: British Film Institute, 1995.

Nochimson, Martha. *Television Rewired: The Rise of the Auteur Series.* Austin: University of Texas Press, 2019.

Nochlin, Linda. *Women, Art, and Power and Other Essays.* New York: Harper and Row, 1988.

Norman, Barry. *The Film Greats.* London: Futura Publications, 1985.

Norman, Mark. *What Happens Next: A History of Screenwriting.* New York: Three Rivers, 2008

North, Michael. "Authorship and Autography." *PMLA* 116, no. 5 (October 2001): 1377–85.

Obst, Lynda. *Hello, He Lied, and Other Truths from the Hollywood Trenches.* New York: Broadway, 1996.

O'Pray, Michael, ed. *Andy Warhol's Film Factory.* London: British Film Institute, 1989.

Ortner, Sherry. *Not Hollywood: Independent Film at the Twilight of the American Dream.* Durham, N.C.: Duke University Press, 2013.

——. "Studying Sideways: Ethnographic Access in Hollywood." In *Production Culture: Cultural Studies of Media Industries*, ed. Vicki Mayer, Miranda J. Banks, and John Thornton Caldwell, 175–89. New York: Routledge, 2009.

Parigi, Laura. "Fake Americans of the Italian Cinema." In *Directed by Allen Smithee*, ed. Jeremy Braddock and Stephen Hock, 209–28. Minneapolis: University of Minnesota Press, 2001.

Park, Clara Claiborne. "Author! Author! Reconstructing Roland Barthes." *Hudson Review* 43 (1990): 377–98.

Parker, Rozsika, and Griselda Pollock. *Old Mistresses: Women, Art, and Ideology*. New York: Pantheon, 1981.

Parrish, Robert. *Growing Up in Hollywood*. Boston: Little, Brown: 1976.

Pascoe, C. J., and Tristan Bridges, eds. *Exploring Masculinities: Identity, Inequality, Continuity and Change*. New York: Oxford University Press, 2015.

Patterson, Orlando. *Freedom*. Vol. 1, *Freedom in the Making of Western Culture*. New York: Basic Books, 1992.

———. *Freedom*. Vol. 2, *Freedom in the Modern World*. New York: Basic Books, 2005.

Paul, Alan, and Archie Kleingartner. "The Transformation of Industrial Relations in the Motion Picture and Television Industries: Talent Sectors." In *Under the Stars: Essays on Labor Relations in Arts and Entertainment*, ed. Lois S. Gray and Ronald L. Seeber, 156–80. Ithaca, N.Y.: Cornell University Press, 1996.

Pawlak, Debra Ann. *Bringing Up Oscar: The Story of the Men and Women Who Founded the Academy*. New York: Pegasus Books, 2011.

Pease, Donald. "Author." In *Critical Terms for Literary Study*, ed. Frank Lentricchia and Thomas McLaughlin, 105–20. Chicago: University of Chicago Press, 1990.

Perkins, V. F. "Authorship: The Premature Burial." *CineAction!* 21–22 (1990): 57–64.

Perry, Louis B., and Richard S. Perry. *A History of the Los Angeles Labor Movement, 1911–1941*. Berkeley: University of California Press, 1963.

Pinch, Adela. "A Shape All Light." In *Taking Liberties with the Author: Selected Essays from the English Institute*, ed. Meredith L. McGill, para. 112–55. Cambridge, MA: English Institute, in collaboration with the American Council of Learned Societies, 2013. https://hdl.handle.net/2027/heb.90058.0001.001.

Pinker, Steven. *Enlightenment Now: The Case for Reason, Science, Humanism, and Progress*. New York: Viking, 2018.

Polan, Dana. "Auteur Desire." *Screening the Past* 12. http://www.screeningthepast.com/2014/12/auteur-desire.

———. *Scenes of Instruction: The Beginnings of the U.S. Study of Film*. Berkeley: University of California Press, 2009.

Pollack, Dale. *Skywalking: The Life and Films of George Lucas*. New York: Harmony, 1983.

Pond, Steve. "Before the Guild." *DGA Quarterly*, Winter 2011, 50–52.

———. "A Guild Divided." In "70th Anniversary Issue," special issue, *DGA Quarterly*, Winter 2006, 92–96

———. "A Guild Is Born." In "70th Anniversary Issue," special issue, *DGA Quarterly*, Winter 2006, 50–52.

Porter, Vincent. "Film Copyright: Film Culture." *Screen* 19, no. 1 (Spring 1978): 90–108.

Poster, Mark. *Cultural History and Postmodernity*. New York: Columbia University Press, 1997.

Powdermaker, Hortense. *Hollywood, the Dream Factory: An Anthropologist Looks at the Movie-Makers*. London: Seeker and Warburg, 1950.

Price, Sally. *Primitive Art in Civilized Places*. Chicago: University of Chicago Press, 1997.

Price, Steven. *The Screenplay: Authorship, Theory, and Criticism*. New York: Palgrave Macmillan, 2010.

Prindle, David. *The Politics of Glamour: Ideology and Democracy in the Screen Actors Guild*. Madison: University of Wisconsin Press, 1988.

Prover, Jorja. *No One Knows Their Names: Screenwriting in Hollywood*. Bowling Green, Ohio: Bowling Green University Press, 1994.

Radosh, Ronald, and Allis Radosh. *Red Stars over Hollywood: The Film Colony's Long Romance with the Left*. San Francisco: Encounter, 2005.

Rafferty, Terrence. "Everybody Gets a Cut." *New York Times Magazine*, May 4, 2003, 58.

Ramsaye, Terry. *A Million and One Nights: A History of the Motion Picture Through 1925*. New York: Simon and Schuster, 1954.

Rapf, Maurice. "Credit Arbitration Isn't Simple." *The Screen Writer* 1, no. 2 (July 1945): 32.

Rebello, Stephen. *Alfred Hitchcock and the Making of Psycho*. New York: St. Martin's, 1990.

Redman, Nick. "Allen Smithee Exposed." *DGA Magazine*, August–September 1992, 23.

Reed, Stanley. *Oriental Rugs: Pleasures and Treasures*. Frankfurt: Wiedenfeld and Nicolson, 1967.

Reeves, Jimmie L. "Rewriting Culture: A Dialogic View of Cinematic Authorship." In *Making Television: Authorship and the Production Process*, ed. Robert J. Thompson and Gary Burns, 147–60. New York: Praeger, 1990.

Rice, Grantland. *Authorship in America*. Chicago: University of Chicago Press, 1997.

———. *The Transformation of Authorship in America*. Chicago: University of Chicago Press, 1997.

Rich, John. *Warm Up the Snake: A Hollywood Memoir*. Ann Arbor: University of Michigan Press, 2006.

Richardson, Brian, ed. "Implied Author: Back from the Grave or Simply Dead Again?." Special issue, *Style* 45, no. 1 (Spring 2011).

———. Introduction to "The Implied Author: Back from the Grave or Simply Dead Again?," special issue, *Style* 45, no. 1 (Spring 2011): 1–10.
Roberts, Jerry, Ted Elrick, and Tom Carroll. "Sixty Years of Action: A History of the Directors Guild of America." *DGA Magazine*, November–December 1996, January–February 1997, 58–82.
Rodden, John. "Appraising Famous Men: Mediating Biography and Society." In *The Politics of Literary Reputation: The Making and Claiming of "St. George" Orwell*, 3–14. New York: Oxford University Press, 1989.
Rohmer, Eric. *The Taste for Beauty*. Trans. Carol Volk. New York: Cambridge University Press, 1989.
Rose, Mark. *Authors and Owners: The Invention of Copyright*. Cambridge, Mass.: Harvard University Press, 1995.
Rosenbaum, Jonathan. "Potential Perils of the Director's Cut." In *Goodbye Cinema, Hello Cinephilia*, 12–24. Chicago: University of Chicago Press, 2010.
Ross, Murray. *Stars and Strikes: Unionization in Hollywood*. New York: Columbia University Press, 1941.
Ross, Steven J., ed. *Movies and American Society*. Malden, Mass.: Blackwell, 2002.
———. "Workers of Hollywood Unite." *DGA Quarterly*, Winter 2011. https://www.dga.org/Craft/DGAQ/All-Articles/1004-Winter-2010-11/10-Questions-Steven-J-Ross.aspx.
Rosten, Leo. *Hollywood: The Movie Colony, the Movie Makers*. New York: Harcourt Brace, 1941.
Rothman, William. *Hitchcock: The Murderous Gaze*. Cambridge, Mass.: Harvard University Press, 1982.
Roud, Richard. *A Passion for Films: Henri Langlois and the Cinémathèque Française*. Baltimore, Md.: Johns Hopkins University Press, 1999.
Rubin, Martin. *Showstoppers: Busby Berkeley and the Tradition of Spectacle*. New York: Columbia University Press, 1993.
Rudell, Michael I. *Behind the Scenes: Practical Entertainment Law*. New York: Law and Business, 1984.
Rugg, Linda Haverty. *Self Projection: The Director's Image in Art Cinema*. Minneapolis: University of Minnesota Press, 2014.
Salokannel, Marjut. "Film Authorship in a Changing Audio-Visual Environment." In *Of Authors and Origins: Essays on Copyright Law*, ed. Brad Sherman and Alan Strowell, 58–77. New York: Oxford University Press, 1994.
———. *Ownership of Rights in Audiovisual Productions: A Comparative Study*. London: Kluwer Law International, 1997.
Sandeen, Cathy A., and Ronald J. Compesi. "Television Production as Collective Action." In *Making Television: Authorship and the Production Process*, ed. Robert J. Thompson and Gary Burns, 161–74. New York: Praeger, 1990.

Sands, Pierre Norman. *A Historical Study of the Academy of Motion Picture Arts and Sciences.* New York: Arno, 1973.

Saper, Craig. "Artificial *Auteurism* and the Political Economy of the Allen Smithee Case." In *Directed by Allen Smithee,* ed. Jeremy Braddock and Stephen Hock, 29–50. Minneapolis: University of Minnesota Press, 2001.

Sarris, Andrew. *The American Cinema: Directors and Direction, 1929–1968.* Chicago: University of Chicago Press, 1985. Originally published 1968.

———. "Foreword: Allen Smithee Redux." In *Directed by Allen Smithee,* ed. Jeremy Braddock and Stephen Hock, vii–xvii. Minneapolis: University of Minnesota Press, 2001.

Saunders, David. *Authorship and Copyright.* New York: Routledge, 1992.

Saunders, David, and Ian Hunter. "Lessons from the 'Literary': How to Historicize Authorship." *Critical Inquiry* 17, no. 3 (1991): 479–509.

Sawyer, Keith. *Group Genius: The Creative Power of Collaboration.* New York: Basic Books, 2007.

Schanzer, Karl, and Thomas Lee Wright. *American Screenwriters: The Insiders' Look at the Art, the Craft, and the Business of Writing Movies.* New York: Avon, 1993.

Schatz, Thomas. *Boom and Bust: American Cinema in the 1940s.* Berkeley: University of California Press, 1999.

———. *The Genius of the System: Hollywood Filmmaking in the Studio Era.* New York: Pantheon, 1988.

———. "The New Hollywood." In *Film Theory Goes to the Movies,* ed. Jim Collins, Hilary Radner, and Ava Preacher Collins, 8–37. New York: Routledge, 1993.

———. "The Studio System and Conglomerate Hollywood." In *The Contemporary Hollywood Film Industry,* ed. Paul McDonald and Janet Wasko, 13–42. Malden, Mass.: Wiley-Blackwell, 2008.

Schiller, Herbert I. *Culture Inc.: The Corporate Takeover of Public Expression.* New York: Oxford University Press, 1989.

Schrecker, Ellen. *Many Are the Crimes: McCarthyism in America.* Princeton, N.J.: Princeton University Press, 1998.

Schultz, David. *Property, Power, and American Democracy.* New Brunswick, N.J.: Transaction, 1992.

Schwartz, Eric J. "The National Film Preservation Act of 1988: A Copyright Case Study in the Legislative Process." *Journal of the Copyright Society of the USA* 36 (1989): 138–59.

Schwartz, Nancy Lynn, and Sheila Schwartz. *The Hollywood Writers' Wars.* New York: Knopf, 1982.

Schwarz, Andreas. *The Role of Authorship During the Shift Towards a New Hollywood.* Norderstedt: GRIN Verlag, 2011.

Scott, Allen J. *On Hollywood: The Place, the Industry*. Princeton, N.J.: Princeton University Press, 2005.

Scott, Joan Wallach. *Gender and the Politics of History*. Rev. ed. New York: Columbia University Press, 1999.

Seabrook, John. *Nobrow: The Culture of Marketing, the Marketing of Culture*. New York: Random House, 2000.

Sellors, C. Paul. *Film Authorship: Auteurs and Other Myths*. London: Wallflower, 2010.

Sestero, Greg, and Tom Bissell. *The Disaster Artist: My Life Inside* The Room, *the Greatest Bad Movie Ever Made*. New York: Simon and Schuster, 2013.

Sharp, Kathleen. *Mr. and Mrs. Hollywood: Edie and Lew Wasserman and Their Entertainment Empire*. Ashland, Ore.: Blackstone, 2013.

Shea, Jack, ed. *In Their Own Words: The Battle Over the Possessory Credit 1966–1968*. Los Angeles: Directors Guild of America, 1970.

Shekarjian, Denise. *Uncommon Genius: How Great Ideas Are Born*. New York: Penguin, 1991.

Sherman, Brad, and Alan Strowell, eds. *Of Authors and Origins: Essays on Copyright Law*. New York: Oxford University Press, 1994.

Sherman, Eric. *Directing the Film: Film Directors on Their Art*. Los Angeles: Acrobat, 1976.

Sherman, Vincent. *Studio Affairs: My Life as a Film Director*. Lexington: University Press of Kentucky, 1996.

Shindler, Colin. *Hollywood in Crisis: Cinema and American Society, 1929–39*. New York: Routledge, 1996.

Shnayerson, Michael. *Boom: Mad Money, Mega Dealers, and the Rise of Contemporary Art*. New York: Public Affairs, 2019.

Shorris, Sylvia, and Marion Abbott Bundy. *Talking Pictures with the People Who Made Them*. New York: New Press, 1990.

Sikov, Ed. *On Sunset Boulevard: The Life and Times of Billy Wilder*. New York: Hyperion, 1998.

Silver, Alain, and Elizabeth Ward. *The Film Director's Team*. Los Angeles: Silman-James, 1983.

Silver, Alain, and James Ursini. *What Ever Happened to Robert Aldrich?* New York: Limelight, 1995.

Simion, Eugene. *The Return of the Author*. Trans. James W. Newcomb and Lidia Vianu. Evanston, Ill.: Northwestern University Press, 1996.

Simon, Joan, ed. *Alice Guy Blaché: Cinema Pioneer*. New Haven, Conn.: Yale University Press, 2009.

Siskin, Clifford. *The Historicity of Romantic Discourse*. New York: Oxford University Press, 1988.

Sklar, Robert, and Vito Zagarrio, eds. *Frank Capra: Authorship and the Studio System*. Philadelphia: Temple University Press, 1998.

Slide, Anthony. *The American Film Industry: A Historical Dictionary*. New York: Limelight, 1990.

———. *Nitrate Won't Wait: A History of Film Preservation*. Jefferson, N.C.: McFarland, 1992.

———. *The Silent Feminists: America's First Women Directors*. Lanham, Md.: Scarecrow Press, 1996.

Smukler, Maya Montañez. *Liberating Hollywood: Women Directors and the Feminist Reform of 1970s American Cinema*. New Brunswick, N.J.: Rutgers University Press, 2018.

Smyth, J. E. *Nobody's Girl Friday: The Women Who Ran Hollywood*. New York: Oxford University Press, 2018.

Solanas, Fernando, and Octavio Getino. "Towards a Third Cinema: Notes and Experiences for the Development of a Cinema of Liberation in the Third World." In *The New Latin American Cinema*, ed. Michael T. Martin, 33–58. Detroit, Mich.: Wayne State University Press, 1997.

Solman, Greg. "Uncertain Glory?." *Film Comment* 29, no. 3 (May–June 1993): 19–27.

Spergel, Mark. *Reinventing Reality: The Art and Life of Rouben Mamoulian*. Metuchen, N.J.: Scarecrow Press, 1993.

Spivak, Gayatri. *A Critique of Postcolonial Reason: Toward a History of the Vanishing Present*. Cambridge, Mass.: Harvard University Press, 1999.

Stahl, Matt. "Privilege and Distinction in Production Worlds: Copyright, Collective Bargaining, and Working Conditions in Media." In *Production Culture: Cultural Studies of Media Industries*, ed. Vicki Mayer, Miranda J. Banks, and John Thornton Caldwell, 54–68. New York: Routledge, 2009.

Staiger, Janet. "Blueprints for Feature Films: Hollywood's Continuity Scripts." In *The American Film Industry*, rev. ed., ed. Tino Balio, 173–92. Madison: University of Wisconsin Press, 1985.

———. "Individualism Versus Collectivism." *Screen* (July–October 1983): 68–79.

———. "Mass-Produced Photoplays: Economic and Signifying Practices in the First Years of Hollywood." In *The Hollywood Film Industry: A Reader*, ed. Paul Kerr, 97–119. London: Routledge and Kegan Paul, 1986.

———, ed. *The Studio System*. New Brunswick, N.J.: Rutgers University Press, 1994.

———. "'Tame' Authors and the Corporate Laboratory: Stories, Writers, and Scenarios in Hollywood." *Quarterly Review of Film Studies* 8, no. 4 (Fall 1983): 33–45.

Staiger, Janet, and David Gerstner, eds. *Authorship and Film*. New York: Routledge, 2002.

Stam, Robert. *Film Theory: An Introduction*. New York: Blackwell, 2000.

———. *Subversive Pleasures: Bakhtin, Cultural Criticism, and Film*. Baltimore, Md.: Johns Hopkins University Press, 1992.
Stamp, Shelley. *Lois Weber in Early Hollywood*. Berkeley: University of California Press, 2015.
Stamp, Shelley, and Toby Miller, eds. *Film and Theory*. Malden, Mass.: Blackwell, 2000.
Stein, Louisa, and Kristina Buss. "Limit Play: Fan Authorship Between Source Text, Intertext, and Context." *Popular Communication* 7, no. 4 (2009): 192–207.
Steinhart, Daniel. *Runaway Hollywood: Internationalizing Postwar Production and Location Shooting*. Berkeley: University of California Press, 2019.
Stempel, Tom. *Framework: A History of Screenwriting in the American Film*. New York: Continuum, 1991.
Stewart, Jacqueline. *Migrating to the Movies: Cinema and Black Urban Modernity*. Berkeley: University of California Press, 2005.
Stewart, James. *Disney War*. New York: Simon and Schuster, 2005.
Stillinger, Jack. *Multiple Authorship and the Myth of the Solitary Genius*. New York: Oxford, 1991.
Stoddart, Helen. "Auteurism and Film Authorship." In *Approaches to Popular Film*, ed. Joanne Hollins and Mark Jancovich, 37–58. Manchester: Manchester University Press, 1995.
Storey, John, ed. *Cultural Theory and Popular Culture*. 7th ed. New York: Routledge, 2015.
Studlar, Gaylyn. "Erich von Stroheim and Cecil B. DeMille: Early Hollywood Cinema and the Discourses of Directorial 'Genius.'" In *The Wiley-Blackwell History of American Film*, ed. Cynthia Lucia, Roy Grundemann, and Art Simon, 293–312. Oxford: Wiley-Blackwell, 2012.
Studlar, Gaylyn, and Matthew Bernstein, eds. *John Ford Made Westerns*. Bloomington: Indiana University Press, 2001.
Tanner, Jeremy, ed. *The Sociology of Art: A Reader*. New York: Routledge, 2003.
Taylor, Clyde R. *The Mask of Art: Breaking the Aesthetic Contract—Film and Literature*. Bloomington: Indiana University Press, 1998.
Thompson, Robert J., and Gary Burns, eds. *Making Television: Authorship and the Production Process*. New York: Praeger, 1990.
Thomson, David. *Sleeping with Strangers: How the Movies Shaped Desire*. New York: Knopf, 2019.
Tomashevsky, Boris. "Literature and Biography." In *Readings in Russian Poetics*, ed. Ladislav Matejka and Krystyna Pomorska, 47–55. Cambridge, Mass.: MIT Press, 1971.

Towne, Robert. "Bogart and Belmondo: Where It Was and Where It's At." *Cinema* 3, no. 1 (December 1965), 4–7.
Trasker, Yvonne. *Fifty Contemporary Filmmakers.* New York: Routledge, 2002.
Trimbur, John. "Agency and the Death of the Author: A Partial Defense of Postmodernism." *JAC: A Journal of Composition Theory* 20, no. 2 (2000): 283–98.
Trouillot, Michel-Rolph. *Silencing the Past: Power and the Production of History.* 2nd ed. Boston: Beacon, 2015.
Truffaut, François. *The Films in My Life.* Trans. Leonard Mayhew. New York: Da Capo, 1994.
Tuttle, Frank. *They Started Talking.* Boalsburg, Penn.: Bear Manor Media, 2005.
Unterberger, Amy, ed. *The St. James Women Filmmakers Encyclopedia.* Canton, Mich.: Visible Ink Press, 1999.
Uzzi, Brian, and Jarrett Spiro. "Collaboration and Creativity: The Small World Problem." *American Journal of Sociology* 111, no. 2 (September 2005): 447–504.
Vaidhayanathan, Siva. *Copyrights and Copywrongs: The Rise of Intellectual Property and How It Threatens Creativity.* New York: New York University Press, 2001.
Valdivia, Angharad N., ed. *A Companion to Media Studies.* Malden, Mass.: Blackwell, 2006.
Wagner, Craig A. "Motion Picture Colorization, Authenticity, and the Elusive Moral Right." *New York University Law Review* 64 (1989): 628, 658 note 174.
Walker, Cheryl. "Feminist Literary Criticism and the Author." *Critical Inquiry* 16, no. 3 (Spring 1990): 551–71.
Wallerstein, Immanuel. *World-Systems Analysis: An Introduction.* Durham, N.C.: Duke University Press, 2004.
Wasko, Janet. London: *How Hollywood Works.* Sage, 2003.
Wasson, Haidee. *Museum Movies: The Museum of Modern Art and the Birth of Art Cinema.* Berkeley: University of California Press, 2005.
Weber, Max. *Economy and Society.* Ed. Guenther Roth and Claus Wittich. Berkeley: University of California Press, 1978. Originally published 1925.
——. "The Sociology of Charismatic Authority." In *From Max Weber: Essays in Sociology*, ed. H. H. Gerth and C. Wright Mills, 245–52. New York: Oxford University Press, 1958. Originally published 1922.
——. *The Vocation Lectures.* Ed. David Owen and Tracy B. Strong, trans. Rodney Livingston. Indianapolis, Ind.: Hackett, 2004. Originally published 1919.
Weimann, Robert. "Text, Author-Function, and Society: Towards a Sociology of Representation and Appropriation in Modern Narrative." In *Literary Theory Today*, ed. Peter Collier and Helga Geyer-Ryan, 91–106. Ithaca, N.Y.: Cornell University Press, 1990.

Weisberg, Robert H. *Creativity: Beyond the Myth of Genius.* New York: W. H. Freeman, 1993.

Wexman, Virginia Wright, ed. *Directing.* New Brunswick, N.J.: Rutgers University Press, 2017.

———. "Directors." Oxford Bibliographies, 2017. http://www.oxfordbibliographies.com.

———, ed. *Film and Authorship.* New Brunswick, N.J.: Rutgers University Press, 2002.

———. "Film as Art and Filmmakers as Artists: 100 Years." *Arachnē* 2, no. 2 (1995): 265–78.

———. Introduction to *Directing*, 1–25. New Brunswick, N.J.: Rutgers University Press, 2017.

———. Introduction to *Film and Authorship*, 1–20. New Brunswick, N.J.: Rutgers University Press, 2003.

———. "Preston Sturges, *Sullivan's Travels*, and Film Authorship in Hollywood, 1941." In *ReFocus: The Films of Preston Sturges*, ed. Jeff Jaekle and Sarah Kozloff, 46–65. Edinburgh: Edinburgh University Press, 2015.

White, Hayden. *The Content of the Form: Narrative Discourse and Historical Representation.* Baltimore, Md.: Johns Hopkins University Press, 1990.

Whitfield, Eileen. *Pickford: The Woman Who Made Hollywood.* Lexington: University Press of Kentucky, 2007.

Whitney, D. Charles, and James S. Ettema. "Media Production: Individuals, Organizations, Institutions." In *A Companion to Media Studies*, ed. Angharad N. Valdivia, 157–87. Malden, Mass.: Blackwell, 2006.

Wild, David. *The Showrunners.* New York: Harper Perennial, 2000.

Wiley, Mason, and Damien Bona. *Inside Oscar: The Unofficial History of the Academy Awards.* New York: Ballantine, 1968.

Wilinsky, Barbara. *Sure Seaters: The Emergence of Art House Cinema.* Minneapolis: University of Minnesota Press, 2001.

Wilk, Max. *Schmucks with Underwoods: Conversations with Hollywood's Classic Screenwriters.* New York: Applause, 2004.

Williams, Linda. "Melodrama." Oxford Bibliographies, 2011. http://www.oxfordbibliographies.com.

Williams, Raymond. *Marxism and Literature.* New York: Oxford University Press, 1977.

Williams, Susan S. *Reclaiming Authorship: Literary Women in America, 1850–1900.* Philadelphia: University of Pennsylvania Press, 2006.

Wittern-Keller, Laura. *Freedom of the Screen: Legal Challenges to State Film Censorship, 1915–1981.* Lexington: University of Kentucky Press, 2008.

Wittkower, Rudolf. *Sculpture: Process and Principles.* New York: Harper and Row, 1977.

Wolff, Janet. "The Death of the Author." In *The Social Production of Art*, 2nd ed, 117–43. New York: New York University Press, 1993.

Wollen, Peter. "The Auteur Theory." In *Signs and Meaning in the Cinema*, 74–115. Bloomington: Indiana University Press, 1972.

——. "The Canon." In *Paris Hollywood: Writings on Film*, 216–32. New York: Verso, 2002.

——. *Signs and Meaning in the Cinema*. Bloomington: Indiana University Press, 1972.

Wong, Cindy Hing-Yuk. *Film Festivals: Culture, People, and Power on the Global Screen*. New Brunswick, N.J.: Rutgers University Press, 2012.

Woodmansee, Martha. *The Author, Art, and the Market: Rereading the History of Aesthetics*. New York: Columbia University Press, 1994.

Woodmansee, Martha, and Peter Jaszi, eds. *The Construction of Authorship: Textual Appropriation in Law and Literature*. Durham, N.C.: Duke University Press, 1994.

Wyatt, Justin. "Economic Constraints/Economic Opportunities: Robert Altman as Auteur." *Velvet Light Trap* 38 (Autumn 1996).

Youngerman, Joseph. *My Seventy Years at Paramount and the Directors Guild of America*. Los Angeles: Directors Guild of America, 1995.

Zinnemann, Fred. *Fred Zinnemann: An Autobiography*. London: Bloomsbury, 1992.

Zuckoff, Mitchell. *Robert Altman: The Oral Biography*. New York: Random House, 2009.

Index

ABC network, 125, 137, 146, 152, 156
above-the-line talent, 40, 44–45, 122
Abrams, M. H., 4
Academy Awards, 33, 175n62, 177n82
Action (DGA magazine), 82, 142, 145
actors, 2, 113, 133; as directorial alter egos, 32; directorial charisma and Hollywood hierarchy, 44–46, 64; low income of SAG members, 44, 188n29; union organizing goals of, 10, 13. *See also* SAG
Adler, Warren, 8
African American directors, 124–25, 141
Alan Smithee Film: Burn Hollywood Burn, An (1997), 77
Aldrich, Robert, 20, 129, 144, 153, 207n84
Alexander (2004), 57
Alexander, Scott, 50, 51
Alfred Hitchcock Presents (TV series, 1950s), 26
Algren, Nelson, 81
Alien (1979), 57
All About Eve (1950), 87

Allen, Woody, 32, 35, 84, 85, 210n99, 223n10
Alliance of Motion Picture and Television Producers (AMPTP), 42, 54, 132, 187n23, 206n67; controversy over credits and, 81, 82, 83; possessory credit and, 142; preservation projects and, 116; writers' strike and, 124
Ally McBeal (TV series), 53
Alpers, Svetlana, 4
Altman, Robert, 35, 36, 43, 174n56
American Cinema, The (Sarris, 1968), 33
American Cinema Editors, 159
American Federation of Labor, 13, 17, 22, 131, 133, 137, 141
American History X (1998), 77, 205n60
Americans for Better Digital Television, 160
American Society of Cinematographers, 157, 159, 160
AMPAS (Academy of Motion Picture Arts and Sciences), 12–13, 14, 133, 135, 177n82; aura of high culture

AMPAS (*continued*)
cultivated by, 24, 175n62; award limited to theatrical releases, 37; controversy over credits and, 78, 79; formation of, 132; producers and, 42
Andy Warhol's Dracula (1974), 80
anti-Semitism, 89, 212n12, 213n16
Antonioni, Michelangelo, 82
Apocalypse Now: Redux (2001), 57
Apted, Michael, 35, 83–84, 124, 129, 154, 227n25
art cinema, 32, 82, 176n72, 181n110
art directors, 5, 73, 74
art house cinemas, 25, 176n72
Arthur, Art, 97
artisans, 2, 5, 19, 64; author designation and, 114; below-the-line, 40; medieval guild system and, 11
artists, Romantic view of, 3, 4, 23, 119, 180n104
Artists Rights Foundation (ARF), 7, 8, 112–14, 203n34; chronology of, 155–61; film preservation projects and, 149; formation of, 148
Arzner, Dorothy, 60, 61–62, 71, 135
Asian American Committee, 125
Asphalt Jungle, The (1950), 110, 158
At the Movies (TV show), 107
audiences, 32, 37, 181n112; as content creators, 119; familiarity with directors' names, 67, 69, 72; television, 52
auteurism, 1, 8; auteur criticism, 4–5; "auteur imports" to television, 52, 191n62; auteur theory, 33–34; directorial style and, 34, 35–36, 183n125; WGA opposition to, 50
authorship, 3, 5, 8, 31; collective models of, 186n13; consumers and rights to, 230n46; court battles of eighteenth century and, 4; credits and names of authors, 66–71; as cultural construction, 9; director's cut and, 56; law and, 109, 175n66; moral rights doctrine and, 229n44; screenwriters' claim to, 46, 48; staging and, 25
Authors League of America, 13, 131
Autry, Gene, 156
avant-garde cinema, 33

Babel (2006), 236n26
Balio, Tino, 169n28
Balzac, Honoré de, 48
Bank, Mirra, 202n26
Barclay, Paris, 8, 126, 154
Barker, Reginald, 167n12
Basic Agreement, 11, 127; credit configuration and, 71, 74, 202n30; on replacement of directors, 45–46
Bass, Saul, 66, 70
Battle of Elderbush Gulch, The (1913), 26
Battlestar Galactica (TV series), 156
Baum, Frank L., 48
Bazin, André, 1
BBS, 35
Beat the Devil (1953), 96
Beatty, Warren, 110
Beaudine, William, Sr., 167n12
Becker, Howard, 185n13
Beethoven, Ludwig van, 180n104
Behind the Candelabra (2013), 53
Behind the Makeup (1930), 71
Beilenson, Laurence, 17, 134
Belasco, David, 68
below-the-line talent, 2, 5, 40, 54
Benioff, David, 53
Bergman, Ingmar, 27, 32, 34, 82
Berkeley, Busby, 15
Berlin Alexanderplatz (1980), 191n62
Berman, Pandro, 20, 41

Berne Convention, 109, 111–13, 155–57, 159, 226n21
Bertolucci, Bernardo, 182n120
Best Years of Our Lives, The (1946), 80
Beverly Hills Hotel meeting (October 1950), 87–89, 211n2, 216n44, 220nn87–89; backstory to, 89–101; denouement of, 104–5; narrative of meeting compared to film genres, 101–4, 105
Biberman, Herbert, 17, 90, 137, 150, 211n4, 218n65
Biden, Joseph, 228n32
Bier, Suzanne, 71
Bigelow, Kathryn, 63, 152, 198n109
Big Eyes (2014), 51
Bill, Tony, 44
Binyon, Claude, 212n9, 215n34
Biograph Company, 26, 48, 67
Birdman (2014), 236n26
Birth of a Nation, The (1915), 25, 26, 81
BlacKkKlansman (2018), 236n26
blacklist, 89, 91, 105, 150, 219n80
Blade Runner (1982), 56
blaxploitation films, 124
blockbusters, 122, 129
Blow-Up (1966), 82
Blue Ribbon Pictures, 14
Bogdanovich, Peter, 58, 228n32
Boleslavsky, Richard, 71
Bonheur, Le (1934), 155
Boot, Das (1981), 58
Bordwell, David, 32, 175n65
Borzage, Frank, 14, 17, 167n12, 170n30, 180n99; abstention from no confidence vote, 215n34; at Beverly Hills Hotel meeting, 212n9; as Directors Declaration of Independence signer, 132
Bourdieu, Pierre, 1, 3, 4, 39, 175n66

Bowman, Rob, 21
Braddock, Jeremy, 200n9, 204n53
Bram Stoker's Dracula (1992), 81
Brannon, Barry, 18
Brave One, The (1956), 79
Brazil (1985), 192n76
Brewer, Roy, 96, 97, 217n54
Brokeback Mountain (2005), 236n26
Broken Arrow (1950), 235n18
Brooks, Albert, 55
Brooks, Richard, 81, 174n56, 207n77, 211n2, 215n37; in Committee on the First Amendment, 213n18; on safety issues, 127
Brown, Clarence, 144, 170n30, 212n9, 217n48
Buckland, Wilfred, 176n69
Burger, Peter, 31
Burton, Tim, 51, 182n120

Cabiria (1914), 48
cable television, 149
Cahiers du cinéma (film journal), 33, 34, 182n117
Caldwell, John Thornton, 3, 52, 172n44
camera angles, 16, 47, 49
cameras, digital, 59
Cameron, James, 58
Campion, Jane, 198n109
Cannes Film Festival, 34, 36–37, 58, 71, 182n120
Cannon Productions, 170n32
capitalism, 118
Capote, Truman, 81, 207n77
Capra, Frank, 5, 6, 23, 40, 86, 94–95, 115; anti-immigrant views of, 219–20n86; authority at Columbia Pictures, 30, 180n98; Beverly Hills Hotel meeting and, 93, 94, 216n44; colorization issue and, 108;

Index 279

Capra, Frank (*continued*)
  congressional representatives and, 224n14; copyright issues and, 224n14; credits and, 69–70, 72, 82; DGA negotiating committee led by, 19–20, 177n79; as DGA president, 17, 30, 40, 75, 153, 169n28; on director's job, 25; founding of DGA and, 169n28; Lupino described by, 62; Mankiewicz criticized by, 100, 101; melodrama genre and, 102; "one man, one film slogan," 2–3, 30–31, 36, 56, 60, 119; as producer-director, 43; on producers and studio executives, 40–41; resignation from SDGA, 139; on reviewers, 27–28; support for greater directorial control, 16; vote against Mankiewicz, 93–94, 215n34, 216n43; on writer–director relationship, 47
Captain from Castile (1947), 128
Carmen (1915), 68, 155
Carné, Marcel, 110, 159
Casablanca (1942), 49, 156, 158
casting, 32, 49
casting directors, 73, 142, 203n40
Cates, Gilbert, 8, 76; colorization issue and, 108, 112; on creative rights, 10, 38; on DGA headquarters building, 29; as DGA president, 8, 29, 108, 112, 123, 153, 154, 188n29; on perks for directors, 123
Caves, Richard, 122
CBS network, 137, 233, 234
cell phones, 119
Chaplin, Charlie, 26, 105, 140, 155, 224n14
Charming Sinners (1930), 71
Chayefsky, Paddy, 52
Children of a Lesser God (1986), 198n109

Children of Paradise (1945), 110, 159
China, 129
Christensen, Jerome, 3, 184n8
Chu, Judy, 161
Cimarron (1931), 235n18
Cimino, Michael, 79–80
ciné-clubs, 33
cinematographers, 5, 113, 114, 115
Cinemeditor Magazine, 55
circus ringmasters, directors compared to, 39
Citizen Kane (1941), 110, 158, 227n25
Clark, Bennett Champ, 213n16
CleanFlicks, 116, 151, 152, 161
clearance letters, 96, 97, 215n31
Clements, Roy, 167n12
Close Encounters of the Third Kind: Special Edition (1980), 56
Coble, Howard, 161
Coen, Joel and Ethan, 76, 182n120
Cohn, Harry, 22, 30
Cole, Robert, 55
Colla, Richard, 188n32
collaboration, in creative activity, 40, 185–86n13
collective bargaining, 146, 147, 202n30
Collector, The (1965), 82
colorization, 6, 107–11, 156–58, 159, 160, 222n5, 226n20
Color Purple, The (1985), 33
Columbia Pictures, 30, 56, 63, 145, 233n10
Come and Get It (1936), 75
commercials, directors of, 27, 66, 125, 130, 173n55
"committee method," 16
Committee on the First Amendment, 90, 96, 213n18
communism, 12, 88, 90; FBI investigation of, 99; in French and Italian motion picture unions, 96; legal

status of Communist Party membership, 213n17; RTDG accused of ties to, 22, 89, 173n49; Waldorf Statement and, 91
composers, 114
conductors, directors compared to, 38, 39
Conference of Studio Unions, 89–90, 136, 217n54
Congressional Creative Rights Caucus, 161
Conlon, Scoop, 30, 180n99
Conner, J. D., 193n79
convergence, in digital era, 119
Conway, Jack, 169n28
Coolidge, Martha, 8, 61, 62, 63, 151, 154
Cooper, Kyle, 66
Cooper, Merian C., 212n9, 214n24, 215n34
Coppola, Francis Ford, 35, 52, 81; on director as circus ringmaster, 39; director's cut and, 57; as president of Cannes film jury, 182n120; studio founded by, 43
Coppola, Sofia, 198n109
copyright, 49, 80, 155, 224n14; Berne treaty and, 109, 226n21; colorization issue and, 157, 158; moral rights doctrine and, 114
Corday, Ted, 22
Corrigan, Lloyd, 17
Costume Designers Guild, 157, 159
court cases, 74, 127, 151, 152, 156
Crane, William, 235n21
Cranston, Alan, 228n32
creative rights mission, of DGA, 2–3, 4, 7, 9, 39; auterism and, 35–37, 60; collaborators' subordination to directors and, 40, 185–86n13; competition from television and, 21, 172n44; digital revolution and, 59–60, 123–24; directors' contracts and, 156; evolving conditions as challenge to, 130; law and, 116–17; policy fields beyond, 121–30; union issues and, 18; writers in conflict with, 46. *See also* "one man, one film" slogan
credits, 3, 65–66, 118, 142; "Allen Smithee," 76–77; co-directors, teams, and replacements, 74–76; "credit creep," 199n4; DGA and credit configuration, 71–74, 149; guilds and controversy over, 77–85; names of authors and, 66–71; possessory credit, 6, 80–85, 136, 142, 143, 151, 152, 207n76
Cromwell, John, 17, 91, 144, 153, 170n30
Cronenberg, David, 182n120
Crossfire (1947), 87
Crouching Tiger, Hidden Dragon (2000), 126
Cruise, Tom, 161
Cruz, James, 201n14
Cuarón, Alfonso, 126, 236n26
Cukor, George, 126
cultural capital, 33, 68
Curtis, Alan, 167n12
Curtiz, Michael, 69

dance directors ("choreographers"), 73, 142
D'Annunzio, Gabriele, 48
Dante, Joe, 113
Dauman, Philippe, 233n10
Daves, Delmer, 27, 235n18
Dawley, J. Searle, 13, 175n61, 201n16
Day, Francisco "Chico," 124, 135
Dayton, Jonathan, 61, 76, 198n109
Death of a Gunfighter (1969), 76–77
DeConcini, Dennis, 228n32

Index 281

de Grassi, Joseph, 167n12
D'Elia, Bill, 53
Del Toro, Guillermo, 236n26
DeMille, Cecil B., 6, 15, 28, 167n12, 181n112, 201n14; anticommunism of, 99, 218n65; at Beverly Hills Hotel meeting, 87–88, 93, 212n9, 212n11; credits in early cinema and, 68–69; DGA lifetime achievement award, 104, 140, 220n90; diminished reputation within the Guild, 179n90; as Directors Declaration of Independence signer, 132; director's job defined by, 24; "director" title and, 68, 201n17; effort to recall Mankiewicz, 92, 93–94, 96, 98, 139, 215n34, 215n36; Ford's change of course and, 95–96, 217n48; Ford's showdown with, 102–4, 219n80; founding of DGA and, 14; gendered persona of, 104, 220n89; jodhpurs and whip of, 40; loyalty oaths urged by, 87–88, 92, 99, 215n35; mockery of Yiddish accents, 103–4, 220n87; in Motion Picture Alliance, 217n48; name and image of, 69; as political conservative, 17, 87; as producer-director, 43; "Rembrandt lighting" and, 25, 176n69; television market and, 22
DeMille, William, 47, 68, 201n14
Dergarabedian, Paul, 55
Derrida, Jacques, 202n22
DGA (Directors Guild of America): African American Steering Committee, 125, 148; Artists Rights Foundation (ARF) and, 112–14, 159; awards sponsored by, 27, 177n82; Cannes Film Festival and, 182n120; charisma of directors and, 5; chronology of, 131–52; Code of Preferred Practices, 42, 149; constitution, 20–23, 173n55; controversy over credits and, 77–85; Creative Rights Committee, 23, 54, 74, 108, 114, 141, 174n56; credits and, 71–74; East Coast (New York) members, 22–23, 173nn51–52; Ethnic Minorities Committee, 145; executive secretaries (executive directors), 154; founding of, 14–17, 170n30; guild versus union identity of, 11–23; headquarters building, 28–30, 29, 179n93; health and pension benefits, 130, 142, 143, 145, 149, 152, 232–33n6; Independent Directors Committee, 35, 150; Latino Committee, 125, 148; membership statistics, 18, 63, 134, 137, 144, 145, 146, 149, 152; name changes, 163n1; Negotiating Committee, 19, 54, 170n32; NLRB and, 17–18, 19, 170n32; "one man, one film" slogan, 2–3; presidents of, 153–54; public relations program, 27–28; Special Projects Committee, 28, 144, 151; wages and working conditions as concerns of, 2, 164n3; Women's Steering Committee, 62, 145. *See also* Beverly Hills Hotel meeting; creative rights mission; SDG[A] (Screen Directors Guild [of America])
DGA Foundation, 151
DGA Honors Program, 174n55
DGA Magazine, 31, 53, 87, 149, 152
DGA Monthly, 152
DGA News, 145, 149
DGA Quarterly, 107, 152
dialogue directors ("dialogue coaches"), 73
Dickens, Charles, 48

Dickie, George, 185n13
Dies, Martin, 135, 213n16
Dieterle, William, 204n48
digital era/technology, 5, 59–60, 123–24
Directed by Alan Smithee (2002), 205n60
Directed by Allen Smithee (anthology), 77
Director, The (journal), 14
directors: as celebrities, 55; of commercials, 27, 66, 125, 130, 173n55; credits and, 65–66; in credits on screen, 6; as "helmers," 38; high reputation of, 1–2; A-list, 19–20, 52, 71, 111; name changes of, 69; property rights and, 106; racial/ethnic minorities, 63, 124–26, 136, 145, 148, 197–98n108; replacement of, 45–46, 188n32; second unit, 75; union organizing of, 13, 21–22; women, 60–64, 145, 148, 152, 194n89, 198nn108–109, 220n88. *See also* television directors
directors, as artists, 2, 9, 115; art valued over profits, 10; auteurs as singular artists, 30–37; credits and, 65; cultural context of, 23–30; early organizational efforts, 11–23; personas created by, 32; screen credits and, 16
directors, assistant, 7, 19, 146, 148, 171n36; at Beverly Hills Hotel meeting, 212n7, 212n9; as SDG members, 134; wages and working conditions of, 18
directors, charismatic authority of, 5, 8, 39–40; actors and, 44–46; editors and, 53–60; hierarchy and, 40–60; patriarchy and, 60–64; producers and, 40–44; writers and, 46–53
Directors' Bill of Rights, 23, 43, 174n57; drafting of, 142; right to director's cut, 56, 192n77

director's cut, 58, 119, 142, 192n75, 224n12; complications associated with, 56–59; cutting time for, 146; editors' authority undermined by, 40; as film reissues, 5
Director's Cut (2011), 179n91
Directors Declaration of Independence, 14, 132
Directors Guild Inc., 14
Directors Guild of Great Britain, 108, 157
Disaster Artist, The (2017), 190n56
Disney, Walt, 104
Disney company, 233n10
diversity, 121, 124–26, 150
Dixon, Ivan, 235n21
Dmytryk, Edward, 53, 87, 90, 91, 137
Dogme 95 group, 71
Dolemite Is My Name (2019), 51
Donner, Richard, 58
Donovan, J. O., 154
Downey, Thomas, 224n15
Dramatists Guild, 49
Duel in the Sun (1946), 204n48
Dunne, Philip, 47, 81, 90
DVDs, 7, 57, 58, 124
Dwan, Allan, 46, 201n14
Dziga Vertov Group, 182n121

Eastwood, Clint, 45, 182n120, 228n32
Eastwood rule, 45
Ebert, Roger, 107, 156
Edelman, Bernard, 106
Edgerton, Gary, 222n5
Edison Company, 67, 201n16
editors, 40, 53–60, 64
Educational and Benevolent Foundation, 28, 136, 144
Ed Wood (1994), 50–51
8½ (1963), 82

Eisner, Michael, 233n10
Eminent Authors, 48
Empire of the Sun (1987), 33
Epstein, Julius, 49
ER (TV series), 191n63
Essanay Studios, 155
Eszterhas, Joe, 77
Ethnic Minority Committee, 125

Fairbanks, Douglas, 155
Famous Players-Lasky, 48, 68
Fanaka, Jamaa, 235n21
Farber, Manny, 33
Faris, Valerie, 61, 76, 198n109
Farrar, Geraldine, 68
Farrelly brothers, 76
Farrow, John, 215n37
Fassbinder, Rainer Werner, 191n62
Feature Film Nominee Symposium, 148
Federal Communications Commission, 141
Federation of European Film Directors, 108, 157
Fellini, Federico, 27, 32, 34, 82
femininity, mass culture associated with, 194n89
feminism, 8, 71
Ferguson, Otis, 33
Fifty Years of Action (documentary), 28
film critics, 1, 33, 35, 48
Film Disclosure Act (1992), 111, 159, 227–28n29
Film Disclosure Act (1995), 160
Film Educators Workshop, 28
film festivals, 25–26
Film Foundation, 116, 158
Film Integrity Act (1987), 111, 157
film journals, 33
Film Preservation Act (1988), 147, 158
film societies, college, 33

film studies, in universities, 25, 48
finances, as DGA concern, 121–24
Fincher, David, 57
Fitzmaurice, George, 201n14
Flaubert, Gustave, 175n66
Fleischer, Richard, 215n37
Fleming, Victor, 75, 217n48
flow, in digital era, 119
Foley, Brian, 233n10
Foote, Horton, 52
Ford, John, 6, 17, 115, 126, 167n12, 215n34; at Beverly Hills Hotel meeting, 88, 89, 93, 212n7, 212n9, 212n11; birth name of, 69; on "committee method," 16; conflict with RKO studio executives, 41; on director as military general, 39; on directors as indivdualists, 31; director's credits and, 65; HUAC and, 94–96, 214n24; as master of Western genre, 26; in Motion Picture Alliance, 95; NLRB hearing and, 170n32; as producer-director, 43; shift to conservatism, 217n48; television market and, 22; as treasurer of DGA, 19, 170n30, 171n36; Western genre associated with, 26, 88, 102–3, 104, 212n8
Forman, Miloš, 106, 161, 174n56, 182n120
Foucault, Michel, 3, 66
Foundation for Americanism, 87
Four Horsemen of the Apocalypse, The (1921), 71
France: international cinephilia centered in, 33–34; moral rights doctrine (*droit d'auteur*), 109, 114–15, 155, 156
franchises, 122
Frank, Barney, 159, 224n15

Frank, Melvin, 213n18
Frank, Ted, 52
Frank Capra: The Catastrophe of Success (McBride), 180n98
Franklin, Michael, 74, 144, 147, 154, 207n84
Franklin, Wendell, 124, 141, 235n21
Frears, Stephen, 182n120
Frick, Carolyn, 222n5
Friendly, David T., 223n10
Friendly Persuasion (1956), 79

Gabler, Neal, 102, 219n81
Gaines, Jane, 175n66, 186n13
Game of Thrones (TV series), 53
Garnett, Tay, 212n9
gay directors, 126
Genette, Gérard, 66, 77, 80
genius, solitary, 3
genres, 23, 26, 186n13
George Stevens: A Filmmaker's Journey (1984), 211n2, 220n87
Gephardt, Richard, 111, 157, 224n15, 228n32
Gerwig, Greta, 198n109
Getino, Octavio, 186n13
Get Out (2017), 236n26
Getty, John Paul, 112–13, 161
Gilliam, Terry, 57
Girl, The (2012), 202n27
Gish, Lillian, 60
Glick, Norman and Earl, 108, 224n14
globalization, 121, 127–30
Godard, Jean-Luc, 34, 182n121, 191n62
Goethe, Johann Wolfgang von, 48
Gogh, Vincent van, 4, 28
Goldman, William, 50
Goldstone, James, 228n32
Goldwyn, Samuel, 75, 80
Goldwyn Pictures, 24

Gone with the Wind (1939), 75
Gordon, Michael, 215n37
Gorin, Jean-Pierre, 182n121
Goulding, Edmund, 126
Gravity (2013), 126, 236n26
Greed (1924), 32
Greenblatt, Stephen, 4
Grey, Rudolph, 50
Grey, Zane, 48
Griffith, D. W., 25, 26, 48, 115, 201n14; credits and, 70, 81; criticized for racial stereotypes, 150; as "first" movie director, 201n16; iconic straw hat of, 40, 184n9; name and image of, 69; as star director, 67
Guild Directors' Council, 76
guild system, medieval, 11, 196n99
Gumpel, Glenn, 147, 148, 154
Gunning, Tom, 67–68
Guy, Alice, 61
Guy-Blaché, Alice, 201n16

Hackford, Taylor, 154
Haines, Randa, 198n109
Hal Roach Studios, 108
Hartford, David M., 167n12
Hartman, Don, 88
Haskin, Byron, 146
Haunting, The (1963), 158
Hawks, Howard, 14, 17, 75, 170n30, 180n99; auteurist praise for, 34; NLRB hearing and, 170n32
Hayden, Jeffrey, 174n56
Haynes, Todd, 53
HBO cable channel, 53, 146
Heat (1995), 161
Heaven's Gate (1980), 80
Heindorf, Ray, 74
Henley, Hobart, 169n28
Hepburn, Katharine, 228n32

Herbier, Marcel L.,' 155
Herrick, F. Herrick, 154, 219n86
Hershman, Brent, 127
High Noon (1950), 235n18
Hill, George, 169n28
Hiller, Arthur, 8, 77, 111, 114, 115, 153
Hitchcock (2012), 202n27
Hitchcock, Alfred, 26, 34, 43, 69; controversy over credits and, 82; copyright and, 224n14; Reville's collaborative relationship with, 71, 202n27
Hock, Stephen, 204n53
Hodsdon, Barrett, 183n125
Holcomb, Rod, 191n63
Hollander, Russell, 154
Hollywood: ascendancy of star actors, 44; classical style of, 23; DGA position in hierarchy of, 2; female executives in, 195n95; gender bias in, 61, 63; HUAC and, 87, 90; industry business practices, 122; labor costs in, 122, 123; promotion of directors as authors, 4; quest for aesthetic validity, 23–25, 117; trade press of, 2, 42; unionization in, 13, 131
Hollywood Highbrow (Baumann), 175n62
Hollywood Reporter, 90, 214n20
Hollywood's New Vandalism (TV show, 1985), 156
Hollywood Ten, 87, 90, 137, 211n4
Hollywood Victory Canteen, 136
Holman, William, 138, 154, 215n35
home movie market, 119
Hones, Sarah, 127
Hopper, Hedda, 90
Horn, Alan, 56
Horne, Gerald, 212n12
Hour of the Furnaces (1968), 186n13

Hoveyda, Fereydoun, 182n121
Howard, William K., 17, 170n30
Howells, William Dean, 25
HUAC (House Un-American Activities Committee), 3, 6, 87, 106, 179n90; establishment of, 135; "friendly" witnesses and, 104; hearings, 50, 89–91, 102, 137, 140; screenwriters as primary targets, 49–50; "unfriendly" witnesses and, 90, 137, 213n17. *See also* Beverly Hills Hotel meeting; blacklist; Hollywood Ten; loyalty oaths
Humberstone, H Bruce, 170n30
Hunt, Marsha, 96, 217n56
Hunter, The (1980), 188n32
Hurt Locker, The (2008), 63, 198n109
Huston, John, 6, 31, 40, 215n37; autobiography, 96–97; at Beverly Hills Hotel meeting, 93, 96; colorization issue and, 109, 110, 112, 157, 158, 223n10; resistance to HUAC, 90, 92, 214n24
Huston Award, 113, 114, 159–61
Huyssen, Andreas, 194n89
Hyams, Peter, 188n32
Hypocrites (1915), 71

Iger, Robert, 233–34n10
Imitation of Life (1934), 235n18
Iñarritu, Alejandro G., 201n19, 236n26
Ince, Thomas, 167n12, 201n16
In Cold Blood (1967), 81, 207n77
Independent Motion Picture Producers Association, 105
indie film movement, 1, 4, 35
individualism, 14
Informer, The (1935), 41
Ingram, Rex, 25, 167n12, 201n14
intellectual property, 106, 109, 149

Inter-Guild Council, 51, 144
International Alliance of Theatrical Stage Employees (IATSE), 12, 89, 131, 132, 135, 217n54; claim to represent all Hollywood workers, 134; New York assistant directors' break with, 141, 143
International Association of English Speaking Directors Organizations, 129
International Filmmakers Union, 129
International Photographers Guild, 159, 160
internet, 60, 119, 150
Inter-Talent Council, 134
It Happened One Night (1934), 169n28
It's a Wonderful Life (1946), 108, 156, 224n14

Jacobs, Arthur, 97
Japan, 115, 129
Jaszi, Peter, 226n22
Jenkins, Barry, 236n26
Jenkins, Henry, 60
Jenkins, Patty, 59–60
Jews, 12, 33
Juenger, Todd, 122

Kagan, Jeremy, 151
Kamuf, Peggy, 201–2n22
Karaszewski, Larry, 50, 51
Kastenmeier, Robert, 157, 224n15
Kaufman, Philip, 45
Kaye, Tony, 77
Kazan, Elia, 28, 35, 98, 140; at Beverly Hills Hotel meeting, 93, 96; colorization issue and, 223n10; Special Projects Committee and, 144; "What Makes a Director" pamphlet, 38

Keays, Vernon, 92, 98, 138, 139, 154, 215n35, 215n38
Kennedy, Edward (Ted), 112, 224n15, 228n32
Kenton, Erle, 180n99
Kershner, Irvin, 72
Key Largo (1948), 158
King, Henry, 17, 128, 167n12
King, Stephen, 81
Klainberg, Lesli, 205n60
Kleingartner, Archie, 232n4
Koch, Howard, 49
Kohner, Paul, 97
Koster, Henry, 180n99
Kozloff, Sarah, 212n2
Krasna, Norman, 213n18
Kulik, Buzz, 188n32

La Cava, Gregory, 14, 17, 43, 170n30, 180n99
Ladybird (2017), 198n109
Laemmle, Carl, 201n16
Lambert, Mary, 81
Lancaster, Burt, 228n32
Landis, John, 127
Lang, Fritz, 54, 180n99, 182n120, 212n9, 220n87
Lang, Walter, 215n34
Lasky, Jesse L., 1, 68–69
Last of Mrs. Cheyney, The (1937), 71
Last Picture Show, The (1971), 58
Latino Committee, 125, 235n22
Laurel and Hardy, 156
law, artists as owners and, 106–17, 222n8
Lawson, John Howard, 78
Leahy, Patrick, 157, 224n15, 227n27
Léaud, Jean-Pierre, 32
Lee, Ang, 126, 236n26
Lee, Rowland V., 17, 180n99
Lee, Spike, 52, 236n26

Index 287

Leisen, Mitchell, 43
Leonard, Pop, 169n28
Leonard, Robert Z., 169n28
Lerner, Joseph, 22
Leroy, Mervyn, 43
Lester, Richard, 58
Levine, Lawrence, 23
Levinson, Barry, 52
Lewis, Avi, 197n106
Lewis, Jon, 212n12
Life of Pi (2012), 236n26
Limelight (1952), 97
Lipset, Seymour Martin, 180n105
Little Miss Sunshine (2006), 198n109
Litvak, Anatole, 213n18
Litvak, Joseph, 212n12
Lloyd, Frank, 41, 43, 180n99
Locke, Sondra, 45
Lord of the Rings: The Fellowship of the Ring, The (2001), 199n4
Los Angeles, history of labor activism in, 12
Losey, Joseph, 182n120, 215n37
Lost in Translation (2003), 198n109
loyalty oaths, 6, 87, 91–92, 94, 103, 211n5, 215n32; court challenges to DGA oath, 105, 142, 221n92; DGA endorsement of blacklist and, 104–5; SDG[A] and, 138, 140; union leaders and, 99. *See also* HUAC
Lubitsch, Ernst, 15, 17, 26, 43
Lucas, George, 52, 72, 113, 156, 203n34; Artists Rights Foundation (ARF) and, 114; studio founded by, 43
Lupino, Ida, 60, 61–62, 220n88
Lynch, David, 52, 182n120

machismo, 104
Maddow, Ben, 227n23
Maher, Karen Ward, 60
Majestic Pictures, 155
Maltby, Richard, 102, 219n81
Maltese Falcon, The (1941), 109, 112, 157
Mamoulian, Rouben, 15, 17, 170n30, 204n48, 220n87; at Beverly Hills Hotel meeting, 88; on DGA headquarters building, 29, 30; on underpaid directors, 20
Manet, Édouard, 25, 175n66
Mankiewicz, Joseph L., 6, 28, 46, 138; best director DGA award (1951), 104; at Beverly Hills Hotel meeting, 87, 88, 93, 98, 212n11; DeMille's recall campaign against, 92, 93–94, 96, 98, 139, 215n34, 215n36; as DGA president, 6, 87, 88, 91, 93–94, 96, 98–101, 139, 153, 218n68; as Hollywood Ten member, 87; loyalty oath and, 99–100, 139, 218n68; SDG Directors Award (1948), 137
Mann, Delbert, 81–82, 142, 153
Mann, Michael, 55, 161
Man on the Moon (1999), 51
Manovich, Lev, 60
Man with the Golden Arm, The (1955), 81
marketing, 1, 193n79
Marshall, George, 26–27, 98, 153, 180n99
Marshall, Penny, 60
Martin, George R. R., 53
Martin, Steve, 84–85, 210n99
Marton, Andrew, 215n37
Marx, Sam, 15
masculinity, 5, 87, 220n89; artists associated with, 194n89; "hegemonic masculinity," 60; Western genre associated with, 101–4
Mastroianni, Marcello, 32
Mathis, June, 71

Mayer, Louis B., 12, 17, 104, 175n61, 233n10
McCall, Ross, 124
McCardell, Roy L., 48
McCarey, Leo, 15, 43, 91–92, 180n99, 217n48
McCarthy, Todd, 109
McCleod, Norman Z., 180n99
McCutcheon, Wallace, 68
McDonald, Frank, 212n9
McGowan, J. P., 154
McNamara, Mary, 53
McQuarrie, Murdock, 167n12
McQueen, Steve, 188n32, 236n26
melodrama genre, 102, 219n81
Menzies, William Cameron, 75
Metzenbaum, Howard, 159
Meyers, Nancy, 61, 76
MGM studio, 12, 157, 169n28; "Ars gratia artis" (art for art's sake) motto, 24; directors on call at, 15, 168n23; lion logo, 67
Micheaux, Oscar, 124, 126
Mickey One (1965), 82
Miéville, Anne-Marie, 182n121, 191n62
Mildred Pierce (2011), 53
Milestone, Lewis, 14, 17, 170n30, 180n99; as Directors Declaration of Independence signer, 132; as "unfriendly" HUAC witness, 90, 137
military generals, directors compared to, 39
Miller, Frank, 75
Miller, Randall, 127
Miller, Robert Ellis, 174n56
Milton, Robert, 71
minorities, employment of, 121
Miracle decision (1952), 222n8
Miracle on 34th Street (1947), 107
Miramax, 35

Mirror and the Lamp, The (Abrams), 4
mise-en-scène, 34, 182n123
Mr. Arkadin (1955), 204–5n53
Mr. Deeds Goes to Town (1936), 69
mobile phones, 151
modernist movement, 23
Modern Romance (1981), 55
"Moments in Time" (short film series, 2011), 179n91
Moonlight (2016), 236n26
Moonves, Leslie, 233–34n10
Moore, Henry, 28
Moore, Schuyler M., 65
Morales, Sylvia, 235n22
moral rights doctrine (*droit d'auteur*), 109–10, 111, 114–15, 229n44
Morrissey, Paul, 80
Motion Picture Academy, 169n28
Motion Picture Alliance for the Preservation of American Ideals, 95, 214n28, 217n48
Motion Picture Association of America, 147
Motion Picture Director, The (journal), 14
Motion Picture Directors Association (MPDA), 13–14, 24, 73, 132, 167n12; formation of, 131; globalization and, 128; nativist Americanism and, 103; women in, 61, 196n97
Motion Picture Producers Association, 19, 131
Motion Picture World, 67
Moulin Rouge (1952), 96
movie palaces, 24, 25
Moving Picture World, 78
Mrazek, Robert, 224n14
Munslow, Alun, 86
Murnau, F. W., 24, 40
Murphy, Ralph, 180n99

Index 289

Museum of Modern Art: film library of, 25; film screenings at, 28
music, 25, 56
Mutual decision (1915), 222n8
Myers, Ben, 173n49

Nagel, Conrad, 175n61
Name Above the Title, The (Capra), 69–70
"nance" figures, 126
National Film Preservation Act (1988), 115
National Film Preservation Board, 115–16, 149, 161, 228n29, 230n52
National Industrial Recovery Act, 12, 132
National Labor Relations Act (Wagner Act), 12, 133, 134
National Recovery Administration (NRA), 132
Nazimova, Alla, 126
NBC network, 52, 137, 140
Neame, Ronald, 228n32
Negulesco, Jean, 215n37
Neilan, Marshall, 201n14
Nelson, Ralph, 129
Neoist movement, 205n55
Nesbit, Molly, 38
Netflix films, 36–37
New Deal, 12
Newman, Joseph, 16–17, 169n28
Newman, Paul, 72, 188n32
new media, 121, 122, 151
Niblo Fred, 167n12, 217n48
Nichols, Dudley, 48
Nightmare of Ecstasy (Grey, 1991), 50
Nixon, Richard, 170n32
NLRB (National Labor Relations Board), 12, 17–19, 22, 134, 135, 139, 170n32

Norton, Edward, 77
Now You See It, Now You Don't (short film), 113
NRA Motion Picture Code, 133
Nugent, Elliott, 180n99
Nye, Gerald, 213n16

Olmos, Edward James, 235n22
One Los Angeles Declration (1997), 161
"one man, one film slogan," 5, 118–19; Capra and, 2–3, 30–31, 36, 56, 60, 119; DGA agenda and, 36; director's cut and, 56, 58
Open Book, An (Huston autobiography), 96–97
Open Hearts [*Elsker dig for evigt*, aka *Dogme 28*] (2002), 71
oral histories, 28, 144, 146
Ortner, Sherry, 8
Oscars, 79, 169n28
Otto, Henry, 167n12
Outlaw Josey Wales, The (1976), 45
Ovitz, Michael, 233–34n10

Pakula, Alan, 182n120
Paramount antitrust decree (1948), 42
Paramount Pictures, 15, 25, 67, 76, 132, 133
Paratexts: Thresholds of Interpretations (Genette), 66
Paris, as center of film culture, 33
Park, Ida May, 196n97
Parrish, Robert, 215n37
Parrot, James, 68
Pat Garrett and Billy the Kid (1973): DVD release (2005), 57
patriarchy, 60–64
Patry, Bill, 116
Patterson, Orlando, 39
Paul, Alan, 232n4

Payback (1995), 192n76
Peacocke, Leslie, 79
Pearce, Chris, 170n32
Peckinpah, Sam, 57
Peele, Jordan, 236n26
Pell, Clairborne, 228n32
Penn, Arthur, 82, 123
People v. O. J. Simpson, The (2016), 51
People vs. Larry Flint, The (1996), 51
Perry, Louis B., 164n3
Perry, Richard S., 164n3
Persona (1966), 82
Peters, Jon, 188n31, 233n10
Peterson, Wolfgang, 57
Pet Sematary (1989), 81
photography, directors of, 73
Photoplay Authors' League, 13, 131, 132
Photoplay magazine, 25, 67, 79
Piano, The (1993), 198n109
Picasso, Pablo, 28
Pichel, Irving, 34, 90, 91, 137, 218n65
Pickford, Lottie, 196n97
Pierson, Frank, 78, 188n31
piracy, 116, 152
Player, The (1992), 36
Pleasantville (1998), 127
Plimpton, Horace J., 78
Plough and the Stars, The (1936), 41
Polanski, Roman, 182n120
Pollack, Sydney, 43, 111, 160, 161, 174n56, 182n120
Pollard, Harry, 180n99
Porgy and Bess (1958), 204n48
Powdermaker, Hortense, 10, 42
Precious (2009), 236n26
Precious Images (1986), 179n91
Preminger, Otto, 81, 107, 156, 224n14
Price-Jones, Michael, 233n10
Prince of Tides, The (1991), 198n109
Princess of Mars, A (2009), 76

Prindle, David, 44, 91
Prisoner of Shark Island, The (1936), 41
producers, 19, 64, 113, 145; associate producers, 41, 187n14; credits and, 80, 200n6, 206n67; DGA attack on authority of, 40–44; line producers, 187n14; SDG and, 136
Producers Guild, 64, 200n6, 206n67
production designers, 5
Professional, The (1994), 192n76
property rights, 106–7, 117
Psycho (1960), 82
"Psychology of the Cutting Room, The" (article, 2002), 55
public relations, 3, 27
Purple Eagle, The (1927), 126

Quo Vadis (1913), 48

race movies, 124
Rachel, Rachel (1968), 72
Radio Directors Guild, 136, 137
ratings system, 150
Ray, Nicholas, 215n37
Reds (1981), 110, 146
"Rembrandt lighting," 25, 176n69
Rembrandt van Rijn, 4
Renaissance, 4, 24
Renoir, Auguste, 28
residuals (royalty payments), 7, 65, 73, 121, 222n5, 232nn4–5; statistics on, 145, 151, 152; for streaming, 152; strikes over, 145, 147, 152; television film contract and, 138; for television shows, 143
Revenant, The (2015), 236n26
reviewers, 27–28, 178n86
Reville, Alma, 71, 202n27
Revue du cinéma (film journal), 34
Reynolds, Gene, 8, 38, 73, 153
Reynolds, Lynn, 196n97

Rhimes, Shonda, 52
Rhoden, Cheryl, 81
Rich, John, 62
Riskin, Robert, 180n98
Rivkin, Allen, 206n64
RKO studio, 14, 41, 132, 157
Roach, Hal, 22
Robb, David, 61
Roberts, Steven, 180n99
Robson, Mark, 88, 212n9, 215n34, 215n37
Rodriguez, Robert, 75–76
Rogell, Albert, 28, 88, 98, 103, 212n9; DGA unity committee attack on, 100–101; diminished reputation within the Guild, 179n90
Rogers, Roy, 156
Rohmer, Eric, 34
Romantic period, 4, 23
Roosevelt, Franklin, 12, 132, 133
Rose, Mark, 4
Rosenzweig, Barney, 115
Rossen, Robert, 90, 91, 137
Rosson, Gladys, 98, 218n65
Rosson, Harold, 98
Rosson, Richard, 75
Rosten, Leo, 43, 123
Roth, Jay, 8, 116, 148, 154
RTDG (Radio and Television Directors Guild), 22, 137, 138, 173n49; DGA's attempt to merge with, 89, 99; NLRB and, 139
Ruggles, Wesley, 43, 170n30, 235n18
Ruiz, Luis, 235n22
Runaway Production Alliance, 129, 151
runaway productions, 121, 128–29, 150
Ryan, Shawn, 53

safety, as DGA concern, 121, 126–27
SAG (Screen Actors Guild), 13, 17, 18, 134, 150, 163n1; AFL joined by, 133; Artists Rights Foundation (ARF) and, 159; colorization issue and, 157; creative rights issues and, 44; formation of, 132; headquarters of, 30; Inter-Talent Council and, 134; loyalty oaths and, 105; minority and women's committees, 235n21; recognition by studios, 135; residuals and, 232n4; safety as concern of, 126, 127; women in, 62
salaries, directorial, 5, 20, 136, 144, 188n29
Sandrich, Mark, 43, 153, 180n99
Sands, Pierre Norman, 175n61
San Francisco Museum of Art, 28
Sargent, Herb, 78
Sarris, Andrew, 33, 35, 77
Sayles, John, 35
Schaefer, George, 153
Schaffner, Franklin J., 153
Schatz, Thomas, 3
Schindler's List (1993), 33
Schlamme, Thomas, 37, 52, 154
Schlöndorff, Volker, 58
Scola, Ettore, 108
Scorsese, Martin, 35, 114, 150, 160, 161; film preservation projects and, 116, 158; as president of Cannes film jury, 182n120; as producer-director, 43
Scott, Ridley, 57
"Screen Authors Agreement, The," 51
Screen Directors Inc., 14, 168n19
Screen Directors International Guild, 105, 142, 173n55
Screen Directors Playhouse (TV series), 140
screenplays, 48–49
Screen Playwrights, 79, 134, 135
Screen Producers Guild, 138, 142

292   *Index*

SDG[A] (Screen Directors Guild [of America]), 133, 134, 135, 163n1; Educational and Benevolent Foundation, 136; Inter-Talent Council and, 134; loyalty oath and, 139, 140; membership statistics, 140; NLRB and, 136; protest against HUAC, 137; television directors and, 138; Unity Committee, 139
Searchinger, Gene, 105
Seaton, George, 215n37
Secret Beyond the Door, The (1947), 54
Seiter, George, 212n9
Seiter, William, 180n99
Selznick, David O., 14, 41, 75
Sense and Sensibility (1995), 236n26
sequels, 122
Serling, Rod, 52
Seven (1995), 66
Seven Beauties (1975), 198n109
Seventh Cross, The (1944), 160, 161
sexual harassment, 64, 199n112
Seydor, Paul, 57
Shaeffer, George, 174n56
Shape of Water, The (2017), 236n26
Shea, Jack, 154
Shepherd, Cybill, 58
Sherman, Vincent, 218n65
Shield, The (TV series), 53
ship captains, directors compared to, 38, 39
Shipman, Nell, 61
Shyamalan, M. Night, 236n26
Shyer, Charles, 61, 76
Sidney, George, 11, 23, 141, 173n57, 215n34; at Beverly Hills Hotel meeting, 93; as DGA president, 11, 27, 141, 153; on DGA public relations program, 27; HUAC and, 214n24; as producer-director, 43

Siegel, Don, 77
Sienkiewicz, Henryk, 48
signatures, authorial, 70, 201–2n22
silent era, 61
Silverstein, Elliot, 7, 8, 18, 23–24; on artistic and economic authors, 115; Artists Rights Foundation (ARF) led by, 112, 157, 159; colorization issue and, 108; contractual rights and, 227n25; Creative Rights Committee led by, 23, 108, 114, 141; on directorial replacements, 188n32; on directors in credits, 74; on rights of editors, 54; Senate testimony on moral rights, 228n32
Simon, David, 52
Simpson, Alan, 112, 159, 224n15
Sin City (2005), 75–76
Singer, Bryan, 55
Sirk, Douglas, 219n84
Siskel, Gene, 107, 156
Six fois deux/Sur et sous le communication (1976), 191n62
Sixth Sense, The (1999), 236n26
Slide, Anthony, 201n16
"Smithee, Allen" (pseudonym), 6, 76–77, 143, 204n53
Snyder, Zack, 57
Société des Auteurs et Compositeurs Dramatiques, 108, 157, 158
Société Film d'Art, 48
Society of Composers and Lyricists, 159
Society of Motion Picture and Television Directors, 159
Soderbergh, Steven, 53, 84
Solanas, Fernando, 186n13
Sometimes a Great Notion (1971), 188n32
Sonny Bono Copyright Term Extension Act (1998), 113, 161

Sony, 35
Soria, Gabriel, 136
Sorkin, Aaron, 52
Sorrell, Herbert, 90
Soviet Union, 129, 143
Spielberg, Steven, 32–33, 37, 52, 69; Artists Rights Foundation (ARF) and, 113, 114, 160, 229n36; director's cut and, 56; as president of Cannes film jury, 182n120; as producer-director, 43; Senate testimony on moral rights, 228n32
staging, 25, 175n65
Stahl, John M., 235n18
Star Is Born, A (1976), 188n31
"Stars and Directors Whose Names Bring in the Public" (*Photoplay* article, 1924), 67, 200–201n14
Star Trek: Director's Edition (2001), 57
Star Trek: The Motion Picture (1979), 57
Star Wars: Episode V—The Empire Strikes Back (1980), 72
Star Wars franchise, 156
State and Main (2000), 45
Steinhart, Miriam Lyons, 28, 179n90
Stevens, George, 31, 88, 180n99; copyright and, 224n14; as DGA president, 54, 153; HUAC and, 214n24; as producer-director, 43; TV stations sued by, 107, 156
Stevens, George, Jr., 108, 211n2, 220n87, 223n10
Stevens, Michael, 179n91
Stewart, Douglas M., Jr., 28
Stewart, James, 224n14, 228n32
Stone, Oliver, 52, 57
streaming, online, 7, 124, 152, 183n134
Streisand, Barbra, 188n31, 198n109
strikes, 18, 122, 124, 131, 132, 232n5; creative rights and, 158; over residuals, 145, 147, 152; studio lockout of craft strikers, 136
studio executives, 18, 36, 40, 113; accounting practices and, 233n7; directors of color and, 125; pay of, 123, 233–34n10
studio system, breakup of, 1, 32, 42
Studlar, Gaylyn, 181n112
Sturges, John, 88, 215n37
Sturges, Preston, 46–47, 86, 105
style, primacy of, 34
Sullivan's Travels (1941), 86, 105
Sundance Film Festival, 35
Sunrise (1927), 24, 175n62
Superman II (1980), 58
Superman Returns (2006), 55
Supreme Court, U.S., 105, 133, 134, 142
Sutherland, A. Edward, 17, 170n30, 170n32, 180n99
Sweets, William M., 173n49
SWG (Screen Writers Guild), 2, 6, 22, 47, 132, 163n1, 166n10; Communist Party and, 12; Inter-Talent Council and, 134; possessory credit and, 136; Radio Writers Guild of America joined by, 140; recognized by NLRB, 135. *See also* WGA (Writers Guild of America)

Taft-Hartley Act (1947), 99, 137, 144, 218n69
Take Two (Dunne), 47
talent agents, 42
Tarantino, Quentin, 75, 182n120
Tarkovsky, Andrei, 32
Task Force on Violence and Social Responsibility, 150
Taurog, Norman, 180n99, 217n48
Tavernier, Bertrand, 108
tax breaks, 35, 128–29, 151

Taylor, Jud, 153
Taylor, William Desmond, 128, 167n12
television, 5, 21–22, 72, 144, 172n44;
colorized films shown on, 156;
credits for commercials, 66; movies
edited for broadcast on, 107, 146;
"walking and talking" camera style,
52, 191n63; writers and, 51–53, 119
television directors, 22, 99, 123, 125,
172n44, 212n7; anonymity of, 21;
SDG representation of, 138
Television Producers Guild, 142
Theatrical Motion Picture Authorship
Act (1995), 160
theatrical releases, 36–37, 183n134
They Were Expendable (1945), 110
This Changes Everything (2019), 197n106
Thomas, J. Parnell, 91, 215n31
Three Bad Men (1927), 126
Three Days of the Condor (1975), 160
Thunderheart (1992), 227n25
tie-in rights, 122
Tin Drum, The (1979), 58
Todd, Betty, 173n49
Topper (1937), 156
Totten, Robert, 76–77
Touch of Evil (1958), 36
Tourneur, Maurice, 25, 167n12
Trevino, Jesus, 235n22
Trouillot, Michel-Rolph, 86
Troy (2004), director's cuts of (2004, 2007), 57
Truffaut, François, 32
Trumbo, Dalton, 79
Turner, Daddy, 167n12
Turner, Ted, 109
Turner Entertainment, 157, 158
Tuttle, Frank, 17, 91, 180n99, 218n65
12 Years a Slave (2013), 236n26
Twentieth Century Fox, 35, 41

Twilight Zone, The (TV series), 127
Two Tars (1928), 68

Under Two Flags (1936), 41
unions, 12, 13, 18, 44, 121; AFL efforts to
unionize in Hollywood, 131; allegations about Communist infiltration
of, 89–90, 136, 138; company unions,
12; continuing strength of unions in
Hollywood, 231n1; corruption and
gangsterism in, 12; drop in membership, 130; in nineteenth century, 11;
television directors and, 21; Wagner
Act and, 133
United Artists, 14, 80
United States, 31, 103; Berne treaty and,
109, 110, 226n21; copyright legislation, 155; drop in union membership, 130; weak labor movement in,
180n105
unit managers, 18, 19, 134, 141, 171n36
Universal Copyright Convention, 156
Universal Studios, 15, 54, 55, 77
U.S. Copyright Act (1976), 143

Valdez, Luis, 235n22
Valenti, Jack, 82, 109
Valentino, Rudolph, 71
Van Dyke, Woody, 17
Variety (trade magazine), 15, 74, 109,
114, 216n43, 236n28
Vertigo (1958), 66, 80
Viacom, 233n10
VidAngel, 116
video-on-demand, 152
videotapes, 56, 119
Vidor, Charles, 215n37
Vidor, King, 41, 115, 167n12, 180n99,
204n48, 215n37; controversy over
credits and, 82–83; as Directors

Vidor, King (*continued*)
    Declaration of Independence signer, 132; as first DGA president, 16, 134, 153, 170n30; founding of DGA and, 14, 16–17, 169n28; as leftist, 17; in Motion Picture Alliance, 217n48; SDG and, 133, 134

Visual Artists Rights Act (1990), 111, 158

Von Sternberg, Joseph, 15, 40, 69, 204n48

von Stroheim, Erich, 32, 69, 181n112

"Vow of Chastity" manifesto (Dogme 95), 71

Wag the Dog (1999), 65

Waldorf Statement, 91, 214n23

Wallace, Richard, 17, 212n9, 219n86

Walsh, Raoul, 15

Warn, Chuck, 149

Warner Bros. studio, 49, 56, 63, 74; assembly line style of production, 15; class action lawsuit against, 145; colorization issue and, 157

Warrens of Virginia, The (stage play), 68

Wasserman, Lew, 43, 82, 111

Watchmen (2009), 57

Waters, John, 212n9

Watt, Reuben, 235n21

Way Out West (1937), 156

Weber, Lois, 38, 61, 71, 196n97

Weber, Max, 39

Weerasethakul, Apichatpong "Joe," 201n19

Weinraub, Bernard, 65

Weinstein, Harvey, 64

Weiss, D. B., 53

Welles, Orson, 26, 36, 43, 51, 110, 158, 204n53

Wellman, William, 17, 43, 93, 170n30

Wells, John, 50, 52

Wertmuller, Lina, 198n109

West Wing, The (TV series), 52

WGA (Writers Guild of America), 17, 46, 50, 229n36; awards program, 137; colorization issue and, 157; controversy over credits and, 77–85, 206n67, 207n84; formation of, 140; headquarters of, 30; moral rights doctrine and, 229n44; name changes, 166n10; possessory credit and, 144, 151; residuals and, 232n4; strike by, 124; women in, 62; Women's Steering Committee, 159. *See also* SWG (Screen Writers Guild)

"What Is an Author?" (Foucault), 3

"What Makes a Director" (Kazan), 38

White, Hayden, 102

Whiteson, Leon, 30

Who Did That? (short film), 113

Widmark, Richard, 77

Wilder, Billy, 92, 116, 148, 215n37; in Committee on the First Amendment, 213n18; as producer-director, 43

Wilkerson, H. R., 90, 214n20

Willebrandt, Mabel Walker, 17, 62, 72, 170n32, 173n49

Williams, Raymond, 186n13

Williams, Spencer, 124

Wilson, Michael, 79

Wise, Robert, 28, 57, 174n56, 215n37; at Beverly Hills Hotel meeting, 88; colorization issue and, 158; creative rights and, 113; as DGA president, 88, 153; Guild exchange program and, 129; as producer-director, 43; Senate testimony on moral rights, 228n32; Special Projects Committee and, 144

Wiseau, Tmmy, 190n56

Wittern-Keller, Laura, 222n8

Wittkower, Rudolf, 4
Wollen, Peter, 34
Wollner, Anthony, 53–54
women, marginalization of: credit attribution and, 71, 202n26; disadvantaged in entering directorial field, 5, 60–64
Wonder Woman (2017), 59–60
Wood, Ed, 50–51
Wood, Sam, 50, 169n28; HUAC testimony, 91, 137, 214nn28–29; in Motion Picture Alliance, 217n48
Woodmansee, Martha, 4
Wordsworth, William, 10
work-for-hire doctrine, 80, 110, 155, 226n22
Workman, Chuck, 179n91
World War II, 19
Wright, Jim, 228n32
writers: credits and, 65, 77–85, 149, 206n67, 207n73; DGA members' advantage over, 2; resistance to directorial charisma, 46–53, 64; television, 5; union organizing goals of, 10, 13. *See also* SWG; WGA
Written By (WGA publication), 46, 52, 113
Wyckoff, Alvin, 176n69
Wyler, William, 6, 35, 75, 80, 215n37; at Beverly Hills Hotel meeting, 93, 96; credits and, 82; Hollywood Red Scare and, 97–98; HUAC and, 90, 214n24, 215n31

Yankee Doodle Dandy (1942), 157
Yates, Sidney, 224n15, 228n32
You Can't Take It with You (1939), 169n28
Young, Collier, 61
Youngerman, Joseph, 27, 40, 95–96, 98–99, 144; as executive secretary of SDGA, 140, 154; on recognition for directors in credits, 65, 73

Zanuck, Darryl F., 41, 65
Zegna, Frank, 235n22
Zero Dark Thirty (2012), 198n109
Zhang, Yimou, 201n19
Zinnemann, Fred, 6, 82, 215n36, 215nn37–18; call for protected canonical films, 108, 224n13; colorization issue and, 108, 110, 157, 160; congressional representatives and, 224n14; on the guild system, 11; John Huston Award given to, 113; moral rights legislation and, 115, 228n32
Zinnemann, Tim, 161
Zodiac (2007), 57
Zukor, Adolph, 24

FILM AND CULTURE

A series of Columbia University Press
Edited by John Belton

What Made Pistachio Nuts? Early Sound Comedy and the Vaudeville Aesthetic
Henry Jenkins

Showstoppers: Busby Berkeley and the Tradition of Spectacle
Martin Rubin

Projections of War: Hollywood, American Culture, and World War II
Thomas Doherty

Laughing Screaming: Modern Hollywood Horror and Comedy
William Paul

Laughing Hysterically: American Screen Comedy of the 1950s
Ed Sikov

Primitive Passions: Visuality, Sexuality, Ethnography, and Contemporary Chinese Cinema
Rey Chow

The Cinema of Max Ophuls: Magisterial Vision and the Figure of Woman
Susan M. White

Black Women as Cultural Readers
Jacqueline Bobo

Picturing Japaneseness: Monumental Style, National Identity, Japanese Film
Darrell William Davis

Attack of the Leading Ladies: Gender, Sexuality, and Spectatorship in Classic Horror Cinema
Rhona J. Berenstein

This Mad Masquerade: Stardom and Masculinity in the Jazz Age
Gaylyn Studlar

Sexual Politics and Narrative Film: Hollywood and Beyond
Robin Wood

The Sounds of Commerce: Marketing Popular Film Music
Jeff Smith

Orson Welles, Shakespeare, and Popular Culture
Michael Anderegg

Pre-Code Hollywood: Sex, Immorality, and Insurrection in American Cinema, 1930–1934
Thomas Doherty

Sound Technology and the American Cinema: Perception, Representation, Modernity
James Lastra

Melodrama and Modernity: Early Sensational Cinema and Its Contexts
Ben Singer

Wondrous Difference: Cinema, Anthropology, and Turn-of-the-Century Visual Culture
Alison Griffiths

Hearst Over Hollywood: Power, Passion, and Propaganda in the Movies
Louis Pizzitola

Masculine Interests: Homoerotics in Hollywood Film
Robert Lang

Special Effects: Still in Search of Wonder
Michele Pierson

Designing Women: Cinema, Art Deco, and the Female Form
Lucy Fischer

Cold War, Cool Medium: Television, McCarthyism, and American Culture
Thomas Doherty

Katharine Hepburn: Star as Feminist
Andrew Britton

Silent Film Sound
Rick Altman

Home in Hollywood: The Imaginary Geography of Cinema
Elisabeth Bronfen

Hollywood and the Culture Elite: How the Movies Became American
Peter Decherney

Taiwan Film Directors: A Treasure Island
Emilie Yueh-yu Yeh and Darrell William Davis

Shocking Representation: Historical Trauma, National Cinema, and the Modern Horror Film
Adam Lowenstein

China on Screen: Cinema and Nation
Chris Berry and Mary Farquhar

The New European Cinema: Redrawing the Map
Rosalind Galt

George Gallup in Hollywood
Susan Ohmer

Electric Sounds: Technological Change and the Rise of Corporate Mass Media
Steve J. Wurtzler

The Impossible David Lynch
Todd McGowan

Sentimental Fabulations, Contemporary Chinese Films: Attachment in the Age of Global Visibility
Rey Chow

Hitchcock's Romantic Irony
Richard Allen

Intelligence Work: The Politics of American Documentary
Jonathan Kahana

Eye of the Century: Film, Experience, Modernity
Francesco Casetti

Shivers Down Your Spine: Cinema, Museums, and the Immersive View
Alison Griffiths

Weimar Cinema: An Essential Guide to Classic Films of the Era
Edited by Noah Isenberg

African Film and Literature: Adapting Violence to the Screen
Lindiwe Dovey

Film, A Sound Art
Michel Chion

Film Studies: An Introduction
Ed Sikov

Hollywood Lighting from the Silent Era to Film Noir
Patrick Keating

Levinas and the Cinema of Redemption: Time, Ethics, and the Feminine
Sam B. Girgus

Counter-Archive: Film, the Everyday, and Albert Kahn's Archives de la Planète
Paula Amad

Indie: An American Film Culture
Michael Z. Newman

Pretty: Film and the Decorative Image
Rosalind Galt

Film and Stereotype: A Challenge for Cinema and Theory
Jörg Schweinitz

Chinese Women's Cinema: Transnational Contexts
Edited by Lingzhen Wang

Hideous Progeny: Disability, Eugenics, and Classic Horror Cinema
Angela M. Smith

Hollywood's Copyright Wars: From Edison to the Internet
Peter Decherney

Electric Dreamland: Amusement Parks, Movies, and American Modernity
Lauren Rabinovitz

Where Film Meets Philosophy: Godard, Resnais, and Experiments in Cinematic Thinking
Hunter Vaughan

The Utopia of Film: Cinema and Its Futures in Godard, Kluge, and Tahimik
Christopher Pavsek

Hollywood and Hitler, 1933–1939
Thomas Doherty

Cinematic Appeals: The Experience of New Movie Technologies
Ariel Rogers

Continental Strangers: German Exile Cinema, 1933–1951
Gerd Gemünden

Deathwatch: American Film, Technology, and the End of Life
C. Scott Combs

After the Silents: Hollywood Film Music in the Early Sound Era, 1926–1934
Michael Slowik

"It's the Pictures That Got Small": Charles Brackett on Billy Wilder and Hollywood's Golden Age
Edited by Anthony Slide

Plastic Reality: Special Effects, Technology, and the Emergence of 1970s Blockbuster Aesthetics
Julie A. Turnock

Maya Deren: Incomplete Control
Sarah Keller

Dreaming of Cinema: Spectatorship, Surrealism, and the Age of Digital Media
Adam Lowenstein

Motion(less) Pictures: The Cinema of Stasis
Justin Remes

The Lumière Galaxy: Seven Key Words for the Cinema to Come
Francesco Casetti

The End of Cinema? A Medium in Crisis in the Digital Age
André Gaudreault and Philippe Marion

Studios Before the System: Architecture, Technology, and the Emergence of Cinematic Space
Brian R. Jacobson

Impersonal Enunciation, or the Place of Film
Christian Metz

When Movies Were Theater: Architecture, Exhibition, and the Evolution of American Film
William Paul

Carceral Fantasies: Cinema and Prison in Early Twentieth-Century America
Alison Griffiths

Unspeakable Histories: Film and the Experience of Catastrophe
William Guynn

Reform Cinema in Iran: Film and Political Change in the Islamic Republic
Blake Atwood

Exception Taken: How France Has Defied Hollywood's New World Order
Jonathan Buchsbaum

After Uniqueness: A History of Film and Video Art in Circulation
Erika Balsom

Words on Screen
Michel Chion

Essays on the Essay Film
Edited by Nora M. Alter and Timothy Corrigan

The Essay Film After Fact and Fiction
Nora Alter

Specters of Slapstick and Silent Film Comediennes
Maggie Hennefeld

Melodrama Unbound: Across History, Media, and National Cultures
Edited by Christine Gledhill and Linda Williams

Show Trial: Hollywood, HUAC, and the Birth of the Blacklist
Thomas Doherty

Cinema/Politics/Philosophy
Nico Baumbach

The Dynamic Frame: Camera Movement in Classical Hollywood
Patrick Keating

Hollywood's Dirtiest Secret: The Hidden Environmental Costs of the Movies
Hunter Vaughan

Chromatic Modernity: Color, Cinema, and Media of the 1920s
Sarah Street and Joshua Yumibe

Rewriting Indie Cinema: Improvisation, Psychodrama, and the Screenplay
J. J. Murphy

On the Screen: Displaying the Moving Image, 1926–1942
Ariel Rogers

Play Time: Jacques Tati and Comedic Modernism
Malcolm Turvey

Spaces Mapped and Monstrous: Digital 3D Cinema and Visual Culture
Nick Jones

GPSR Authorized Representative: Easy Access System Europe, Mustamäe tee
50, 10621 Tallinn, Estonia, gpsr.requests@easproject.com

www.ingramcontent.com/pod-product-compliance
Lightning Source LLC
Chambersburg PA
CBHW021936290426
44108CB00012B/859